American Industry in
International Competition

*Cornell Studies in
Political Economy*

A SERIES EDITED BY

PETER J. KATZENSTEIN

American Industry in International Competition: Government Policies and Corporate Strategies, edited by John Zysman and Laura Tyson

Closing the Gold Window: Domestic Politics and the End of Bretton Woods, by Joanne Gowa

Governments, Markets, and Growth: Financial Systems and the Politics of Industrial Change, by John Zysman

International Regimes, edited by Stephen D. Krasner

American Industry in International Competition

GOVERNMENT POLICIES AND CORPORATE STRATEGIES

Edited by

JOHN ZYSMAN and
LAURA TYSON

CORNELL UNIVERSITY PRESS

Ithaca and London

137080

First published 1983 by Cornell University Press.
Published in the United Kingdom by Cornell University Press Ltd.,
Ely House, 37 Dover Street, London W1X 4HQ.

International Standard Book Number 0-8014-1577-2
Library of Congress Catalog Card Number 82-22044
Printed in the United States of America
Librarians: Library of Congress cataloging information appears on the last page of the book.

The paper in this book is acid-free and meets the guidelines for permanence and durability of the Committee on Production Guidelines for Book Longevity of the Council on Library Resources.

Contents

Preface   7
Contributors   11

1. American Industry in International Competition   15
   LAURA TYSON AND JOHN ZYSMAN

2. The Politics of Competitive Erosion in the U.S. Steel
   Industry   60
   MICHAEL BORRUS

3. Decline in an Expanding Industry: Japanese Competition
   in Color Television   106
   JAMES E. MILLSTEIN

4. Trade and Development in the Semiconductor Industry:
   Japanese Challenge and American Response   142
   MICHAEL BORRUS, JAMES E. MILLSTEIN, AND JOHN ZYSMAN

5. The Politics of Protection in the U.S. Textile and Apparel
   Industries   249
   VINOD K. AGGARWAL, WITH STEPHAN HAGGARD

6. Adjustment in the Footwear Industry: The Consequences
   of Orderly Marketing Agreements   313
   DAVID B. YOFFIE

7. Beyond the Age of Ford: The Strategic Basis of the
   Japanese Success in Automobiles   350
   DAVID FRIEDMAN

8. Italian Small Business Development: Lessons for U.S.
   Industrial Policy   391
   MICHAEL J. PIORE AND CHARLES F. SABEL

9. Conclusions: What to Do Now?   422
   LAURA TYSON AND JOHN ZYSMAN

   Index   429

6

Preface

During the 1970s, the performance of the American economy deteriorated. The deterioration manifested itself at both the macroeconomic level and the microeconomic level. On the macro level, the aggregate growth rate declined, the average rate of inflation climbed sharply, the productivity growth rate dropped, and the unemployment rate registered new postwar highs. On the micro level, declining growth rates, rising unemployment rates, falling profit rates, and competitive difficulties in international trade characterized a growing number of sectors. In part, sectoral economic difficulties were a natural outgrowth of macroeconomic difficulties. To an extent, sectoral performance reflected cyclical disturbances in the American economy and in the rest of the world due to the two oil price shocks of 1973–1974 and 1979–1980 and resulting macroeconomic adjustments. In part, however, sectoral economic difficulties were the outgrowth of longer-run forces in the domestic and world economies, changing the patterns of international competition and comparative advantage. Increased competition both from the advanced industrial countries and from several of the newly industrializing countries aggravated the economic difficulties of several important economic sectors and contributed to the continued erosion of the U.S. share of exports and production in world markets.

Not surprisingly, sectoral economic difficulties have generated political pressure for economic policy responses to the needs of individual industries. In the ensuing policy debate, industrial policy has become a fashionable catch phrase. Although rarely precisely defined, industrial policy has come to reflect the view that the structural and competitive adjustment problems of individual sectors require policy measures tailored to their needs. Implicit in this view, of course, is the presumption

7

that industrial policy requires an understanding of competitive market dynamics and policy options in particular sectors of the economy.

The case studies in this volume contribute to the continuing policy debate on the sources of competitive difficulties in individual sectors and industrial policy responses to them. Each of the case studies provides a fascinating account of the particular set of domestic and international factors underlying changes in the competitive position of U.S. industry in a particular sector. Taken individually, the case studies illustrate the kind of industry-specific analysis required for the effective formulation and evaluation of industrial policy at the sectoral level. Taken together, the case studies reveal some significant general conclusions about the sources of U.S. competitive difficulties and about the general thrust of U.S. policy responses to them. These general conclusions provide the focus of the introductory chapter, which highlights the overall economic and political lessons to be drawn from the individual case studies.

The major conclusion that emerges from the case studies is a disturbing one. In response to actual or imagined competitive difficulties of individual sectors in international trade, the U.S. government appears to have only one policy option: the introduction of some kind of protectionist measures. Equally disturbing is the fact that the case studies reveal the ineffectiveness of such measures in promoting the kind of structural adjustments required to improve economic performance under changing international economic conditions. In contrast to the limited policy options of the U.S. government, several of the case studies highlight the broad range of policy instruments used in other industrial economies, most notably in Japan, to promote needed adjustments at the sectoral level. These alternative instruments are especially important for effective policy response to economic developments in high-technology industries, such as the semiconductor industry, which are the growth industries of the future. Without such instruments, the U.S. government is forced to take a passive attitude to sectoral economic performance until such time as mounting economic difficulties necessitate a protectionist political response. As a result, U.S. industrial policy focuses on industries in decline rather than on industries on which future growth and competitiveness depend.

Current international pressures for protectionism in a variety of industries threaten the maintenance of the liberal international economic order created under U.S. world leadership after World War II. As competitive pressures in particular U.S. industries mount, domestic pressures for protectionism make it increasingly difficult for the United States government to hold the line against international protectionist tendencies. Under current conditions the policy conclusion emerging from the case studies presented in this volume is clear. Domestic political support for a liberal economic order requires that the U.S. government arm itself with a variety of instruments to promote economic adjustment at the sectoral level rather than to impede it with protectionist measures. If, instead, the government persists in its pattern of responding to sectoral developments only after they have become acute enough to muster the strength of a protectionist coalition and only with protectionist measures, then the liberal economic order will continue to disintegrate, as political support for it within the United States continues to erode.

This book, though written by separate contributors, was conceived initially as a single project. Only the chapter by Michael Piore and Charles Sabel was added afterward. The initial question common to all the efforts was: Are there government policies that could sustain the international competitiveness of these sectors without compromising commitments to high wages or a clean environment? Frank Wolek, then Deputy Assistant Secretary of Commerce, and his assistant Phil Goodman first encouraged our interest in these issues. They provided material support for the initial examination of a number of these sectors. The chapter on the semiconductor industry found support from Wells Fargo Bank, the Joint Economic Committee of the United States Congress, the State of California, and the German Marshall Fund. In particular we would like to thank Louis Coleman, Peter Weitz, and James Galbraith. The automobile analysis was initially funded by the MIT program on the Future of the Automobile, and specifically by Alan Alshaler. The overview analysis was originally encouraged by Jeffrey Hart when he was with the President's Commission on a National Agenda for the 1980s. A multitude of scholars have contributed their time, encouragement, and criticism. Since each chapter represents a separate debt, they are too numerous to be noted separately. Cleo Stoker, then Administrative Director of the Institute for International Studies, and her successor Karin Beros helped keep order in the long process of manuscript completion. Gene Tanke helped turn a series of studies into a book and did his best to keep the prose of academics from obscuring our purposes.

The short introductions to each chapter dealing with a specific industry were written by the editors.

JOHN ZYSMAN
LAURA TYSON

Berkeley, California

Contributors

VINOD K. AGGARWAL is an assistant professor of political science at the University of California at Berkeley. He received his Ph.D in political science from Stanford University. His dissertation focused on international regimes in textile and apparel trade.

MICHAEL BORRUS is a graduate of Harvard Law School, the University of California at Berkeley, and Princeton University. He has consulted on issues of international trade policy for the Joint Economic Committee, the Office of Technology Assessment, and the State of California.

DAVID FRIEDMAN is a graduate student in political science at the Massachusetts Institute of Technology.

STEPHAN HAGGARD is an assistant professor of government at Harvard University. He received his Ph.D. in political science from the University of California at Berkeley.

JAMES E. MILLSTEIN is a graduate of Columbia Law School, the University of California at Berkeley, and Princeton University. He has consulted on issues of international trade policy for the Joint Economic Committee, the Office of Technology Assessment, and the State of California.

MICHAEL PIORE is a professor of economics at the Massachusetts Institute of Technology. He has written extensively on issues of labor economics in advanced industrial societies.

CHARLES SABEL is an associate professor in the Program on Science, Technology, and Society at the Massachusetts Institute of Technology. His most recent book is *The Division of Labor: Its Progress through Politics*. He was recently awarded a grant from the MacArthur Foundation.

LAURA D'ANDREA TYSON is an associate professor of economics at the University of California at Berkeley. Her most recent work is *The Yugoslav Economic System and Its Performance in the 1970s*.

DAVID B. YOFFIE is an assistant professor at the Harvard Business School. He received his Ph.D. in political science from Stanford University. His dissertation focused on trade conflicts between advanced and newly industrializing economies.

JOHN ZYSMAN is an associate professor of political science at the University of California at Berkeley. His other works include *Political Strategies in Industrial Order: Market, Industry and the State in France* and *Governments, Markets and Growth: Finance and the Politics of Industrial Change*.

*American Industry in
International Competition*

CHAPTER ONE

American Industry in International Competition

LAURA TYSON AND
JOHN ZYSMAN

THE PRE-EMINENCE of the United States in international industrial competition and the insulation of American markets from foreign
competition have ended. In industrial sectors as diverse as autos, steel,
consumer electronics, textiles, and apparel, American firms now face
intense foreign competition. These sectors, which account for a substantial share of industrial production and employment, have become vulnerable to developments abroad. According to recent estimates, although the share of foreign trade in GNP remains lower in the United
States than in any other advanced country, more than one U.S. manufacturing worker in five is now employed in a trade-impacted industry.[1]

The competitive difficulties of individual sectors reflect a broad
change in the international economic position of the United States. The
present trade deficit, which has now endured for more than a decade,
is an indication of deep economic shifts. At one time we might have
dismissed the foreign-trade threat as simply a temporary phenomenon,
a matter of war-torn or backward countries catching up to a dominant
America. But it has been over thirty-five years since the war ended.
Our national shares of world production and exports in many sectors
have declined steadily, while the shares of the fast-growing economies
of Japan, Germany, and France have expanded. During the past dec-

[1]This is certainly a conservative figure. By 1977, employment in textiles, apparel, and
iron and steel represented about 15 percent of the labor force. If automobiles are also
included as a trade-impacted industry, then adding employment in automobiles to employment in these other sectors indicates that significantly *more* than one out of every five
manufacturing workers is currently employed in a trade-impacted industry.

ade, all of the advanced countries have had to cope with the consequences of an aggregate slowdown in world economic activity. All of them have also had to cope with intensifying trade conflicts, which have resulted not only from the general slowdown but also from changing patterns of international trade. The adjustment problem in the United States, however, has been aggravated by persistently low growth rates, which have remained below those of the other advanced countries throughout the postwar period. Perhaps even more disturbing, the pace of productivity increase in the United States has continually lagged behind productivity growth in the other advanced industrial economies. Changes in the U.S. trade position and pattern of growth point to an abiding need to restructure U.S. productive capacities to reflect higher oil prices and new patterns of international competition.[2] Countries that effectively adjust to these new patterns will continue to grow in industrial strength and wealth. Those that fail or are slow to adjust will suffer relative declines. Our national economic well-being will rest on our capacity to accomplish the necessary sectoral restructuring and competitive revitalization.

The industry case studies in this volume depict the problems of adjustment and change in seven industrial sectors—consumer electronics, steel, semiconductors, footwear, textiles, apparel, and autos. Each of these sectors is exposed to international competition. The well-being of firms in these sectors depends on defending home markets against foreign firms and selling in markets abroad. Unlike sectors such as housing, which are insulated from international trade, the well-being of the industries considered here depends on their capacity to win and hold markets against the efforts of foreign rivals. The jobs and wages of American workers in these industries depend on the market strength of American companies, of course. However, the employment and income prospects for American workers depend not only on the well-being of American firms but also on their strategies of production. The choice between producing in the United States or manufacturing and purchasing products abroad is not simply a matter of discovering how to produce at least cost, as we shall see in the discussion of consumer electronics and autos. The choice of where and how to produce also reflects both the ability of firms to innovate in production and the policy incentives they face for moving abroad or staying at home. A

[2]There is an extensive and growing literature on this subject, which would include numerous studies completed at the GATT as well as the work continuing at Chatham House under the direction of Louis Turner. See Louis Turner et al., *Living with the Newly Industrializing Countries* (Royal Institute for International Affairs, 1980). See also Commissariat Général du Plan, *Rapport du Groupe d'Etudier l'Evolution des Economies du Tiers Monde et l'Appareil Productif Français* (Paris, 1978).

firm may have several production strategies that will allow it to stay profitable; but for labor, the source and technology of production is all-important, because it establishes whether there will be jobs and determines the value labor will be able to add, which in turn structures the wages a firm can pay. The consequence is that the interests of management and labor in American industries—those that produce in the United States for sale in the United States or abroad—tend to converge. In multinational companies, however, those same interests may diverge. The cases of consumer electronics and steel were initially chosen to examine this difference.

Three themes are highlighted in this book. The first theme is that national differences in the relations between business and government reflect basic political choices that influence the position of a nation's firms in international markets. The studies of steel, consumer electronics, semiconductors, and automobiles focus directly on the competition between the United States and Japan and on the influence of government policy—which has been regulatory and defensive in the United States, and developmental and expansionary in Japan—on market outcomes.

The second theme is that the United States has responded to growing pressures of international competition primarily with protectionist policies. Such defensive policies have dampened our industrial capacity for adjustment and change. They exist in part because we have no apparatus for developing, and no coalition for supporting, policies that actively promote American international competitiveness. The study of textiles and apparel considers the political development of the protectionist coalition in those industries, demonstrating the insidious tendency of protectionist policies to distort markets in ways that require increasing protection. In the United States, Orderly Marketing Agreements (OMAs) that involve bilateral agreements to restrict imports into the United States are a typical form of trade protection. The introduction and consequences of such arrangements are considered in more than half the cases discussed here. The footwear case most explicitly explores this form of protection, demonstrating that OMAs insulate American producers from incentives to adjust while providing powerful inducements to our competitors to adopt strategies that make them even more competitive and dangerous. Although OMAs have usually been introduced with the intent of giving American companies time to adjust to changing market conditions, most often they have hindered adjustment in the United States and have strengthened the position of our competitors.

The third theme is that the basic technological choices which companies make about products and production processes often differ dramatically among the advanced countries. The strong competitive position of Japanese firms in automobiles and their dominance of the consumer electronics sector have resulted from technical choices that are radically different from those made in the United States. A large national market that developed very early in the United States induced producers to develop standard products that would capture the core of that market. The aim was to capture a large volume of sales with a limited range of products, thereby achieving economies of scale. The specialty markets that American companies attacked were usually at the high-price end of the national market. The Japanese have consistently entered this market by designing products, such as portable television sets and fuel-efficient cars, specifically targeted at its low-price end. Their overall strategy, as described in Chapter 7, has been to fragment the market into a series of submarkets which could be attacked with specially designed products. Creating submarkets has been more than a marketing trick; it has required production and design strategies to match. Slowly, Japanese producers have moved from the low-price end to the high-price end of the market, often encouraged by quantitative restrictions on their low-price exports to the United States.

In the immediate postwar years, American security and economic interests coincided. Our extraordinary postwar power allowed us to construct an open international economic system. In those years, American business was pre-eminent in international markets. As firms became international and multinational, they provided political support for free trade policies. Yet even then the commitment to free trade was not unlimited, and in those sectors where free trade occasionally proved politically troublesome, American leadership made exceptions to its own principles. In general, though, we could afford to use access to the American market and assistance to foreign producers as devices to promote the development of our allies.[3]

In recent years, the number of sectors in which American industry faces intense foreign competition in its home market has grown. Textiles and apparel may have been first; these sectors were clamoring for protection in the 1950s, when imports took only a small share of the market. They have now been joined by segments of the steel, auto, footwear, and electronics industries, to name only a few. Without a revitalization of the U.S. world market position in these and other sectors, it will be difficult to maintain our commitment to an open international trading system. The system—which has largely been the

[3]On this issue, two competing explanations of events are offered: one by Fred Block, *The Emergence of International Economic Disorder* (Berkeley: University of California Press, 1977); and one by Stephen Krasner, "External Strength and Internal Weakness," in Peter Katzenstein, ed., *Between Power and Plenty* (Madison: University of Wisconsin Press, 1978).

product of our political leadership in the free world and which remains essential to maintaining our wealth and security in the future—is now threatened. It is threatened by domestic political pressures to insulate our markets in response to the competitive difficulties of important and politically powerful industries.

Historically, and much to our national economic advantage, political resistance to industrial change in the United States has been hard to organize. Industrial development has usually meant competition between domestic regions; one region's loss has often been another region's gain. Because of regional economic competition, it has been difficult to organize political support for a national policy toward industry.[4] But in recent years conditions have changed. Declines in our international competitiveness in certain sectors have made industrial development an issue of national rather than regional significance. Firms adversely affected by international competition have turned to the federal government for support and protection. Political pressure for a more active involvement of the federal government in the detailed development of individual industries has grown. This pressure has produced growing interest in industrial policy and an active trade policy. Although seldom precisely defined, industrial policy reflects the view that competitive adjustment problems require policy measures tailored to the needs of individual sectors or firms. An active trade policy means the explicit use of foreign economic policy to promote competitive adjustment in domestic industries.

Industrial policy, as we use the term here, means government policy aimed at or motivated by problems within specific sectors. It does not imply that the appropriate solutions to such problems are sector-specific, although that is a possibility. In some cases, structural adjustments may require a set of *sector-specific* policy measures defined by the needs of individual sectors or the needs of individual firms. In others, *aggregate policies,* such as fiscal or monetary policies, which affect the whole economy, or *market-promotion policies,* which seek to improve the workings of the market system, may suffice.

The general orientation of economic policy in the United States during the postwar period has been a macroeconomic one. Keynesian demand management policies of both the monetary and the fiscal variety have been introduced to offset cyclical swings in output, in employment, and more recently (and with less success) in prices. In addition, social welfare programs, such as unemployment compensation, Social Security, and Medicare, have been used to achieve various distribu-

[4]This argument is taken from John Zysman's essay on U.S. regional policy completed for the OECD. See John Zysman, "American Regional Policy," *Social Sciences and Policy Making* (Paris OECD, 1981).

tional objectives. The underlying premise of policy has been that most economic decisions at the microeconomic level, meaning either the industry or the firm level, are best made through the market mechanism. Having said this, however, it is important to note that throughout the postwar period there have been many policy measures that have had significant microeconomic or sectoral effects, whether these were intended or not. One need think only of how restrictive monetary policies, introduced for macroeconomic objectives in 1966, 1970, and more recently in 1981, adversely affected the housing and construction industries; or of how the investment tax credit, designed to stimulate aggregate investment demand, has worked to the relative benefit of some firms and industries.

There have also been unintended sectoral effects of policies introduced to realize aggregate economic objectives other than macroeconomic demand management. Regulatory policies to promote environmental goals, for example, have aggregate objectives but important industry-specific side effects. A commitment to cleaner air and water in the aggregate has stimulated the introduction of regulatory measures with disproportionately large effects on the costs and profitability of particular sectors, notably the steel industry (which accounts for more than one-fifth of all domestic industrial pollution) and the automobile industry.[5]

Finally, policy measures with explicit and intended sectoral effects, although interpreted as exceptions to the macroeconomic orientation of economic policy, have played a role in shaping the postwar U.S. economy. The case of policies in the agricultural sector comes immediately to mind. The United States, like most other Western industrial economies, has introduced a set of coordinated policies with the explicit purpose of influencing production levels, input usage, prices, and incomes in the agricultural sector. Procurement and research and development policies have intentionally influenced the aeronautics industry in both its civilian and military lines of production. More recently, the complicated set of price controls, taxes, and direct regulations on the use and distribution of oil have affected the operation of the energy industry. And finally, the extension of federal loan guarantees to Chrysler is an example of a policy measure that is simultaneously sector-specific and firm-specific. What these policies have in common is the fact that they are explicitly directed at certain characteristics of economic performance in a specific sector of production. They are thus sector-specific policies, and as such they should be distinguished, at

[5]Office of Technology Assessment, *Technology and Steel Industry Competitiveness* (Washington, D.C.: Government Printing Office, 1980), p. 20.

least in principle, from other types of policies aimed at the realization of aggregate objectives, regardless of whether such policies have specific sectoral effects.

Thus the simplest distinction between sectoral policies and aggregate policies is this: sectoral policies are addressed to the performance of an individual economic sector, whereas aggregate policies are addressed to the realization of economic objectives that affect all sectors—such as macroeconomic stability, balance of payments equilibrium, or environmental protection. Industrial policies, according to this definition, are simply sectoral policies aimed at certain industries. In this sense, the United States has had an industrial policy, whether by default or intent, in several important industries. Whether the policy has been coordinated and systematic, or uncoordinated and haphazard, is another matter. Coordinated policy requires that the government have a clear view of its objectives in particular sectors, and that it structure its sector-specific and aggregate policies so that they are consistent with one another and with these objectives. Most of the industrial policies introduced by the U.S. government during the postwar period have not satisfied this condition. To the extent that the United States has had an industrial policy, it has been haphazard.

Before going on to analyze industrial policy in more detail, it will be useful to identify a final category of policy measures that has considerable importance in Western industrial economies. For want of a better term, these policy measures may be called *market promotion* policies. They encompass government policies designed to improve the workings of the market system. As such, they are aggregate in intent, aimed at improving the operation of the entire economy; but most often they are directed at individual markets, such as the labor market, the capital market, certain regional markets, or certain industrial markets. Such policies include: labor market policies, which produce employment services, job relocation and retraining subsidies, and other incentive programs to increase the mobility of labor; capital market policies, such as government loan guarantees to small business, to offset distortions in private capital markets; regional development policies to counteract barriers to the mobility of capital and labor among regions of different developmental levels; and antitrust policies to combat actual or potential market distortions arising from uncompetitive market conditions.

Market promotion policies, like the broader category of aggregate policies of which they are properly a subset, may have industry-specific effects but their objectives are aggregate. It is important to keep the distinction between industrial policy and market promotion policies in mind, because much of the current debate blurs this distinction to the detriment of informative policy discussion. The semiconductor indus-

21

try, for example, is currently investing at a rapid rate, and individual companies are taking substantial risks. In policy discussions, the industry claims that its growth is limited by the availability of investment finance. A sector-specific policy response to this claim would imply special programs aimed at the semiconductor industry. Market promotion policies, by contrast, would be aimed at influencing the capital markets to provide more risk and growth capital to all expanding sectors, including the semiconductor industry.

Market promotion policies might be deemed preferable to sectoral policies for two reasons. First, they are more consistent with the market principle that insofar as possible government policy intervention should not discriminate between sectors or firms. Behind this principle is the rebuttable presumption that discriminatory government policies tend to distort otherwise correct market signals, leading to a misallocation of resources. Second, market promotion policies free the government from the need to develop the costly information base required for industry-specific policy formation.

As this discussion suggests, the fact that a specific sector faces a specific problem does not provide a prima facie case for an industry-specific response. Industrial policy, as we use the term here, means policy aimed at problems in specific industrial sectors. It does not necessarily imply that the appropriate solutions to these problems are sector-specific. Usually, industrial policy will be an amalgam of aggregate policies, market promotion policies, and sector-specific policies. What distinguishes industrial policy is the *government's capacity to evaluate the problems of individual sectors,* not the kinds of policies introduced to solve them.

The position elaborated in this chapter is that although appropriate aggregate and market promotion policies are essential, the government must also establish the capacity to make and evaluate policy with an eye to its consequences for particular sectors. Unless the government can formulate its own view of the critical structural objectives of national economic policy, the only alternative will be for it to leave the definition of policy to the politically strongest segments of industry. A likely policy result, the studies in this volume suggest, is protection for troubled industries. A basic purpose of policy, and one measure of its success, must be the encouragement of strategies that leave American firms, using high-wage American labor, competitive in international markets. At a minimum, pursuit of this purpose requires that the government develop an explicit understanding of the competitive dynamics of crucial sectors engaged in international trade. At a maximum, it requires that mechanisms be established to govern sectoral intervention so that when sectoral policies are required, they can be effectively conducted.

Without a standing government capacity to understand competitive dynamics and to intervene judiciously, policy will remain hastily formulated in response to political pressures of the moment, without an understanding of the market issues at hand.

Policy for industry is not simply a technical instrument of rational economic strategy. We must recognize that a number of sectoral policies, or aggregate policies with industry-specific effects, already exist in a whole range of arenas, from the environment to antitrust. If we do not wish to be confronted with a choice between a dirty environment and dangerous workplaces on the one hand, or plants closed in the face of international competition on the other, we must devise these policies with an eye to international competition. Furthermore, in an economy buffeted by international trade, we will continually face demands for protection. Unless we have a capacity to devise sound policies aimed at promoting internationally competitive firms, we shall adopt make-do policies that succeed in blocking change within firms or resource allocation between sectors. To pretend that we can reduce political pressures for intervention by posing stark choices between protection or free trade is only to guarantee that when intervention comes it will be ill-conceived and badly implemented, or that in the end the only politically feasible choice will be protection. To pretend that workers and firms should follow the dictates of price signals is to ignore the fact that both business groups and unions have the political power to influence the marketplace. A single case for an industrial policy, then, is that we already have one. The only open question is whether we shall have policies that equitably encourage firms to make competitive adjustments, or policies that insulate firms from market pressure.

INDUSTRIAL POLICY AND INTERNATIONAL TRADE: CHANGING THE TERMS OF THE POLICY ISSUES

The increasing pressures of international competition on domestic industry are the motivating factor behind contemporary interest in industrial policy and active trade policy in the United States. Although this is understandable from a political point of view, it arouses suspicions about the desirability of industrial policy from an economic point of view. By now, the received theory of international trade is well known. Equally well known is its presumption that free trade leads to mutual economic gains among trading nations. It is this presumption that is the starting point for most economic discussions about the appropriate policy responses to the competitive difficulties of individual firms or sectors. Predictably, these discussions usually end with the

23

conclusion that no policy action is desirable because it would serve only to reduce the gains from free trade. In order to evaluate this sort of conclusion and its relevance for contemporary policy debate, it is necessary to contrast the theory of international trade with the political and economic realities of trade under contemporary circumstances.

Traditional theory reveals only the benign face of trade: mutual gains arise from maximizing the general welfare through expanded exchange; the pie is always expanding, so the absolute size of everyone's share grows. But this theory, built as it is on fundamentally static assumptions, masks a malign face of trade. The outcomes of trade competition not only reflect but also actively shape the lines of national development. A dominant position in vital, expanding industries may give long-term advantage to a whole economy. There can be real losers as well as real winners from trade, and the lines of trade development can be shaped by national policy. Both images of the effects of trade—mutual gains, and winners and losers—have validity. Nothing here should suggest we are unaware of the enormous benefit to all the advanced countries from significant reductions in barriers to trade. But we cannot afford to ignore the policy implications of the structural adjustments required by increasingly open international competition.

The basic conclusion here is that government policies actively shape the outcomes of international trade. Public interventions do not simply distort the workings of otherwise efficient markets. Instead, they permanently alter the terms of international competition and irrevocably change the very structure of the market. Since this conclusion is central to much of what follows, and also runs against received or popular wisdom, it is necessary to digress briefly to some basic economic propositions about international trade. Consequently, we beg the tolerance of the non-economist over the next several pages; we want to make the basis of our policy position unmistakably clear. Readers who wish to be spared even a brief brush with economic theory may skip ahead to the last paragraph of this section, where our conclusions are stated as a premise for our more detailed consideration of policy.

According to the modern theory of international trade, free trade encourages countries to export in sectors in which they have a comparative advantage and to import in sectors in which they have a comparative disadvantage. Comparative advantage is usually assumed to depend on relative factor proportions or availabilities, under the assumption that all countries have access to the same production technology and differ only in their endowments of factors of production. The modern variant of comparative advantage theory, referred to in the economics literature as the Heckscher-Ohlin theory, assumes the existence of two or more factors of production—usually, at a minimum, labor and capital—and argues that countries will tend to export goods embodying their relatively more abundant factors and to import goods embodying their relatively more scarce factors. Ricardian trade theory, in contrast, explains comparative advantage in terms of a single key factor of production, which is usually labor, although in more recent usage it has come to explain trade based on natural resource endowment as well. In Ricardian theory, the precise pattern of specialization in production and trade depends on comparative costs measured in terms of the factor of production in question.

Both the Heckscher-Ohlin and the Ricardian theories of international trade assume that mutual gains from free trade accrue to national trading partners. In both theories, even the country with an absolute disadvantage, in the sense of a higher domestic cost of production for all traded commodities, gains from free trade by exporting those goods in which its absolute disadvantage is least. Not surprisingly, then, discussions based on these theories are likely to take a dim view of the need for government policy in response to the difficulties of domestic industries in international trade. Interfering with the market can only distort the pattern of free trade; ameliorating the difficulties of specific industries can be accomplished only by relinquishing national gains. According to this view, the competitive problems of individual industries in international trade are the market consequence of changing patterns of comparative advantage. For example, in a recent essay, Branson argues that the trend in U.S. trade at both the aggregate and the sectoral levels represents a return to and a strengthening of the lines of comparative advantage that were temporarily disturbed by World War II.[6] The postwar decline in the U.S. share of world exports, and in its share of manufacturing in markets such as steel, automobiles, and consumer goods, has been part of the process of postwar reconstruction in Europe and Japan. What is more, both the United States and the rest of the world have been made better off as a consequence of this process. As a result, apart from the general promotion of trade, the best policy is no policy.

Although the received theory of international trade is a useful starting point for understanding trends in international competition, an informed policy discussion must go further in order to analyze policy questions overlooked in the conventional theoretical framework. The first such question is that of adjustment costs. It is possible to argue convincingly that the decline of the U.S. apparel and footwear industries is the result of our comparative disadvantage vis-à-vis the develop-

[6]See William Branson, "Trends in United States International Trade and Foreign Investment Since World War II," in Martin Feldstein, ed., *The American Economy in Transition* (Chicago: University of Chicago Press, 1980).

25

ing countries in the production of labor-intensive goods; or that the decline of the U.S. steel industry is the result of a Heckscher-Ohlin disadvantage vis-à-vis Japan in the production of capital-intensive goods produced with standard technology. Such arguments, however, do not address the question of the adjustment costs the United States must bear as a result of changing trade patterns and the resultant decline of important industries. The second question overlooked by traditional theory is whether government policy, over time, can influence comparative advantage in most sectors of importance to the advanced countries. Let us consider these two questions in turn.

Changing trade patterns imply structural changes in how people earn their living and lead their lives. Such changes pose important economic and political problems. The crucial economic problem becomes one of determining the net gains from trade after deducting adjustment costs. Under contemporary institutional arrangements, these costs are quite high in most advanced industrial economies. The crucial political problem becomes one of determining how these net benefits shall be distributed both within a single economy and between it and its trading partners.

Once these adjustment issues enter the picture, the traditional benevolent vision of free trade takes on a more divisive cast, at both the national and the international level. An obvious example would be the recent international discussion of "oversupply" in certain world industries, such as shipbuilding and steel. The policy task hidden behind the euphemism "oversupply" is to determine how established producers in certain countries can accommodate the entrance of aggressive new firms from other countries into their traditional markets. How can the development objectives of new market entrants be reconciled with the insistence of established producers that they maintain production in trade-impacted industries, at least long enough to make the adjustment transition less painful? The struggle over the pace of adjustment and the distribution of its costs lies at the core of new international economic and political conflicts.

Although adjustment costs are frequently overlooked in discussions of comparative advantage, they can be easily incorporated into the theoretical framework: the theoretical explanations of changing patterns of trade remain intact, and the policy issues are broadened to determine how to measure and distribute the adjustment costs of structural change. There are other policy issues, however, that the traditional theory is powerless to grapple with. These questions arise as soon as one moves away from the static orientation and the assumption of perfect competition that characterize traditional trade theory. Once dynamics and market imperfections are allowed to enter the picture, both the theoretical models and their implied policy prescriptions become confused.

The static nature of traditional trade theory is reflected in the assumptions of fixed technology and fixed factor endowments that are part of both Ricardian and Heckscher-Ohlin theory. For example, the Heckscher-Ohlin theory assumes a standard production technology to which all countries have access, and given factor endowments in each country. Under these assumptions, the theory posits that free trade will lead to increasing specialization among trading partners, as both factor prices and hence production costs of traded goods converge. The theory treats the determinants of factor endowments as exogenous and overlooks the important fact that technologies are not the same among nations producing the same goods. As a consequence, certain critically important policy issues are placed beyond the reach of theoretical analysis.

One such issue is the impact of government policies on the process of both physical and human capital accumulation over time. Government policies can gradually turn a temporary comparative disadvantage in capital-intensive or education-intensive commodities into a comparative advantage. In short, national comparative advantage is in part the product of national policies. There are only a few sectors in which comparative advantage is given in the form of fixed natural resource endowment. In most sectors, comparative advantage rests on relative capital endowments, and these are the result of accumulated investment. Seen in this light, the growing comparative advantage of Japan in many capital-intensive and education-intensive goods in the postwar period, and the declining share of U.S. producers in the world markets for these goods, are the result of different national investment efforts influenced by different national policies.

The influence of government policies on the dynamics of comparative advantage over time becomes even more pronounced once one allows for the possibility of differing production technologies across countries. Both new product technologies and new process technologies are usually embodied in fixed capital. Embodied technological progress implies that policies to stimulate investment and capital accumulation will change comparative advantage over time both by changing relative factor endowments and by changing technological conditions. An economy with a high investment rate can gradually transform itself into an economy with a comparative advantage in capital-intensive and technology-intensive industries, while at the same time an economy with a low investment rate can gradually lose its initial advantage in those industries. This scenario has at least some applicability to the economic fortunes of Japan (the high-investment economy) and the

United States (the low-investment economy) during the postwar period. Needless to say, the relatively low investment rate in the United States has also meant relatively low productivity growth and a decline in the abolute cost advantage of U.S. producers in several international markets. The result has been the loss of international competitiveness in these markets, as firms have found themselves unable to meet competition given their capital, technology, and relatively high-wage labor. As this discussion suggests, national differences in policies to promote investment in physical and human capital influence the patterns of comparative and absolute advantage over time and the international performance of individual industries.

The role of national policies in the process of developing a comparative advantage is forcefully demonstrated in the case of Japan. In 1950, the Japanese were at a comparative disadvantage in steel production: they lacked the economies of scale to assure low-cost production, and they were dependent on raw materials imported by sea. A generation later, giant ships and port facilities had lowered the cost of imported raw materials, and rapid expansion had provided new technologies that lowered production costs. Both the policy choices of the government and the strategy choices of firms promoted investments that gradually gave Japan a comparative advantage in steel production. The gradual transition to a comparative advantage was reflected in changes in the competitive position of Japanese steel firms in international trade.

To understand this transition process, it is first necessary to distinguish between the notions of comparative advantage and competitive advantage. Comparative advantage refers to the relative export strength of a particular sector compared to other sectors in the same nation and is usually measured after adjusting for market-distorting government policies. For the purposes of our discussion, competitive advantage refers to the relative export strength of the firms of one country compared to the firms of other countries selling in the same section in international markets. According to this interpretation, the competitive advantage of the firms of a particular country in a particular sector may be the result of that country's absolute advantage in that sector. In contrast to the usual notion of absolute advantage, however, the notion of competitive advantage allows for the presence of economic policies that help or hinder the international performance of different firms. Thus the competitive advantage of the firms of a particular country in a particular market may be the result either of real absolute advantage or of policy-induced and hence distorted absolute advantage. Indeed, policy-induced advantage can become real absolute advantage over time.

Whether competitive advantage is real or policy-induced at any mo-

28

ment in time, the competitive dynamics of industry form the link between static and dynamic comparative advantage. Over time, shifts in competitive advantage for particular firms in particular industries can accumulate into a change in national comparative advantage. The crucial point is that comparative advantage rests on the accumulation of investments, and that a long-run strategy can slowly alter a country's comparative advantage by altering its capital stock. Generous endowments of specific raw materials may give firms in one country a competitive advantage over international competitors. Thus in paper products, a firm with domestic access to ample timber resources will presumably have lower timber costs (a real Ricardian absolute advantage). In electronics assembly, cheap labor may give developing countries a competitive advantage in the labor-intensive phases of production (a real Heckscher-Ohlin absolute advantage). In steel, however, the Japanese position does not depend on cheap labor or raw materials, but rather on carefully developed infrastructure and market position (a policy-induced absolute advantage). Port facilities give Japan cheap access to imported raw materials required for steel production; in automobiles, an elaborate national policy to promote the components sector provides a substantial competitive advantage to all companies.

The main point, again, is that accumulated investment, whether in physical infrastructure or in the infrastructure of related markets and firms, is crucial to determining both competitive advantage and comparative advantage over time. In essence, a nation creates its own comparative advantage by the efforts of industries and government to establish competitive advantage in the market. Where the eroding competitive positions of individual firms unravel a web of infrastructure, the outcome can be a long-term loss in competitive advantage which amounts to a shift in national comparative advantage. This is especially true in industries composed of a few large firms. Although there may be no comparative disadvantage underlying the initial competitive difficulties of a particular firm, these difficulties can have a cumulative effect that leads to a national disadvantage. The costs of recapturing a lost market share will go up if the infrastructure, in the form of suppliers and distribution networks, is undermined. The collapse of suppliers may affect the industry's collective ability to sustain its technological position. As this discussion suggests, in advanced industrial economies, comparative advantage—a concept much in vogue and often loosely used—is to be understood as the cumulative effect of both company capacities and government policy choices, not simply as the effect of given endowments in capital, labor and resources.

Although the determinants of changes in competitive and comparative advantage have been largely overlooked in most models of international trade, they have been the focus of at least one branch of trade theory—namely, product-cycle theory.[7] Product-cycle theory focuses on the role of technology and innovation in the dynamics of trade. According to this theory, trade in manufactured goods typically follows a set pattern: a country that introduces a good becomes at first a net exporter of it but eventually loses its net export position when production of the good becomes standardized and moves to those countries that have a comparative advantage, given the factor intensities required by the standard technology. In the period before technology becomes standardized, the innovating country enjoys the benefits of imperfect competition that accrue to a single seller, and if increasing returns to scale exist, these benefits may persist for quite some time before competitors are able to enter the market. The entry of new competitors ends the period of monopoly rents based on technological innovation. As might be expected, given the critical role of innovation in the product-cycle theory and given the apparent links between innovation and the process of both physical and human capital accumulation, countries that pursue investment policies in both arenas are likely to be the product innovators and to earn the resultant rents. Moreover, in addition to investment policies, a variety of other national policies—such as tax policies on capital income, depreciation policies, and policies to support research and development—may influence the pace of technological change in a given country and hence its competitive advantage in high-technology industries. In simpler terms, policy can clearly affect the number and variety of products in which a country initiates the product cycle.

Policy will also affect the pattern of trade that each cycle produces. How long one country can hold an advantage in the production of a particular good, or how quickly another producer can catch up, is not determined by some inevitable economic process. Markets can be manipulated, imperfections created, to influence these outcomes. In these dynamic conditions, there are no longer automatic mutual gains from exchange.

Consider, for example, potential market imperfections resulting from production economies of scale. Significant competitive advantages may be gained by the firms of a particular country if their domestic market is protected and they are allowed to develop a scale large enough to capture cost advantages. Under these protected conditions, a greater portion of market demand will appear stable to each domestic producer. Greater market predictability should lead to faster standard-

---

[7]For more on the product-cycle theory, see Ray Vernon, "International Investment and International Trade in the Product Cycle," *Quarterly Journal of Economics*, May 1966.

ization and automation of production to capture maximum scale economies. The risk that protected domestic producers will be stuck with unneeded capacity will be reduced. It is also important to emphasize that the potential for the firms of one country to reap scale advantages can depend on that country's ability to organize and operate large-scale production, finance, and marketing systems. The Japanese, for example, seem to have a special managerial capacity to organize world-scale production and marketing of standard products. Obstacles to developing a managerial capacity of this type may prove a handicap in international trade. Indeed, a recent Brookings Institution study of Britain suggests that the concentration of strikes in large-scale facilities may represent an underlying disadvantage in maintaining large-scale production.[8] One might contend that the trade ascent of Japan and the trade decline of Britain are in part linked to their relative abilities to produce at large-scale output levels.

Learning-curve economies, like production economies of scale, can be the source of competitive advantage in imperfect markets. In the presence of learning economies in rapidly changing final products, such as integrated circuits, quick market entry and an initial dominant position may provide a producer a market advantage during a long phase of the product's life cycle. Or, more ominously for those who follow the leader, early entry may provide advantage through a long phase of an industry's development. Our underlying argument, of course, is that as production volumes increase, and modifications in product and process technology occur, costs decline. This argument applies most powerfully to the rapidly expanding advanced-technology industries. Once again, in sectors where learning-curve economies are likely to be significant, government policy can play an important role in stimulating or hindering their realization in domestic firms, and hence in affecting the competitive advantage of these firms in international markets.

To sum up the overall policy conclusion of this section: comparative advantage is not static but dynamic, and government policies that influence the competitive advantage of particular firms in particular sectors can alter the pattern of comparative advantage over time. Seen in this light, the policy prescription implied by international trade theory is no longer obvious. If a sector appears to be in decline as a result of a developing comparative disadvantage, the government might decide to exercise a hands-off policy, if politically feasible, on the grounds that this is the policy response that will maximize the gains from trade. If a

[8]Richard E. Caves, "Productivity Differences among Industries," in Richard Caves and Lawrence Krause, eds., *Britain's Economic Performance* (Washington, D.C.: Brookings Institution, 1980).

longer-term and dynamic perspective informs policy decisions, however, the government might decide to introduce a variety of aggregate, market-promotion, and sector-specific measures to promote the changes in factor endowments or technology that will lead to a comparative advantage in the future. And even when the long-term perspective is eschewed in favor of static considerations, a hands-off policy response may be infeasible, and the government may be required at the very least to introduce measures to ease the adjustment process and distribute the costs of it in some equitable fashion. All in all, the competitive difficulties of individual industries in international trade pose thorny economic and political problems for governments; and in the United States, as elsewhere, they are problems for which theory offers no ready solution.

CHANGING COMPARATIVE ADVANTAGE AND THE CURRENT PROBLEMS OF AMERICAN INDUSTRY IN INTERNATIONAL TRADE

The international pressures on U.S. industries which have provoked an interest in industrial policy can be understood as the result of changing patterns of comparative advantage. These patterns, in turn, are best understood by distinguishing between two kinds of international competition: competition between U.S. firms and firms in the other advanced countries, and competition between U.S. firms and firms of newly industrializing countries.

To analyze the dynamics of competition between firms of the advanced industrial world, we have argued that it is necessary to go beyond the simple Ricardian and Heckscher-Ohlin theories, which focus on relative factor endowments and static technology, to consider the role of economies of scale, learning-curve economies, and technological innovation in shaping the comparative advantage of individual countries and the competitive advantage of individual firms. For example, in many sectors important to trade between the advanced industrial economies (such as automobiles, steel, and semiconductors), economies of scale give firms in rapidly growing, highly protected domestic markets a competitive advantage in international markets. A company able to pursue rapid domestic expansion can introduce the most advanced technologies available and can use its strong domestic position to capture scale economies that will provide a long-term competitive advantage. Dominant domestic positions can thus become the basis for expanding export positions in international markets. Thus, in the case of Japan, a large and relatively protected domestic market has provided domestic producers with an opportunity to develop the scale economies and technologies on which their competitive position vis-à-vis U.S.

firms in world markets is based. Rapid growth in Japan, combined with policy-induced protection of domestic producers, has thus allowed production costs in several key sectors to fall below production costs of U.S. firms competing in the same sectors. As comparisons between Japanese and American firms indicate, diverging production costs among the advanced industrial economies in several sectors have been the result of scale economies and embodied technological progress enjoyed by firms in rapidly growing economies.

Of course, it can be argued that whereas diverging production costs may give certain countries absolute competitive advantage within several industries or segments of them, this does not mean that these countries will have a comparative advantage in all of them. A real danger, however, is that over a wide range of important national industries the United States will lose its competitive advantage. A second danger is that sectors in which the United States is falling behind are high-employment sectors in which competitive decline will have significant aggregate effects on employment and output—at least in the short run considered relevant by policy-makers. Clearly, this is a possibility in autos and steel. The third and greatest danger is that as a result of differing growth rates, our competitors will gain a comparative advantage not simply in a single business or even in a range of businesses but in a general type of business—business in which high-volume, standardized production yields quality and cost advantages. The risk is that comparative advantage in modern mass-production sectors will hinge not on wage rates but on the operational control of complex systems that reduce per-unit labor costs substantially. In this regard, comparing Japanese labor requirements with U.S. labor requirements for production in a wide range of sectors is quite sobering. Also sobering is the fact that in technology-intensive products, the U.S. trade deficit with Japan increased from $2 billion in 1970 to $13.5 billion by the end of the 1970s. Although the U.S. trade surplus in technology-intensive products increased from $4 billion to $19 billion during this period, the vast increase in exports of these products has been to OPEC countries and other less developed countries, not to the advanced industrial economies.[9]

A second source of trade pressure on the United States comes from the newly industrializing and developing economies in sectors in which relative labor endowments and low wage rates are the basis for a Ricardian or Heckscher-Ohlin cost advantage in production. Evidently, in some segments of footwear, textiles, apparel, and electronics, labor-cost

---

[9]These figures are cited in formal comments on postwar trends in U.S. competitiveness made by Peter Peterson in Martin Feldstein, ed., *The American Economy in Transition.*

differences mean a loss of competitive and comparative advantage for the advanced industrial economies, including the United States. In the United States, as elsewhere, the direct effects of the loss of competitiveness in labor-intensive goods on the trade balance have been offset by growth in the exports of capital-intensive and technology-intensive industries to the less developed countries. In contrast, the indirect effects of the loss of competitiveness on the pace of adjustment and its resultant costs remain substantial. In addition, as an indirect consequence of competition from less developed countries in labor-intensive goods, the advanced countries have become less able to accommodate shifts in trade patterns with one another. Thus, trade difficulties with the newly industrialized countries and with the other advanced industrial countries, although the result of different underlying economic conditions, have aggravated one another, making the problems of adjustment broader in scope and less susceptible to easy policy resolution.

Foreign Industrial Policy as a Rationale for Government Policy Response

The policies of promotion and subsidy pursued by the governments of our trade partners pose a policy problem for the United States. Some have argued that these policies amount to "unfair competition" in international trade. The basic idea behind this charge is that market signals are distorted and the market is imperfect because of foreign government interference to promote or protect national industries. Others have argued that such interventions reduce the cost of goods to American consumers, and therefore represent foreign contributions to our domestic welfare, which we should accept with thanks. In a perfectly static world this latter view might be correct. But in a dynamic world, if such policies help create comparative advantage for our foreign competitors in sectors critical to our long-run economic and technological development, then this view is incorrect. Such policies work to reduce our economic well-being over time. In addition, market distortions induced by the policies of foreign governments may impose unacceptable adjustment costs on the U.S. economy. In the presence of such distortions, the presumption that markets automatically work well is called into question, and domestic government policy may be required to achieve preferable market outcomes.

The policy-making dilemma under these conditions is considerable. Stated in its extreme form, the choice is this: either accept the policy initiatives of foreign governments as part of market conditions, without taking any compensating policy measures at home; or respond to foreign initiatives with offsetting, compensatory domestic policy measures. Unfortunately, there are no simple analytical rules to guide us in making this choice. Instead, it must be made with reference to the details of the situation—what industries or firms are involved, what foreign government policies are being pursued, what are the implications for market dynamics, and what are the likely costs and consequences of compensatory domestic policies.

Despite the fact that nothing very general can be said about the advisability of using domestic policy to cope with policy distortions from abroad, thinking about the issue can be clarified by distinguishing between two kinds of foreign industrial policies: policies intended to promote industrial developments or adjustments, and policies intended to protect the existing organization of production. Of course, many a policy of protection has been touted in the name of promotion, and policies of promoting adjustment have an odd way of becoming instruments of financial protection for existing producers. The categories overlap, but the distinction remains useful. In economic terms, the policies of protection, by label or in fact, represent simple market distortions. In political terms, such policies represent more than just a reward to the politically powerful. Rather, they are often part of a social compact about how the costs and strains of industrial change will be shared. As such, protective subsidies may be seen as a contribution to social peace, a payment to avoid destructive industrial conflicts, and a means to assure that market adjustment can continue. Providing cushions against the costs of change may be part of the political process of assuring that necessary industry change will continue smoothly.

Our concern here is with policies of promotion. Policies of promotion and adjustment may be seen as doing three things: (1) assisting the emergence of new industries, particularly growth-linked industries; (2) assuring that national firms remain competitive during the process of transition and transformation in an industry; and (3) easing or smoothing the exit of resources from declining industries.

The case studies presented in this volume highlight the role of Japanese industrial policy in promoting the expansion of growth-linked industries. Common policy objectives and instruments are apparent in all the individual cases of Japanese intervention. Policy is used: (1) to assure resources for expansion from national financial markets; (2) to assure a domestic market through various protectionist policies; (3) to assure competition between domestic producers; and (4) to assist and encourage exports through both general and industry-specific policies.[10] Taken together, these policy objectives and instruments reflect a powerful development strategy. Steel is widely accepted as an industry in which

[10]This formulation is drawn from the cases presented in this volume and in Ira Magaziner and Tom Hout, *Japanese Industrial Policy* (Berkeley: Institute for International Studies, 1981).

Japanese policy has altered national comparative advantage in a specific and conscious way.[11] Policies for the shipbuilding industry have also served to help establish competitive and comparative advantage in other industries. The shipbuilding success has helped reduce costs for Japan as a whole by affecting the prices of imported commodities and the costs of exports, just as steel has provided an inexpensive material to other industries. In shipbuilding, short delivery dates crucial to initial market entry have been assured by providing assistance to firms to stockpile vessels.[12] The auto case has more nuances. Japanese automobile producers are now the leading low-cost producers in the world. They are able, for example, to sell quality cars at competitive prices *over* an 11 percent tariff wall and a 10 percent transport bill—which suggests that at the factory gate Japanese cars are at least 20 percent cheaper than European cars. What, though, has been the role of the government in the auto industry? Japanese government efforts to restructure the main producer-assemblers have never come to much, and this has been taken as evidence of the unimportance of government policy in this case. Yet a closer look shows the hand of the government in developing a domestic market, in insulating that market during its early fragile years, and in restructuring not the assemblers but the components sector. And without the competitive components sector, the assemblers could not have made their world breakthrough.[13]

In the semiconductor industry (Chapter 4), the elements of the Japanese development strategy are all in place. The patterns of international trade suggest how domestic markets become insulated as producers enter new product markets. The patterns of domestic trade among the electronics houses suggest the presence of international market arrangements that permit seemingly agreed-upon specialization amidst competition. Substantial government research and development assistance have served as part of an effort to close the technical gap with American companies. Indeed, the combination of trade and industry policies represents a substantial long-term threat to the American integrated circuit industry. For the moment, as suggested by Borrus, Millstein, and Zysman in Chapter 4, American firms have responded successfully. The danger is that American firms will not be able to turn specific product advantages into a strong overall market

---

[11]See Chapter 2 in this volume, by Michael Borrus; and Magaziner and Hout, *Japanese Industrial Policy.*

[12]See Kozo Yamamura, "General Trading Companies in Japan," in Hugh Patrick, ed., *Japanese Industrialization and Its Social Consequences* (Berkeley: University of California Press, 1976); and John Zysman, *Governments, Markets, and Growth: Finance and the Politics of Industrial Change* (Ithaca: Cornell University Press, 1983), Chap. 5.

[13]See Magaziner and Hout, *Japanese Industrial Policy.* These points were also made in private interviews, between John Zysman and auto industry executives.

position within Japan. The closure of the Japanese market to American firms makes the battle for the future of the industry a struggle over American and European markets between Japanese and American firms. Permitting the Japanese to retain a secure home base in world competition means that a single slip by American producers can undermine their long-term position, whereas a Japanese slip can be compensated for and overcome later.

All of the case studies in this volume suggest that the Japanese have a marked advantage in managing large-batch and mass production. Magaziner and Hout present systematic evidence that labor hours per product in Japan are substantially lower than in Europe and the United States.[14] Anecdotal evidence suggests that this advantage is reinforced by more refined timing in the production process that reduces inventory levels of component parts. This, of course, has substantial financial advantages. One real hope is that the Japanese advantage lies not in the unique characteristics of Japanese workers but in distinct Japanese managerial strategies, for it will be easier to copy managerial techniques than to alter the sociology of the workforce. The contrast in management strategies is particularly evident in the consumer electronics case, where two distinct managerial responses are evident in the competition between American and Japanese firms. The Japanese gained a long-term competitive advantage by adopting product design that incorporated solid-state technology, while the Americans tried to solve their competitive difficulties by finding cheaper sources of foreign labor.

Although the evidence in this volume does not permit us to analyze in detail the trade implications of different national strategies for managing adjustment, something can be said about the political and institutional barriers to effective adjustment policies in England and the United States. These two countries depend on private markets to bring the underlying resources of plant, equipment, and labor back into productive use without particular attention to maintaining the competitive position of individual firms. When the importance of the particular industry or the scope of the rearrangement requires public intervention, there are few instruments for managing the affair. When mature industries have found themselves in competitive trouble, American policy has for the most part focused on trade protection: OMAs; ad hoc agreements in textiles, apparel, and footwear; and trigger pricing in steel. Only in the auto industry—the Chrysler case—has there been an effort to manage the process of market change by supporting and reorganizing a producer. The Chrysler case and the earlier Lockheed

[14]See Magaziner and Hout, *Japanese Industrial Policy.*

case are distinctive for the enormous public political effort required to conduct what were seen as unique interventions. The recent restructuring of the steel industry by the French government provides a useful contrast. When the major firms failed under the weight of truly extraordinary levels of debt (estimated at over 100 percent of annual turnover, with debt servicing representing 20 percent of annual turnover), the government stepped in to reorder the financial circumstances of the firms, change the management, and protect the banks and markets from the impact of potential failure. The effort was organized within the government bureaucracy and conducted without public scrutiny, as if the state were acting as a merchant bank. The sums mobilized in this effort were between two and a half billion dollars (French government estimates) and five billion dollars (English-language business press estimates).[15]

The United States cannot be sanguine about the possibilities of using bilateral and multilateral trade negotiations to protect its industry from the policy interventions of other nations. The United States does not have the power to force other countries to play the trade-and-industry game in accordance with its own free-market, non-interventionist rules. In the end, U.S. policy may have to be predicated on the view that if other countries are unwilling to adopt our rules, then we may have to consider the consequences of their rules and policies in formulating our own.

Government Policy and Industrial Dynamics

Making a defensible case for economic policy intervention is only the first step in the formulation of an effective policy response to sectoral economic difficulties. A much more difficult step is the design and implementation of such a response. The policy measures chosen must be consistent with the rationales that underlie them. In addition, whenever such measures have an industrial or sectoral orientation, as opposed to an aggregate one, they must be framed with an understanding of particular industries or firms; the level of policy analysis must move to the level of industry and firm dynamics.

At the industry level, it may be useful for the purposes of government policy-making to distinguish three categories of industrial change: *growth, transition,* and *decline*. In a *growth* industry, output and demand are expanding. In addition, product and process technologies are usually changing rapidly, and the competitive positions of individ-

---

[15]See John Zysman, *Governments, Markets, and Growth*, for a complete discussion of these estimates and their sources.

ual firms are in flux. In other words, growing industries are frequently those characterized by high market risk and uncertainty. These conditions characterize the technology-intensive industries that are the growth industries of the advanced industrial economies, including the United States. Most frequently, the rationales for government intervention in a growth industry rest on some kind of externality argument— the basic rationale being that the gains to the national economy from the expansion of a particular sector may not be fully reflected in the market signals faced by individual agents. The greater the uncertainty and risk confronted by these agents, the more likely this is to be the case. Private risk to the individual firm can be substantial even when there is a long-term certainty about the growth prospects of an industry from a national point of view, as in the case of the semiconductor industry. Besides their externality features, growth industries characterized by product differentiation and production-curve and learning-curve economies imply a market structure that does not guarantee socially desirable outcomes. Thus for a variety of reasons, government policy intervention to promote the efficient expansion of growth sectors may be required.

Not all growth industries are the same. Some have significant input-output or productive linkages with other sectors and their expansion can shape the development of the entire economy. The semiconductor industry is a case in point. Its consequences for the economy are not the same as those of the breakfast food industry. The expansion of the semiconductor industry will reduce the costs of electronic information processing and will thereby affect production costs throughout the economy. Put in cautious language, the social returns from this industry are likely to exceed the private returns by a significant margin over the long run. This provides a powerful rationale for policy to encourage its continued expansion by making the necessary capital and labor available to it. Put more boldly, growth-linked industries are the engines of Schumpeterian economic progress; their expansion generates new means of producing and distributing goods, and they are the basis of structural change in the economy.

An industry in *transition,* in our terminology, is a mature industry undergoing basic changes in its product or production processes. In such an industry, the industrial structure is stable, and patterns of competition have been entrenched as the result of accumulation of experience among producers. During periods of transition, changes in the characteristics of product demand or in the most efficient production system occur, and these changes alter the patterns of competition. Shifts in the competitive positions of individual firms develop, frequently leading to shifts in employment and output levels. This process of change and adjustment may entail substantial short-run adjustment costs, especially if the process is rapid.

In the case of industries in transition, government intervention is frequently justified on grounds that the costs of adjustment are too onerous for individual firms or that the social welfare costs created by adjustment are appropriately the government's responsibility. For both efficiency and equity reasons, government policy may be desirable to smooth the transition process. This policy rationale may be extremely appealing when firms that are potentially profitable and competitive in the long run confront short-run difficulties due to rapid and unpredictable changes in market conditions. This rationale has played an important role in debates about the need for government policy in industries, such as automobiles and consumer electronics, where the process of transition has been triggered by sudden sharp changes in the terms of international competition.

In the automobile case, the pattern of American demand shifted suddenly (and many argue unpredictably) to the advantage of foreign competitors, making the standard products of American producers less attractive than the standard products of foreign companies. Adjusting product characteristics and production processes to meet the new pattern of demand requires a long period of transition before American firms can achieve competitiveness under the new market conditions. However, a sudden surge of imports may leave inadequate time for the necessary adjustments in products and production process to occur. As profits decline and consumers substitute foreign goods for domestic ones, short-term market developments can thwart the financing of necessary longer-term adjustments. This is especially true when changes in short-term market conditions are sharp and sudden. The market system is much better equipped to handle changes that occur in incremental steps.

When the underlying objective of policy is to maintain a large segment of domestic employment and production by aiding the adjustment process, the obvious policy—protection—is probably the worst one. Protection mutes market signals and simply blocks change. It is much better to provide direct subsidies or exceptional tax arrangements when policy seeks to maintain domestic production during an adjustment period. There may be abuse, but such policies are more likely than protection to reshape the industry along the lines the market requires. Protectionist policies to aid the adjustment process all too frequently turn into policies that mute market signals and eliminate the need to adjust.

An industry in *decline* is the last of our three industrial categories. In a declining industry, output, employment, and demand are falling over time, and there may be nothing an individual firm can do to maintain its market. From a national perspective, decline may be precipitated by foreign firms that are able to underprice national competitors. As argued earlier, the primary competitive advantage enjoyed by the newly industrializing and less developed countries is relatively cheap labor in industries with homogeneous output and standard-production characteristics. In these industries—such as apparel, footwear, and consumer electronics—international market conditions may necessitate decline in the advanced industrial countries unless protectionist barriers are erected to distort market signals. Most frequently, the rationale for policy in declining industries is based on adjustment cost considerations. The policy problems are how to move capital and labor to more profitable uses and how to accomplish the move in an equitable way.

Arguments about the need for government policy in a declining industry also frequently focus on national security considerations. National firms argue that their decline in international competition poses a national security problem by making the nation dependent on foreign sources of supply. These arguments and many others, often used by trade-impacted sectors to press for protectionist government policy, should be viewed with suspicion, if only because industrial decline rarely if ever implies the actual disappearance of an industry. The process of decline at the industrial level usually obscures the fact that certain firms or segments in the industry are maintaining or even expanding their markets. This point is forcefully demonstrated in the studies of steel, consumer electronics, textiles, apparel, and footwear in this volume. Each of these industries is in decline at the aggregate level, but each of them contains firms or segments that have worked out strategies for coping with changing international conditions.

The distinction between overall industrial performance and the performance of individual firms suggests that effective government policy with an industrial orientation must be based on a detailed understanding of firm-level as well as industrial-level dynamics. This brings us to the questions of why a particular firm may find itself in difficulty, what it might do to eliminate this difficulty, and—assuming there is a justification for it—how government policy might facilitate the adjustment process.

To understand firm-level dynamics, policy-makers must identify the various factors that can create a competitive position for an individual firm. Three such factors might be identified to start a discussion: raw material costs, labor costs, and complex production costs. Some businesses, like paper and pulp or oil, depend primarily on the accessibility and quality of particular natural resources. Others, like textiles and footwear, depend primarily on the cost of labor. Most manufacturing businesses in the advanced industrial countries, however, depend on several important and interrelated factors, including the scale of production, the technology employed, the distribution system, the product mix, and research and development. Understanding firm-level and industry-level dynamics requires an understanding of the role of these various factors in setting and changing the terms of market competition. From a policy-making viewpoint, the consequence of different and changing sources of competitive advantage for the individual firm is that no set of industry-wide statistical measures or indicators is an adequate guide to policy. Measures such as the age of facilities, research and development as a percent of sales, debt-equity ratios, and trade balances do not describe a competitive dynamic. At best, they describe average symptoms of an industry group.

Government Response to International Trade Difficulties

Although there is considerable agreement on the existence of competitive difficulties and structural decline in some important U.S. industries, there is disagreement about what the government response should be. Running through our discussion of competitive difficulties and appropriate government responses is a view of the role of the market, which ought to be made explicit here. Given the market principles underlying the U.S. economic system, the basic perspective motivating much of the policy debate is the perspective of market failure or government by exception: as long as the market mechanism functions successfully, it is preferred to government policy. Even this perspective, however, admits the necessity and desirability of government policy action under certain economic circumstances. Unfortunately for the elegant application of theory to policy, the range of exceptions is wide in practice. When exceptions become the rule, we need a rule for coping with the exceptions, or at least a means to judge the implications of the most difficult cases. Traditional static economic analysis obscures the dynamic and competitive character of the process by which national comparative advantage is created. Like traditional trade theory, it is concerned with maximizing welfare within a given static environment. Government by exception remains the characteristic policy rule consistent with this theoretical tradition.

Let us consider what some of the circumstances of market failure are. For example, when a declining sector's substantial adjustment costs are the result of price and wage barriers to capital and labor mobility, a market-oriented perspective is consistent with the introduction of market promotion policies to speed the adjustment process. This rationale for government policy is based on efficiency considerations and is distinct from an equity rationale for policy. On efficiency grounds, the socially optimal allocation of resources under changing national and international market conditions may require the movement of both capital and labor resources from industries in relative decline to more profitable employment opportunities. Market imperfections or rigidities may interfere with this movement by distorting the price, wage, and profitability signals that guide private market decisions. Under these circumstances, an efficiency argument can be made for applying corrective government policies. But even in the absence of such imperfections, government policy may be warranted in order to guarantee that the social benefits from the market adjustment process do not accrue disproportionately to some while the costs of the process fall disproportionately on others. Such costs include the income lost by workers during their transition to new jobs and any retraining and relocation costs that are associated with this transition. If the movement of capital is added to the analysis, there are the additional costs of income lost by capital during its transition to alternative uses. In the absence of government policy, these social costs of adjustment are paid by the labor (and capital) resources that are forced to find alternative employment under the new conditions. There is, of course, nothing necessarily equitable in this market resolution. If the government determines that a different distribution of costs and benefits is desirable, then it can introduce policies to achieve this distribution. This equity motivation for policy is behind the trade-adjustment assistance program that is part of the Trade Act of 1974. Income supplements and retraining and relocation grants, as well as aid programs for communities, are designed to reduce the costs paid by individual workers and communities as a result of industrial decline caused by changing conditions of international competition. Such policies are particularly important because workers in many trade-impacted industries are older, unskilled, and unable to find alternative employment opportunities easily.[16]

Barriers to sectoral adjustment and the resulting social and private costs of adjustment have provided a powerful rationale for market promotion policies in all the advanced industrial countries. Recently, another rationale for government policy has focused on the use of government macroeconomic policies, especially taxation policies, to promote investment and economic growth. The rationale for policy change has been an aggregate one, and the preferred policy instruments have been aggregate rather than industry-specific in character.

[16]For a complete breakdown of the characteristics of trade-impacted workers, see Charles Frank, *Foreign Trade and Domestic Aid* (Washington, D.C.: Brookings Institution, 1977).

Accelerated depreciation allowances and investment-tax credits are particular examples of supply-side policies based on this rationale. Tax cuts and government expenditure reductions to stimulate savings and investment at the macro level are broadly conceived of as supply-side policies. Such policies are not examples of industrial policy, as the term is used here, because they are not framed to deal with the problems of individual sectors or industries. Nonetheless, as the earlier discussion of the dynamics of comparative advantage suggests, supply-side policies, although aggregate in perspective, can have significant sectoral effects on the competitive positions of capital-intensive and technology-intensive industries over time. Thus, supply-side considerations are a powerful rationale for government policy to promote industry at the aggregate level, and the competitive difficulties of particular industries in international trade are undoubtedly a source of political and economic pressure in support of such policies.

The economic rationale for industry-specific policies, as distinct from market promotion and aggregate economic policies of the type discussed here, is industry-specific market failure. Government policy aimed at a particular industry or sector is required when market conditions fail to produce socially desirable outcomes in that industry or sector. Market failure may be the result of externalities, the presence of public goods, or the existence of market imperfections. Each of these factors has been used to press for industry-specific policies in industries that are facing competitive difficulties in international trade. For example, the use of government funds to promote research and development in high-technology industries has been urged on the grounds that the social returns of research and development exceed the private ones. This is a straightforward externality argument that is supported by empirical work. It is also supported by recent theoretical work on the behavior of markets in which firms compete mainly in process or product innovation rather than in prices. Under such conditions, the usual presumption that markets work optimally is suspect. In the words of two highly respected theoretical economists: "in those sectors of the economy where technological change is important, the analysis of competitive market equilibrium is of limited applicability . . . and a fundamentally different kind of analysis is required."[17]

A second type of market failure occurs in the case of so-called public goods that are produced inadequately or not at all by private producers because of two peculiar characteristics: first, such goods are "nonrival," in the sense that one person's use of them does not diminish

[17]This point is made by Partha Dasgupta and Joseph Stiglitz, "Uncertainty, Industrial Structure, and the Speed of R & D," *The Bell Journal of Economics* 11, no. 1 (Spring 1980), pp. 1–28.

someone else's ability to enjoy them; and second, they are "non-exclusive," in the sense that those who choose not to pay for them cannot be kept from using them. So far as the debates about industrial policy are concerned, arguments using a public goods rationale for government intervention focus on national security or defense. For example, a recent study of the steel industry by the Office of Technology Assessment argues that government policies to aid the U.S. steel industry are necessary in part because steel is vital to national security. This kind of argument, applied in other countries, is in large part responsible for the fact that 45 percent of world capacity in steel production (more than 50 percent of European capacity) is nationalized.[18] A similar argument is frequently made for government policies to promote the semiconductor industry, on the grounds that its products have important military applications. For example, a recent study argues that the loss of U.S. competitiveness in the commercial semiconductor industry would lead to possible foreign control over the development of some state-of-the-art military hardware in the United States.[19]

The fact that the output of a particular industrial sector is vital to national security implies that the social benefits from its production are greater than the private benefits, and that government policies are required to maintain the socially necessary level of production. Nonetheless, there are at least two steps between the assertion of a national security interest and the conclusion that government policies are required. First, it must be demonstrated that in the absence of such policies, market indicators will not support the level of domestic production required for national security reasons. Existing studies of the steel and semiconductor industries are not conclusive on this point. Second, it must further be demonstrated that in the absence of sufficient domestic production, the necessary output could not be obtained through foreign trade channels. For example, if it were necessary, could the United States rely on imports of steel and semiconductor products from its allies or from other nations on fair market terms? Given the vagaries of international economic and political relations and the importance of uninterrupted supplies to the effectiveness of national defense, a risk-averse strategy might require that government industrial policies guarantee domestic output availability (including stockpiling) at levels dictated by national defense considerations.

The third general category of market-failure arguments for govern-

---

[18]This figure is taken from Office of Technology Assessment, *Technology and* ·*l Industry Competitiveness*, p. 102.

[19]See Julian Gresser, "High Technology and Japanese Industrial Policy: A Strategy for U.S. Policy Makers," A Report submitted to the Assistant Secretary for East Asian and Pacific Affairs, U.S. Department of State (unpublished, 1980).

ment policies rests on the existence of imperfections in private product or factor markets. In product markets, such imperfections may take several well-known forms, including barriers to entry from increasing returns to scale, product differentiation, and advertising. As even the most elementary treatise on economics indicates, in the presence of such imperfections, there is nothing necessarily socially optimal about the functioning of the private market. Thus the existence of such imperfections becomes a powerful rationale for government policies. For example, it is this rationale which underlies antitrust policy in the United States, a general market promotion policy with significant industry-specific effects.

The issue of antitrust and related patent regulations arises in debates about industrial policy because of the increasingly popular view that the energetic pursuit of antitrust measures has put U.S. industry at a disadvantage vis-à-vis its competitors in Europe and Japan. According to this view, a narrow focus on domestic market structure and a failure to acknowledge the existence of foreign competition have led policymakers to an overly restrictive stance on mergers among U.S. firms in some industries. As a consequence, it is argued, U.S. firms have not been able to exploit the scale economies realized by foreign firms. This argument has been stressed in recent discussions of industrial policy for the semiconductor industry. In particular, in Chapter 4, Borrus, Millstein, and Zysman argue that vertical integration between semiconductor producers and users in consumer electronics and computers is a source of competitive advantage exploited by Japanese firms. As the capital and research costs of semiconductors increase, the economies of scale from this type of integration are likely to become large, thereby increasing the Japanese competitive advantage, unless antitrust guidelines are relaxed so that the U.S. industry structure is allowed to adjust in the same direction.

Imperfections in the capital market provide another reason for government policy. Such imperfections may take several forms. Private capital market institutions frequently appear to discriminate between large and small business borrowers. Because of insufficient information, lenders face risk and uncertainty about returns. If they lend to large firms with large flows of internal savings and market reputations, they have confidence that the borrowers will be able to repay their loans, regardless of the success or failure of the actual project for which funds are lent. In contrast, if they lend to small firms, the perceived risk of default may be greater, even though this perception may simply reflect the fact that there is less market information about small firms. Since market information is costly to acquire, lenders may simply prefer not to lend to small borrowers as part of their profit-maximizing strategy in a world of imperfect information. Capital market imperfections may also exist as a consequence of a business preference for reinvesting internal funds even if there are outside investment opportunities with higher rates of return. This preference for reinvestment may reflect the objectives of business decision-makers, who at least in the short run are more interested in growth or sales than in profit maximization. It may also simply reflect the fact that such decision-makers have better information about reinvestment opportunities than about opportunities in other firms and industries, and given their information, they will choose the most profitable reinvestment alternatives.

Alleged imperfections in the capital market that result from the preferred access to external capital enjoyed by large "mature" firms and industries, and from their preference for reinvesting internal funds, have played an important role in recent debates about the need for a new government finance organization along the lines of the Reconstruction Finance Corporation. According to proponents of such an organization, government intervention in the capital market is required to guide funds from large, declining industries, to smaller, higher-productivity industries whose growth is limited by their access to capital.[20] Firms in the latter industries, it is argued, are discriminated against in the capital market because they are relatively small and new, hence lacking the reputation necessary to compete for external funds. In addition, many of these firms are found in high-technology industries, where there is greater than average risk on investment projects.

The issue of risk introduces the possibility of another type of capital market imperfection—the failure of the private capital market to finance projects that are excessively risky by the standards of private industry. Industrial policy discussions frequently cite the need for government policies to guarantee capital availability for high-risk projects in high-technology or new-technology industries, such as semiconductors and industries involved in the development of alternative energy sources. For example, some analysts have argued that the future expansion of the semiconductor industry may be limited by capital, because the new higher capital costs of entry cannot be covered by the venture capital market that has heretofore provided the bulk of funds. According to this argument, the venture capital market is not capable of supplying private capital to high-risk, high-return projects, beyond a certain size, and that size is fast approaching in semiconductors. One possible policy response to this situation would be to reduce still further the taxation of private returns in the venture capital market—raising

[20]For a discussion of the proposed Reconstruction Finance Corporation, see Lester Thurow, *The Zero Sum Society* (New York: Penguin Books, 1981).

the after-tax return to stimulate more lending. Another would be to introduce some kind of government capital organization or program to insure some of the risk.

A final capital market argument for government policy intervention focuses on the time horizon of private market borrowers and lenders. For example, the study of the steel industry by the Office of Technology Assessment argues that the share of equity finance in total finance in the steel industry has tended to favor investments that have a quick payoff over long-term investments that are needed to renew the technological position of the industry. (According to the OTA study, even though the debt-equity ratio for the entire steel industry rose from 36.5 to 44.0 percent during the past ten years, the U.S. industry has a debt-equity ratio only one-half that of the Japanese industry.) This is a specific example of a general argument that the low debt-equity ratio of many U.S. industries means that investments are evaluated according to the criterion of short-term profitability of interest to shareholders rather than according to the criterion of long-term profitability which concerns the nation. The policy prescription seems to be that government intervention might be called for to offset the bias for short-run projects built in by the structure of finance.

Summarizing the above discussion, it is apparent that at least in theory there are several possible rationales for government policies that respond to sectoral adjustment problems caused by changing conditions in international markets. The first step in any national debate over the need for government policy under such circumstances should be to identify the particular rationales at issue. This step is critical because it forces the proponents of policy to be specific about their objectives and about their view as to why the market system alone will fail to realize them.

GOVERNMENT INTERVENTION AS POLITICAL NECESSITY

Thus far our discussion has focused on government intervention as an explicit economic strategy developed in response to market failures or company failures in international markets. In this section, we consider the political rationale for such intervention and the domestic political problems that influence the government's ability to make effective economic policy aimed at the problems of particular sectors or industries in international trade. As earlier sections of this chapter suggest, the government has many policies with explicit or unintended sectoral consequences. These policies have many different domestic purposes, such as regulating competition, assuring consumer or worker safety, and encouraging regional development or better transportation and housing. In some cases, the purposes of these policies may simply conflict with the objective of industrial adjustment and international competitiveness. In such cases, we may have to accept disadvantages in international competitiveness in order to pursue other goals, such as certification of the safety of drugs. Or we may have to accept the fact that some social purposes must be subordinated to the continued well-being of U.S. industries in international markets. In other cases, however, the conflicts between policy objectives may be illusory, the unnecessary result of the ways we traditionally conduct policy. In these cases, by examining existing approaches to policy we may achieve more satisfying outcomes without abandoning diverse multiple objectives.

In sum, as individual sectors are jolted by shifts in international competition there will be political pressures for sector-specific policies to sustain employment and production. There is no doubt that we will continue to have some sector-specific policies. The only question is whether these policies will respond to the short-run demands for protection or whether they will be used to promote long-run competitive adjustments.

Reshaping Existing Policy

Let us consider the case of regulation, taking our example from new-style regulation (administration of the processes of production and product characteristics to assure worker, consumer, and community well-being), rather than old-style regulation (regulation of prices and market entry) to assure approximate competitive processes. Regulatory processes that are suitable to an insulated domestic market may be inappropriate in international competition. It is not the objectives of regulation that we question here, but the way in which we achieve them. Let us consider automobile pollution and mileage regulation (auto safety would fall into a different category and require a different analysis). Pollution and gas mileage regulation were introduced because market competition was not taking account of externalities in auto usage. The problem was classic and simple. Evidently, the public good of a clean environment could be achieved only if each individual's auto usage was less polluting. Given a choice, however, no individual had an incentive to purchase anti-pollution devices. Each person's pollution was simply not great enough to affect the air he breathed. If everyone else bought non-polluting cars, the individual buyer had no incentive to do so, because he benefited from clean air anyway. If no one else took measures to avoid polluting, self-restraint had little consequence. In the case of gas mileage, the gap between domestic and world oil prices gave misleading signals to consumers. As long as gas prices were low enough, the gas mileage of each car was relatively unimportant. Again, the public problems of diminishing oil reserves and rising import bills were public consequences that did not enter the private calculus of individual auto buyers.

An obvious response to both problems was to require product characteristics that would force the consumer to incorporate these social externalities in his choice. The question was not what to do, but how to do it. Choosing to mandate product characteristics shifted the problem from the consumer to the producer: the producer had to adjust the automobile to meet the new product characteristics mandated by government. In this way, the U.S. government sought to achieve the public goals of clean air and improved gas mileage by influencing the behavior of firms rather than the behavior of consumers.

The assumption underlying the policy choice was that either the producer would bear the costs of producing pollution-free, high-mileage cars, or alternatively, that those costs would be passed on to the consumer in the form of higher product prices. In either case, the firm was to act as the collector of a user tax in order to bring private and public costs more closely into line. Although the objective of this type of regulation has been the achievement of a public goal, the firms have been expected to solve resulting product development problems separately and at their own expense. In essence, we have made the pursuit of a public goal that was not being achieved through the market an element of market competition between firms. All firms are not equally capable of collecting these special taxes, which reflect the extra costs associated with publicly mandated purposes, and we must consider whether their different abilities in this area should affect who wins and loses in the market. To remain in business and collect the implicit "pollution and mileage" tax, producers must adjust their products or production techniques. Certainly, a prima facie argument can be made that competitive necessity will drive firms to adjust products to incorporate mandated characteristics more rapidly, and that firms which cannot meet these public purposes should be penalized in private market competition. Whatever the merits of this argument, however, there are problems in trying to achieve the public purposes of incorporating externalities in the cost of the automobile through the process of market competition between producers. Many of these problems are by now well known.

First, since many of the costs of product development are fixed, the smaller the total sales of an individual producer the higher the per-auto cost of incorporating new product features. Similarly, the cost will be a larger share of total available investment funds for smaller firms, and this will reduce their ability to respond to other problems. As a result of the greater burden imposed on smaller firms, such firms may lose their competitive edge relative to larger ones. For example, since General Motors is already so strong that its pricing and model policies are shaped in part by the need to assure the continuing viability of its competitors, regulation of this sort simply increases the strength of its position. Thus one policy objective, assuring a domestic industry composed of several competitors, is endangered by the way a second policy objective is pursued. In contrast, policies to promote joint research and development efforts, or public loans or tax deferments to defray the immediate capital outlays required to redesign the automobile, will not necessarily affect the relative profitability of different-sized firms. They do, however, imply a different distribution of the costs of regulation, and they also raise the danger of collusive behavior among producers.

Regulation can create a substantial disjuncture in markets by redefining acceptable products. The need to develop new products to meet new conditions of market regulation can press hard on the capacity of individual firms to adjust. Policies of assistance intended to help firms quickly carry out necessary changes in a product or a production process can facilitate the regulatory purpose. The question here is not whether we ought to have environmental regulation; it is assumed that we should. Nor is the question one of who should pay for such regulation; distributional questions are not the focus of this regulatory example. The real focus is the impact of such regulation on competition in domestic and international markets. As this discussion suggests, we must re-examine regulatory processes with an eye to their implications for the competitiveness of individual firms or sectors in international trade.

A similar argument can be made about old-style antitrust regulation. Again, the question is not whether we should have policies to promote competitive markets, but rather how to define the relevant market. Two large domestic producers in an insulated domestic market may be able to exert market power. Those same two producers struggling to maintain position in international markets may not be able to exert such power. In industries involved in international trade, market power must be defined and measured in terms of international markets rather than domestic ones.

Industrial Change: Political Resistance and International Competition

The real political challenge to the formulation of effective industrial policy is reconciling the demands of those dislocated by international trade with the necessity of continued industrial adjustment. Industrial change and adjustment are not painless processes, and labor threatened by a loss of jobs or businessmen threatened by declining profits will seek political help to preserve their position. To the worker put out of his job or the industrialist who sees his plants close, the aggregate economic gains from industrial change are of little import. To those who pay, how the costs of adjustment are shared is a critical issue. We must expect those who bear the costs of adjustment to seek policies that cushion them from the shock of change. Policies offering subsidy or protection in response to sharp dislocations in employment or production are inevitable. Presumably, as the number of industries adversely affected by international trade increases, the base of a protectionist coalition will expand. The result is that an administration's political ability to refuse protection to particular groups will dwindle as the number of groups seeking help increases.

Perhaps ironically, an industrial policy may be a crucial political ingredient in maintaining political support for adjustment and free trade. Certainly, industrial policies have played such a role abroad. The political ability of the French Planning Commission to generate support for aggregate policies and market promotion policies that sustained growth has been a remarkable achievement. This political achievement has been at least as significant as its technical efforts in specific sectors. In the cases examined in this volume, American government policies have responded to short-run demands; they have not sought the basis of longer-term adjustment policies. In the absence of conscious government strategies for adjustment, the result has been protectionist policies that have not served the interests of consumers and often not even the needs of producers.

One might argue that creating the capacity for developing sectoral policies generates demands for policy intervention. In fact, in the U.S. government, permanent departments to receive applications for assistance already exist—client-based bureaucracies linked to congressional committees provide a permanent application center. The policy issue is how to counterbalance narrowly defined and negative policy. If the supposed risk of the government's development of a long-run view is presented as an argument in favor of doing nothing, the cases in this volume suggest that short-run policies of subsidy and protection will often become long-run policies.

The assumption here is that there are substantial national gains to be realized from transforming political demands for protection into demands for competitive adjustment. That the American government has not taken the initiative in developing a political basis for adjustment and promotion policies to counteract the political support for protectionist policies is evident from the case studies presented here. Take, for example, the U.S. government's repeated use of Orderly Marketing Agreements (OMAs) as an instrument of protectionist policy. OMAs have been introduced in the cases of footwear, textiles, apparel, and consumer electronics. An OMA is an explicit agreement between two countries about the volume and composition of their trade in particular goods, such as shoes or automobiles. Protection against foreign competition in the form of an OMA can be used to help a politically vocal, well-organized, and visible interest group while imposing the costs of such help on a large, unorganized, and unidentifiable group of consumers, each of whom shares in these costs to an uncalculated extent. Because the groups benefiting from protection are organized, whereas the groups paying for it are diffuse, protection tends to be a politically expedient choice. The costs of alternative policies, such as tax and credit policies, to other industries or consumers (or both) can be more easily observed and resisted. Thus although protection is a second-best strategy by economic criteria, it is a workable and often superior political strategy.

The broad lines of postwar U.S. policy, however, have called for an open trading system and a continuous reduction in the barriers to trade. Thus we continuously treat protection as an unfortunate deviation from the general thrust of policy. In order to minimize the scope of trade barriers, and to suggest their temporary and limited character, we have often turned to bilateral agreements, such as OMAs, to restrict imports.

OMAs seem to reconcile immediate demands for protection with a longstanding commitment to free trade. Ironically, they can also seriously damage the protected industry. As we have argued above, sudden and unexpected surges of imports can destroy firms that would be able to make competitive adjustments over time. OMAs seldom effectively block these initial surges and can only create damaging side effects. OMAs simply transfer the adjustment problem to foreign competitors. Once these competitors have made the necessary adjustments, they pose even more dangerous threats to domestic industry.

OMAs tend to have three main consequences. The first is well understood: the restriction of imports from one country encourages new producers to spring up quickly in other places. The second is even more serious: if one limits the volume of imports, it is in the interest of foreign producers to move into higher-value goods to achieve the largest possible value of total sales. Finally, foreign producers may alter the composition of the goods they produce to escape the quantitative limits on certain imports. For example, David Yoffie shows in Chapter 6 that after the imposition of OMAs on the import of leather shoes, foreign producers added rubber soles to place these products in the non-protected rubber category. Overall, OMAs force our foreign competitors to adjust, and this accentuates the long-run problems of the domestic industries they are designed to protect.

In the absence of an explicit strategy for adjustment and promotion, it is likely that temporary policy measures to ease adjustment will continue to impede it altogether. Moreover, the link between protection and actions to restore competitiveness is weak precisely because while protectionism generates the funds required to finance such actions, it simultaneously reduces the incentives to take them. Protection reduces competition, and reduced competition means less, not more, pressure for necessary changes. The only way to guarantee that the profits generated from a protectionist policy are used for the objectives motivating that policy is to link the extension of protection to an explicit and monitored plan for adjustment. To be successful, protection should be granted only on a conditional basis. An adjustment plan and timetable should be the quid pro quo for the additional profits earned by the domestic producers as a consequence of protection, and evidence of deviations from the plan should lead to a reconsideration and possible termination of protection. The general principle of the conditionality of adjustment policies goes beyond the issue of protection and trade. In the absence of explicit objectives for industrial policy, the dislocations of change are most likely to produce policies that retard adjustment to changed patterns of competition. Moreover, unless trade policy is linked to domestic policy and an understanding of competitive dynamics, it will be largely counterproductive.

The necessity for an explicit understanding of the competitive dynamics of a sector, and the capacity to use trade policy as an instrument for domestic development, is nowhere clearer than in the growth industry of semiconductors, which we have discussed several times already. In this industry domestic firms have felt a capacity pinch as demand has expanded. Indeed, applications for semiconductors have diffused so rapidly that there is likely to be a rapid fluctuation between capacity and overcapacity for several years. The danger is that Japanese firms exporting from a highly organized domestic base will be better able to plan expansions aimed at capturing U.S. market share. The Japanese challenge has received extensive press coverage; but in fact, in quality and capacity the U.S. firms have responded vigorously, maintaining market share. The real danger lies in the closed nature of the Japanese market. So long as the market remains closed, or effectively closed to U.S. suppliers, Japanese companies can expand in a more orderly fashion, in secure possession of a substantial world market share. Trade policies that force open the Japanese market with threats to close our own market may be necessary to prevent an insulated Japanese industry from gaining unfair advantage in our markets.

Here is a case where government initiative can prevent trade policy from being purely defensive.

In sum, we must accept political resistance to change and demands to provide assistance in international competition as natural, perhaps inevitable. National policy must seek to construct strategies that will permit executive-branch leadership to promote structural change by thwarting protectionist alliances. Government policy must serve to unravel the political obstacles to change: it should not be simply a reflection of protectionist demands.

AMERICAN POLICY AND INDUSTRIAL ADJUSTMENT

The first sections of this chapter have examined analytically the changing context of trade and the political basis of government strategies for trade and industry. Here we examine the basic pattern of American policy and its implications for our trade position. In the period culminating with the Smoot-Hawley tariff in 1934, the terms of the national policy debate assumed the right to protection and required that individual instances of free trade be justified on an exceptional basis. The post–World War II trade discussion reversed the framework of the Depression years. The creation of the Bretton Woods–GATT trade and money apparatus sought to correct the workings of the international economy that were thought to have contributed to the unraveling of national economies in the interwar years, and also to establish a firm economic base for a security alliance. Following that fertile period of institution-building, the American trade debate became one of general support for free trade, with justification required for particular protectionist exceptions.[21] Both American strategic and economic positions shifted in the years that intervened between Smoot-Hawley and Bretton Woods. An international business constituency favoring free trade emerged. The industrial purposes of a considerable constituency and the national purpose as defined by those making foreign policy overlapped.[22] The free trade thrust itself culminated in the Kennedy Round of tariff negotiations.[23] Substantial reductions in external barriers were achieved. Equally important, responsibility for trade was shifted away from Congress toward the President and the Treasury,

[21]See Raymond Bauer, Ithiel de Sola Poole, and Lewis Dexter, *American Business and Public Policy* (Cambridge, Mass.: MIT Press, 1972).

[22]These issues are analyzed succinctly by Krasner in Peter Katzenstein, ed., *Between Power and Plenty;* and by Block in *The Emergence of International Economic Disorder.*

[23]See John W. Evans, *The Kennedy Round in American Trade Policy* (Cambridge, Mass.: Harvard University Press, 1971), for a description of the negotiations.

55

and trade negotiations were conducted by a direct presidential appointee, the Special Trade Representative. The bureaucratic coalition represented the institutional commitment to open trade, which could force protection to be debated in terms of exceptions.[24] The Kennedy Round tariff reductions, in fact, shifted attention away from external restraints to internal policies that acted as restraints on trade.

Overall, the general thrust of American policy since the war has been aimed at creating a world that favors free trade—meaning the free flow of goods and finance (labor is a notable exception in all our policies). Yet from the cases examined in this volume, it is clear that in specific manufacturing sectors, policies have run a different course. The exceptions are more numerous than one would have expected from the rhetoric (see Table 1). Promotion of American interests abroad came in the form of general rules to encourage the expansion of international trade, which was thought to favor American companies. Importantly, alongside international agreements to free the flow of goods were policies to support the multinationalization of American business. More precisely, American rules were structures to favor direct foreign investment. Two forms of support were crucial: first, the tax laws tended to encourage overseas investment rather than domestic adjustment; and second, the trade laws were arranged to allow American firms to invest overseas, producing part of their product at these offshore locations, and to be taxed on only the value added abroad when the goods re-entered the American market. A third element of support for direct foreign investment was provided by U.S. aid programs that helped the developing countries establish export platforms.

Sector-specific policies, in contrast, have largely protected rather than promoted. Policies conceived to respond to particular sectoral problems have served mainly to insulate American firms from foreign goods and producers. Yet given the general commitment to free trade, restrictive policies have been established on narrow grounds and for purposes as limited as political pressure would permit. There has been a tension between the specific pressures, often channeled through the Commerce Department, and the general commitment embodied by the Treasury.

Specific protectionist policies have often been justified on grounds that they would ease transition or permit adjustment. In the cases examined in this volume, the policies seemingly did neither. In whatever language they were couched, they had the effect of protecting existing producers and the existing arrangements of production. In essence,

[24]This coalition is described in both I. M. Destler, *Making Foreign Economic Policy* (Washington, D.C.: Brookings Institution, 1980), and Stephen D. Cohen, *The Making of United States International Economic Policy* (New York: Praeger, 1977).

Table 1. External and internal U.S. policies in regard to various industries,

Policy	Textiles	Apparel	Footwear	Steel	Autos	Television	Integrated circuits
External							
Protection	Extensive, ending with Multifiber	Extensive	Extensive, mostly OMAs	Trigger pricing, aimed first at Japan, then at Europe	No	Limited to 807 clauses	807, but not important
Direct foreign Investment	Yes; crucial to pattern of adjustment in U.S. markets	Yes	Yes	No	No	Yes	Yes
Promotion of trade abroad	No	No	No	No	No	No	No
Internal							
Financial protection	No	No	No	No	Chrysler Loan Act	No	No
Intervention to promote domestic industry	Nominal	Nominal	Nominal	No	No	No	Military until 1970 and since 1980; military market proportionally small now

policy protected profits in the hope that American firms would themselves make the appropriate adjustments. Yet the snowball of protection described by Aggarwal and Haggard in Chapter 5 makes it clear that for the most part the policies simply served to raise industry profits while eliminating the need to adjust. In steel, as Borrus suggests in Chapter 2, foreign markets were abandoned and domestic markets insulated. Protection served to raise profits that helped some firms leave the industry with their winnings rather than reinvest to make steel more competitive. In Chapter 3, Millstein paints a similar picture in the television segment of consumer electronics, where the pursuit of cheap-wage strategies in lieu of domestic investment in more sophisticated production technologies led inexorably to disaster. Thus, ironically, many of the strategies of external protection damaged the very industries that sought them, as the earlier discussion of OMA's indicates. Such strategies often forced our competitors to adjust, which only made things worse for domestic firms in the next round of competition. The short-term solutions to political pressure have encouraged a step-by-step march toward broader protection. A second example of how external protection has hurt domestic industry is evident in Chapter 3, where Millstein demonstrates how the Trade Act of 1974 encouraged offshore production. In consumer electronics, this production ultimately encouraged American firms to adopt product and production strategies that slowed down the introduction of solid-state television and the automated production processes that solid-state products permit.

American policy has not sought adjustment from industry as the quid pro quo for protection, nor has the government sought to intervene to promote adjustment. Rather we have established a pattern of incentives that has encouraged two kinds of adjustment. First, it has encouraged American firms to meet cheap-wage competition by moving abroad rather than innovating. Second, it has encouraged foreign firms to innovate in products and production processes to meet American markets and beat American protection.

The sector studies presented in this volume were selected because they represent industries that have faced intense foreign pressure in their domestic markets. With the exception of the electronics sector, these are largely mature industries whose primary markets are domestic. Until recently, for example, exports in textiles served mainly to absorb slack when American demand sagged. A different sample, one might argue, would find a different result, a less striking pattern of protection. In growing and expanding industries that are seeking markets abroad, policy may look very different. Or, one may argue, growing sectors at any rate need less specific assistance and are the beneficiaries of general rules. Such arguments can only be definitively refuted by a different study sample. Nonetheless, there is certainly a prima facie case that in manufacturing there is limited specific support from government for growing sectors and that defensive policies primarily consist of external protection. With the exception of aircraft and military equipment, we believe that our overall policy findings would have been the same if we had chosen different industries to study.

As the cases included in this volume suggest, American policy has responded to the specific domestic adjustment problems provoked by international trade with protectionist measures. Such measures have sometimes been justified in the name of industrial adjustment or of easing corporate transition, but they have not been reinforced by domestic policies to encourage such shifts. There has been no government leadership to help guide firms toward a new market competitiveness. The resulting policy gap can be variously evaluated, depending on one's policy and political views. The Chrysler case represents the extreme limit of intervention. Here the government used financial protection to help a firm retain market share, but the central initiative remained with the company. Chrysler's policies were clearly altered by its negotiations, and it pushed further toward a small-car strategy. Yet the government did not seek to change management or force a restructuring through mergers.

The overriding intent of the case studies in this volume is not to argue which policies have worked in which case. It is rather to show that the range of American policies, given the nature of the problems and the array of government strategies abroad, is quite narrow and has a common theme: apparently, we can have protection or nothing. Domestic intervention has not been an alternative to trade restrictions, a means of derailing pressures for external protection. (When the French entered the Common Market, their domestic apparatus of sector intervention served to contain political reaction to German competition by providing financial protection and internal assistance in adjustment.)

The implications for our purpose here are twofold. First, the American executive branch will have difficulty targeting industries, product segments, or firms that it perceives to be crucial to policy. The U.S. system is organized precisely to block such discrimination. The limits are both political and legal. Second, the executive will have difficulty pulling together strands of policy for a continuously changing set of purposes. Purposes in industry policy must be defined by a shifting set of market needs, not by pre-established administrative and regulatory criteria. The free trade versus protection dichotomy is a product of our political structure; but it is also consonant with our political ideology, which abhors direct intervention in corporate choices as a violation of managerial prerogatives.

59

CHAPTER TWO

The Politics of Competitive Erosion in the U.S. Steel Industry

MICHAEL BORRUS

The steel, television, semiconductor, and automobile chapters all focus on industrial competition between the United States and Japan and on the role of government in shaping the options available to firms in those industries. Because Japan's emergence as the primary rival to America's industrial pre-eminence is the subject of intense policy controversy, the editors believe that their own view of the issue should be explicit. As Chalmers Johnson has remarked, the Japanese experience contains both "soft" and "hard" lessons for the United States. The soft lesson—which emerges from a predominant concern with management style, worker attitudes, or the legal forms of inter-company collaboration in Japan— suggests that the United States can offset the Japanese advantage by imitating specific features of the Japanese economic system, to the extent that such features do not reflect unique cultural traditions. The hard lesson, by contrast, is that the Japanese advantage rests on basic political choices that are fundamentally different from the political choices made in the United States. The Japanese have actively pursued industrial development and international competitiveness as a tenet of national security. They have mobilized their economy by methods and policies that are at odds with the basic political guidelines for policy-making in the United States. Their mobilization strategy has allowed them to capture what have been called the advantages of economic backwardness. Because many of their industries were in their infancy in the 1950s, the Japanese were able to use foreign trade and licensing strategies to borrow and apply the best available foreign technology. By the 1970s, after many years of pursuing this strategy, Japanese industries had equipment that was more modern than that of many of their American counterparts. As shown in the steel industry study that follows, the Americans, like the Japanese, introduced the most advanced steel technologies whenever in recent years they built new plants. After World War II, however, relatively few new facilities were built in the United States, while in Japan a major new investment boom developed.

Rapid Japanese expansion involved more than effective borrowing of technology. The sudden burst of domestic demand for mass-produced goods, ranging from motorcycles to television sets and later to automobiles, permitted the Japanese to innovate in product design and production processes. The consequences of such innovation are evident in the studies of television and automobiles in this volume. Real competition between growing firms over rapidly expanding new markets is sufficient to account for many of the Japanese advantages in production management. Indeed, organizational management theory predicts that flexible and innovative management arrangements develop more readily in companies growing quickly in unstable environments, which has been the Japanese case, than in static companies in stable environments, which has often been the case in mature American industries.

The Japanese economic miracle, though, was not achieved simply by companies competing with one another in burgeoning domestic markets. The "high-growth system" was fostered by a variety of coordinated government policies, as the analysis of the semiconductor industry indicates. The government played a powerful role in preventing the domestic market from being overrun by foreign competition and in assuring the resources needed for companies to expand. Japan's credit-based financial system, which encouraged and permitted long-term management strategies, was structured by the government to support rapid growth. Even the system of labor relations, with its famed "quality circles," has its political roots. The underside of the system of lifetime employment security is a system of temporary workers and small firms that absorb the shocks of economic fluctuations in the Japanese economy. The shop floor integration of labor on terms set by management is inextricably connected to the political weakness of the left. In summary the hard lesson to be drawn from an analysis of the Japanese economic miracle is that a successful response to the Japanese challenge will require real political choices about the appropriate use of government policy in the U.S. economy.

The following chapter considers how the political structure of the American steel industry, even more than the market problems it has faced, has set the terms of the debate over U.S. policy which has been triggered by the Japanese challenge.

ONE CONSTANT feature of U.S. trade policy since World War II has been the autonomy granted U.S. corporations to pursue their own strategies for adjusting to changing conditions of competition in the international economy. The grant of such autonomy has been an ideological concomitant of the liberal or "free trade" international economic regime that U.S. policy-makers have fashioned and defended in the postwar period. The national economic gains to be had from industrial specialization and comparative advantage, based on national resource endowments in capital and labor, have presumably been a primary concern of U.S. policy-makers. According to this view, firms must be free to pursue adjustment along their industry's life cycle precisely because their autonomous actions, as if by an invisible hand, will maximize the static well-being of the nation.

This chapter is intended in part to challenge such a perspective by illuminating the performance and experience of the U.S. steel industry over the past three decades. The case study which follows acknowledges the simple proposition that nations want to participate in the international economy on their own terms and that national governments can and do intervene to alter markets to their own advantage. One of the prerequisites for industrial growth in the development stage has always been the construction of domestic capacity in strategic industries such as steel. In the course of acquiring such industries, governments have intervened in ways that have shifted comparative advantage between nations. In the postwar period, the rapid rise of the Japanese steel industry to international competitive pre-eminence is one example. Equally, in the course of *ongoing* industrial adjustment, the political interaction between the domestic sector and the state may drastically alter comparative advantage among competing industrial sectors of different nations. This is not to slight the role, emphasized by economists, of relative factor costs, technological innovation, and scale economies in determining the international competitiveness of national industries; it is rather to suggest that the political choices made by industrial firms and by policy arms of the state may be important determinants of an industry's long-run competitiveness in international markets.[1]

A second proposition flows from this perspective. The ability and willingness of firms in a sector to evolve along a production cycle toward the higher value-added technologies most appropriate for advanced industrial economies is altered by the political interaction over industrial adjustment between business and the state. The firms and governments that participate in the actual processes of industrial adjustment are real political actors, not merely constituent inputs to the formal analytic of economic theory. Firms, indeed entire sectors, may be unable to manage adjustment successfully and unwilling to accept the consequences of their failure. When, as in the U.S. steel industry, these firms control a significant portion of economic production, em-

---

[1] Thus, in industrial economies, comparative advantage should be understood as the cumulative effect of company capacities and policy choices, not simply as the effect of resource endowments in capital and labor.

ploy a significant portion of the labor force, underwrite the economic health of entire communities, and have the consequent political power to dominate policy, such unwillingness will frustrate the ideology and the goals of theorists and policy-makers alike.

This role of politics in the process of industrial adjustment and in the evolution of a national industrial sector's life cycle will be our central concern here. We shall focus in particular on the experience of the U.S. steel industry over the past twenty-five years. During this time, that industry has fallen from an aggregate position of international competitive dominance to a position in which its largest integrated producers retain their domestic market share only with government assistance. In that same time span, by contrast, a tightly oligopolistic Japanese steel industry has risen from backwardness to become, in the aggregate, the world's most efficient and technologically advanced steel producer. The supplanting of U.S. dominance by the Japanese should be understood initially as a failure by the largest integrated U.S. producers to manage the transition between two distinct technological phases of steel-making in a way that could have left them internationally competitive.[2] As the next section suggests, the shift from open-hearth to the "greenfield" method of basic oxygen steel-making that began during the mid-1950s was a transitional phase in the global steel industry's life cycle. The experience of the largest U.S. producers since that time has been in part an attempt to catch up with Japanese success in managing this transition, and in part a political battle to forestall the effects of their own failure to do so. The political success of the large U.S. producers initially allowed them to protect their market share, and then in the late 1970s to undertake long-deferred adjustment on terms that enabled them to retain their profitability. In essence, their political strategy was the primary factor enabling them to cope with a new phase in the industry's life cycle for which they were technologically and structurally unprepared. Of course, the political success of the large integrated producers came at the expense of others: domestic steel consumers, labor, and the older steel-making communities whose production had sustained U.S. predominance during the earlier, open-hearth phase of the industry's life.

The first section of this chapter describes the present comparative positions of the Japanese and U.S. steel industries and examines the key political and economic factors that led to Japanese ascent and U.S. decline through the late 1960s. The second section describes and analyzes the political strategy chosen by the largest U.S. steel producers in

[2]By an industry "in transition" we mean a mature industry undergoing basic changes in product or process that require sustained investment and whose cumulative effects alter the terms of competition in the industry.

63

the 1970s to cope with their competitive decline. It examines in detail the political battle in 1977 between the producers and the state over the terms of strategy of industrial adjustment for the U.S. steel sector. The third section analyzes the strategy of adjustment that emerged in the United States in late 1977—particularly as embodied in the Comprehensive Program for the Steel Industry, known as the Solomon Program—and evaluates the adjustment that followed through 1981.[3]

STRUCTURE AND STRATEGY

The U.S. steel industry is composed of a large range of producers who manufacture, with differing degrees of technological capability, an extensive range of products in different regions of the country for numerous and varied end-users. In order to address the issue of international competitiveness, the existing structure of the U.S. steel industry must be disaggregated. Only by pulling the industry apart analytically is it possible to identify segments of it—both producers and products—which are or can be competitive. As we shall see, such a disaggregation has so far been avoided by policy-makers and spokesmen for the industry, largely because the most politically influential steel producers are also the least competitive. Their ability to push the policy debate away from the problem of domestic competitive inefficiency and focus it on allegedly unfair foreign trading practices has resulted in government actions that have compensated for competitive inefficiency but have failed to encourage competitiveness.

Sources of Decline and Competitiveness

The preliminary analysis of the industry offered here will identify both competitive and non-competitive segments. In this regard, three

[3]The major sources for this chapter, which will henceforth be cited by author only, are as follows: Anthony M. Solomon, "Report to the President: A Comprehensive Program for the Steel Industry," December 1977. Charles Bradford (Merrill Lynch, Pierce, Fenner and Smith, Inc.), "Japanese Steel Industry. A Comparison with Its United States Counterpart," June 1977. Howard W. Piper, II, Paul W. Marshall, and John P. Merrill, Jr. (Putnam, Hayes, and Bartlett, Inc.), "Economies of International Steel Trade," 1977, and "The Economic Implications of Foreign Steel Pricing Practices in the U.S. Market," August 1978. Hans Mueller and Kiyoshi Kawahito, "Steel Industry Economics: A Comparative Analysis of Structure, Conduct and Performance," January 1978. U.S. Council on Wage and Price Stability (COWPS), *Prices and Costs in the United States Steel Industry,* October 1977. U.S. Federal Trade Commission (FTC), *Staff Report,* "The United States Steel Industry and Its International Rivals," November 1977. Joel Clark, *Report on the Ferrous Metals Industry* (National Academy of Engineering, 1980). Office of Technology Assessment (OTA), *Technology and Steel Industry Competitiveness,* June 1980. And various trade journals, including *Iron Age, Metal Bulletin,* and *Metal Statistics.*

distinct industry segments may usefully be identified: major integrated producers; small, nonintegrated mini-mills; and alloy-specialty steel companies.

Major integrated producers are high-volume producers of simple carbon steel. They operate in all three of the industry's principal production branches: blast furnace pig-iron production, steel-making and casting (rolling), and finishing. They account for approximately 85% of total industry steel tonnage shipments (of which about 5 to 7 percent are alloy-specialty). The seven largest integrated firms account for approximately 75 percent of total industry shipments, although this figure both overstates and understates the degree of concentration in particular product lines and market areas.[4] For example, the concentration of these seven firms in heavy flat-rolled products is probably higher, and their concentration in light flat and non-flat products is lower. Only two of the seven largest firms, Armco and Republic, have over 10 percent of their shipments in alloy and specialty steels. The largest firms are also extensively integrated backward into the extraction and processing of principal raw material inputs, particularly iron ore and coking coal. Some of these producers are integrated forward into a network of service centers which sell steel to a variety of smaller firms.

Small nonintegrated mini-mills are lower-volume producers of a narrow range of non-flat and light flat carbon steel who now account for approximately 13 percent of total industry shipments, a share that is still growing.[5] These producers bypass the pig-iron stage by processing scrap in electric furnaces. As a result, they are heavily dependent on the domestic scrap market or the larger integrated producers for their raw materials.

Alloy-specialty steel companies are normally low-volume producers of high value-added, technology-intensive steels. They account for approximately 3 to 4 percent of total industry shipments, but over 9 percent of industry dollar sales.[6] They process iron ore, coking coal, scrap, and various ferroalloys, depending upon the specialty-alloy product in question.

As an aggregate group, the largest integrated producers are the hardest hit by import competition in the domestic market. As a per-

[4]These seven firms are United States Steel (USS), Bethlehem, National, Republic, Inland, Armco, and LTV (which has recently acquired the Lykes Corporation to join with its Jones and Laughlin steel division).

[5]The OTA estimates that the mini-mills may account for up to 25 percent of domestic production by 1990. OTA, p. 256.

[6]The percentage of dollar sales attributed to each segment of the industry in the available statistics is always confounded by the inclusion of the largest producers' non-steel revenues, which are significant. It is likely that the percentage of dollar sales of the specialty-alloy producers is significantly greater than 9 percent.

centage of respective industry shipments, three times more carbon steel is imported (more than 20 percent in 1978) than alloy-specialty steels (approximately 7 percent). Moreover, the composition of carbon steel imports is heavily weighted toward the product mix of the integrated producers, in particular, sheet and strip, plate, structural steel, and pipe. Mini-mills suffer relatively little import competition, because unless scrap is scarce they can produce the mix of their products more cheaply than the integrated mills.

For the major integrated producers, compared to other industry segments, capital costs are very high and rising, operating costs are high and rising, and profitability (return on sales, equity, and investment) is low. In 1979, an extremely good year for steel, integrated producers averaged an 8.1 percent return on investment compared to 13.95 percent for the mini-mills and 9.8 percent for the alloy-specialty companies. In 1980, a worse year for steel, integrated producers had an average 6.1 percent return on investment compared to 11.16 percent for the mini-mills and 10.6 percent for alloy-specialty producers. While these latter two industry segments are expanding their capacity at high and moderate rates respectively, the aggregate capacity of the large integrated producers is contracting through marginal plant closings. (Among the majors, only Inland has expanded capacity.)

Compared to the largest Japanese companies, the world's most efficient steel producers, the integrated U.S. producers suffer from significantly outmoded capacity, poor location and layout, mismatched products and markets, and significant technological backwardness in energy productivity, resource utilization, and finishing capability.[7] The degree to which these problems affect competitiveness differs among U.S. producers, depending upon the facility, product, and market area in question. The particular strengths of the largest producers, which can be indirectly determined by examining the adjustment strategies each is pursuing at present, will be assessed later, in the third section. We shall begin by suggesting the general extent of their competitive problems.

The great majority of Japanese steel originates in fully integrated, fully rationalized, "greenfield" plants of 1965 vintage or later.[8] By contrast, the only comparable U.S. facility is Bethlehem's Burns Harbor plant, which began operation in 1968 and accounts for perhaps 5 per-

[7]The five largest Japanese steel companies are Nippon, Nippon Kokan, Kawasaki, Sumitomo, and Kobe.

[8]"Greenfield" plants are those involving wholly new construction at a new location, from the ground up, of an optimally laid out, fully integrated steel production facility that rationalizes production from raw materials input at the pig-iron stage to finished steel output. Greenfield plants are normally designed to accommodate capacity expansion through "brownfield" additions (facilities added to existing plant sites).

cent of U.S. production. Large-scale economies and greater and more efficient use of modern technology increase the advantages of the Japanese methods of steel production.[9] Thirty-two of the world's largest and most efficient blast furnaces are located in Japan, compared to only five in the United States. Over 80 percent of Japanese steel-making plants use the efficient basic oxygen furnace, compared to 64.7 percent of U.S. plants.[10] Indeed, almost 15 percent of U.S. production still uses the ancient open-hearth process. These figures are especially revealing in view of escalating energy costs: the basic oxygen furnace yields an approximate 85 percent energy saving per ton of crude steel over the open-hearth process. Approximately 58 percent of Japanese finished steel is now continuously cast, compared with no more than 17 percent in the United States.[11] This is another revealing comparison, for continuous casting uses only 45 percent of the energy used in the standard process. The Japanese are also world leaders in adapting computer technology to control the steel production process.

The efficiency advantages of the Japanese methods of steel production become clear in a comparison of yield, productivity, and resource utilization. On the average, 100 tons of crude steel yield from 78 to 87 tons of finished steel in Japan, compared to 68 to 73 tons of finished steel in the United States.[12] The average Japanese employee turns out 400 tons of steel per year compared with 250 tons for the average U.S. worker. Japanese labor costs comprise approximately 12 percent of total production costs, compared with about 35 percent in the United States. Although the U.S. producers probably have an advantage on the price of raw materials, the Japanese tend to use them far more efficiently. For example, the Japanese must use about 1,100 pounds of coal to produce one ton of pig-iron, for which U.S. producers require from 1,550 to 1,700 pounds of coal.

In some particular cases, integrated American producers can match Japanese efficiency. For example, National Steel's production mix and relatively high use of continuous casting yield figures roughly comparable to those of Japanese producers in a normal year. Bethlehem's Burns Harbor plant has a direct labor productivity of 600 tons per man per year. As a single producer, Inland Steel is in a superior position

[9]Except where noted, figures on Japanese and U.S. steel production are from Bradford.
[10]The U.S. figure is from Clark, p. 16.
[11]*New York Times*, January 1, 1981, p. 28. Note, however, that U.S. mini-mills continuously cast over 50 percent of their production, compared to about 9 percent by the integrated producers. See OTA, pp. 10, 86.
[12]Low-end figures are Bradford's; high-end figures are from Mueller and Kawahito, "The International Steel Market: Present Crisis and Outlook for the 1980's," Conference Paper Series No. 46, Business and Economic Research Center, Middle Tennessee State University, May 1979.

vis-à-vis its domestic competitors and suffers relatively little from Japanese competition: its facilities are modern, integrated, and concentrated in a single plant; and its Chicago location is in the center of its major markets and relatively removed from import penetration because of higher shipping costs to the Midwest. There are other cases of successful competitiveness by U.S. producers, but the overall state of U.S. production is not competitive on the basis of production costs.

Furthermore, building greenfield capacity in emulation of the Japanese model is not a practical solution to U.S. problems. The capital and construction costs of such an undertaking are simply too high in the United States; domestic capital markets will not finance such expansion, and United States Steel, the only producer that could finance a greenfield plant from internal funding and debt, has dropped any plans to do so. Indeed, steel manufactured in an all-new plant would cost significantly more than steel from existing modernized plants, because production cost savings would be more than offset by high capital costs per ton.[13]

By contrast, the congressional Office of Technology Assessment (OTA) suggests that the capital costs of new mini-mills range from $154 to $275 per annual ton, which is 10 to 20 percent of the cost per ton of a new integrated plant.[14] The competitive vitality of the mini-mills and specialty producers stands in marked contrast to the problems of the major U.S. integrated firms. As we shall argue in section three, the Japanese greenfield model of steel production may no longer be the appropriate model for a changing U.S. economy's role in a transitional international economy. But let us begin by examining the market changes and historical sources of competitive decline for the large integrated producers.

THE BACKGROUND OF CHANGING U.S. AND WORLD STEEL PRODUCTION

In 1955, when the reconstruction phase in the steel industries of Western Europe and Japan was completed, the United States accounted for over 40 percent of world crude steel production. While world steel production grew dramatically from 1950 to 1976, expanding speedily from less than 300 million net tons in 1955 to 750 million tons in 1976, U.S. production grew only minimally. Except for two

[13]See the analysis in COWPS, pp. 79–83.
[14]OTA, p. 93.

brief periods of excess demand in 1968–1969 and 1973–1974, U.S. steel production has not grown since the mid-1960s. From 1977 to 1980, the industry was producing an average level roughly equal to that of 1964 (between 120 and 130 million net tons), only 9 percent above 1955 levels.[15] From 1950 to 1959, U.S. steel-making capacity grew by 46 million tons. As will be indicated shortly, expansion choices during this period are crucial to an understanding of the relative decline of individual firms, because they represent missed opportunities for enhanced internal competitiveness in the 1960s and 1970s. From 1960 through 1977, capacity grew by only 10 million tons; during this period capacity utilization rose above 90 percent in only three years (1969, 1973, and 1974). Since 1977, the capacity of the major producers has been contracting through marginal plant closures.

From the late 1950s until 1968, apparent consumption of steel in the United States grew by approximately 50 million tons. Imports began to enter the domestic market in significant quantities, growing steadily from approximately 3 million tons in 1960 to a peak of almost 18 million tons in 1968. The largest import increases occurred in 1959, 1965, and 1968 (and again in 1971), the years in which the industry's collective bargaining agreements with the United Steelworkers of America expired. The pattern of increases in imports is attributable to hedge-buying by domestic steel-users concerned with the possible disruption of domestic steel supplies by strikes. In this regard, however, it is crucial to note that once a higher level of imports gained access to the U.S. market, that level was generally maintained, and indeed was raised in later years. Apparent domestic consumption of steel leveled off around 1968, and there has been no growth trend in apparent consumption since that time. Since 1968, steel imports have fluctuated around levels comparable to that year, representing from 14 to 20 percent of domestic consumption (with fluctuations corresponding to domestic import barriers, price controls, and cyclical demand).

The growth in import penetration of the U.S. market paralleled major structural changes in world steel production and trade from the 1950s through the early 1970s. While U.S. output levels remained relatively constant, the U.S. share of world steel production fell steadily through the 1960s to about 18 percent in the early 1970s. Japan has become the world's third largest producer (growing 1,038 percent since

---

[15]The steel market is subject to wide cyclical fluctuations. Output is highly responsive to cyclical demand in the capital and consumer goods industries that steel serves. The years 1973 and 1974 exhibited the first concurrent cycle peaks in the industrialized capitalist world since 1956 and 1957. Lesser demand peaks occur in the United States roughly every five years (hence production in 1978 and 1979 was high).

1955), with a share that stabilized around 16 percent in the 1970s. Combined production by countries in the European Economic Community (EEC) now captures a share just under 20 percent, which reflects a steady decline of over 7 percent since 1955. The change in relative U.S. and EEC market shares also reflects the addition of about forty steel-producing nations since 1950. Many nations that formerly relied on steel imports have become, or are attempting to become, self-sufficient and perhaps capable of exporting steel. Excluding the United States, the EEC, and Japan, the share of "non-communist" countries in "free-world" steel production rose steadily from 8 percent in 1950 to 21 percent in 1976. Internationally, because the distribution of growth in consumption has not been closely matched by the distribution of growth in production, an increasing number of nations have contributed to a changing pattern of trade.

World steel exports have grown from 13 percent of total production in 1955 to 22.5 percent in 1975. About 40 percent of Japanese production is exported, and this represents a full quarter of all world steel exports. The export share of EEC production has risen steadily from 30 percent in 1955 to over 50 percent in 1975, although the EEC share of world exports has declined slightly to about 45 percent.

For both the Japanese and the EEC, exports were a vital means of generating additional economies of scale to bring costs down and keep employment high at home by making maximum use of large-scale facilities. This characteristic of production for export explains the willingness of Japan and the EEC to engage in fierce price competition in export markets: they want to maintain the market shares that are essential for efficient large-scale production. In contrast (for reasons to be examined in the next section), U.S. exports have not participated in the growth of world export trade: except in the few years of short world supply, U.S. steel industry exports have shown no appreciable growth since 1959, and generally have remained at the levels of the 1950s. The export share of U.S. production is normally only 2 to 4 percent. Since 1959, the United States has been a net importer of steel, and until the middle and late 1970s most of the growth in import penetration of the domestic market has consisted of steel exports from Japan and the EEC.

A fairly clear-cut interplay of market and political factors with company and government strategies underlies the shifts described above. Two distinct periods (the 1950s and the 1960s) will now be examined in the context of that interplay, and the U.S. and Japanese situations will be contrasted. To understand why the United States has done poorly in steel since 1959, we must also understand why the Japanese have done so well.

The 1950s: Last Phase of American Supremacy in Steel

For over seventy years, through the 1950s, the U.S. steel industry was the world leader in steel technology, plant size, and production. "Its comparative advantage was based on a large home market, abundant raw materials and skilled labor, access to the world's largest and best organized capital market, and the benefits derived from a continuous stream of innovation in other sectors of the economy."[16]

In the 1950s the U.S. industry was also characterized by some form of administered pricing, in which United States Steel or a cartel of the largest integrated producers could set prices, because they faced only an insignificant competitive fringe of other domestic suppliers and imports.[17] The combination of comparative advantage and successful oligopoly in the home market was highly profitable. However, the industry's oligopolistic structure, which accompanied U.S. supremacy in steel, was to become a singular structural barrier to the industry's ability to respond to foreign competition in the 1960s.

Expansion decisions in the 1950s must be understood in this context. In general, existing facilities were regionally dispersed and of an optimal size and layout for open-hearth steel-making. The largest producers had developed and refined the open-hearth production process; metal engineers and production workers had been trained in its fine points; construction companies could build open-hearth plants with little waste.[18] Two basic technologies were available for capacity expansion decisions by the largest producers: the established processes (including open-hearth or OH), where the learning curve had delivered highly efficient production and low-cost steel; and the basic oxygen-furnace process (BOF), which was relatively untried. The BOF process promised lower-cost production in the future, and for that reason it threatened to destabilize the industry's pricing structure. The largest producers opted overwhelmingly for the time-tested OH process, and only smaller producers, like the tiny McLouth firm, gambled on the BOF process.

Relations between the steel industry and the U.S. government in the 1950s were ambivalent. Although the federal government, as a matter of policy, had helped the states to suppress labor unrest in the industry's formative years, it had tolerated the growth of a fairly powerful steelworkers' union in the 1930s and 1940s. The federal government financed the construction of steel plants during World War II, sold them after the war to the largest producers at a fraction of their cost,

---

[16]Mueller and Kawahito, p. 1.
[17]See the discussion in FTC, *Staff Report*, chap. 4.
[18]I am indebted to my colleague Aton Arbisser for this argument.

and provided low-interest loans and accelerated depreciation for expansion in the 1950s. Even so, President Truman had tried to seize the mills in 1952; because steel was an oligopolistic, mature industry in a postwar economy of rapid growth, its pricing practices began to be watched closely. From 1955 to 1960, while the wage-price index for all industrials rose by 9.7 percent, the steel mill products index rose by 24.9 percent.[19] In the 1960s, steel would become a favorite target of "Keynesian" government administrators seeking to check inflation.

The experience of the 1950s was quite different in Japan. Steel was targeted early in the postwar period as a critical redevelopment priority. In addition to rebuilding Japan's industrial infrastructure, steel was to serve two other functions. The industry was to generate foreign exchange for Japan through its export growth; and it was to supply low-cost steel to Japan's automobile, shipbuilding, machine-tool, and other steel-using industries in order to enhance their global competitiveness.[20] The Ministry of International Trade and Industry (MITI) and the steel industry, in close consultation, developed a series of rationalization plans. Growth was encouraged by various tax and depreciation incentives and by manipulating tariffs to encourage the inflow of cheap raw materials and to exclude foreign steel and steel-using products. Growth was financed approximately one-third through internal funds and equity, and two-thirds through low-interest debt (held in equal parts by government and private banks).

The Japanese experience in steel compared to the U.S. experience during the 1950s (and 1960s) may be understood in part as an instance of the advantages of backwardness. With little sunk investment compared to U.S. producers, and lacking a comfortably oligopolistic, market-sharing, industrial structure within a relatively mature market such as existed in the United States, the Japanese were relatively unconstrained by past success from moving into a new phase in the steel industry's life cycle. However, the success and speed of the Japanese move must also be seen as the fruit of state intervention to secure international competitiveness. As Zysman notes, the constant theme of Japanese policy in the decades after World War II was consciously to create comparative advantage in high value-added industries rather than to remain focused on the labor-intensive industries that might seem appropriate to an economy short of materials and capital.[21] Thus,

[19]See COWPS, p. 19.

[20]James von B. Dresser, Jr., Thomas M. Hout, and William V. Rapp, "Competitive Development of the Japanese Steel Industry" (Boston Consulting Group, 1971), pp. 201–220.

[21]John Zysman, *Governments, Markets, and Growth* (Ithaca: Cornell University Press, 1983); see also the chapter on Japan by T. J. Pempel in Peter Katzenstein, ed., *Between Power and Plenty* (Madison: University of Wisconsin Press, 1978).

72

Japanese state intervention in steel closed the domestic market to preserve it for Japanese firms, provided relatively cheap investment capital, staged investment through a series of rationalization plans to avoid overcapacity, and also helped to manage excess capacity when it did occur. The most important features of the state's repertoire of policy instruments were control over credit and control over imported materials. Access to long-run, low-interest funding was selectively extended by the state through Japan's credit-based financial system, to encourage the steel sector's growth. Such funding was particularly vital during the expansion phases of steel industry development, when individual firms did not have the necessary internally generated liquidity, and private investors were wary of extending credit (in the absence of a government commitment to share or assume the risk of failure).[22] Moreover, foreign exchange controls permitted the Bank of Japan to limit the borrowing of steel producers from foreign lenders, and thereby assured producer cooperation with state strategy. Finally, controls over the importation and allocation of coal and iron ore were similarly critical, because Japan imports 98 percent of its iron ore and 84 percent of its coal.[23]

Thus, through the means described above, and especially during the second half of the 1950s, Japanese steelmakers began to adopt the BOF process and to rationalize steel production toward large, integrated greenfield plants. By the end of the 1950s Japan was ready to embark upon a massive capacity expansion program, using new technology, strategic location, and layout, and taking advantage of ever greater economies of scale to become the world's most efficient low-cost steelmaker. In contrast, by the end of the 1950s, the U.S. industry had completed its major postwar expansion committed to an older process phase of steel-making, just when steel production, courtesy of the Japanese, was about to jump abruptly into the next process phase of its life cycle.

The 1960s: Japanese Expansion and American Catch-Up

In the 1960s Japanese steel production grew from 24 million to over 100 million net tons. The pattern of consultation between MITI and industry, and of tax incentives for expanding firms, continued. Capac-

---

[22] By contrast, the unwillingness of private financial markets to allow private U.S. steel companies to put more than 30 to 40 percent of their funding in long-term debt—thereby forcing them to rely on large internally generated funds—is a significant structural block to the U.S. industry's ability to emulate Japanese growth.

[23] Dresser, Hout, and Rapp, "Competitive Development of the Japanese Steel Industry," p. 207.

ity growth was financed largely (up to 80 percent) by long-term, low-interest debt. In this way, the Japanese industry constructed large, technically advanced, integrated plants in modern deep-water port locations (to facilitate the necessary imports of raw materials as well as the export of steel products), bringing construction costs rapidly down as they advanced along a "learning curve." Huge blast furnaces realized economies of scale in pig-iron production, and BOF mills devoted to limited product ranges and long production runs achieved huge economies of scale in steel production. The adoption of continuous casting and rationalized, high-capacity usage of primary rolling and finishing plants brought down the costs of finishing raw steel. Falling world prices for raw materials (caused in large part by the aggressive pursuit of long-term contracts by Japanese trading companies) enabled additional reductions in production costs. Much lower wage costs than in the United States combined with huge productivity increases in the modern integrated facilities to generate significant labor-cost advantages.[24] Falling bulk transportation costs (generated in no small part by the Japanese industry's pioneering innovation of the giant bulk carrier for raw materials), and aggressive marketing by Japanese trading companies (which buy and sell perhaps 80 percent of Japanese steel), significantly enhanced the Japanese position in world markets. Indeed, the Japanese achieved a decade-long sustained decline in steel prices.[25] The result, by 1980, was that Japanese steel producers had an absolute advantage over their U.S. counterparts in labor, raw materials, and capital costs, the major factor-cost categories. This translated into an approximate 40 percent average production cost advantage (nearly $50.00 per ton) over the largest U.S. producers.

The 1960s was a critical decade for U.S. producers as well, as they tried to develop a strategy to deal with import penetration and the new Japanese model of steel production. In the early 1960s, faced with aged and technically inferior plants, the domestic industry embarked on a serious strategy of catch-up to the new model of steel production. The largest U.S. producers managed the transition out of open-hearth steel production in a way that undoubtedly seemed rational to risk-averse oligopolistic managers. Each U.S. integrated producer had a tremendous sunk investment in open-hearth capacity and in facilities, location, and layout that were optimal for open-hearth production. In the aggregate, they shifted over to the new process phase of the industry's life cycle in a way that allowed them to exhaust the useful life of that sunk investment. Thus, capital expenditures were significant in the 1960s,

---

[24]Labor costs and productivity during this period are compared in FTC discussion.
[25]Dresser, Hout, and Rapp, p. 205.

rising gradually through the first half of the decade and topping $2 billion annually from 1965 to 1969 (in 1972 dollars).[26] This parallels closely the pattern of import penetration and represents a response to it. Yet, with the exception of Bethlehem's Burns Harbor plant, which began producing in 1968, none of that capital expenditure represented the addition of greenfield capacity. Instead, expenditures went to replace obsolete facilities, to tack advanced rolling and finishing facilities onto old plants, and, especially toward the decade's end, to install costly environmental protection equipment. Much of the replacement and "rounding out" decisions adopted modern technology (basic oxygen furnace, electric furnace, and continuous casting) at an efficient rate, although the largest producers lagged considerably behind the smaller ones in rate of adoption.[27] However, the productivity improvements that accrued to the pattern of plant replacement were considerably less than would have been achieved by the construction of new, integrated facilities. Given existing location, layout, plant infrastructure, and supportable size, aggregate U.S. producers could not hope to match the scale economies and rationalized production of the Japanese. However, individual producers and specific plants could be competitive where production was well located, well laid out, and modernized. Bureau of Labor statistics data for 1967 estimated that value added per production worker was three times larger in the most efficient U.S. mills than in the least efficient ones.[28]

An industry-labor entente ensued in the face of import competition after 1959 and led to rising wages, although minimal productivity gains in the modernizing facilities kept labor costs relatively constant. Price rises outpaced the general inflation rate by a few percentage points, partly to sustain high dividends for equity investors, and partly to generate internal funds for the necessary capital expenditures.[29] Indeed, it appears as if retained earnings and equity were the principal sources of capital for the U.S. steel industry in these years. U.S. banks were reluctant to finance an industry in competitive trouble, especially one with low profitability, and as a result sources of debt capital for steel "dried up" by mid-decade.[30] Successive administrations jawboned the industry

---

[26]COWPS, p. 16.

[27]See the discussion in FTC, *Staff Report;* and Walter Adams and Joel Dirlam, "Big Steel: Invention and Innovation," *Quarterly Journal of Economics* 80, no. 2 (May 1966), pp. 167–189.

[28]"Technological Change and Manpower Trends in Five Industries," *Bureau of Labor Statistics Bulletin* No. 1856 (BLS, 1975).

[29]This, at least, is the standard rationale used by the industry to account for price rises greater than those necessary to cover increased costs.

[30]This argument is presented by Robert Cohen, New York University, in an unpublished study.

75

for its pricing practices, yet it is most likely that import competition and the loosened oligopoly pricing structure that resulted from disparate patterns of firm modernization were the principal factors limiting excessive price rises in this period. As a result, profitability was low throughout the decade, consistently far below the all-manufacturing average.

Toward the decade's end, then, a number of trends converged. Despite expensive modernization, U.S. producers had failed to narrow the Japanese production cost advantage (which had, in fact, widened). Import competition was severe, and apparent domestic consumption of steel was leveling off. Environmental compliance costs were rising, and perhaps 35 percent of the industry's capacity was still technologically outmoded, but debt capital was unavailable. By the late 1960s, recognizing that its decade-long catch-up attempt had failed, the industry shifted its strategy from catch-up to protection of its home market.

The failure of the catch-up strategy pursued by the largest U.S. producers may be understood as a structural inability to move between the old and the new process phases of the industry's life cycle. The industry's structure was the result of an era of U.S. predominance in steel, during which the major producers had moderated their competitive instincts in favor of a comfortable oligopolistic market-sharing arrangement. In the absence of foreign competition, so long as they modernized apace they could have moved into a future phase of their industry's life cycle while retaining their respective market shares. Instead, they were suddenly faced with an international competitor who, thanks to state promotion, had *created* a new phase in the steel industry's life cycle for which U.S. producers were wholly unprepared. For catch-up to be successful, the U.S. industry needed to restructure. Instead, the major producers tried to enter the new phase of their industry's life cycle from within the structure that had served them so well in the older phase.

When this strategy failed, they exercised their *political* muscle to protect their oligopoly of the domestic market and thus to insulate themselves for a time from the need to restructure. Whereas the Japanese had used state-led political action to create and dominate a new phase in the steel industry's life cycle, U.S. producers used political action to defer their adjustment to the changes in international competition. As the second main section will demonstrate, the largest U.S. producers' political ability to frame the issues and dominate the policy debate allowed them to protect themselves at the cost of the nation's competitiveness in steel. Before examining that story, however, we should take a closer look at the economics of import penetration in the U.S. market and at its significance for the major U.S. producers' political strategy.

The Economics and Politics of Import Penetration

A look at price-cost behavior during the last decades can lead us to important insights into the competitive behavior of U.S. and world producers. During the 1960s, Japanese and European steel producers had a significant factor cost advantage over U.S. producers, and the explosive growth in import penetration of the U.S. market followed. The relative cost advantages of the foreign producers declined when the dollar was devalued in 1971, and this stemmed for a time the growth in imports. However, from 1972 to 1977, factor input costs rose sharply in energy, coal, iron ore, scrap, and labor, and these costs far outpaced limited productivity increases in the United States. During the same period, the rise in finished domestic U.S. steel prices totaled 79 percent, significantly outpacing the average industrial price increase by over 24 percent. Much of this price rise reflects a pass-through of costs. Import penetration seems to be precisely a function of the interaction of costs with pricing practices. In general, the world steel market exhibits the pricing characteristics of competition, with world export prices rising and falling during economic expansions and contractions. Especially during global recessionary periods, there has been intense pricing competition among foreign suppliers of the U.S. market. U.S. producer prices, however, have been far more inflexible than world export prices.[31] Although import competition and differences in cost competitiveness among American producers have generated some discounting from domestic price lists since the late 1960s, these discounts have been taken from continually rising list prices.[32] Imports have generally increased when domestic prices have risen relative to world market prices.[33] As world prices fell during economic contractions in 1969–1970 and 1974–1975, domestic prices remained comparatively stable. The resulting gap led to increased imports, from 13 million net tons in 1970 to 18 million in 1971, and from 12 million net tons in 1975 to 19 million by the end of 1977.[34]

The stickiness and upward trend in prices, even in the face of severe import competition and under-used capacity, suggest the behavior that critics of the steel industry have long implied: a persistent refusal to meet price competition in the market. Such behavior, for example, illuminates the industry's failure to be export competitive. Through the

---

[31] See COWPS for a discussion of pricing activities.

[32] Discounts usually are given to major buyers, and include: sub rosa price-cutting; absorption of certain item costs, including freight; charging less than cost for "extras"; warehousing without charge; and selling high-quality steel at lower quality prices. For more detail, see FTC, *Staff Report*, p. 195.

[33] See COWPS, note 4.

[34] AISI, *Statistical Report*, 1978, p. 8.

1950s and 1960s, American steel exports were typically priced at U.S. list plus freight to the point of delivery. As the Senate Finance Committee conceded in 1967, "generally no attempt is made to align export pricing on the substantially lower prices quoted in third markets [other than market of the exporter and the United States] by the European or Japanese steel producers."[35]

The largest producers have consistently advocated full-cost pricing in the domestic market as well as in foreign markets. This advocacy has held even when competitive pricing could drive imports out of the U.S. market, or could increase U.S. shares of foreign markets, and even when under-used capacity exists to accomplish either of these objectives. This behavior by the major producers suggests that they are in an extremely vulnerable competitive position. Their actions suggest a long-run explanation of their behavior: as oligopolistic producers, the major integrated firms seek over the long term to refrain from any activity that might unnecessarily destabilize respective market shares.[36] There is a related short-run argument as well. Since much excess capacity is outmoded, the costs of bringing it into production are high. The industry has generally brought that capacity into production only when high market prices could cover the increased costs and return an acceptable level of profit. Since labor can be laid off without increased industry costs, it is probably more profitable in the short run to produce at less than capacity for a higher-priced domestic market than to produce at fuller capacity for lower-priced markets. Thus it appears that for U.S. producers, the cost-lines of production with outmoded capacity *reverse* the normal capacity-profitability theory—namely, that costs fall as the scale of production increases. If variable costs on their older capacity are significantly high, *it is more profitable (or less costly) for the largest producers to be under-utilized in the absence of high enough prices.*

In essence, given their similar production-cost characteristics, both the major producers' short-run profitability and their long-term market shares are dependent upon maintenance of the full-cost domestic pricing structure.[37] Although price-cutting could drive out imports and increase the use of capacity, it would almost certainly upset the price

[35]Quoted in Walter Adams, "The Steel Industry," in Adams, ed., *The Structure of American Industry* (New York: Macmillan, 1977), p. 115. Although I have seen no evidence, I suspect that the bulk of the industry's exports in normal times are tied to various export-financing, U.S. aid programs.

[36]A fascinating historical treatment of the industry in these terms is given in Mary Yeager's paper prepared for the American Political Science Association Annual Meeting, September 1979.

[37]Bradford makes this point on p. 21; see also the remarks by Robert Crandall, "Competition and 'Dumping' in the U.S. Steel Market", *Challenge* (July-August 1978), pp. 13–20.

structure. Such price-cutting makes no economic sense, if the resulting lower prices are insufficient to return a profit on use of the added capacity, or if the resulting lower price structure diminishes the profitability of capacity already in use. Price-cutting makes even less economic sense if it acts in the long run to destabilize a comfortable, oligopolistic allocation of market shares.

If it has been neither profitable nor stabilizing to engage in competitive pricing, it has been economically prudent for the largest producers to call for protection of the domestic market—and the industry has done exactly that since the mid-1960s. Protection serves to reduce competitiveness in the industry and in the past had always resulted in higher prices. In such an environment, it becomes profitable for the big integrated domestic producers to bring outmoded capacity into production; and it becomes possible to re-establish oligopoly control over the domestic market and market shares. Note that in these circumstances, oligopoly control need not be overtly collusive; it can be the natural consequence of industry structure. If the largest producers face similar costs, and if lower-cost domestic producers are operating at near full capacity (as, for example, Inland has done even in recession), there is no incentive for individual producers to compete on price. Higher prices mean higher profits all around, and this is accomplished without threat to market shares.

The industry's argument for protection has not, of course, been based on the line of analysis we have made. The argument adopted by the industry was most fully articulated in a study commissioned by the American Iron and Steel Institute, the industry trade association and lobby, for use in the policy battle over an adjustment strategy for steel in 1977.[38] Its argument rests on an assumption of unfair competition through unfair trading practices. The industry alleges that high, protected home-market prices enable foreign producers to capture growing shares of the American market by pricing exports below average costs. In effect, high home-market prices subsidize low export prices. During periods of excess supply, this argument is tied to foreign producers' desire to bring excess capacity into production (for the purpose of covering high fixed costs associated with high levels of debt and the political commitment to maintain full employment in so basic an industry as steel): "Some producers are able to maintain protected prices in their home market while using lower prices to displace competition in the export market. . . . (In particular, they sell) steel in the U.S. market at prices below their average costs . . . whenever necessary to increase capacity utilization."

[38]Piper, Marshall, and Merrill; the following quotations are from pp. i, v, and vi.

The essence of this argument is that exporting producers engage in dumping steel on the U.S. market. Were American producers to match the resulting unfairly low steel prices, they would not be covering their costs of production and so could not generate the profit necessary to satisfy stockholders and stay in business: "Domestic producers cannot meet (such behavior) and still fulfill the profit and capital formation requirements of operating in the U.S. political and economic system." The costs of allowing such behavior are even greater, however, for when there is excess demand, these same foreign producers will withhold steel supplies, allocate them to other consumers, and drive up the price of steel in the U.S. market for American consumers: "In periods of tight supply, prices will be substantially increased and the amount of steel provided by foreign producers will be reduced." Such behavior, the argument goes, has deleterious long-run effects on the U.S. economy. This point is frequently combined with an argument that carefully chooses to avoid any mention of the neo-classical economists' notion of the national economic benefits of free trade. For example: "Even if the nation is willing to accept the major losses of steelworker employment and adverse pressure on our trade balances which greater dependence on imported steel would entail, the ultimate risk to the U.S. economy . . . is unacceptable." Then, in an interesting twist of logic, the industry completes its argument by eliminating any questions of comparative ability to compete and lays the blame for U.S. problems solely on imports that are presumed to be unfair: "The growth of steel imports during the 1960s constrained the growth of shipments by U.S. producers, thereby inhibiting productivity improvements, profitability, and investment in new capacity." The call for protection, then, necessarily follows. In the words of Bethlehem's president, Lewis Foy, "All we are asking for is a chance to compete on fair and equal terms here in our own country."[39]

The industry's argument about the behavior of foreign competitors in periods of tight supply finds no support in existing evidence; it appears to be a self-serving characterization for the purpose of implementing a political strategy of protectionism. From 1959 to the mid-1970s, the rise in steel imports was interrupted three times, in 1960–1961, 1969–1970, and 1973. In the first two instances, imports declined in response to recessionary conditions of reduced demand. Only in 1973 did imports decline and prices rise during a boom period.[40] The major factors here, however, were the prior devaluation of the

[39]*National Journal* 9, no. 24 (June 1977), p. 924.

[40]Hans Mueller and Kiyoshi Kawahito, "Errors and Biases in the 1978 Putnam, Hayes, and Bartlett Study on the Pricing of Imported Steel," Monograph Series No. 17, January 1979.

dollar, and domestic price controls that held steel prices below the world level, thus limiting the attractiveness of the U.S. market. Moreover, as the study by the Council on Wage and Price Stability indicated: "The importance of these two events is highlighted by noting the 96 percent increase in U.S. exports between 1972 and 1974. The response of foreign firms to more attractive prices outside the United States was little different than that of domestic producers."[41] Indeed, in this period, U.S. producers themselves could be accused of "undesirable" trading practices: they, too, diverted significant steel from the domestic market to seek the higher profits available in world markets, thereby intensifying the steel shortage within the United States. (Exports rose from 2.8 million tons before and after 1973–1974 to a peak of 5.8 million tons in 1974.) Any validity to the industry's argument concerning tight supply would rest on the ability of foreign producers to act in concert to restrict supplies to the U.S. market. In fact, foreign steel producers have not historically been able to maintain such cartel-like behavior except for very short periods.[42]

The industry's argument about "dumping" deserves a closer examination because of what it reveals about the industry's attempt to focus policy debate on the "fairness" of the competitive behavior of foreign steel producers. It is characteristic of the ideology of U.S. trade policy to focus on the issue of "fair" competition. The problem of dumping reveals the difficulties inherent in such a focus when competitive behavior is filtered through the normative lens of U.S. law.

The 1921 Anti-Dumping Act defines dumping as export sales at prices below those in the home market. Apparently the framer of this legislation hoped, through this definition, to guard against cases in which high home-market prices subsidized a foreign producer's ability to price-cut in export markets and thereby "steal" market shares away from the export market's native producers. However, excess demand and tight supply might drive prices up in a home market, while competition under conditions of excess supply could drive prices in the export market down below those of the home market. Alternatively, prices could be held "artificially" high in the home market by formal agreement among producers, by informal oligopoly control over pricing, or by government fiat. U.S. policy-makers might well consider such behavior "unfair" as a means of competing. But during the 1970s, perhaps 60 percent of steel exports from the United States were priced at less than the partly protected and oligopolistically set domestic price

[41]COWPS, p. 48.
[42]See Kent Jones, "Forgetfulness of Things Past: Europe and the Steel Cartel," *The World Economy* 2, no. 2 (May 1979), pp. 139–154.

level in non-shortage years—apparently to compensate for competition in export markets.[43]

The difficulty of assessing the existence of dumping is compounded by amendments in the 1974 Trade Act, which state that if home prices are below average production costs, dumping is then defined as export sales at prices below a fair "constructed value." The constructed value is defined as direct production costs plus 10 percent overhead and 8 percent profit (which is, in fact, a very high return for steel except in peak years). As Robert Crandall points out, however, these price comparisons are extremely difficult to determine accurately: "Price data are not easily obtained or interpreted. . . . There are literally thousands of products . . . many of these are produced in the same facilities, making cost comparisons difficult. Moreover, the quality and variety of the steel, as well as the bargaining power of the buyer, have a substantial influence on market price."[44]

Given these difficulties, a shorthand approximation of dumping compares foreign average production cost advantages over the United States with importation charges. If the dollar value of the advantage gained through lower-cost production is smaller than the value of importation charges which are added to imported steel, and if imported steel is being sold at prices below those of domestic producers, a prima facie case of dumping is alleged. In 1977, average Japanese costs were significantly below American costs and were probably low enough to dismiss any significant dumping charges based on this shorthand approximation. However, European costs were approximately equal to American ones, and EEC steel was undoubtedly being "dumped" in the United States. Assume, however, that EEC steel producers were merely setting export prices at marginal cost, as neo-classical economics suggests competitive producers would do. Is such behavior unfair? In essence, both the shorthand approximation of dumping and amended U.S. law act to prohibit arguably competitive behavior in the form of marginal cost pricing of steel by foreign producers in the U.S. market. Consider the following anticompetitive anomaly which would work under U.S. law, assuming that competitive firms set price at marginal cost. With high fixed costs, prices set at marginal cost will be below average costs. In a recession, average costs will rise because high fixed costs are spread across a smaller output. Thus in a recession, U.S. law could actually require foreign suppliers to *raise* prices to meet the average-cost-of-production test of dumping.

It should be apparent that the abstract notion of "fair" competition is

[43]FTC, *Staff Report*, p. 74.

[44]Crandall, "Competition and 'Dumping' in the U.S. Steel Market," *Challenge* (July–August 1978).

given a determinative, normative meaning when U.S. actors politically delimit a range of acceptable producer behavior. Whoever is able to define those limits in any given political battle is going to dominate the policy outcomes. But the need to characterize foreign actions as fair or unfair merely underscores the simple point that other nations have chosen not to play by U.S.-imposed rules. Indeed, behind the U.S. emphasis on "fairness" one finds an insistence that other nations must not create new rules of their own, and an unwillingness on the part of U.S. industry to adjust structurally in a way that restores competitiveness to the industry within the terms of the new rules. Was it "fair" to create comparative advantage as the Japanese did in steel? This question is much less interesting from a policy point of view than the fact of Japanese success at creating new rules for the industry. When the major U.S. steel producers focused on "fairness" of import penetration, they masked their failure to manage the transition from old to new rules of competitiveness in their industry's life cycle.

Seen in this light, the U.S. producers' strategy of characterizing foreign import penetration as "unfair" under U.S. dumping laws becomes a question-begging tactic with an appealing reasonance for U.S. policymakers: it limits the policy debate on steel to the issue of restoring "fair" competition and thereby avoids a hard look at the state of the major U.S. producers' own competitiveness. Thus, when the industry cast its argument into the typical ideological mold of U.S. trade policy, it acquired a powerful political tool to divert the policy debate over adjustment in steel to the major producers' own ends. In the next section we shall examine the ways in which politics and economics intertwined in 1977 to permit such a diversion.

THE LIBERAL POLITICS OF RESCUING THE STEEL INDUSTRY

In order to grasp fully the nature of the adjustment strategy chosen by the U.S. government in the 1970s and embodied in the Solomon Report, it is crucial to examine the political context from which this strategy emerged. This section will describe the competitive problems during the 1970s. It will examine the ways in which this strategy allowed large American producers to defer their adjustment to the changes that had occurred in the international steel market. The actions taken by the largest producers deeply affected the ways in which government policy-makers chose to define the industry's problems and to develop responses to them. In turn, policy actions taken by governments at home and abroad represented political actions that directly altered the character of national steel markets and influenced the business strategy choices made by firms in the industry.

Background to the Bargain over Adjustment: Politics Intervenes to Alter the Market

When steel import penetration of the U.S. market jumped in 1967, the domestic industry and the United Steelworkers of America mounted a campaign for protectionist legislation. To forestall the imposition of mandatory import quotas by Congress, the State Department negotiated three-year Voluntary Restraint Agreements (VRAs) with steelmakers in Japan and the EEC. The VRAs took effect in 1969 and provided for specific tonnage limits with a 5 percent annual growth. This induced importers to concentrate on a higher value mix of imports in order to maintain foreign exchange earnings while adhering to quantity limitations. In addition, imports from producing nations not covered by the VRA's grew to 4.2 million net tons in 1971, an increase of almost 70 percent.

This episode foreshadowed the strategies and actions of both the industry and the U.S. government that were to characterize the political battle over adjustment in 1977. The industry and the union combined to urge protection through Congress. An executive branch characteristically committed to "free trade" negotiated protectionist departures to forestall even stronger protectionist legislation in Congress. The rationale for both congressional and administrative action was to restore slumping competitive profitability and shore up a "necessary" domestic industry. The VRAs were supposed to encourage adjustment by providing breathing space in which the domestic industry could improve its competitiveness by modernizing its facilities. Yet U.S. producers recognized that such efforts were unlikely to be successful—they represented, after all, a mere replication of the catch-up strategy that had failed during the 1960s. Thus capital expenditures for the industry were below the 1968 level throughout the six-year VRA period. Moreover, because the VRAs forced foreign competitors in the EEC and Japan toward a higher value-added mix of steel exports, U.S. policy actually pushed those producers further along the product life cycle of the industry. Ironically, the policy desired by the largest U.S. producers to protect their position in the domestic market only served to encourage a foreign presence in product areas that U.S. producers might otherwise have been able to keep for themselves.

After the VRA campaign, the industry and its union continued to engage in a joint political approach to their competitive problems. As will become clearer below, this joint political strategy sought government intervention to alter the terms of competition in steel. In particular, it sought to minimize the domestic industry's need to adjust, by requiring a full-cost steel pricing structure that allowed relatively un-

84

competitive domestic producers to retain domestic market shares and to operate at a profit.

Under pressure from the joint industry-union lobby during the formation of the 1974 Trade Act, steel was established as one of the domestic sectors that could legitimately require separate sectoral negotiations at the Multilateral Trade Negotiations. An effort to pursue separate steel negotiations followed the legislation. As a joint statement to the Carter administration summarized in 1978:

> Since October 1975, the American Iron and Steel Institute and the United Steelworkers of America have called for steel sector negotiations. We cited at that time the serious nature of the worldwide steel crisis and the need for sector negotiations leading to . . .
> (a) creation of a standing Steel Committee within the framework of GATT;
> (b) establishment of a multilateral safeguard mechanism for handling problems of market disruption; and
> (c) elimination of all steel tariffs over a period of time, conditioned upon the realization of the above.[45]

The call for multilateral steel negotiations coincided with an EEC request in 1975 to solve global steel problems within the framework of the Organization for Economic Cooperation and Development.[46] These problems had emerged at the end of the global steel boom of 1972–1974. The economic recession that followed continued into 1977 and occasioned similar responses throughout the foreign steel industries.[47] The Japanese, the EEC, and other exporters (such as South Korea, Spain, South Africa, Canada, and Mexico) cut most world market prices, reduced projected production targets, and scaled back plans for capacity expansion. The EEC was particularly hard hit because its producers had significant excess capacity, and because like the U.S. producers, they needed to modernize significant plants. In 1976, the EEC and Japan negotiated a bilateral agreement to restrain Japanese exports to Europe. By the end of that year, the EEC formulated the Simonet Plan to monitor and rationalize the practices of its steel producers.[48] This action was followed in April 1977 by the Davignon Plan, which included subsidies for production research and investment,

---

[45]Statement of AISI and USWA on Steel Sector Negotiations and Steel Tariff Policy, January 10, 1978, p. 1.3.
[46]Conversation with Robert Crandall, March 31, 1979.
[47]Testimony of the Department of State's William Barraclough. Reported in U.S. Congress, House Ways and Means Subcommittee on Trade, Hearings on World Steel Trade: Current Trends and Structural Problems, 95th Congress, Sept. 20, 1977, pp. 126–128.
[48]U.S. Congress, House Ways and Means Subcommittee on Trade, Hearings on Oversight of the Antidumping Act of 1921, pp. 80–81.

a restructuring of the EEC industry to match its market more closely, and "temporary" market interventions to set voluntary delivery targets and minimum prices. In addition, the Davignon Plan included long-term actions to organize the closure of outdated facilities, to encourage mergers, to coordinate state aid for adjustment assistance, and to re-train laid-off workers.

These responses were presented as a serious effort to restore com-petitiveness to the troubled EEC industry through government-encour-aged adjustment, but the restoration of competitiveness was not the only possible outcome. Indeed, the Davignon Plan also encouraged discussions with other exporters aimed at reaching bilateral agreements like the EEC-Japan deal of 1976. By the middle of 1977, such talks were underway with Brazil, South Africa, South Korea, Spain, Aus-tralia, and Comecon producers (who sell in Western Europe when in-ternal Comecon demand falls).[49] These unilateral and bilateral actions could, instead, be a step in the direction of what the French Prime Minister, in early 1977, called "organized free trade" in steel.[50] The long-run intent would be to fix world shares and prices (which amounts to cartelization) in order to maintain profitable domestic steel indus-tries and minimize the need for adjustment.[51] This intent corresponded with the vision of the largest U.S. producers, who called for sectoral negotiations in steel. It was a vision, as will be shown, that was pursued with vigor even after the Solomon program was adopted.

The domestic response in the United States to these events has its roots in the cyclical boom period in steel that stretched from November 1972 to October 1974.[52] World demand was high, and imports and some domestic steel were diverted from the price-controlled U.S. mar-ket. A domestic steel shortage developed in April 1973, and U.S. pro-ducers began to allocate steel based on historical customer purchases. Most domestic discounting practices were stopped, and steel deliveries were slowed as pressure began to mount for the lifting of price con-trols. Domestic users who had relied on imported steel were, in effect, punished by the domestic industry: they were denied purchase in-creases. This occurred despite a drop in auto demand following the energy crisis in the first quarter of 1974, which should have created some slackness in domestic steel supplies. Instead, the auto companies took their allocated quantity of steel and resold it at a profit. Price controls were removed in August 1974, and the industry's prices jumped 30 to 40 percent. By the beginning of 1975, demand eased and

[49]Barraclough, in U.S. Congress, Hearings on World Steel Trade, pp. 126–128.
[50]Quoted in *The Economist*, December 31, 1977, p. 75.
[51]Conversations with Robert Crandall, March 31, 1979.
[52]Description derived mainly from FTC, *Staff Report*, pp. 79–80, 187–194.

prices dropped marginally as discounting and non-price concessions began to reappear.

One crucial result of the practices during this period was the reluctance of "punished" domestic buyers to return to foreign sources of steel. As the United States recovered from recession relatively more quickly than its industrialized allies, and domestic steel demand picked up by 1976, foreign exporters began to price steel considerably below domestic firms in order to compete for wary U.S. customers. As lower-priced imports began to enter their market, domestic producers began to present an increasing number of relief petitions under various U.S. trade laws. Once again, in the face of import competition, U.S. producers chose a political strategy to try to reduce imports in their markets. Their action constrained the ways in which U.S. policy-makers could respond to the industry's problems.

Import relief actions had actually started at the end of the steel boom, in January 1975, when United States Steel filed seven countervailing duty petitions with the Treasury Department against six EEC producers and Austria. U.S. Steel argued that rebates of value-added taxes on steel exports were subsidies subject to countervailing duties under U.S. law. The Treasury dismissed the steel petitions in June 1975, and U.S. Steel subsequently filed suit in customs court under the court review clauses of the 1974 Trade Act. In July 1975, American specialty steel producers and workers filed a petition with the International Trade Commission (ITC) for special relief against imports from stainless and alloy tool steel producers in the EEC, Japan, Sweden, and Canada. The ITC ruled affirmatively in January 1976 and recommended protectionist quotas. President Ford attempted to avoid outright protectionism by negotiating Orderly Marketing Agreements with the countries involved. Only Japan agreed, and three-year quotas were subsequently imposed on the other importers in June. Also in January 1976, steel was exempted from the general and special preferences that give exporters in less developed countries duty-free access under the terms of section 503 of the 1974 Trade Act. In October, the American Iron and Steel Institute filed a petition with the Special Trade Representative under section 301 of the 1974 Act alleging that the 1976 agreement between Japan and the EEC was unfairly diverting steel to the U.S. market. As imports accelerated at the start of 1977, the domestic steel industry and labor intensified their joint campaign for import relief.

1977: Political Bargaining for a Strategy of Economic Adjustment

The year 1977 was a crucial one for domestic steel for several purely domestic reasons as well. The industry contract was up for renewal in the spring, but this was to follow the union's own leadership elections in February.[53] I. W. Abel, the head of the United Steelworkers of America (USWA) since 1965, was retiring and his named successor, Lloyd McBride, faced a stiff challenge from an insurgent rank-and-file slate headed by steelworker Ed Sadlowski. Sadlowski's platform denounced much of the community of interest that had developed between steel and labor during Abel's tenure. McBride won a narrow victory, but only by running up substantial margins in such non-steel outposts of the union as the machine-tool and container industries. The contract negotiations that followed were greatly influenced by the close election. U.S. Steel had apparently been moving toward a "buyout" package that consented to "lifetime" job security (for existing steelworkers) in return for a sweeping overhaul and elimination of existing regulations that blocked management's ability to use and transfer workers as it wished. Abel had been willing to exchange existing workplace control for job security, but Sadlowski's challenge forced him to abandon much of the plan. The contract was finally settled in April. The industry agreed to increase security benefits and to wages that would boost costs by 10 percent per year through 1980, in return for some increased workplace control. This outcome of the industry's own political bargaining had a direct effect on its ability to compete internationally. The rise in labor costs meant more costly steel and thus gave new strength to the joint campaign for protection. Indeed, shortly after ratification of the contract, McBride began to appear with industry leaders and the joint campaign for import relief intensified. The industry wanted to raise domestic prices to cover the costs of the new contract and restore flagging profitability. The union hoped to restore unity in its ranks and actually expected to save steel jobs. If protection could be won, neither party would immediately have to face the cruel confrontations and choices of an industry in competitive trouble.

Through the first half of 1977, U.S. Steel's Edgar Speer (chairman of the American Iron and Steel Institute), other leaders of big steel, and the union all rallied to the call for "fair trade," and pushed for protection using "national security" and "health of the economy" arguments. They also continued to urge the Special Trade Representative, Robert Strauss, to call for separate sectoral negotiations on steel at the Multilateral Trade Negotiations. Strauss was unwilling to fracture the overall negotiations and instead advised big steel to seek relief under the antidumping laws. In March, Gilmore Steel filed the test-case anti-dumping petition against carbon steel plate imports from Japan.

[53]See David Ignatius, "Who Killed the Steel Industry?," *Washington Monthly* 11, no. 1 (March 1979); and *Wall Street Journal*, various issues, November 1976 to April 1977.

In June, Speer outlined a four-point program to Strauss for dealing with the alleged "diversion" of Japanese steel from the EEC to the United States. The program included a 40 percent reduction of Japanese exports to the United States, compensatory damages, a limitation of EEC exports to 1975–1976 levels, and an investigation of other bilateral agreements in negotiations.[54] In mid-year, the Carter administration agreed to the formation of an Organization for Economic Cooperation and Development Ad-hoc Group on Steel, temporarily removing domestic pressure for separate sectoral negotiations at the Multilateral Trade Negotiations (MTN).

The administration's position on steel was closely tied to the MTN.[55] The Special Trade Representative and the State Department, in particular, had to avoid protectionist actions in the United States while negotiating for trade concessions abroad. Unilateral government action to protect depressed steel industries was accelerating abroad, especially in Europe, and U.S. negotiators wished to avoid an atmosphere of protective retaliations. The administration's domestic fight against inflation was another critical variable in its steel position. U.S. Steel announced 6 and 7 percent price rises in May and July, a move that Chairman Schultze of the Council of Economic Advisors called "inconsistent" with the fight on inflation.[56] In fact, steel prices had risen 12.5 percent since September 1976 and both the Council of Economic Advisors and the Council on Wage and Price Stability (COWPS) were determined to stem the impetus to inflation that this represented. In early August, President Carter ordered the COWPS study and recommended that government purchasers seek the lowest-priced steel they could find. From this perspective, too, the administration wanted to avoid protectionist actions and the price rises that would probably result from them. The administration's problem was compounded, however, by plant cutbacks that affected significant numbers of steelworkers. If the administration wanted to avoid protectionist legislation in Congress, an accelerated adjustment assistance package had to be formulated. In early 1977, the departments of Commerce and Labor began work on just such a package.

The pressure for import relief swelled suddenly in mid-August with the start of a pattern of major plant closings and cutbacks, which closely followed the relative degree of technical inefficiency among the major producers. From August to the end of September, at least fourteen major steel mills were closed down, and operations were cut back

---

[54]U.S. Congress, Hearings on World Steel Trade, pp. 138–139.
[55]Special Trade Representative Robert Strauss's remarks in U.S. Congress, Hearings on World Steel Trade, pp. 36–37.
[56]*Christian Science Monitor*, July 25, 1977, p. 11.

at many other plants. The largest shutdowns occurred at the Bethlehem Steel plants in Johnstown, Pa., and Lackawanna, N.Y., where
7,300 steelworkers were laid off, and at the Lykes Corporation's plant
in Youngstown, Ohio, where an additional 5,000 workers lost their
jobs. The Alan Wood Steel Company, the nation's oldest producer,
went bankrupt, affecting an additional 2,300 workers. Kaiser closed
three West Coast mills, and Jones and Laughlin closed a Michigan mill.
Armco and National cut back operations in Kentucky and West Virginia. U.S. Steel closed three mills in the East and one in the West; it
also threatened to close its Chicago South Works, which would lay off
another 8,500 workers, unless steps were taken "to stem the flow of
foreign steel."[57] A total of 20,000 steel jobs were lost in a few months,
and tens of thousands of citizens were indirectly affected in the communities involved. The problems in steel seemed to be reaching crisis
proportions.

In mid-September, a group of public officials and local union leaders
from sixty steel towns formed the Steel Communities Coalition and
began to push for community assistance through Congress. Simultaneously, members of Congress from the hardest-hit steel states met with
representatives from big steel and the United Steelworkers and formed
the bipartisan Congressional Steel Caucus. By mid-October, the Caucus
membership swelled to over 120 members of Congress. Congressman
Charles Vanik of Ohio, Chairman of the House Ways and Means Subcommittee on Trade, called a hearing in late September on "World
Steel Trade: Current Trends and Structural Problems." At the hearing
Vanik confronted Strauss and representatives from the Council of Economic Advisors and the State, Treasury, Commerce, and Labor departments: "We simply can't wait for the administration to come up with a
position while more steel mills throughout America close down and
create problems of unemployment and havoc. (Protectionist Congressional action is imminent.) The President will not have the power to
stop this force once it starts, and if it starts, it is going to snowball and
affect every item of trade in the whole glossary."[58]

In fact, congressional legislation had already begun to snowball. By
early October, at least five major protectionist bills were introduced by
members of the Steel Caucus.[59] During this congressional maneuvering, pressure on the administration mounted from within. At the end
of September, Treasury ruled (in its preliminary finding on the Gilmore case) that the Japanese had indeed been guilty of "dumping"

[57]U.S. Congress, Hearings on World Steel Trade, p. 42.
[58]*Ibid.*, p. 71.
[59]*Congressional Quarterly*, November 19, 1977, pp. 2467–2469.

carbon steel plate in the United States. In anticipation of the ruling, U.S. Steel and Georgetown Steel had filed separate anti-dumping petitions against Japan and France respectively, in mid-September. A spate of anti-dumping petitions, mostly against the EEC and Japan, followed the Treasury's ruling; there would be sixteen petitions before the Treasury by mid-November and nineteen by December. The EEC began to threaten retaliation in anticipation of the additional anti-dumping filings. From the perspective of the Multilateral Trade Negotiations, the mounting pressure for protectionism was disastrous. Indeed, as Richard Heimlich, Special Trade Respresentative's steel expert, confirmed in early October, "the timing couldn't be worse."[60]

In the midst of these conflicting pressures, President Carter called a special White House Conference on Steel on October 13. Carter appointed Treasury Undersecretary Anthony Solomon to head a Task Force on Steel which was to formulate a comprehensive program for the industry. By the meeting's end, the industry's position had altered slightly, although it still disclaimed responsibility for steel's problems. In Speer's words: "We find ourselves where we are because the executive branch in several administrations has failed since the early sixties—for almost two decades—to enforce our nation's fair trade laws."[61] He then argued against "unworkable," easily evaded quotas, and against any Orderly Marketing Agreement "that has as its purpose or effect turning from reliance on our free market economy to allocate steel toward reliance on the judgment of a government agency." There was, he argued, "no substitute for a free market-oriented economy. . . . A free market is the cornerstone of our economic system."[62] Note here that Speer's rhetoric disguises the extent to which he is seeking government intervention to alter the domestic market in steel so as to minimize the need for adjustment by the industry. Political action to exclude competitive steel imports creates a domestic steel market that serves uncompetitive domestic producers.

What kind of adjustment strategy could possibly emerge from the White House meeting? The answer revolves around the degree to which, through their political strategy and actions, the largest producers had come to define the terms of the debate on steel for almost all of the political actors involved. The United Steelworkers had identified its interests with those of the integrated steel producers. The Congressional Steel Caucus also identified the problem along the industry's lines: at the White House Conference, the Caucus recommended that the President formulate a "national steel policy" to do the following: (1)

[60]Quoted in *Business Week*, October 10, 1977, p. 39.
[61]United States Steel press release, October 13, 1977, p. 11.
[62]*Ibid.*

restrict steel imports; (2) provide assistance to communities where steel plants had closed; (3) consider tax measures to stimulate investment and increase the cash flow in the steel industry; and (4) help plants which need to modernize but do not have enough capital to do so.[63] Moreover, the positions of labor, Congress, Commerce, Labor, Treasury, the Council on Wage and Price Stability, the Council of Economic Advisors, and even the Special Trade Representative consistently reflected the industry's bottom-line requirement: profitability had to be restored to the industry without significant interference in management's autonomy to recover and adjust as it wished; furthermore, it was the government's responsibility to pick up much of the cost of adjustment for the firms, workers, and communities involved.

In these conditions, Solomon's program could only reflect a thoroughgoing identity with the interests of the largest producers. Because their focus was on "unfair" trade and they presumed that adjustment had to be fashioned by the firms themselves, Solomon's committee could not formulate a strategy of government intervention to encourage competitiveness or adjustment directly for the benefit of the economy as a whole. Moreover, the program had to console the EEC and Japan long enough to allow Strauss negotiating room at the Multilateral Trade Negotiations in an atmosphere relatively free from the threat of retaliation. Even as more anti-dumping petitions were being filed to bring pressure on Solomon's task force, an early November meeting of the GATT Anti-Dumping Committee drove the retaliation point home. Japan and the EEC pressed earlier charges that the 1974 Trade Act amendments to the U.S. anti-dumping law violate the intent of the GATT anti-dumping code (by enabling retaliation even where substantial injury was not proved).[64] Commenting on the negotiating of the Multilateral Trade Negotiations' tariff reduction agreement (which was reached on November 29), Jacques Ferry of the European Steel Industry Association said: "What has been happening in the past few weeks on the steel front threatens to alter relations between Europe and the U.S. in a dangerous manner."[65] In the midst of these pressures, and partly in response to anti-dumping petitions, the EEC's use of production capacity fell below 60 percent, threatening some 80,000 steelworkers.[66] On November 8, Congressman Vanik called hearings on "Oversight of the Anti-Dumping Act of 1921." At the hearings, he

[63]Congressional Steel Caucus, internal papers, "Actions Taken by the Congressional Steel Caucus," 1978, p. 1.2.

[64]National Journal, Oct. 22, 1977, p. 1637; U.S. Congress, Hearings on Oversight of the Antidumping Act of 1921, p. 12.

[65]Quoted in Business Week, November 14, 1977, p. 48.

[66]National Journal, November 14, 1977, p. 48.

pressed Treasury officials for a mechanism that could initiate anti-dumping investigations of imported steel that came in below a "fair value" price. Rumors that Solomon was considering a "trigger-pricing mechanism" had been leaked to the *Washington Post* the day before, partly to gauge public response. As November wore on, and top-level Japanese and EEC officials caucused with the administration in Washington, Solomon began to barter with the industry. He offered to recommend a trigger-pricing mechanism if the industry would drop its existing anti-dumping petitions. In late November, U.S. Steel announced that it would indeed drop its anti-dumping petitions against Japan if it was satisfied with the "fair price" levels of the trigger-pricing mechanism.[67] By early December, the United Steelworkers and the Congressional Steel Caucus indicated qualified support for the trigger prices, and Japan and the EEC announced their willingness to cooperate. On December 5, Solomon presented his task force's comprehensive program to the President. The program was received cautiously, because the industry still had to bargain for acceptable trigger-pricing levels in the first months of 1978. Not coincidentally, a week after the program was released, the International Trade Commission announced postponement of its anti-dumping investigations until after the turn of the year.[68] Those petitions were subsequently dropped by mid-1978, after acceptable trigger prices went into effect.

In summary, then, by the end of 1977 government intervention to alter the terms of trade in the domestic steel market had been implicitly authorized by the participants in the steel debate. Simultaneously, however, the universe of acceptable actions that such interventions might take had been expressly limited by the politics that preceded it. The strategy for adjustment that emerged did not really address the issue of restoring competitiveness, although it would satisfy the aims of the industry's major producers. The next section will examine the strategy set forth in the Solomon Program, describe its impact on the industry after 1977, and draw some general conclusions about the political economy of industrial adjustment.

THE SOLOMON PROGRAM: LIBERAL TRADE ADJUSTMENT AND THE INDUSTRY'S FUTURE

The Comprehensive Program for the Steel Industry, or Solomon Program, outlined four major objectives, as follows:

[67]*Wall Street Journal,* November 25, 1977, p. 4.
[68]*Barrons,* December 19, 1977, p. 7.

1. Our primary objective is to assist the steel industry in a manner which will stimulate efficiency and enable the industry to compete fairly. . . .

2. A second objective is to help ease the burden of adjustment to market trends for both industry and labor. . . .

3. A third objective is to provide meaningful incentives for plant and equipment modernization through appropriate tax, investment, and financial assistance. . . .

4. A fourth objective is to expedite relief from unfair import competition, but to do so in a manner which will . . . be consistent with our *overall objective of maintaining an open world trading environment based upon normal trading practices* [italics added].

It then made two additional, crucial points: (1) "We must *avoid any* direct governmental involvement in the industry's decisions. Our role is not to direct the industry's actions, but to help create an environment within which a free industry can operate efficiently. . . . And (2) "*We must avoid measures which stimulate inflation.*"[69] In a few sentences, the task force had neatly outlined some of the major features of American trade policy in the late 1970s. A domestic industry, its home market disrupted by foreign competition, was to be indirectly nursed back toward competitive health. The government would remove market imperfections and pick up many of the costs of adjustment, while reaffirming its commitment to management autonomy. The administration could pursue its commitment to a liberal trade policy, and address serious balance-of-payments and inflation problems, while simultaneously deflating the pressure for outright protectionism. This last point became even clearer when the Program went on to state, "the comprehensive program . . . requires no specific legislative measures and can be implemented quickly."[70] The Solomon Program was designed to be immune to protectionist alterations in Congress.

The Program's immediate aim was to restore profitability to the industry whether or not it was competitive. The underlying assumption was that the industry would commit increased income to close an expected "$1.8 billion gap between industry cash flow and investment requirements."[71] Modernization could then take place, and the industry's competitiveness would be restored. The centerpiece for this effort was the trigger-pricing mechanism; if "unfair" competition could be eliminated, then the industry's production and cash flow would naturally increase. With the trigger-pricing mechanism, the Treasury Department would establish a reference price list to monitor what have

[69]Solomon, pp. 7–8.
[70]*Ibid.*, p. 9.
[71]*Ibid.*, p. 23.

now become 84 categories of basic steel products, representing 90 percent of basic steel imports. The prices would be based on the estimated average costs of production for each product of the world's most efficient producer, Japan, plus 10 percent overhead, 8 percent profit, and "extras" covering freight, insurance, and handling costs to four areas of the United States (the West, the East, the Gulf Coast, and the Great Lakes). Imports entering the United States below their reference price would immediately trigger a "fast track" anti-dumping investigation (to be conducted within two or three months instead of the normal seven to nine months). If the mechanism worked as planned, "unfair" competition in the domestic market would be alleviated.

In fact, the choice of a trigger-pricing mechanism based on Japanese costs was a strategic one for the administration. The prices allowed the relatively less efficient EEC producers to continue the export of steel at prices below their own costs of production. This minimized the protectionist impact on the troubled EEC industries; a strict enforcement of U.S. anti-dumping law might otherwise have resulted in an effective embargo of EEC steel.[72] This could only have led to further deterioration of the European industry and to increasing social unrest in Europe. Through the pricing mechanism based on Japanese costs, American policy-makers could avoid such dislocation and the retaliation it was likely to engender, while still addressing the concerns of U.S. producers, labor, and Congress.

The Solomon Program addressed these concerns through additional recommendations for a revitalization of the depressed industry and for assistance of communities and steelworkers. These included tax incentives to increase company cash flow for modernization; expanded industrial loan guarantees from Commerce's Economic Development Administration; a rationalization and re-examination of the environmental policies and procedures that affect steel; expanded trade adjustment and community development assistance under existing programs; an expediting of the Justice Department's evaluation of proposals by steel companies for mergers and joint ventures; and the establishment of a "tripartite" industry-labor-government committee to ensure a "continuing cooperative approach" to the industry's problems.

The adjustment program must, however, be viewed in the context of what is realistically possible for the industry. Solomon's task force knew, as the report by the Committee on Wage and Price Stability indicated, that: "a reduction of imports to historical levels . . . would not significantly improve the domestic industry's economic position. Even if domestic production rose to fully compensate for the reduction

---

[72]Conversation with Crandall, March 31, 1979.

in imports, the percentage impact on domestic output and employment would be small and the fall in unit cost from higher volumes
would be modest. The financial position of the industry would be
strengthened if the reduced import competitiveness allowed them *to
increase prices.*"[73]

Indeed, although the trigger-pricing mechanism did not substantially
alter the flow of imports until 1979, it did provide a price floor that
allowed domestic producers to sell at levels closer to list price, thereby
restoring profit margins. Moreover, in conjunction with the rapid appreciation of the *yen*, trigger prices rose to match the price rises of
domestic producers. In essence, the pricing mechanism served to sustain domestic price increases and to raise import prices, by putting a
floor under competitive price-cutting. Such a result was foreseen by the
International Trade Commission in a memo on the Solomon Program
in January 1978, that was largely ignored: "The successful implementation of the plan would be to fix the compromise 'reference prices' as
minimum prices . . . a result inconsistent with the policies of the antitrust laws of the United States."[74] The most immediate result of government intervention, then, was to allow price rises to restore profitability to the industry by eliminating import competition that could
hold prices down.

Solomon's task force also understood another point that the Wage
and Price Stability report had highlighted: "The proposition that the
U.S. steel industry's problems would be solved by faster modernization
is naive."[75] The construction costs of modernization have far outpaced
the cost inefficiencies of the majority of the industry's outmoded
plants, thus creating a disincentive to modernize by rounding-out existing plants. As indicated earlier, the costs of building new greenfield
facilities were even higher than those of modernizing existing plants.
Thus, even major profitability increases under the trigger-pricing
mechanism *could not be expected to lead to significant modernization.* As the
task force undoubtedly realized, higher prices and increased profit—
which were the goals of big steel—would not be used to create a significantly more competitive domestic industry.

These outcomes suggest that the Solomon Program's major intent was
to generate the profit necessary to enable company-led adjustment of
the industry. The Program assumed that any possible increase in competitiveness, however limited, would naturally follow from company-led
adjustment. We may now examine the impact of such reasoning.

[73]COWPS, pp. iii; second emphasis, mine.
[74]*Congressional Quarterly,* January 21, 1978, p. 185.
[75]COWPS, pp. 79–83.

Liberal Trade Adjustment

The government policy actions taken in accord with the Solomon strategy represent political actions that bear directly on economic adjustment. Through the trigger-pricing mechanism, the government entered the market to define the terms of entry for foreign steel, to alter conditions of competition for the benefit of domestic producers, and indirectly to generate the resources necessary for profitable adjustment by domestic firms. The politics of 1977 enabled the government to intervene on behalf of the industry at large, with the historically consistent stipulation that adjustment at the sectoral level would be carried out by the steel firms themselves. Under these conditions, the efficacy of adjustment for the industry and for the domestic economy as a whole was crucially dependent upon the adjustment choices of the individual firms in the industry. However, these choices were to emerge from market conditions that were themselves the product of the major producers' political strategy and consequent government action.

As indicated above, the actions taken by the government served to raise prices and eliminate price competition in the domestic market.[76] In effect, they compensated domestic producers for their competitive inefficiency. By restoring a semblance of competitiveness to the troubled domestic industry, government intervention actually served to *discourage* the sort of adjustment that would otherwise have been necessary. Artificially high prices made outmoded marginal plants artificially competitive, and allowed relatively inefficient U.S. firms to continue turning out products in which they no longer had a comparative advantage. In this regard, it is important to note that in the years following the enactment of the trigger-pricing mechanism, the industry has continued to seek policies to promote its competitiveness by protectionist measures. For example, the American Iron and Steel Institute's Fair Trade Enforcement Act proposes a definition of "injury" (resulting from import competition) that includes "any past, present, or potential loss of customers or customers' participation to imports . . . (any) increase in imports either actual or relative compared to domestic production, or long-term domination of the market for a product . . . or growth in the level of inventories of such goods in the United States."[77]

---

[76]In fact, the effects attributed to the trigger-pricing mechanism are often confused with the effects of sharp and steady declines in the value of the dollar. Since world export prices are dollar-denominated, they will rise as the dollar falls. However, since the dollar's value bears a positive relationship to the relative success of the U.S. adjustment to changing world economic conditions, the points raised in this discussion are not materially affected.

[77]See the discussion in Ingo Walter, "Protection of Industries in Trouble. The Case of Iron and Steel," *The World Economy* 2, no. 2 (May 1979), p. 170.

It is difficult to see how such a definition would allow foreign producers to engage in *any* competitive behavior in the U.S. market.

There is no available, detailed study of the effects of maintaining artificially high steel prices in the U.S. market. Since the enactment of trigger pricing, some of the probable consequences of such a policy can be identified. First, significant income has been transferred from consumers to steel producers. This result was anticipated by the Federal Trade Commission study which estimated that the costs to consumers of a trigger-pricing mechanism would be at least $1 billion annually. The impact on the international competitiveness of American producers who use steel in their products—especially heavy capital goods, consumer durables, and higher-valued finished steel—has undoubtedly been damaging and has not been taken into account by policy-makers. What is the competitive effect, for example, of Nippon Steel's ability to sell plate and sheet to Japanese auto companies at prices up to 30 percent below U.S. Steel's price to American auto companies? The potential injury to steel consumers, caused by government protection of the profitability of the domestic steel industry, can be justified only if the transfer of income from those consumers is used by steel firms to adjust in a way that eventually restores competitively priced steel to the domestic market.

In fact, some company-led adjustment in the domestic industry has occurred, primarily because basic steel is not particularly profitable for the largest producers, given their existing product mix and facilities. As a consequence, the profits generated by government action have not been used to expand or substantially modernize basic steel-making capacity. Instead, profits have been used to cover the costs of closing outmoded facilities, to restore high dividend levels, and to finance the movement of these firms into more profitable, mostly non-steel investment areas.[78]

The recent actions taken by U.S. Steel to acquire Marathon Oil provide an important illustration of this point. These actions are only one component of U.S. Steel's corporate strategy of the past decade to diversify out of steel-making. U.S. Steel is one of the world's largest raw materials producers, and even apart from the Marathon Oil deal, it is using its corporate earnings in an effort to double its half-billion-dollar petrochemical business by the early 1980s. Its shift to raw materials is striking:

[78]This conclusion is supported by evidence provided in the following sources; company annual reports; *Moody's Industrial Manual; Iron Age;* Peter Marcus (Paine Webber Mitchell Hutchens, Inc.), *World Steel Dynamics,* November 30, 1978, A-13; and Helen Shapiro and Steven Volk, "Steelyard Blues: New Structures in Steel," *NACLA Report on the Americas* 12, no. 1 (January-February 1979).

U.S. Steel earmarked a bare 1 percent of its capital expenditures for ore development in the period after World War II. Today, the proportion is about 50 percent. As board Chairman Edgar Speer candidly explained: "When foreign steel flooded our market and we couldn't compete, spending for additional finishing capacity didn't seem too attractive economically. But we wanted a piece of the growth we saw in world steel. So we decided the way would be to become a supplier of raw materials."[79]

U.S. Steel's non-steel holdings have generated important corporate income in recent years while its steel business has lost money. Rather than expanding its commitment to steel, the company has been retrenching its steel operations. In November 1979, it closed fifteen older plants, eliminating 12,500 jobs, and it has tabled plans to build a greenfield plant in Ohio. Steel-making now accounts for only 11 percent of total company operating income.[80]

A similar retrenchment in steel production has characterized the other major integrated producers protected by the trigger-pricing mechanism. Thus Bethlehem laid off 10,000 people (10 percent of its workforce) in 1977 and closed down a significant part of its capacity, including many of its structural fabrication plants. The trimmed-down company, with a heavy orientation toward capital equipment markets, has been among the most profitable of the large producers. It has heavy raw materials interests, and its non-steel sales accounted for about 20 percent of revenues by 1980. Bethlehem's Burns Harbor greenfield plant, though among the most modern facilities in the United States, is now in need of reinvestment, and many of Bethlehem's other plants will not survive competition. The company will continue to retrench in steel, and is likely to begin more extensive diversification out of steel.

Through corporate acquisitions, National Steel has moved heavily into aluminum and manganese, into construction, and most recently, into banking (with the acquisition of United Finance Corporation, the nation's eleventh largest savings and loan company, in March 1979). National Steel possesses significantly modern steel-making facilities, especially in its Midwest division, and it makes the most extensive use of continuous casting of any of the major producers. Major diversification will continue, but the company is likely to maintain its existing, modernized facilities.

Armco has invested heavily in the production of oil field equipment and related products, and in fact, it is so diversified that it dropped the

[79]Quoted in Edward Greer, "Placebos for a Sick Industry," *The Nation* 226, no. 8. (March 4, 1978), p. 237.
[80]*Time Magazine*, November 30, 1981, p. 64.

word "Steel" from it corporate name in 1978. Its management is committed to further extensive diversification, especially because its long-term potential in basic steel production seems poor. Armco's specialty steel production (stainless silicon and specialty bars) is strong, however, and has accounted for the bulk of the company's steel profits in recent years.

Republic Steel's basic steel-making costs are probably greater than those of its domestic competitors, but its specialty division is strong. It has not engaged in significant diversification, and as a result has minimal non-steel earnings. The company will attempt to cut costs and modernize, but will also seek more investment outside steel. Similarly, Jones and Laughlin, a division of the huge LTV conglomerate, is burdened with significantly older plant and high costs. LTV will continue to acquire a wide range of companies (it recently tried to acquire Grumman), but it is unlikely to put any significant corporate earnings into its steel-making arm. If Jones and Laughlin is to modernize, capital will have to come from the division's own earnings (unless the parent company decides to milk those earnings to cover its own debt, as the Lykes Corporation did with its Youngstown plant).

Inland Steel is in a superior position versus its domestic competitors. Its facilities are modern, integrated, and concentrated in a single plant. Its Chicago location is in the center of its major markets and is relatively removed from import penetration because of higher shipping costs to the Midwest. Inland has maintained relatively high operating rates, even in recession, and has been consistently more profitable than its major competitors. Inland's commitment to steel production was reinforced when a series of diversification moves undertaken in the late 1960s and early 1970s lost money. It is completing a major one-million-ton capacity expansion program, and its ability to remain competitive in basic steel is probably secure. However, Inland may well move toward a tentative diversification strategy now that its steel expansion is completed.

As these company profiles suggest, the kind of reinvestment necessary to restore international competitiveness among the major producers has simply not occurred, despite trigger pricing and other policies to inflate steel industry profits by restricting foreign competition.

In sum, private control over capital allocation in pursuit of aims that differ from those of the state, and the state's own conflicting goals, militate against a coherent redevelopment policy in steel. As we have argued here, the Solomon Program's basic assumption that competitiveness would follow company-led adjustment—an assumption that underlies most U.S. policy efforts to promote economic revitalization in declining industries—has not borne fruit.

Disaggregation as an Alternative Strategy

The aggregate policies developed and implemented in the Solomon Program to assist company-led adjustment make little sense when they fail to restore competitiveness to the troubled U.S. sector. Indeed, it can be argued that by deferring and reorienting adjustment, U.S. policy has injured the more competitive segments of the steel industry. Since U.S. policy has delayed shakeout in the industry, the major producers have not been forced as quickly to give up markets they would probably have lost in the absence of government protection. Thus the mini-mills, specialty producers, and potential new entrants have been denied opportunities to increase market share and to test their competitive strength against foreign producers. Rather than fruitlessly pursuing policy strategies aimed at assisting the non-competitive segments of the industry, government policy in steel ought to disaggregate the sector and focus on segments of the industry that remain competitive.

Any strategy to restore competitiveness should take advantage in particular of four strengths: (1) the existing competitiveness of the mini-mills and specialty producers; (2) the advanced steel-making technologies in the production and finishing stages; (3) the requirements of the nation's technology-intensive economy; and (4) the close linkage between regional steel production and the needs of regional steel users. Some tentative possibilities are sketched below.

The expansion of the mini-mill and specialty segments of the industry should be encouraged, since they remain the most competitive and profitable segments of the industry. Given capital costs, the only financially sound additions to basic carbon steel production technology are electric furnaces in the steel-making phase and continuous casting in the finishing phase—which are the strengths of mini-mill production. The present extent of scrap dependency limits the growth that would be possible through electric furnace production; but the United States should have a distinct advantage in coal-based direct reduction of iron ore, which could alleviate the scrap dependency problem. A combination of direct ore reduction and electric furnace production could offer lower production costs but equal quality in a wide range of steel products that can now be made only in an integrated plant. Financing of direct reduction development, which might be too risky for individual companies to pursue, is a classic area for government action. Similarly, the complex technologies upon which specialty producers depend can serve to focus government policy. Indeed, the specialty producers may well become export competitive.

Given the trend of international competition (discussed in the next section), the prudent long-run course of government action is to encourage a shift away from the lowest-valued basic steels toward higher-valued finished and specialty steels. One advantage in this regard lies in the specific requirements of our technology-intensive economy. Those requirements are expressed in the particular characteristics required of different finished steels (for example, the automotive requirement that sheet steel for auto bodies be 'corrosion-resistant on the inside and paintable on the outside). Steel product innovation to meet the changing needs of user requirements generates steel production. U.S. producers are best situated to meet the requirements of domestic steel users, and this can be encouraged by research and development assistance that matches steel producers to steel user needs. Similarly, since investment in finishing capacity is economically sensible, it should be encouraged as part of the overall shift from basic to finished and specialty steels. Since this is where the value is added, this is where the profit lies. In the long run it is more economically sound to import cheap semi-finished and low-value steel and produce competitive finished products.

Distinct competitive advantages accrue to regionally located producers who specialize in a limited number of products closely matched to the requirements of the regional markets. Therefore, abandonment of particular regional markets and product market-segments by the major producers should be encouraged by the gradual phasing-out of import controls. As markets are given up, the gaps will be filled by foreign competitors *and* smaller U.S. firms that are competitive because they combine technologically advanced low-cost production with regional location within the market segment in question, and because they specialize in a product mix appropriate for that market. It is in this area of adjustment that government could concentrate its efforts: it could make research and development expenditures to encourage innovation in small-firm production, provide tax incentives to locate production in specific markets, and encourage user-guided assistance in developing the products most suitable for specialization.

Finally, it must be emphasized that any alternative strategy to restore competitiveness cannot be carried out in a political vacuum. The major producers will continue to dominate the outcomes of policy unless a stronger political coalition is built on the side of competitiveness. *Government alignment with the mini-mills, specialty producers, and regional producers will be politically feasible only if labor and older steel-making communities are brought into the coalition.* The point, of course, is to undercut the existing alliance of labor unions and whole communities with the big steel producers. Since that alliance has served to benefit only the major producers, it will not be difficult to draw labor and communities into a competitiveness coalition *if their interests are served in good faith.* Their basic need—and the equitable policy as well—is for comprehensive community and regional adjustment assistance focused on retraining workers and redeveloping depressed local areas. This strategy should focus on developing local enterprise that can be operated and owned by the communities and workers themselves, so that they will no longer be susceptible to the devastating effects of economic adjustment managed by large corporate interests. This kind of redevelopment should also be combined with a "brownfield" modernization strategy of preserving local labor and capital infrastructure wherever it can be competitive and whenever the greenfield redevelopment strategy is too costly.

Internal Strengths and External Weakness:
The Protection of Profits at the Cost of Competitiveness

Although the major producers experienced a brief period of renewed profitability during their five-year cyclical business peak in late 1978 and early 1979, from the second quarter of 1979 through the second quarter of 1980 they saw their profitability decline by about 63 percent, with some outright losses on steel-making operations. By early 1980, despite the trigger-pricing mechanism, imports were again flooding the domestic steel market. In March 1980, in a faithful replication of the strategy that had served the major producers so well in 1977, U.S. Steel filed anti-dumping suits covering five major product categories and seven foreign-country producers. On the same day, apparently to gain bargaining leverage, the Carter administration suspended operation of the trigger-pricing mechanism. All of these actions spurred the behind-the-scenes maneuvering of the Steel Tripartite Advisory Committee, which had been seeking a compromise solution to the problems in steel since its creation pursuant to the Solomon Program. In September 1980, the Tripartite Committee issued its *Report to the President on the United States Steel Industry.*

The Report differed little in its analysis and conclusions from the Solomon Program—which has remained the essential model for policy for the steel industry. The Report cited a capital shortfall for modernization needs of approximately $2 billion annually, and sought to restore profitability to close the capital gap. Its major recommendation was the restoration of the trigger-pricing mechanism at a 12 percent higher price level, modified to include a "surge" mechanism: if there was a surge of imports when the import share of the U.S. market was above 15.2 percent and domestic producers were operating at less than

86 percent of capacity, the Commerce Department would look immediately into trade law violations, and companies would be free to file dumping complaints without fear of suspension of the trigger-pricing mechanism. In effect, the large producers had finally won a volume-based trigger. The Report also recommended relaxation of pollution-control requirements and liberalization of depreciation rules plus an investment tax credit. In return for these concessions, U.S. Steel withdrew its anti-dumping suits. Here, as in the Solomon Program before it, there was no guarantee that firm-led adjustment would attempt to restore competitiveness to the bulk of the U.S. steel industry. Indeed, as we have suggested, the major firms in the industry, supported by favorable government policy and tacit public subsidy, continued to move toward diversification and high dividend payouts and away from any significant commitment to steel modernization.

After a strong start in 1981, thanks in part to the Tripartite Committee's recommendations, the domestic steel industry slumped badly, along with the rest of the U.S. economy, in the second half of 1981. The industry shipped just 87 million tons in 1981 (down from 100 million tons in 1979); imports accounted for about 20 million tons (up about 30 percent from 1980); and by year's end domestic mills operated at just 55 percent of capacity with almost 22 percent of the industry's production workers laid off.[81]

To such dismal performance figures should be added long-run shifts in the terms of international competition in steel, shifts that are likely to increase the problems of U.S. steel-makers in the 1980s. The trend in steel production is toward state-owned or heavily state-supported industries. This means that U.S. companies will have to compete with state-supported enterprises that will be free of the constraints imposed by the U.S. system of private enterprise. In particular, state-supported enterprises will present two challenges. First, they can more easily meet the capital requirements of modernization and expanding steel production because the state will underwrite borrowing, while providing support during cyclical down periods. Second, they will be under less pressure to generate high profits, at least in the less developed countries, because they will provide necessary employment, will provide necessary foreign exchange earnings (following the Japanese example of the 1960s), and will underwrite steel-using domestic industries. The United

[81]*Wall Street Journal*, December 31, 1981, p. 3. In these conditions it was hardly surprising that President Reagan's Commerce Department chose to file unfair trading practice suits in November 1981 against foreign steelmakers in France, Belgium, Brazil, Romania, and South Africa. The ITC, in its preliminary ruling in late December 1981, found a reasonable indication of material injury—the lessened injury standard of the 1979 Trade Acts. This finding would staunch import penetration in the product categories considered.

States, of course, will be the single largest market for these producers of basic steel.

Since 1977 the U.S. government has intervened in its domestic steel market in ways which have compensated major U.S. producers for competitive inefficiency, but which have not begun to address the basic problems of international competitiveness we have identified. Through their political strategy the major U.S. producers have been able to define the problems of the steel industry in a way that suits their interests, and consequently they have thoroughly dominated the outcomes of policy-making. Their focus has been on restoring short-run profitability at the expense of long-run competitiveness. The objective of state policy in steel has been to assist and ensure the profitability of the major producers during adjustment that is planned and executed by the firms themselves. Since the state has intervened toward this end, and because the major steel companies have been granted the autonomy to adjust as they see fit, the major producers have effectively controlled the implementation of "public" policy. Despite meager and temporary trade adjustment assistance, the costs of adjustment have fallen on consumers, labor, and "abandoned" older communities whose production had sustained earlier U.S. predominance in steel.

Looking at U.S. trade policy in the 1970s, observers like Stephen Krasner have called the vacillation between policies of free trade and protection "incoherent."[82] Our study of the U.S. steel industry suggests, however, that U.S. trade policy has not been incoherent. Instead, the United States appears to have pursued free trade where that has benefited its major industrial and financial enterprises; but it has deviated from the norms of free trade whenever necessary to protect the profitable implementation of adjustment strategies by firms in relatively uncompetitive domestic sectors like steel. On the whole, competitiveness has not been restored. Such an outcome is unnecessary, however, as the example of Japan's success at creating comparative advantage in steel since World War II suggests. In short, Japan has focused on promoting structural adjustment, whereas U.S. policies have focused on protecting profits by postponing structural adjustment or making it unnecessary. As this study suggests, government policies of the type adopted over the last decade will not succeed in helping the U.S. economy, for they can only protect profits at the expense of international competitiveness.

[82]Stephen Krasner, "United States Commercial and Monetary Policy. Unraveling the Paradox of External Strength and Internal Weakness," in Peter Katzenstein, ed., *Between Power and Plenty* (Madison: University of Wisconsin Press, 1978), p. 54.

CHAPTER THREE

Decline in an Expanding Industry: Japanese Competition in Color Television

JAMES E. MILLSTEIN

The previous chapter has shown how the Japanese were able to take advantage of the late development of their steel industry to introduce the most advanced technologies available. The next chapter, on the television industry, shows how they had begun to create their own technological advantages even as they began importing technology from abroad. Government promotional policies certainly contributed to the technological infrastructure on which industrial success was built, but the basic product and production strategies adopted by the Japanese firms can be distinguished from those of their American competitors. While American firms were competing among themselves for shares in the market for high-priced, large television sets with high profit margins, the Japanese began to distribute small, inexpensive sets through large U.S. retailers under private labels. Small sets required an early turn toward solid-state components and away from increasingly outmoded tube-based technologies. Equally important, the Japanese aggressively automated their production processes, thereby gaining advantages in quality and cost. Slowly the Japanese broadened their market base, selling larger and more expensive sets and moving into the large color sets favored by American manufacturers.

It is argued here that policies of protection designed to assist the adjustment of U.S. firms encouraged the Japanese to broaden their production and marketing lines. Orderly Marketing Agreements, such as the one employed in the color television industry, have had the perverse effect of encouraging competitors to move from low-value to high-value products. If quantitative limits are imposed on units sold, it makes sense to produce high-value items. It is also argued that American policies designed to facilitate offshore production as a defensive ad-

106

justment strategy for American firms discouraged them from moving aggressively toward the automation of production.

The politics of protection in television have differed from the politics of protection in steel. In steel, domestic producers could not plausibly move production offshore, and so they found themselves allied with labor. In television production, the interests of American producers were divided: multinational companies sought above all the right to assemble products offshore with inexpensive labor; but domestically based companies, joined by American labor, sought protection. Large-scale importers, such as Sears, found themselves allied with their Japanese suppliers. In the end, protection was won, but it came in a form that was not nearly strong enough to offset the Japanese advantages.

IN 1966 the Japanese Ministry of International Trade and Industry coordinated and helped finance a research and development program aimed at developing an all solid-state technology for application in monochrome and color television sets.[1] This application of all solid-state circuitry to television receivers had two competitive advantages: it increased *product* safety and reliability; and it contributed to a cost reduction in *process* technology. By 1971 Japanese television manufacturers had converted approximately 90 percent of their color television production to the all solid-state technology. U.S. manufacturers, on the other hand, did not make the shift as quickly; RCA and Zenith, for example, did not offer complete all solid-state product lines until 1973-1974.

The early move to all solid-state television by Japanese manufacturers has been seen as "the turning point in the technological advancement of Japanese over American industry."[2] In its wake, Japanese firms have taken the lead in developing new consumer electronics products associated with the television receiver, such as the videotape recorder and the video disc. Neither of these products would be commercially or technologically possible without the application of semiconductor technology. Indeed, since the development of the all solid-state receiver, semiconductor technology has provided the foundation for new product innovation and development in the video field.

Technology, though only one element contributing to a firm's com-

[1] "Integrated Circuits for Television Receivers," *I.E.E.E. Spectrum,* May 1969.
[2] "Sources of Competitiveness in the Japanese Color Television and Tape Recorder Industry," paper prepared by World Developing Industry and Technology, Inc., for the U.S. Department of Labor (October 1978), p. 65. Hereafter cited as Dept. of Labor, "Sources of Competitiveness."

petitive position in the market, was a key to the past success of American firms in the consumer electronics market; and so we should not discount the importance of the technological advances made by Japanese firms.

Just as it was engaged in the development of all solid-state technology in the late 1960s, the Japanese Ministry of International Trade and Industry (MITI) is now engaged in coordinating and financing a research and development effort that may have similar consequences for U.S. firms in the consumer electronics and semiconductor markets. In 1976, the Japanese government allocated almost $400 million to a four-year program of semiconductor research into Very Large Scale Integration production techniques, processes, materials, and devices. The effect of this support in enhancing the position of Japanese firms in the semiconductor market has already been noted by many observers.[3] And although the effect of this semiconductor research effort on firms in the consumer electronics market is less clear and direct, its importance should not be underestimated. As Colin Mick has noted, "the five largest semiconductor producers in Japan" (who are the primary beneficiaries of MITI's research and development assistance) "are also the five largest manufacturers of consumer electronics products—the major future market for semiconductors."[4]

The semiconductor markets and consumer electronics markets inceasingly hold the competitive key to each other's future. On the most elementary level, semiconductor technology is the foundation upon which future new product and process development will occur in the consumer products market. In turn, consumers are the most rapidly growing market for semiconductor sales—sales which allow semiconductor firms to lower their production costs by increasing their production volumes. Vertically integrated firms with strong consumer products divisions and strong semiconductor divisions may therefore have real competitive advantages in each market. In this regard, the Japanese firms, having achieved a pre-eminent position in the consumer electronics products market over the past ten years, have established a strong position from which to challenge U.S. semiconductor and computer firms in the home information and entertainment market of the future.

Among the U.S.-owned firms currently in the video market, only RCA and GE have the requisite organization to compete with the present Japanese challenge. Among the U.S.-owned firms in the semicon-

---

[3]For instance, see Colin Mick, "Threats to the Market Preeminence and Predominance of U.S. Semiconductor Industry," and Mark Blackburn, "Japanese Chips Gain Hold in U.S.," *New York Times*, September 9, 1969, Section III, p. 1.

[4]Mick, "Threats to the Market Preeminence," p. 17.

ductor market, only a few, such as Texas Instruments, have success-fully entered the market for consumer electronic products. However, with growth in the market for personal computers, new entrants with new product technologies may also help to revitalize American partici-pation in the consumer electronics market of the 1980s. One way or another, it is clear that technological innovation will play a major role in shaping the consumer electronics industry of the future.

As our analysis of the U.S. television receiver industry in the next section will clarify, recent developments in the international market for consumer electronics and semiconductors will force new policy re-sponses if the existing U.S. industry is to remain competitive. As a consequence, the current form of U.S. trade adjustment assistance in the television receiver sector (the successive Orderly Marketing Agree-ments with Japan, Taiwan, and South Korea) has done little to remedy the competitive problems posed by Japanese firms to the few U.S. firms remaining in the industry. To anticipate the analysis of the next section briefly, the structure of both Japanese and U.S. firms in the color television market is multinational; the imposition of bilateral quotas, as a consequence, has altered only the source from which imports arrive in the American market. With the accelerated investment since 1976 by Japanese firms in final assembly plants in the United States, the "pro-tection" afforded by bilateral quotas on complete sets has been virtually eliminated. Furthermore, as the remaining U.S. firms have increased their already heavy dependence on foreign television components, the U.S. sector has become little more than a site for the final assembly of television sets to be sold in the American market. The Orderly Market-ing Agreements (OMAs) have done little if anything to alter these trends, which were well under way before the agreements could be implemented. There are two crucial policy questions, then, which the OMAs have failed to address. First, do the U.S. firms have the techno-logical and capital resources to move into the next generation of con-sumer electronic products? Second, if they do, is there an alternative production strategy, compatible with a high-wage labor economy, which can both enhance American value-added and also lengthen the period, during the new video products' life cycle, in which production can be retained in the United States?

An effective trade-adjustment assistance program in the consumer electronics sector cannot ignore these questions. The OMAs, by obscur-ing them, have not directly helped U.S. firms adjust to the new com-petitive conditions in the industry.

In the second main section of this chapter, "The Politics of Industrial Adjustment," we will explore the politics behind the implementation of this politically expedient and economically ineffective form of trade adjustment assistance. To anticipate its conclusions briefly, a rational and economically prudent government policy should include three features. First, there should be a policy environment conducive to forward integration into consumer products manufacturing by U.S. semiconductor and computer firms, which would also be conducive to a backward integration of U.S. consumer electronics firms into semiconductor manufacturing and development. This process of integration could entail mergers, acquisitions, technology transfers, and joint ventures between firms that are already strong in their respective markets, and so the Justice Department's Antitrust Division should develop procedures and guidelines within which the process of integration may proceed. Second, there should be a revamped export promotion program, including tax incentives for the development of foreign markets, and extra depreciation allowances for capital equipment used in production for export to the extent possible consistent with the U.S. obligation under the GATT. Third, there should be collaboration between management, labor, and government in tailoring government policy to fit the strategic needs of U.S.-based industry and to implement that policy so that it equitably distributes the costs and benefits of adjustment. Since 1971, labor and management in the industry have been at odds with government trade adjustment policy, which has offered them only small benefits. Policies which sustain competitive American firms that follow product and production strategies compatible with the wage levels of American labor can be the basis of collaboration rather than conflict.

In the section that follows, we begin with a brief description of the historical roots of the current position of U.S. firms in the television receiver industry and the parameters of U.S. policy that have contributed to the patterns of development and adjustment in the industry. We then examine at some length the domestic political structure that produced the Orderly Marketing Agreements, so as to clarify the past positions of both labor and management vis-à-vis government trade policy and to identify the political obstacles that the current organization of U.S. trade policy places on the road to an effective sectoral policy. We shall argue that the position of the U.S. firms in the sector is partly a by-product of government policy, and also that policy solutions adopted for an earlier era are not adequate to the present tasks.

INTERNATIONAL COMPETITIVENESS IN POLITICAL PERSPECTIVE

In reviewing the history of the U.S. television receiver industry, we shall emphasize the role of U.S. policy in shaping both the direction of its development and the adjustment problems it now confronts. Our analysis posits that the political structure (domestic and international) within which industrial adjustment occurs shapes the direction, pace, and cost of the adjustment process.

The influence of government policy is by no means limited to adjustment strategies. It also strongly influences the manner in which firms translate their factor costs and technological resources into competitive strategies in both domestic and international markets. Government policy is therefore an important constituent of the relative international competitiveness of national sectors; in the case of the television receiver sector, it is crucial. The position to be argued here is that the decline of the U.S. sector and the rise of the Japanese sector have been as much a product of government policy (in the United States, in Japan, and in certain less developed nations) as a result of the relative factor cost differentials and technological resources of the two nations.

In discussing the impact of government policies on the dynamics of industrial development and international competition in the consumer electronics sector, it is important to distinguish between different types of government intervention. Government policy may affect market outcomes in three separate but related areas. It may directly influence the domestic environment of the sector (through subsidies, loans, and tax incentives); it may control the link between the domestic sector and the international marketplace (by tariffs and quotas); and it may influence the organization of the international system itself.[5]

Since the end of World War II, U.S. policy-makers have intervened chiefly in the third of these areas: envisioning and working toward the creation of a liberal international economic order, a "free trade" regime in which barriers to the free movement between nations of goods, services, technology, and capital would be minimized, and in which transactions would be carried out by private as opposed to state owned firms.[6] Although much progress has been made, this vision of a "free trade'" regime remains imperfectly realized. And although U.S. policy makers have generally eschewed the first two types of market intervention mentioned here, these forms of intervention remain a relatively common practice among our allies in the advanced industrial nations and have become integral elements in the development strategies of a number of less developed countries. The political structure of international trade —the varying levels of tariffs and quotas among nations as

[5] John Zysman, "Inflation and Adjustment: The Politics of Supply," unpublished paper, p. 29.
[6] Stephen Krasner, "United States Commercial and Monetary Policy: Unraveling the Paradox of External Strength and Internal Weakness," Peter Katzenstein, ed. *Between Power and Plenty* (Madison: University of Wisconsin Press, 1978), p. 52.

well as their different trade, tax, and investment policies—has influenced the dynamics of the market in television products.

The U.S. television receiver industry has moved through a number of distinct phases, each of them related to the overlapping life cycles of two products, monochrome and color television. The monochrome industry grew rapidly in the postwar period, spurred by domestic prosperity and the availability of wartime technology and production experience. In the 1950s the domestic industry enjoyed a technological and capital advantage which allowed it to develop and market its products without pressure from foreign import competition in the American market.

During the "growth" phase of the monochrome market, the General Agreements on Tariffs and Trade (GATT)—the institutional forum that U.S. policy-makers hoped would foster trade liberalization—had barely gotten off the ground. Given the strategic exigencies of postwar reconstruction in both Europe and Japan, the United States tolerated the maintenance of high tariff barriers in Europe and the imposition of restrictive import quotas and foreign direct-investment controls in Japan. As a consequence of the political structure of international trade in the 1950s, U.S. firms, in order to exploit their lead in production experience and television technology in foreign markets, were compelled to invest in production facilities in Europe (thereby getting in under the tariff wall) and to license their technology to the Japanese so as to generate residual earnings in a market closed to foreign imports and investment. Moreover, provisions of the U.S. tax code—the foreign tax credit and tax deferral, adopted in part to encourage the influx of investment capital to a reconstructing Europe—enhanced the strategy of foreign direct investment.

The sale of technology to Japan and the investment in local production plants in Europe, although it generated residual earnings for U.S. firms in the short run, had two undesirable long-term consequences for the domestic sector: (1) it hastened the closing of the technological gap between U.S. and foreign manufacturers, thereby further eroding the foundation of the domestic sector's comparative advantage in the world economy; and (2) it locked the domestic sector into the position of producing almost exclusively for domestic demand, thereby precluding the realization of higher economies of scale and "learning curve" efficiencies, which might have sustained the competitive position of the domestic sector for a longer period in the life cycle of its products.

The entry of the Japanese television receiver industry into the world market in the early 1960s, when it broke through the protective veil of sectoral development policies initiated by the Japanese government in the mid-1950s, coincided with the first major multilateral steps by the advanced industrial nations toward tariff reduction and trade liberalization. The Kennedy Round of GATT negotiations (1962–1967) took a major stride toward eliminating the protective tariffs and quotas that prevailed in the 1950s and had particular success in liberalizing trade in manufactured products and intermediate inputs.

The changed political structure of international trade in the 1960s was conducive to the growth of an electronics export industry in Japan. But of greater importance in its success was the package of promotional and protectionist policies put together by the government of Japan in the mid-1950s to encourage the development of its consumer electronics sector. The Machinery Temporary Measures Act of 1956 provided financial assistance in the form of direct grants and long-term, low-interest loans to Japanese manufacturers, stimulating both the acquisition of foreign technology and the investment in research and development. The Provisional Measures Law Concerning the Promotion of the Electronic Industry, enacted in 1957 and effective until 1969, provided financial assistance for the development of targeted "growth" products, allowed extra depreciation based on increased exports, and provided tax exemptions for expenditures to develop overseas markets.

Behind a strong "protectionist" regime that imposed controls on foreign direct investment, set import quotas, and put restrictions on import and currency exchange licenses, the Japanese government intervened directly in the domestic environment of its electronics firms so as to encourage the development of an internationally competitive consumer electronics sector. With transistor and monochrome television technology licensed from the major U.S. consumer electronics firms—RCA and GE—the Japanese firms rapidly moved down the learning curve of printed circuit board assembly, applying transistor technology to create both product innovations and process efficiencies. The net result was a relatively compact, lightweight monochrome television set highly suitable for export; given the additional economies of scale achieved in producing for both the "protected" domestic market and the relatively "open" export market, this product could be sold at a very competitive price in the American market. Japanese monochrome television exports grew rapidly in the period following the implementation of the government's electronics industry promotional program, moving from a negligible share of the U.S. monochrome market in 1961 to over 11 percent of it in 1966.[7]

The year 1966 was a crucial turning point in the history of the U.S.

[7]U.S. Tariff Commission, *Television Receivers and Certain Parts Thereof*, Publication No. 436 (November 1971), p. A-20. Hereafter cited as Tariff Commission. Pub. 436.

television receiver industry. The steady growth of Japanese import penetration in the U.S. monochrome market in the early 1960s and the significant price competitiveness of the Japanese product (in large part a reflection of relatively low labor costs in Japan) required a major adjustment in the production and marketing strategies of the firms in the domestic sector. The response by these firms took two directions: a number of U.S. manufacturers began in 1967 to transfer monochrome assembly and intermediate component production to "export plat-forms" in Mexico and Taiwan; and domestic manufacturers rapidly expanded production of color television receivers in their domestic plants.

The shifting of unskilled, labor-intensive activities to low-wage countries was a "process" innovation that enabled U.S. firms to defend their domestic market positions in the mature monochrome product lines against price competition from Japanese imports. This form of process innovation, as opposed to any other, was in part underwritten by the tax and tariff policies of the government of the United States—notably the provisions of the U.S. tax code favoring direct foreign investment as a mode of industrial adjustment to international competition, and the foreign tax credit and tax deferral provisions. The taxation and trade policies of foreign governments also encouraged this kind of "process" innovation. For example, in 1965, with initial planning assistance from Arthur D. Little, Inc., and a professor at the University of California respectively, the governments of Mexico and Taiwan each put together a package of tax, investment, and tariff policies designed to encourage foreign direct investment in local manufacturing for export.

In Taiwan, foreign export producers are granted tax holidays for as long as five years. Under the provisions of Mexico's Border Industrialization Program and those of Taiwan's Export Processing Zones, export producers are granted duty-free import and duty-free export licenses. Although the greatest incentive to foreign direct investment in "offshore production" facilities is the relatively low-wage labor available in the international market, government tax and tariff incentives were found in surveys of U.S. corporate managers to be of just slightly less importance in the choice of locations, specifically Mexico and Taiwan, for investment in "offshore production" operations. Consistent with these findings, soon after the implementation of programs designed to promote foreign and direct investment in manufacturing for export, Taiwan and Mexico became the primary sites of U.S. offshore production.

For the firm considering foreign direct investment in offshore production facilities for export back to the United States, tariffs and taxes are analogous to transport costs within a national-level analysis of such a firm's behavior. In combination, the tax deferral provision of the U.S. tax code and the tax holidays granted in Mexico and Taiwan to foreign investors acted to eliminate the tax costs of offshore production. Moreover, with the amendment of the Tariff Schedules of the United States in 1963 to include the value-added tariff provisions under items 806.30 and 807.00, the tariff costs of offshore production in Mexico and Taiwan for export back to the United States were virtually eliminated.

Traditionally, the movement of manufacturing to low-cost labor areas abroad has been explained in terms of the product cycle.[8] The product cycle theory suggests that as a product moves into the "mature" phase of its life cycle, as monochrome television had by the early 1960s, labor costs become the primary factor influencing the relative price competitiveness of the product. Given the high labor costs of production in the United States relative to labor costs in Japan, Mexico, and Taiwan during the 1960s, the product cycle theory seems to explain quite nicely why American firms began to move monochrome television assembly plants offshore beginning in 1967.

The product cycle theory, however, too readily suggests that reducing wage costs is the only means of reducing labor costs. In other words, the explanatory value of the theory rests on the assumption that product and process technologies are sufficiently fixed as to limit the possibility of cost-effective innovations that would be compatible, in competitive terms, with high-wage labor. The shift by U.S. firms to low-cost labor was, in fact, only one of a number of process innovations that might have sustained the price competitiveness of their monochrome product. Clearly, as among other possible alternatives, it involved the least risk, and given the tax and tariff policies of the United States compared to those of Mexico and Taiwan, it minimized additional capital expenditures.

There can be no doubt that price competition from Japanese imports, in part a function of lower wage rates in the Japanese industry, compelled U.S. firms to reduce unit production costs in order to remain competitive in the domestic market. However, to explain the type of adjustment strategy that was chosen and the pace of its implementation, we must refer to the political structure within which the necessity of adjustment emerged. That structure strongly influenced and conditioned the outcomes. It cannot be discounted. The tax and tariff policies of the United States, in tandem with the economic development programs of certain less developed countries within the American sphere of strategic interest, strongly favored foreign direct investment

[8]See, for example, Seev Hirsch's article in Louis Wells, ed., *The Product Cycle and International Trade* (Boston: Harvard Business School, 1972).

as a mode of industrial adjustment to import competition in the American market during the 1960s.

The wave of offshore production of television components and monochrome receivers by foreign subsidiaries and affiliates of U.S.-owned firms, which began in 1967, dramatically changed within the short span of five years the composition of "foreign" imports sold in the American market. Whereas in 1966 some 99.9 percent of all imported television sets came from Japan, monochrome imports from U.S.-owned subsidiaries operating primarily in Taiwan and Mexico immediately captured 5.1 percent of import market in 1967, the first year of offshore operation. By 1972 these same monochrome imports from U.S. subsidiaries and affiliates had captured over 52 percent of market.[9] While Japanese monochrome imports declined as a percentage of total monochrome imports from 1967 onward, they nonetheless increased absolutely from 1.2 million units in 1967 to over 2.5 million units in 1971.[10] The steady increase in both Japanese and U.S.-foreign subsidiary imports in the American market had a devastating impact on domestic monochrome production: yearly domestic output declined steadily from 6.7 million units in 1966 to less than 1.7 million units in 1976.[11] Domestic consumption of monochrome receivers, however, did not actually reach its peak until 1972, and although demand has since dropped, more than 6 million monochrome units were sold in the domestic market in 1976.[12] Where monochrome production remained in the United States, the percentage of domestic value-added in the final product also steadily declined, as domestic manufacturers increasingly relied on components and subassemblies manufactured abroad.[13] The export opportunities which it was assumed would accrue to U.S. component manufacturers under the Trade Schedule of the United States, item 807, simply did not appear. The strategy of using offshore production and foreign sources was far more cost efficient. In the short time between 1967 and 1972, domestic production of most television components and subassemblies, with the exception of picture tubes,

[9]These figures are minimum estimates of the volume of U.S. multinational corporation intra-company trade in monochrome television units, representing only those imports entered under TSUS item 806. The actual volume during this period was probably somewhat greater. For 807 imports, see Tariff Commission Pub. 436, pp. A-62–63; and U.S. International Trade Commission, Publication No. 808 (March 1977), pp. A-94–95 (hereafter cited as ITC Pub. 808).

[10]These figures reflect only monochrome sets imported directly from Japan. The number of imports from Japanese-owned firms is actually higher, including a certain percentage of imports from Korea and Taiwan.

[11]ITC Pub. 808, p.A-89

[12]*Ibid.*

[13]See, for example, the import statistics in U.S. Tariff Commission, *Television Yokes, Tuners, and Horizontal Output Transformers*, Publication No. 502, (July 1972), p. A-29.

virtually disappeared, as U.S. firms either shifted production offshore or simply sought their intermediate inputs abroad.

In the mid-1960s, as U.S. firms began to move their monochrome assembly and component manufacturing plants offshore, the advent of color broadcasting in the United States hastened the movement of color television into the "growth" phase of its life cycle. The rapid expansion of domestic color production, however, was equally a response by U.S. firms, in the area of product innovation, to the growing Japanese challenge in the domestic monochrome market. Domestic production of color television receivers expanded from 750,000 units in 1963 to over 5 million units in 1966. As the Japanese were beginning to make significant inroads in the American monochrome market, U.S. manufacturers were riding the first waves of a domestic color television boom that would not peak until the recession of 1974–1975.

As in the early years of the monochrome market, the foundation of the competitive position of U.S. firms in the color television market lay in their pioneering development of new product technology. In 1962, before the full impact of the government of Japan's Measures for the Promotion of the Electronics Industry had been realized in the U.S. monochrome market, RCA (following the pattern it had set in the monochrome market) licensed its color television technology to the Japanese just as it was beginning its first mass production runs in the United States. At the time, Japanese monochrome imports were just beginning to make headway in the U.S. market, a full ten years after U.S. manufacturers had moved into mass production of monochrome sets. The technological lead time which had been a critical element underwriting the strength of U.S. manufacturers in the development and growth of the domestic monochrome market, however, was not to prevail in the new color product market. Japanese monochrome exports had not captured as much as 15 percent of the U.S. monochrome market until some fifteen years after the U.S. industry had moved into the mass production of monochrome sets. In color television, Japanese exports captured 15 percent of the U.S. color market only five years after the U.S. industry had moved into mass production. With color television targeted by the government of Japan as an export "boom" item, the Japanese industry quickly adapted the product and process experience it had gained in monochrome production to the development of the new color product. Facilitated by the credit and commodity tax incentives in the government's package of promotional policies, and supported by government grants for solid-state research and development, the Japanese industry quickly moved into the commercial development and application of all solid-state technology to their color product. Whereas a U.S. manufacturer, Motorola, had developed the first all solid-state color television prototype in 1966, a Japanese firm, Hitachi, was the first to produce it commercially in 1969. By 1970, a full 90 percent of the color sets produced in Japan had incorporated the new technology. The two leading U.S. firms—RCA and Zenith—did not offer a complete all solid-state line of color products until model year 1973. As mentioned earlier, the early willingness of Japanese management to undertake the costs of product and process innovation entailed in the conversion to all solid-state construction was "the turning point in the technological advancement of Japanese over American industry."[14] There can be no doubt that the government of Japan's promotional policies facilitated the quick development and conversion by Japanese manufacturers to the new solid-state technology.

The conversion to all solid-state sustained the relative price competitiveness of the Japanese sets in the American color market during a period when Japanese labor costs were rising. The short-term costs of conversion were more than compensated, in the long term, by the further automation of the production process and the resulting productivity gains which the use of all solid-state allowed. While following the American lead in the strategy of moving offshore to produce mature components and products, the Japanese firms also assured the continued competitiveness of their domestic production operations by adopting and developing a process technology compatible with their increasingly high-wage labor. In the Japanese sector, the shift to all solid-state was as much a "process" innovation as a "product" innovation.

Beginning in 1970, the Japanese color television manufacturers overcame the scale advantages that had been part of the competitive edge enjoyed by the U.S. firms producing color sets in the United States. With color television targeted by MITI as an export growth item, Japanese manufacturers rapidly expanded production of color sets well in excess of Japanese domestic demand. Japanese output of color sets more than quadrupled, from 1.3 million sets in 1967 to over 6.3 million in 1970. Japanese exports during the same period quintupled, from 300,000 in 1967 to over 1.5 million units in 1970.[15] In turn, U.S. output of color sets, after reaching the five-million-unit mark in 1967, flattened out and remained relatively stable through 1971, when only 5.6 million units were produced in domestic plants. Imports, primarily from Japan, had in the meantime captured over 17 percent of U.S. domestic demand for color sets by 1970. Well before U.S. domestic demand for color receivers had peaked, Japanese imports had captured a sizable share of the U.S. domestic market. Well before any of

[14]See Dept. of Labor, "Sources of Competitiveness", p. 65.
[15]*Japan Economic Yearbook 1971*, pp. 208, 289.

the U.S. firms had fully converted to all solid-state color television production, the movement "offshore" in response to Japanese import competition was once again underway.

In part, the competitive problem has been a by-product of the marketing and production strategies that U.S. firms have pursued. In the mid-1960s the already significant investment by U.S. firms in production facilities in Europe worked against the development of Europe as an export market for their domestic color production runs. Moreover, the willingness to collect royalties from the license of television technology to Japanese firms seems to have worked against a strong commitment on the part of U.S. firms to try to penetrate the Japanese market. Whether there is any merit to the claim that Japanese manufacturers have been "dumping" television products in the United States or not, the failure of U.S. firms to penetrate the Japanese television market has no doubt contributed to the possibilities of international price discrimination on the part of Japanese television manufacturers. Unchallenged by U.S. manufacturers in their home market, Japanese manufacturers may very well have been able to earn higher profits in their domestic sales—to help underwrite the costs of acquiring technology and converting to all-solid-state, and to help sustain the price competitiveness of Japanese products in foreign export markets.

It has often been noted that "marketing efforts by U.S. firms tend to push U.S. consumers indiscriminately as close as possible to the upper end of any product line where the profit margins are higher. The relative vacuum created at the lower end is rapidly filled by competitive imports."[16] In the monochrome market, domestic producers had concentrated their efforts in the 16-inch and larger screen sizes, whereas Japanese imports were primarily concentrated in the 13 inch and smaller screen sizes.[17] Because the price of a color set is considerably higher than that of a comparably sized monochrome set, it should not have been surprising that the lower-priced, small-screen end of the market would experience the fastest percentage growth in unit sales. Domestic manufacturers, however, as had been their practice in monochrome production, concentrated their efforts on the "big-ticket items."[18] The failure to produce and market small-screen color receivers in the early years of the color boom was a serious marketing error, which left an opening in the U.S. market that the Japanese rapidly filled.

The difference between Japanese and American marketing strategies reveals again a more fundamental difference in production strategies. While the Japanese color sets were introduced at the low-priced end of

[16]See Dept. of Labor, "Sources of Competitiveness," p. 20.
[17]Tariff Commission Pub. 436, p. A-57, Table 3.
[18]ITC Pub. 808, p.A-35.

the market, the rapid expansion of sales volume at this end of the U.S. market during the period 1967–1970 permitted the Japanese firms to take advantage of scale economies that helped generate sufficient earnings for them to upgrade and further automate their production processes as the all solid-state technology became available. Using more cost-efficient production equipment than their U.S. competitors, they have been able since 1971 to move up the product line and successfully compete on the basis of price with U.S. manufacturers.[19]

The strategies adopted by U.S. manufacturers in response to Japanese import competition have contributed as much to the long-term decline of the U.S. domestic sector as have the comparative factor advantages of the Japanese economy. The production and marketing strategies of the two industries stand in sharp contrast and cannot be discounted in the explanation of the decline of the domestic sector. In essence, the two industries have been moving down two different "learning curves," to the ultimate advantage of Japanese industry. On the one hand, as World Developing Technology and Industry, Inc., has noted in its study of the Japanese industry, "the constant drive to expand exports has contributed to production efficiencies as expanded production volumes permitted firms to move down the learning curve, thereby reducing unit costs and permitting Japanese firms to accumulate production experience more rapidly and improve their competitive position against foreign firms at home and abroad."[20] On the other hand, as Robert Stobaugh has noted, "U.S. manufacturers are advancing along the 'learning curve' in terms of knowing when to go overseas to fight foreign import competition."[21]

In the 1960s, the shift of monochrome production offshore was compensated for by the rapid development of domestic color production. The "process" innovation that involved the transfer of production abroad was accompanied by a "product" innovation that for a time sustained production in the domestic sector. But well before domestic demand for color receivers had flattened out, Japanese imports began to challenge U.S. firms in the new color product market. U.S. firms could barely hold onto the "growth" phase of the color product life cycle. Domestic production in the television receiver sector peaked in 1968; thereafter, the expansion of domestic color production which continued until 1973 could not compensate for the losses in domestic

[19]Between 1971 and 1975 the average unit value of imported Japanese television sets steadily increased from $75 to over $95, reflecting the changing mix of Japanese imports toward the higher value-added end of the product line. See ITC Pub. 808 p. A-97, Table 10.

[20]Dept of Labor, "Sources of Competitiveness", p. 72.

[21]Robert Stobaugh, *Nine Investments Abroad and Their Impact at Home* (Boston: Harvard University Press, 1976), p. 110.

output and employment entailed by the strategies of offshore production and "foreign sourcing."

Economists and U.S. policy-makers alike explain the decline of the U.S. consumer electronics sector in terms of the comparative factor cost differentials favoring electronics manufacture outside of the United States. In such an explanation the relatively high cost of labor in the United States becomes a villain in the sector's dramatic declines. Given this premise, the policy needs of labor and of the domestic and multinational segments of the market diverge. Government's role becomes one of managing the decline of domestic production. The fact remains that it was not until three or four years after the Japanese had achieved significant labor productivity advances through the "process" applications of solid-state technology that U.S. firms began to convert to all solid-state and abandon the more labor-intensive assembly operations involved in the use of vacuum tube components. In this regard, the government of Japan's research and development program encouraging product innovations and manufacturing process adaptations contrasts strongly with the philosophical detachment with which U.S. policy-makers have watched the sale of new product technology to foreign firms and the shift by U.S. firms to component manufacture and product assembly overseas. The decline of the domestic color television receiver sector was not simply the inevitable result of relative factor cost differentials but a combination of two factors: the success of Japanese policy-makers and managers in transforming the relative factor endowment of the Japanese economy, and the failure of U.S. policy-makers and managers to perceive and respond to the competitive challenge to the domestic sector entailed by that transformation.

THE POLITICS OF INDUSTRIAL ADJUSTMENT

The signing of the Orderly Marketing Agreement for color television products between Japan and the United States in 1977 was a by-product of numerous attempts, beginning in 1968, by labor and management in the United States to enlist government aid in organizing a response to the challenge posed by Japanese imports. The delay of nearly a decade in the provision of some form of trade adjustment assistance, and the eventual choice of an Orderly Marketing Agreement as the specific form of relief to be provided, can be understood by examining three factors: (1) the change in the structure of U.S. trade policy that made it easier after the passage of the 1974 Trade Act for trade-impacted sectors to elicit government assistance; (2) the divergent policy demands of labor and management; and (3) the intra-industry division between the domestic television manufacturers and the major U.S. multinational electronics firms in the sector. Given the importance of government policy in shaping industry outcomes, the political dynamics that shaped these policies ought to be examined in order to consider how different policy initiatives would fare. Embedded in the particulars of policy were political questions about the targets of relief, the types of damage that would be compensated, and the types of adjustment that would be promoted.

These questions suggest the several purposes that must be accommodated if a positive adjustment strategy is to be sustained politically. These purposes include jobs for American labor, support for the firms in the industry that produce only in the domestic market, and an internationally competitive position for the multinational and technologically advanced firms. In a declining industry under attack from imports, the interests of different actors and segments can diverge as each scrambles to find some shelter, but in an expanding industry, or when policies sustain domestic positive adjustment, these interests can coincide.

Between 1962 and 1974, under the terms of the Trade Expansion Act of 1962, U.S. trade policy had two effects on the industry. It encouraged the use of "export platforms" by U.S.-owned manufacturers, and it blocked appeals by organized labor and certain television manufacturers for government intervention to help the industry adjust to the competitive challenge of Japanese imports. The provisions of the Trade Expansion Act were informed by the economic and political assumptions of "free trade." These limited the state's role in international trade matters to two general areas of intervention: trade adjustment assistance or import relief; and the enforcement of U.S. fair trade laws—the Anti-Dumping, Countervailing Duty, and Unfair Trade Practice Acts.

The terms of the Trade Expansion Act, however, left enforcement of the fair trade laws within the discretionary control of the executive branch, and it also limited trade adjustment assistance and import relief (under the "escape clause") to cases in which tariff reductions negotiated in the Kennedy Round of GATT (1962–1967) were the primary cause of the increase of imports. This causality stipulation severely limited the ability of import-competing industries and workers to receive even the minimal assistance provided for in the Act: in only two of twenty import-relief cases brought before the Tariff Commission between 1962 and 1974 was relief found to be mandated, and between 1962 and 1969 the Tariff Commission denied *all* petitions for worker adjustment assistance. The initial political outcomes were structured by these trade laws.

The political responses of management and labor in the domestic television receiver sector diverged sharply during this period. In general, management tried to counter the Japanese challenge through recourse to U.S. fair trade laws, and the unions in the industry tried to win import relief and adjustment assistance. In 1971 the three major unions in the television industry (the International Union of Electrical, Radio, and Machine Workers; the International Brotherhood of Electrical Workers; and the International Association of Machinists and Aerospace Workers) filed a petition for import relief under section 301 of the Trade Expansion Act of 1962. The petition alleged that imports of television receivers had seriously injured the domestic industry and that a restoration of the 1930 rate of duty (35 percent ad valorem) was necessary to remedy the loss and prevent further injury. The unions were not joined in this petition by any representatives of the firms in the domestic industry, however. By 1972, RCA, Zenith, GE, Admiral, Sylvania, Motorola, and Magnavox all shifted portions of their monochrome and component operations offshore in an effort to protect their market shares and profitability in the United States. A 35 percent ad valorem tariff would have significantly altered the economics of this strategy.

According to section 301 of the 1962 Act, government import relief could not be granted unless it could be demonstrated that the increase in imports was "a result in major part of concessions granted under trade agreements." During the period considered by the Tariff Commission in its investigation of the unions' petition, tariff reductions negotiated and implemented were insignificant: the effective rate of duty on television receivers and apparatus declined from 10 percent of value in 1962 to 6 percent of value in 1971—hardly a sufficient explanation for the dramatic increase in the volume of imports sold in the American market during this period. As a consequence, the Tariff Commission could not rule that import relief was mandated. It did, however, recognize the economic facts of the situation, and took note in its final report of the statutory bind in which it was caught.

> Import data show that television receivers from all sources have increased in every year from negligible quantities in 1961 to over 4.5 million receivers in 1970; imports during January–June 1971 indicate a continuing increase. Although television receivers are being imported in increased quantities, it is our opinion that the increase in imports is not "as a result in major part of concessions granted under trade agreements" as required by Section 301 (b) (1) of the 1962 Act. Failure to meet this statutory condition is the basis of our negative determination.[22]

[22] Tariff Commission Pub. 436, p. 4.

The Commission's report also noted that factors other than the stipulated "trade concessions" had influenced the increase of imports. Among these other factors the commissioners cited the following. (1) "A variety of export incentives on the part of the Government of Japan and the Japanese television industry to bolster production well in excess of home market requirements." (2) "A more rapid increase in labor productivity in the television industry in Japan as compared with the industry in the United States," and the relatively lower wage rates in Japan. (3) The licensing of U.S. technology to Japanese firms, first in monochrome receivers in 1953 and then in color in 1962, which provided the Japanese industry with a technological base for production. And finally, (4) the rapid increase in "imports from foreign subsidiaries of U.S. firms in the U.S. television industry."[23]

What is clear from the Commission's 1971 report is that the combination of the promotional policies of the Japanese government and the cost-reducing response of U.S. firms in taking production offshore had adversely influenced employment and output in the U.S. domestic sector. In this regard, it is important to note that the movement of Japanese electronics firms offshore had been only slightly less dramatic than the shift of American manufactures offshore. The difference was that Japan's shift had not undermined the international competitiveness of its domestic industrial sector. The Japanese government, through its coordination of tax, investment, and tariff policy, had helped keep Japanese domestic production facilities in the forefront of product innovation and world market growth.

Between 1970 and 1973 workers in the U.S. domestic television receiver and component industries filed more petitions for trade adjustment assistance than workers in any other domestic sector, with the exception of those in shoe manufacturing. Of the eleven petitions filed with the Tariff Commission for worker adjustment assistance, not one was met with an affirmative determination; the eligibility stipulations of the 1962 Act proved too restrictive. The Commission's investigations revealed that imports which were directly competitive with those articles formerly produced in domestic facilities had increased substantially; but again, as in the import-relief case, the commissioner could not agree that the increase of imports was a result "in major part of concessions granted under trade agreements." The commissioner frequently found that other factors, such as the shift to "offshore" production facilities and "foreign sourcing" strategies by U.S. manufacturers,

[23]*Ibid.*, pp. 6, 13, 15.

were more important than the minimal tariff reductions negotiated and implemented in the Kennedy Round.[24]

While domestic labor unions were filing their unsuccessful petitions for import relief and adjustment assistance, several U.S. manufacturers were seeking "relief" from Japanese imports by filing anti-dumping and countervailing duty petitions with the Treasury Department.[25] In 1971, the Tariff Commission found in favor of a dumping petition filed by Zenith, which charged that Japanese television sets were being sold in the United States at prices lower than those charged for comparable sets sold in Japan. The Treasury Department, charged with determining the extent of the price differential and imposing compensatory fines, did not act on the Tariff Commission ruling until 1978. It claimed that its delay was related to the technical problem of determining the actual price differential; but as we shall see, it was as much a question of policy as of mechanics.

In 1972, Magnavox, Sylvania, and Zenith filed a petition with the Treasury Department alleging that a number of Japanese government practices combined to have the effect of subsidizing Japanese television exports and that a countervailing duty should be imposed on those affected articles exported into the United States. The countervailing duty petition provoked a split in the industry's "peak association," the Electronics Industry Association. Joined by two manufacturers of components, Zenith, Magnavox, and Sylvania organized the Electronic Industry Committee for Fair International Trade, a thinly disguised lobby for the countervailing duty petition. The divisions which the petition created between U.S. television receiver manufacturers were related to the different degrees of multinationality among U.S. manufacturers. Among the major U.S. manufacturers with offshore production facilities, Zenith, Magnavox, and Sylvania were the least internationally diversified, and thus the most sensitive to the price competitiveness of Japanese imports in the American market. (In fact, the Japanese government's alleged de facto "export subsidy" to Japanese manufacturers was not unlike the government practices from which a number of other American manufacturers benefited in their offshore production operations in Mexico and Taiwan.) As with the dumping petition, however, the Treasury Department was slow to respond to the contervailing duty complaint. When it finally did act in 1976, it rejected the argument that Japan's practice of remitting its commodity tax on manufactured ex-

---

[24] See U.S. Tariff Commission, Publication No. 502, p. 16.

[25] For the shifts in the ratio of imports to domestic consumption by item, see U.S. Tariff Commission, *Comparison of Ratios of Imports to Apparent Consumption, 1968–1972* (Washington, D.C.: Government Printing Office, 1973).

ports constituted a "bounty" or a "grant" within the meaning of the U.S. countervailing duty statute.

In 1973, congressional consideration of legislation that would eventually become the Trade Reform Act of 1974 clarified the divisions which had emerged between U.S. industry management and the unions. In testimony before the House Ways and Means Subcommittee on Trade, the Electronic Industry Association (EIA) and the unions presented almost completely opposing views on the legislation. The EIA advocated a five-point program: (1) retention of the present tax treatment of U.S. multinationals; (2) retention of the rules covering the transfer of patents to foreign affiliates of U.S.-based corporations; (3) the continuation of TSUS items 806.30 and 807.00 (the value-added tariff provisions); (4) strict enforcement of the dumping and countervailing duty rules; and (5) the development of more powerful government incentives for export and for research and development. The unions countered with three proposals: (1) an equalization tax on profits made by U.S. foreign subsidiaries; (2) the elimination of TSUS items 806.30 and 807.00; and (3) the imposition of strict import quotas on products like or directly competitive with articles produced by import-sensitive domestic industries. The final bill, the Trade Reform Act of 1974, did not fundamentally alter the existing tax and tariff treatment of U.S. multinationals, but it did relax the eligibility requirements under which import-sensitive domestic industries or workers might secure import relief and trade-adjustment assistance. Moreover, in response to complaints from a number of industries (including firms in the television industry) that the Treasury Department tended to drag its feet on dumping and countervailing duty cases, the legislation placed strict time limits on Treasury Department investigations, expanded the International Trade Commission's jurisdiction to cover these areas, and included the right to judicial review of the Treasury's findings.

Among students of U.S. trade policy there seems to have been general agreement on one point: "The forty-year period of liberalism in American commercial policy between 1934 and 1974 was made possible by a change in the institutional arena of policy-making. The shift of power from the legislative to the executive branch of government partly insulated policy-makers from protectionist groups and thus facilitated the steering of a liberal course in the international political economy."[26] The Trade Reform Act of 1974, although it continued to delegate broad negotiating authority to the executive vis-à-vis tariff

[26]Peter J. Katzenstein, "Conclusion: Domestic Structures and Strategies of Foreign Economic Policy," in Katzenstein, ed., *Between Power and Plenty*, p. 303.

schedules, reasserted the role of congressional oversight in trade policy matters and legislated strict procedural boundaries in areas where earlier legislation had granted broad discretion to the executive. The Trade Reform Act of 1974 altered the institutional arrangements governing the policy-making process, so as to give greater weight to the needs and demands of import-sensitive domestic sectors and thereby altered the politics of industrial adjustment in the television industry.

The recession of 1974–1975 hit the domestic television receiver industry particularly hard, in part because it had never developed a significant export market for its products. With the drop in domestic consumer spending, production in the industry dropped dramatically, from 10.7 million units in 1973 to less than 7.5 million units in 1975. Many smaller firms were caught by the recession in the middle of the expensive conversion to the new all solid-state technology. The drop in domestic demand hit them the hardest, and several were forced to sell their plants and inventories.[27]

As reported in *Television Digest*, the cutback in domestic production during the recession opened the domestic market to a new wave of Japanese color TV imports in 1975.[28] "Japanese television equipment manufacturers responded to the recession by retooling and automating production possiblities. The U.S. industry's reaction was to cut costs by moving offshore to low-wage economies and locking into then-current designs and production techniques, and to release R and D personnel as a further cost-reduction measure."[29] Moreover, a number of private-label domestic retailers—Sears, Montgomery Ward, and K-Mart—switched their purchases of color television sets from domestic to foreign suppliers in 1975–1976. These responses led to a dramatic increase of imports in the domestic color market in 1976. In 1973, its peak year, domestic production accounted for just under 85 percent of the domestic color demand; in 1976 it accounted for less than 64 percent of domestic demand. The sale of imported color television sets leaped from 15 percent of the domestic demand in 1973 to over 36 percent in 1976.[30] Domestic employment in the industry in turn dropped from 35,711 in 1973 to 23,713 in 1976, a loss of more than 33 percent of the workforce employed in television assembly. Some of this decline has been attributed to productivity gains made by domestic manufacturers; but it is is more than likely that these productivity gains represented in major part the increased use of foreign components,

[27]Dept. of Labor, "Sources of Competitiveness", p. 65.
[28]*Television Digest*, 15, no. 19, p. 9.
[29]Dept. of Labor "Sources of Competitiveness", p. 20.
[30]ITC Pub. 808, p. A-90, Table 4.

parts, and subassemblies in domestic manufacturing plants. In any case, domestic employment and production dropped significantly and color imports rose dramatically throughout 1976.

These dramatic changes in the domestic color television market in 1975–1976 were met by a series of legal actions under the new Trade Reform Act of 1974. For the first time in the industry's history, a management-labor coalition was formed. Called COMPACT—the Committee to Preserve American Color Television—it was a hybrid, combining the labor unions that had filed the first import-relief petition in 1970 and the basic membership of the defunct Electronic Industry Committee for Fair International Trade, which had filed the countervailing duty petition with the Treasury Department in 1972. In September 1976, COMPACT filed a petition with the International Trade Commission under section 201 (the "escape clause") of the Trade Reform Act of 1974. The petitioners alleged that "the color television segment of the industry cannot survive as a viable domestic industry unless immediate relief from imports is afforded. Petitioners have no desire to see their plants and jobs relocated to foreign shores."[31] The remedy that COMPACT sought was an imposition of quantitative restrictions on *all* imports of *finished* color television receivers.

The coalitional alignments that formed around the COMPACT petition are an indication of the severe political disunity prevailing in the domestic sector. First, the petition united under the aegis of the Industrial Union Department of the AFL-CIO all ten labor unions organized in the domestic component and television receiver industry; it represented workers in the domestic plants of every U.S. manufacturer of television receivers and of many of the numerous television component manufacturers. Second, the labor unions were joined by three component manufacturers and three U.S.-owned domestic color television manufacturers. Although Zenith and Sylvania both operated offshore production facilities, they remained the only U.S.-owned manufacturers that still assembled all of their complete color TV sets in the United States; import relief in the form of quantitative restrictions on complete color receivers would have had little impact on their color operations. The three component manufacturers represented in the petition, however, were all dependent upon domestic color production for sale of their parts; the increase of color imports would probably shrink the market for their components and was therefore a serious competitive threat.

The other major domestic manufacturers of color television sets did

---

[31]"Petition for Import Relief" by COMPACT, submitted to the International Trade Commission (September 1976), p. 11.

not join the COMPACT petition, and each had sound economic reasons for not becoming a party to its cause: all produced or purchased a significant portion of their color sets or component parts offshore; moreover, of the twelve domestic manufacturers in 1976, four were U.S. subsidiaries of foreign-owned multinational corporations. In general, tariffs and other barriers to the flow of international trade are a decided nuisance to multinational corporations. COMPACT represented a coalition of the domestic workforce and the segment of the domestic color television industry that was least dependent on offshore production for its supply of color sets. Those opposed to the COMPACT petition were the major domestic retailers represented by the National Retail Merchants Association and the shadow group of multinational corporations, both U.S. and foreign-owned, which operated in the American market.

Perhaps the most strenuous opposition to the COMPACT petition came from within the executive branch of government itself, where decision-makers were still trying to defend the historical commitment of the United States to a "free trade" regime, even at the expense of "fair trade" in television. The story of the government's reactions to the COMPACT petition for protection exemplifies the ability of the executive branch to resist a trade-impacted industry's plea for assistance.

GROWING PRESSURES FOR PROTECTION AND GOVERNMENT RESPONSES: THE ROAD TO THE ORDERLY MARKETING AGREEMENT WITH JAPAN

In March 1976, before the COMPACT petition was filed, Sylvania filed a complaint with the International Trade Commission under section 337 of the Tariff Act of 1930 (unfair trade practices in import trade) against five Japanese color television manufacturers. Under section 337, as amended in the Trade Reform Act of 1974, when the International Trade Commission determines that a violation has taken place, it may unilaterally prohibit the import of articles in violation or may issue cease-and-desist orders to all parties it determines to be in violation of the statute. The President may revoke the ITC's action for policy reasons within a period of sixty days; but the 1974 Act clearly empowers the ITC to take its initial action independently of the President.

The Sylvania complaint provoked a major jurisdictional and policy dispute within the Ford administration. At the time, the multilateral trade negotiations (the Tokyo Round of the GATT) were under way in Geneva, and the ITC's consideration of alleged unfair trade practices by the Japanese put American negotiators in a delicate position. The

Treasury, State, and Justice departments all tried to dissuade the ITC from investigating and acting on the Sylvania complaint. A letter to the Chairman of the ITC from a deputy assistant to the Attorney General clarified the preferences guiding the Ford administration's handling of trade policy: "The allegations in the complaint dealing with economic benefits received by the respondents from the government of Japan should be dismissed as a matter of law by the Commission; and the allegations regarding predatory pricing behavior as part of a broader conspiracy to monopolize the U.S. portable television receiver market should be dismissed as a matter of policy, in the exercise of the Commission's jurisdiction." Treasury Secretary Simon, in his letter to the ITC (exhibiting a remarkable shortness of memory about the earlier dumping and countervailing duty petitions by Zenith and Sylvania), charged that the Treasury Department "traditionally performs the function of protecting U.S. industry from unfair international trade practices. The intrusion of the Commission into this area can only be viewed as a new and significant non-tariff barrier to trade."[32] Treasury, of course, had "traditionally" and consistently delayed or ignored petitions for protection from the domestic television industry. In fact, it was precisely to remedy the Treasury Department's historic tendency to sit on "unfair trade practices" cases that the Trade Reform Act of 1974 specifically extended the ITC's jurisdiction to such cases under section 337. Simon's jurisdictional claim had little historical or legal merit. However, it does show that the policy commitment of U.S. central decision-makers to a liberal international economic order, at the expense of the legislated commitment to "fair trade" and to the survival of domestic industries, was still strong in the Ford administration. The Trade Reform Act of 1974, however, clearly limited the discretionary authority which the executive branch had previously exercised in pursuing the liberal vision. The ITC, citing the 1974 Act, affirmed its jurisdictional right to investigate the Sylvania complaint, but it later postponed its investigation while it pursued the "escape clause" investigation initiated at the request of COMPACT.

On March 8, 1977, the ITC ruled unanimously that "color televisions, complete and incomplete, were being imported into the United States in such increased quantities as to be a substantial cause of serious injury to the domestic industry producing articles like or directly competitive with the imported articles."[33] Under the revised eligibility requirements in the Trade Reform Act of 1974, the increase in imports need not be "a result in minor part of concessions granted under trade

[32]*Electronics News*, October 4, 1976, p. 22.
[33]ITC Pub. 808, p. 1.

agreements" but only a "substantial cause of serious injury, or threat thereof, to the domestic industry" in order to mandate the provision of import relief to the industry in question. The ITC's report documented that during the period 1971–1976, the domestic color industry had experienced significant unemployment and underemployment.

The remedy which the majority of the ITC commissioners recommended to help the domestic *color* television industry was a tariff rate increase to 25 percent ad valorem, to be gradually reduced to 10 percent over the course of a five-year period, at the end of which time the prevailing 5 percent rate would be restored. The recommended tariff increase, according to the commissioners, would compensate for the average price difference between an imported and a domestically assembled color set: "Domestic receivers would be more price competitive with the imported products and therefore preferable to the consumer who buys on the basis of price." Further, the overall profitability of the television industry would be enhanced as domestic output increased and production facilities were used more extensively. . . . The virtue of a tariff (as opposed to the quota recommended by the petitioners) is that it would allow the market to sort out its own sourcing relationships while accomplishing the primary objective of remedying the serious injury to the television producers."[34] This last point is crucial to understanding the ITC's preference for tariff remedy; recognizing that all domestic producers had, in the previous five-year period, shifted to offshore production of subassemblies and television components, a tariff on complete and incomplete receivers would allow domestic producers to retain the cost advantages of these foreign arrangements and at the same time make their domestic final assembly operations more price-competitive. It would not, however, necessarily lead to a technological reconstruction of the domestic industry. Such an outcome might be more likely to occur as a result of the increased profitability of tariff-protected, American-based production, but a tariff is only a means by which to assure domestic corporate profits, not a means by which to direct the use to which those profits are put.

Shortly after the ITC's final report was issued, the Board of Governors of the Electronic Industry Association (EIA) voted to endorse the ITC's injury finding, with RCA casting a dissenting vote on the grounds that it supported "free trade." The more substantive divisions between the firms in the "domestic industry" were revealed by the board's inability to reach agreement on the ITC's remedy recommendation. As reported in *Electronics News,* the divisions that emerged on this issue reflected the different degrees of multinationality among the

[34]*Ibid.,* pp. 30,25.

different firms.[35] A number of the EIA members (Sony, Motorola, Magnavox, and Sanyo) are U.S. subsidiaries of foreign-owned multinationals that import complete and incomplete color sets into the United States. A number of other members (Admiral, RCA and GE) have substantial offshore operations that might be adversely affected by the tariff increase. Zenith and Sylvania, both EIA members and parties to the COMPACT petition, were "delighted" with the injury and remedy findings, for neither manufactured or purchased color sets abroad.

With the multilateral trade negotiations still under way in 1977, the positive determination of injury and the tariff-increase remedy recommended by the ITC put the Carter administration in a difficult policy position: a tariff increase on color television sets in particular would contradict the general commitment to tariff liberalization which had underwritten the U.S. position in the GATT negotiations. Moreover, the tariff increase, by raising the average price of a television set sold in the United States, could contribute (albeit minimally) to an already high and persistent inflation rate. Perhaps most important, such a mode of relief might work against the efforts already being made by U.S. firms to adjust to the new competitive conditions in the U.S. market (offshore production and use of other and foreign sourcing arrangements). Thus an ambiguity in the language of the Trade Reform Act of 1974 arose in cases where the "domestic industry in question" was less domestic than multinational; given the criteria governing the presidential decision to provide relief, the legislation is unclear as to which is the primary consideration, protecting the "domestic industry" or protecting the U.S. *firms* in the domestic industry. The descriptive phrase "domestic industry" as applied to those firms constituting the U.S. television receiver industry is misleading; by 1977, this domestic industry consisted of eleven multinational firms for whom the domestic market was but one source of sales revenue and one location for a particular stage of production. Given this industrial structure, the provision of import relief to the "domestic industry" through the limited and indirect means of either a tariff or quota was burdened with ambiguity from the start.

The tension between the mounting pressure for protection and the historical policy commitment to free trade was exacerbated by the events of April 1977. Preliminary statistics released by the Department of Commerce in late April revealed that imports of color television sets in the first quarter of 1977 had jumped almost 50 percent over the level of imports in the same quarter of 1976: the increase of color imports that had begun in 1975 and had grown dramatically in 1976

[35]*Electronics News,* March 21, 1977, p. 23.

showed no sign of slowing down in 1977. Moreover, after the Treasury Department had finally rejected the 1972 Zenith-Sylvania countervailing duty complaint in 1976, Zenith exercised the option of judicial review of Treasury decisions provided for in the Trade Reform Act of 1973 and appealed the decision in the U.S. Customs Court in New York. On April 12, 1977, the Customs Court unanimously ordered Treasury Secretary Blumenthal to impose countervailing duties on Japanese electronic equipment. The significance of the ruling went well beyond the specific case involved. As a *New York Times* editorial the following week noted: "The practice of returning indirect taxes on exported goods is common in most industrialized countries. If the court's standard were generally applied, it could affect between 60 percent and 70 percent of all products imported into the U.S."[36] Such imports would include television components and receivers produced by U.S. subsidiaries in Mexico and Taiwan for export back to the United States.

During the first week of June 1977, a special twenty-nation working group of GATT announced that the Japanese practice in question was in full accord with the provisions of GATT, and that the imposition of countervailing duties by the United States, as mandated in the Customs Court decision, would be in contravention of these same provisions. The working group concluded that if the Customs Court decision were not overturned, Japan would have the right to take retaliatory action in compensation for this U.S. violation of the GATT rules. The Carter administration first contemplated introducing special legislation in Congress to nullify or delay the impact of the court's decision, but it later chose the more expedient path of court appeal. With a number of industries pressing for protection, Congress was not likely to be receptive to a legislative end run around the court's decision. The administration won its case a few months later in the Court of Customs and Patent Appeals, and although Zenith continued to press its case up to the Supreme Court, that court affirmed the appellate court's determination that the Japanese practice was an "act of state" and therefore exempt from prosecution under U.S. law. Nonetheless, when the Customs Court decision was first rendered in April 1977 it put additional pressure on the administration in making its determination in the import-relief case. Indeed, it enhanced the likelihood that the solution would be politically expedient and economically innocuous.

The provision of import relief by the U.S. government does not involve a formal quid pro quo between the firms in the trade-impacted "domestic industry" and the government. As part of the process of

---

[36]*New York Times*, April 24, 1977, p. 31.

deliberation within the Office of the Special Trade Representative, firms are *requested* to provide officials with a plan and schedule of their response should import relief be provided; but after import relief is granted the government has no special power to compel the firms to perform as their plans and schedules have indicated. The purpose of government policy is to facilitate the process of adjustment as managed by the firms in the "domestic industry" and is in no way meant to compromise the unilateral discretion of management to determine the basic direction of the enterprise: "economic planning is the thing to avoid, the market system works best." The plans and schedules submitted by the firms in the industry are not a subject of negotiation but simply of discussion; they constitute *only* relevant information that government officials may take into consideration when formulating policy. The role of import relief is primarily "to take uncertainty out of the market for awhile, to give management space to make its moves to restore its competitive position."

The "moves" that domestic firms had been primarily making to restore their competitive position were offshore production and "foreign sourcing." In its final report to the president, the International Trade Commission fully documented the offshore movement of U.S. firms in response to Japanese import competition.[37] Nonetheless, import relief to the domestic industry would be provided "to help U.S. companies adjust to foreign competition and not to disadvantage American companies sourcing abroad." It is here that the ambiguity of "protection" for a domestic industry dominated by multinational firms unravels: import relief is granted not so much to protect a domestic industry as *to protect the profitability of the firms operating in the domestic market.* In a sector dominated by multinational firms, state policy cannot protect domestic employment and value-added and at the same time not interfere with the management production strategies that have historically taken production abroad. The competing claims on government policy—that the state not interfere with "autonomy of management," and that the state act "to prevent or remedy serious injury to the domestic industry in question"—seem to be inherently at odds where the industry in question includes eleven multinational firms. To say the least, the COMPACT import relief case presented the Carter administration with an unusual policy dilemma.

On May 20, 1977, President Carter announced the signing of an Orderly Marketing Agreement with the government of Japan limiting the number of Japanese color television receivers shipped to the U.S. market from Japan for three years beginning July 1, 1977. The Presi-

[37]ITC Pub. 808.

dent chose this form of relief in order "to remedy serious injury to the domestic industry and its workers." Special Trade Representative Robert Strauss, who negotiated the agreement with Japan, characterized the accord as "a fair and equitable arrangement—one which does not unnecessarily limit trade or raise consumer costs, but which also gives American firms and workers time to adjust to international competition without market disruption caused by sudden surges in import penetration."[38] Under the terms of the Orderly Marketing Agreement, a limit of 1.56 million units per year was placed on "complete" but not necessarily fully assembled receivers, and a limit of 190,000 units per year was put on "incomplete" receivers. These two categories together were targeted to total 1.75 million units per year over the three-year period ending in mid-1980. In addition to the quantitative limit on imports from Japan, separate assurances were concluded with the understanding that the Japanese government would encourage investment by Japanese TV makers in production facilities in the United States, which would require substantial levels of U.S. labor to complete and assemble semi-finished imports. The limit on "incomplete" sets could be exceeded if the completion of the final product by American labor accounted for at least 40 percent of the value-added. Thus although the U.S. government could not exact a quid pro quo from U.S.-owned manufacturers to retain production in the United States in exchange for import relief, it was able to exact a quid pro quo from the government of Japan—that is, expansion of Japanese television products in the United States above the level specified in the Orderly Marketing Agreement would be tied to the proportion of U.S. value-added in Japanese products.

Although the President explained that "imports from Japan were the principal cause of concern," the members of COMPACT—the original petitioners for import relief—did not see the situation in the same light. COMPACT had petitioned for an annual import quota of 1.3 million color television sets from *all* countries and had criticized the President's agreement, which limited only sets from Japan and put the limit at 1.75 million units. The labor unions in COMPACT recognized that the movement offshore by American television manufacturers was as much a part of the "serious injury" experienced by the "domestic industry" as the increase in the volume of imports from Japan. President Carter's form of relief did nothing to reverse or affect the offshore trend; indeed, it enhanced it. Therefore, as might be expected, "the U.S. color television industry applauded the agreement" with Ja-

---

[38]Office of the Special Representative for Trade Negotiations, Press Release no. 249 (May 20, 1977), p. 1.

pan. Spokesmen for RCA and GE called the Orderly Marketing Agreement a "good compromise."[39]

That the Orderly Marketing Agreement with Japan (OMA) failed to address the real source of the problems of the "domestic industry" was soon made clear. In September 1977, three months after the OMA went into effect, Zenith—the largest domestic color television manufacturer and a supporter of the COMPACT petition—announced that it was laying off a fourth of its domestic work force and transferring a substantial part of its color production to Taiwan and Mexico. Zenith's reason for the move illustrates both the inadequacy of the OMA as form of import relief and the Carter administration's too facile identification of imports from Japan as "the principal cause of concern" to the domestic industry. As reported in *Television Digest*, "Zenith's shift to low-wage foreign feeder plants was dictated by U.S. competitors." Zenith President John Nevin said the move was dictated by "increasingly significant cost advantages gained by other manufacturers from production in low labor cost areas."[40] Indeed, Zenith was only following a pattern of trade adjustment that the other members of the domestic industry had pursued in previous years. RCA, regarded as the most profitable company in the industry, several years before had implemented a cost-cutting offshore production program to which the Zenith program announced in September 1977 was virtually identical. As reported in the *New York Times*, "R.C.A. laid off a substantial number of workers and moved many operations overseas. The company said it is now [May 1977] reaping the benefits of the program."[41]

Nevertheless, Zenith's announcement caught the office of the Special Trade Representative by surprise; during the policy deliberations leading up to the signing of the OMA with Japan, Zenith had given no indication that such a mode of "trade adjustment" was to be part of its response to the provision of "import relief" to the domestic industry. The contradiction between the commitment not to interfere with or disadvantage the "foreign sourcing" relationships developed by U.S. manufacturers and the goal of remedying or preventing serious injury to the "domestic industry" was resolved in the OMA in the favor of the former and at the expense of the latter.

The Zenith move left only one U.S.-based color television manufacturer without substantial dependence on imports of television subassemblies from its foreign subsidiaries—Dutch-owned Magnavox. That the OMA failed to address itself to the problems posed for the domestic industry by the offshore production strategies of the U.S.-owned

[39] *New York Times*, May 21, 1977, p. 25.
[40] *Television Digest*, 17, no. 40, p. 9.
[41] *New York Times*, May 21, 1977, p. 25,

corporations selling in the American market testifies to the primary goal of import relief: to protect the profitability of American firms in the industry, rather than to protect production, employment, and value-added in the domestic television receiver industry.

The offshore production strategy, however, was at best a short-term profit-maximizing move: in the effort to restore profitability quickly, it was the most cost-efficient "process" innovation open to U.S. firms. In the longer term, however, in terms of sustaining capacity to translate technological innovation into the development of new "growth" products that can be produced and marketed in the United States, the offshore production strategy is highly questionable. As evidenced in both the RCA and Zenith programs, the movement offshore has been accompanied by a cutback in research and development personnel and expenditure, the closing of domestic production plants, and the transfer of existing product and process technologies abroad. In the short term, profitability in mature product lines may be enhanced, but in the longer term the capacity of these firms to move into new product lines may be undermined.

The lesson of Zenith for the domestic television receiver industry was, as a headline in *Television Digest* suggested, "Go Multinational or Die." The Orderly Marketing Agreement with Japan was, at best, an assurance to U.S. firms that they would have a sufficient degree of certainty about the level of Japanese imports while they pursued the multinational strategy of market adjustment. It certainly did not enhance the American market as a location for television production, except for those Japanese firms wishing to expand their sales in the United States above the levels specified in the OMA. With Zenith's switch to importing chassis and printed circuit board subassemblies from Taiwan and Mexico, the multinationality of the "domestic industry" was complete by 1977: "Admiral makes both color and black and white sets in Taiwan; most of G.E.'s circuit boards come from Singapore; Magnavox imports from the Taiwan plant of its parent Dutch Phillips; Curtis Mathes has a feeder plant in the Netherlands Antilles and imports chassis from Mexico; Sylvania-Philco makes televisions in Taiwan, color chassis and parts in Mexico; and as it did even before its 1977 move, Zenith makes black and white television and some color circuit boards in Taiwan, picture tube guns and deflection parts in Mexico."[42]

The Orderly Marketing Agreement with Japan was by law and presidential proclamation supposed to protect "domestic" plants and workers from "import injury." Although separate assurances were ex-

[42] Ibid.

tracted from the government of Japan to encourage Japanese manufacturers to invest in U.S. production facilities, the OMA had no separate provisions for encouraging U.S.-owned manufacturers to expand their production in the United States rather than their assembly and production operations in Mexico, Taiwan, and Singapore—all sources of U.S. imports but left untouched by the administration's original form of import relief. Moreover, the Orderly Marketing Agreement—a bilateral, government-to-government agreement—failed to consider the structure of the import industry in another regard: it placed no immediate limits on color sets imported from Japanese-owned plants located in third countries—and most of the major Japanese television manufacturers have production facilities in South Korea and Taiwan, among other places. Given the international organization of the television industry, among both U.S. and Japanese firms, the OMA as a form of "import relief" was mostly form and little substance.

In the first year of the OMA with Japan, color sets imported from Taiwan and Korea more than compensated for the cutback in imports from Japan. Under the "equity clause" of the original OMA, and under pressure from both Japan and COMPACT, the Carter administration was compelled in December 1978 to negotiate additional OMAs with the governments of Korea and Taiwan. Given the multinational structure of the industry worldwide, the flexibility of intra-firm trade was sufficient to undermine the effectiveness of any single bilateral agreement limiting imports. Therefore, the administration was forced to follow the OMA with Japan with additional OMAs with Taiwan and Korea to make its original "import relief" stick. The OMA with Japan, nonetheless, did accelerate the pace of investment by Japanese firms in assembly facilities in the United States. Six of the major Japanese consumer electronics firms now assemble color televisions in the United States. Recent estimates place their share of domestic shipments at around 2 million units, or just slightly under 30 percent of all domestic shipments in 1978.[43] In turn, imports from Japan during 1978 totaled 1.4 million units. Color television sets assembled by Japanese firms in the United States and those imported from Japan in 1978 constituted together just under 30 percent of domestic consumption: what was lost in import volume under the OMAs has been gained through domestic assembly. U.S. value-added, however, has been only slightly enhanced, because for the most part the Japanese have shifted only their production of picture tubes and cabinets to their assembly operation in the United States. With the continuing movement of U.S. firms offshore for the production of color parts and chassis, it is unlikely that domestic

[43]*Wall Street Journal,* January 9, 1979.

value-added constitutes more than 40 percent of the total volume in any domestically assembled set.

Throughout the past decade, as U.S. firms have been struggling, through a program of cost-reducing efforts, to maintain their price competitiveness in a maturing color product market, the Japanese have moved ahead of U.S. firms in new product development. As the Machinery Temporary Law of 1956 and the Temporary Measures for the Promotion of the Electronics Industry 1957–1969 succeeded in facilitating the closing of the technology gap between U.S. firms and Japanese firms in monochrome and color television production, so the Electronic Industry and Specified Machinery Industry Promotion Temporary Measure Law 1971–1979 has succeeded in facilitating the advancement of the Japanese industry over U.S. firms in the development of the next generation of video products. Japanese firms have completely preempted U.S. firms in the video tape-recorder market. Hence, while the OMA has limited the U.S. market for Japanese-based color television production, Japanese exports of the higher value-added videotape recorder product (over one million units in 1980) have more than compensated for the limits on color telelvision sales. While the OMA has to some extent helped U.S. firms improve their profits in the color product line, it remains doubtful whether they have in fact helped U.S. firms adjust to the *new* competitive conditions in the consumer electronics market.

In this regard, limited assistance to firms in a trade-impacted sector—which fairly describes the spectrum of U.S. trade-adjustment assistance programs—stands in marked contrast to the coordinated development assistance programs of the government of Japan. Japanese policy-makers, in consultation with industry, have worked at maintaining Japanese-based production in a competitive position in the international consumer electronics market. By promoting the acquisition and improvement of foreign technology, MITI has helped assure that Japan's domestic sector will remain a leader in new product development and market growth. By 1970 Japanese color television output surpassed that of the United States; in 1968, when U.S. manufacturers were only slowly converting to integrated circuits, Japanese industry, through a coordinated program of research into the applications of integrated circuits to television functions, produced a prototype all solid-state color receiver; by 1971 it had made the conversion in virtually all of its sets. In essence, firms in the U.S. domestic sector have been playing catch-up ever since, trying to gain in cost-reduction what the Japanese have taken away with economies of scale and process efficiencies. And, in the meantime, American firms have lost their head start, evident in their early leadership in the 1960s, in color television production and in new product development for the 1980s.

CONCLUSIONS

The mode of Japan's promotion of its electronics industry is a type of intervention in the domestic environment of its firms which, while not in contravention of the principles of "free" international trade, has helped facilitate the development of advantageous terms of trade for the firms producing in its domestic sector. In this, Japan has not been alone: development assistance, export promotion, joint funding of research and development, and tax incentives are common features of sectoral policy among many nations trading in the international market. Such policies, as the history of the U.S. color television sector indicates, really do influence outcomes in the marketplace. However, as U.S. trade policy is currently organized, they are policies that the United States is hard pressed to respond to in a rational and coherent manner.

The structure of U.S. trade policy in the postwar era has left U.S. policy-makers in the position of having to strike a delicate balance between their commitment to "free trade" and the pressures put on them to provide legislated remedies for trade-impacted sectors—remedies which necessarily involve some form of protectionist subsidy. The Orderly Marketing Agreements on color television units exemplify the limits on such policy and the difficulties that result from the effort to strike such a precarious balance. For although U.S. firms have regained a measure of profitability in the color product market since the implementation of the OMAs, Japanese firms have moved rapidly ahead in the development of the next generation of consumer electronic products associated with the television receiver—the video disc and the video-tape recorder. The OMAs have encouraged an offshore production strategy by U.S. firms trying to adjust to the competitive conditions in the color market, but they have in no way helped reconstruct the domestic sector so as to assure it a competitive position in the new video products market. In terms of this latter end, two policy issues not addressed by the OMAs must be considered. (1) Is there a production strategy compatible with high wage labor which can restore the international competitiveness of production in the domestic sector? (2) Do the remaining U.S. firms in the television receiver market have the necessary capital and technological resources to enter and compete in the new home electronic markets of the future?

Answers to these questions were not to be found in the courts, where the outcome of the dumping case against Japanese television manufacturers and U.S. importers was delayed so long that the final penalties assessed had no demonstrable deterrent value. Nor were answers to be found in Orderly Marketing Agreements, which only put a government imprimatur on a short-sighted adjustment strategy long underway. Instead, rational answers require that U.S. policy-makers recognize two facts: (1) that U.S. "fair trade" laws give little protection against an official sectoral policy in another nation designed to promote the international competitiveness of its domestic sector; and (2) that the provision of import relief by simple recourse to tariffs and quotas assures nothing but an orderly and profitable sectoral decline. As the Japanese experience with its electronics sector suggests, there are other types of government intervention that may enhance the international competitiveness of firms producing in a targeted domestic sector. It is toward these types of intervention, combining promotion with temporary protection, that adjustment assistance programs should be directed, so as to create a greater probability of sustained American participation both in existing markets and in the new product markets of the future.

CHAPTER FOUR

Trade and Development in the Semiconductor Industry: Japanese Challenge and American Response

MICHAEL BORRUS, JAMES E. MILLSTEIN,
JOHN ZYSMAN *with the assistance of*
Aton Arbisser and Daniel O'Neill

For over twenty-five years after its inception in the late 1940s, the U.S. semiconductor industry enjoyed a position of unchallenged technological pre-eminence and international market dominance. U.S.-based firms retained international leadership through several stages of technological innovation, market growth, and the consequent restructuring of their industry. In the mid-1970s, however, that leadership was challenged for the first time by large multidivisional Japanese electronics firms. The share of the world market for integrated circuits held by U.S. firms declined between 1974 and 1978 while the Japanese share grew, largely at the expense of American producers. Then, in the late 1970s, these Japanese producers captured a significant percentage of the domestic U.S. market for large-scale integrated circuit memories, or LSI-MOS. (For definitions of technical terms and abbreviations, see the Glossary, pp. 245–248.)

These events signify much more than a loss of profits for U.S. firms in particular product categories in a single industry. They indicate the potential for an irreversible loss of world leadership by U.S. firms in the innovation and diffusion of semiconductor technology. Because the products of this industry are

A somewhat different version of this chapter appeared as *International Competition in Advanced Industrial Sectors: Trade and Development in the Semi-conductor Industry*, a study prepared for the Joint Economic Committee, U.S. Congress, February 18, 1982. This study was reprinted in Policy Papers in International Affairs, no. 17, of the Institute of International Studies at the University of California at Berkeley under the title *U.S.–Japanese Competition in the Semiconductor Industry: A Study in International Trade and Technological Development*, 1982.

the crucial intermediate inputs to all final electronics systems, competition in the semiconductor industry will be at the center of competition in all industries which incorporate electronics into their products and production processes. Indeed, trade in integrated circuits and electronics in general is typical of competition in industrial goods between the advanced countries. Market success in the products which these countries exchange between themselves depends on the management of complex processes of product development and manufacturing rather than simply on national differences in factor costs such as wages or raw materials. The corporate capabilities that afford a national advantage in high technology can be promoted by government policies for industry and trade. National competition in this industry is typical of the trade conflicts we may anticipate in all of the growing high-technology industries on which advanced countries depend. Indeed, the case of this one industry suggests that government policies can shape a nation's comparative advantage in trade. General issues aside, however, this study argues that the outcomes of industrial competition in electronics will have a unique national importance.

FOR TWO GENERATIONS, analysts have foreseen a new industrial revolution based on the processing of information. Although the computer has been the symbol of this transformation, the semiconductor has in great measure been responsible for it. Innovation in and diffusion of semiconductor technology has helped to create markets in data processing, automated production, and robotics; and it has fundamentally altered communications, instrumentation, transportation, consumer goods, and military systems. The videogame may be no more than a new diversion, but the automated factory portends fundamental changes in the organization of work. The semiconductor industry is therefore strategically vital to the future growth of knowledge-intensive industrial development within the U.S. economy. For the foreseeable future, the relative economic strength of all advanced industrial economies will rest in part on their capacity to develop and apply semiconductor technology to product design and production processes. Thus the loss of leadership in this one industry would mean the loss of international competitiveness in many of the advanced technology sectors that have been the basis of a U.S. advantage since World War II. This chapter therefore analyzes the evolution of competition in an industrial sector that will undoubtedly remain an important focus of international negotiation for many years.

The most salient measure of the U.S. semiconductor industry's competitive performance has been a constant and steady decline in the price of an electronic function—for example, from $15.00 in 1965 to 2 cents in 1980. (The consumer's interest is best defined as the cost of an electronic function and the extension of the tasks that electronic systems can perform.) This remarkable performance has been based on the creation of new products rather than on the more efficient production of existing products. It is the steady advance in technology that has made possible the dropping cost of components and the expanding pool of applications. For example, there are limits to the reduction in costs and applications of discrete semiconductor components, whatever efficiencies in production might be achieved. Advances in production technology and the resulting cost competition between producers of the standard product of the moment have stimulated product technology, as some companies have tried to avoid price competition by offering product innovations.

The foundation for this dynamic advance has been the distinctive structure of the U.S. semiconductor industry. For our purposes here, there are three critical components of that structure: (1) the set of independent, "merchant" semiconductor producers; (2) the set of electronic systems producers who incorporate the merchants' products as intermediate inputs; and (3) the two largest systems producers, ATT and IBM, who have played a crucial role through their broad-based, widely shared research and development.

The merchant firms have given the industry its dynamism, for their central advantage over larger-scale systems producers has been that they have continuously advanced existing component technologies and introduced them into new uses. In providing an ongoing stream of competitive component innovations, these firms have forced final systems producers to be similarly competitive in the speed and inventiveness with which they incorporate component innovations into their final products. It is in this central role as innovators and diffusers of semiconductor technology that the merchant producers have contributed to the advance of the knowledge-based sectors of the U.S. economy. Their capacity to sustain their entrepreneurial role through successive stages of the industry's development has rested in the most widely accepted view on achieving a *commodity* position for the products they innovate. These products must achieve a widespread use that permits volume production; the innovating firm must capture a substantial part of the mass market if it is to have sufficient returns to help finance the next round of innovation and diffusion. Some firms, by contrast, have found a niche in specialized market segments, which together represent nearly 40 percent of open market sales, and have succeeded without participating in the commodity market. It is our view that a strong national presence in the commodity semiconductor markets is still required to maintain the pace of advance in the underlying technologies on which all firms depend. The issue is significant because the

Japanese challenge, as we shall discover in the third main section, is primarily in standard commodity products, albeit products of enormous sophistication. American firms have been most successful in responding to rapidly shifting market needs, whereas the Japanese have had their greatest success in the more standard products in established markets. The challenge is all the more serious since the industry has become increasingly capital-intensive, which favors Japanese capacities and strains some American firms.

ATT and IBM have played a special role in the semiconductor industry's dynamism. That role is a by-product of their effort to preserve their existing final product advantages through extensive research and development. Since neither firm competes in the merchant component market—a result of court decree or corporate choice informed by antitrust considerations—both have incentives to trade their technologies for technological developments made by other firms. Such exchanges serve to protect ATT and IBM against radical breakthroughs elsewhere in the industry, and serve simultaneously to spread their own technological advances to the merchant sector.

The structural linkages between ATT, IBM, the merchant firms, and the set of systems houses are unique to the U.S. industry. It is doubtful whether the dynamic character of the industry's competitive performance—the constant development of new applications and markets—could have been sustained without each component. In addition, the U.S. government has played an important, and initially determinative, role in the industry's development. However, that role is best characterized as one of indirect influence through tax and military policies; and whether it is sufficient to help sustain the industry's dynamic character in the future depends upon our evaluation of the competitive threat the U.S. industry faces from abroad.

Japanese entry into the U.S. market is part of a conscious national strategy of establishing comparative advantage in the knowledge-intensive and technology-intensive industries. The 300-page *Vision of MITI Policies in the 1980s* is explicit about this goal: "It is extremely important for Japan to make the most of her brain resources, which may well be called the nation's only resource, and thereby to develop creative technologies of its own. . . . Possession of her own technology will help Japan *to maintain and develop her industries' international superiority* and to form a foundation for the long-term development of the economy and society. . . . This spirit of basing national development on technology should be our aim in the 1980s"(emphasis added).[1]

---

[1] Industrial Structure Council, *The Vision of MITI Policies in the 1980s* (translated by the Industrial Bank of Japan, Limited), March 1980. Hereafter cited as *MITI Policies.*

This developmental goal is really an evolution of Japan's general policy of promoting economic development, which could be seen in shipbuilding, steel, and automobiles a generation earlier. Developmental strategies organized around closure of Japanese domestic markets and promotion of Japanese production became more than tactics for nourishing infant industries. In an economy dependent on the export of manufactures to pay for raw materials, MITI chose industries for domestic development that could serve to expand overseas sales. The Japanese system became one of controlled competition, a system of a managed but unstable competitive equilibrium. Intense competition between firms in targeted sectors was directed and limited both by state actions and by collaborative efforts of the firms and the banks. State bureaucrats did not dictate to an administered market; rather, they consciously manipulated market forces to shape the development of particular sectors.

The Japanese created a system in which, when it works at its best, the state helps in a detailed way to establish conditions of investment, risk, and collaboration that promote the long-term development and international competitiveness of favored industries. As we shall demonstrate, the structure of the Japanese domestic market gives domestic electronics producers a substantial advantage in international competition. To the extent that arrangements in the Japanese market which favor domestic producers are the result of conscious policies of the government or the corporations, these arrangements represent political tactics of industrial development and should be made the subject of international trade negotiation.

During the 1970s, the Japanese electronics and semiconductor industry moved from a consumer product orientation and a technological position of relative inferiority in components toward a state-of-the-art capability in components, telecommunications, and computers. State policies helped to protect, promote, and rationalize the industry. High-volume production of commodity components manufactured with U.S.-made production equipment to U.S. design standards characterized the successive stages of this transformation. (Indeed, for their production of advanced devices the Japanese still rely heavily on U.S. equipment in some manufacturing stages and still tend to follow U.S. design standards.) Stable sources of plentiful capital for expansion and high-volume production in a closed domestic market—a market rationalized among firms in both their component and their final systems production—served finally to allow Japanese export penetration of the U.S. market. Such structural characteristics also served to cushion the Japanese industry from technological or market errors: Japanese firms could compensate for the consequences of a market misjudgment or of a new U.S. technological innovation by returning to a Japanese domestic market insulated from foreign competition. Formal and informal control over the degree and character of foreign access to the domestic Japanese market prevented U.S. firms from consolidating their innovations and victories in the international marketplace and translating them into entrenched positions in the Japanese market.

Certainly the structure of the distribution system and other features of the Japanese economy represent "natural" obstacles to foreign penetration, but there can be little doubt that government and corporate policy reinforced this closure. Although direct discrimination is now being reduced and direct government administration of the economy is receding, the arrangements that give structural advantages to the Japanese have endured. It should be understood that these arrangements were not produced by a backward economy, an infant industry, or small-scale firms in need of protection. Rather, by the end of the 1970s, all of the top six electronics firms in the highly oligopolistic Japanese semiconductor industry were multi-billion dollar companies. Thus the story of Japanese electronics development is as much a political story as a study in marketplace competition.

In sum, the Japanese companies have emerged as strong international competitors in semiconductors by enjoying the benefits provided by a state that organized its relations with the business community and tried to structure the market to promote accelerated economic development. State policies and private market arrangements established a relatively stable and predictable domestic market environment. In this environment, large integrated firms have prospered in international markets chiefly with *production strategies that focus competition on cost and quality of commodity products rather than with entrepreneurial strategies that focus competition on the diffusion and advance of new technologies and the rapid adjustment to shifting markets.*

The implications of this analysis are that the Japanese have emerged as strong international competitors in semiconductors, with unique production strengths and market strategies based on Japan's domestic market structure. The medium-term Japanese competitive threat is to the merchant sector of the U.S. industry. By bringing their high-volume production strengths to bear in competition for large shares of merchant semiconductor markets in commodity products in an increasingly capital-intensive industry, Japanese firms could come to dominate U.S. component commodity markets; they could deny U.S. merchant firms the margins that have historically underwritten their capacities to create new products and make new markets. Thus, over the long term, significant Japanese domination of merchant commodity markets—if it occurs—might well rob the U.S. electronics industry of the unique

147

capacity for innovation and diffusion that has been the hallmark of its merchant firms. If the U.S. semiconductor sector, where relative advantage lies in dynamic interaction between merchant firm and user, loses its markets to the Japanese firms whose relative advantage lies in production efficiencies in commodity products, the pace and character of innovation throughout the U.S. electronics industries could be slowed. The most serious damage of a loss of competitive advantage in integrated circuits would be that the integrated Japanese electronics companies—which produce both components and final systems products—would come to dominate systems markets over the very long run.

The character of the Japanese threat in this industry, however, should not be overstated. Nor, indeed, should U.S. policy be based directly on countering the potential threats outlined above. Markets for semiconductor technology are expanding at such a rapid pace that there may well be room for all competitors. Moreover, as a relatively young, dynamic sector serving growing markets, the U.S. semiconductor industry is vastly different in kind from the mature, relatively uncompetitive domestic U.S. industries that succumbed to competitive pressures from Japanese firms during the 1970s. Whereas other U.S. industrial sectors like steel have sought protection, this industry with its unique structure retains a dynamic ability to outstrip static Japanese advantages in offering a stable product line. Integrated-circuit technologies are young, rapidly changing, and still overwhelmingly the product of U.S.-based research and development. The issue which U.S. policy must confront, then, is how to reconcile Japanese and European ambitions to create internationally competitive electronics sectors with U.S. interests in maintaining technological and marketplace leadership.

The United States has a clear strategic interest in retaining leadership in the semiconductor industry and in maintaining an industrial structure that has facilitated the diffusion and innovation of this most vital technology. There is simply no reason to allow the evolution of this sector to be dictated by the policies of foreign governments. This chapter suggests policies aimed on the one hand at easing domestic constraints on the U.S. industry's ability to grow and compete, and on the other hand at opening international markets in Japan and the EEC to rigorous competition from U.S. firms. Such policies would serve to make domestic and international markets work more efficiently. If, to remain viable in the face of policy strategies abroad, U.S.-based firms require U.S. policies that ease constraints and open foreign markets, then failure to adopt such policies could generate serious long-run costs to the U.S. economy. If U.S.-based firms do not in fact need assistance, then the policies suggested here would serve only to facilitate market developments already underway and to speed the arrival of an electronics era. In this context, it is our view that American defense procurement can no longer play the catalyst role of guaranteed first user. Competitive civilian development of advanced technology will not automatically emerge from defense expenditures.

More generally, events in the semiconductor industry provide the United States with a timely opportunity to reconsider U.S. policy responses to the generic problem of foreign governmental promotion of specific industrial sectors. Foreign growth policies aimed at accelerating the shift out of agriculture into capital-intensive industries (such as autos) were acceptable in an era of U.S. economic hegemony, but they pose new problems when they serve as strategies to forge leadership in the advanced technology sectors upon which the U.S. future rests. The United States must not copy foreign growth strategies developed by other cultures for their particular national circumstances. Rather, working within the constraints of the U.S. political economy, the goal of policy should be to assist U.S. firms to compete successfully in international markets while equitably dispersing at home both the benefits of successful competition and the costs of adjustment. In an industry like semiconductors where the United States leads, such government action will be much less costly than the significantly more intrusive intervention that would be required later were the United States to lose its leadership.

Our discussion of domestic development and international trade competition tells three interrelated stories. First, it details the evolution, operation, and distinctive character of the U.S. and Japanese semiconductor industries (the first and second main sections). National differences in the relations between government and industry, we shall discover, have major consequences when corporations compete in international markets.

Second, it describes how the Japanese utilized a controlled domestic market and financial leverage to enter the U.S. market in the late 1970s; it evaluates the character of U.S. and Japanese competitive interaction in the U.S. market; and it draws out the implications of this interaction for the U.S. industry's ability to retain its technological and market leadership (the third main section). The trade battle in this essential industry is as much a political struggle between government policies of protection and promotion as it is a marketplace struggle between firms. Indeed, this case is prototypical of the industrial sectors in which the advanced countries will compete in the future and also of the type of trade politics that will be generated.

Third, the final main section considers how U.S. policy might reconcile U.S. interests in maintaining leadership in this industry with Japanese and European ambitions of sustaining their own industrial expansion in an epoch of electronics. Such a policy will have a trade component and a domestic policy component. The trade policy needs of this industry, it should be noted, are diametrically opposed to the types of policies demanded by the more traditional industries such as textiles, steel, and even automobiles. The political question for domestic policy is how the needs of American high-technology sectors for open international markets can be reconciled with the demands of mature industries for various forms of protection. There should be little doubt that American policies of selective protection in sectors where we are weak internationally make it harder to insist on policies of open trade in sectors where we are strong. In the early years of the semiconductor industry, domestic policy had two parts: Defense Department procurement and product development; and antitrust policies, formulated without direct reference to the development of the industry, which established the unique role that ATT and IBM were to play. As the industry developed commercial markets that outstripped defense procurements both in dollar volume and technological importance, the industry focused its attention on the market, not on Washington. Now, under pressure from Japanese competitors building on a more concerted national effort, domestic policies to support U.S. electronic development are again needed.

THE DEVELOPMENT OF THE AMERICAN SEMICONDUCTOR IINDUSTRY

Since the birth of the integrated circuit at Texas Instruments and Fairchild in 1958, the United States has dominated the development and marketing of integrated circuit devices. Technological innovation in integrated circuit design and production processes has kept U.S. firms at the leading edge of growth in the world market. In 1980, U.S. firms still accounted for 70 percent of the world's production of integrated circuits.

The international competitive advantage that U.S. firms have enjoyed in the design and production of integrated circuits has stemmed, in large measure, from the early developmental trajectory along which the industry was pulled. From 1958 to 1964, support for product development and high-volume demand from both the United States Department of Defense and the National Aeronautics and Space Administration created a "market pull" effect on the initial phase of integrated circuit development which spawned entry and sped the commercial diffusion of the new technology. Defense and space program procurement in the early 1960s offered an assured demand for the integrated circuit at premium prices, which helped to underwrite the risk and cost of product development in the private sector and served to broaden the industrial base over which technological innovation in integrated circuit design and production continued to advance.

It should be noted, however, that although early defense and space administration demand for the integrated circuit was the most direct stimulus to industrial growth, other environmental factors that were unique to the United States domestic market shaped the structural impact of this early government support. Ready availability of venture capital, a high mobility of technical personnel between firms, liberal licensing of transistor and integrated circuit technology by the U.S. firms which had pioneered their developments, as well as antitrust constraints on potential ATT and IBM entry into the open market for microelectronics, all contributed to the creation of a domestic environment in which new entry and competition were fostered by the initial demands of the defense and space programs.

After this first stage in the industry's development, the factors sustaining the early pace of integrated circuit innovation and diffusion in the United States rested with the unique industrial structure and commercial market dynamism which demand from the military and space markets had fostered. In both Europe and Japan, integrated circuit production is dominated by large, vertically integrated electronic systems manufacturers; in the United States the bulk of integrated circuit production has been carried out under the auspices of an independent set of merchant firms, whose primary business is the manufacture and open-market sale of microelectronic components. These merchant producers have been a crucial stimulus to a technological and competitive dynamic unique to the United States integrated circuit industry.

The integrated circuit industry's historical development has been strongly influenced by the markets it has served. As we have noted, early government development support and market demand for integrated circuits helped to pull the U.S. microelectronics sector into the production and design of integrated circuits well in advance of microelectronics producers in Europe and Japan. Thereafter, demand from a more highly developed computer and industrial electronics equipment market in the United States helped to sustain the pace of innovation and market growth for integrated circuits; despite military procurement during the Vietnam war, the role of "creative first user" of the latest in integrated circuit designs fell to the commercial market. Demand from the computer and industrial markets in turn spawned a new wave of merchant entrants into the production of integrated circuits (ICs). Between 1966 and 1972, over thirty new IC firms entered the domestic market.[2]

To focus simply on the demand-pull effects of the military and computer markets on innovation and sales growth in the U.S. integrated circuit industry is to lose sight of the dynamics of competition between IC manufacturers, and particularly between the merchant firms that set the pace of technological advance. Product and process innovation and competition between the merchant firms have progressively lowered the cost and enhanced the performance of an electronic function. As competition on cost and performance drove the price of an electronic function downward, the demand for integrated circuits became greater and greater; by achieving commodity positions as market demand for the latest in IC-device technology expanded, the merchants earned a sufficient return on their risk-taking to help finance the next round of product innovation and market development. Thus competitive rivalry between the merchant firms themselves as well as between the merchants and the more established vertically integrated electronic systems companies such as RCA, Westinghouse, and General Electric, accelerated the pace of both *innovation* in and *diffusion* of integrated circuit technology. As an independent, low-cost source of advanced IC technology, this unique merchant segment had the dynamic effect of introducing new competitive risks into the environments of established component and system producers. By lowering technological barriers to entry in systems markets and creating the potential of new cost and product performance competition in those markets, the merchants altered the technological and competitive environment of dominant electronic systems/manufacturers such as IBM and Western Electric, creating greater uncertainty and greater competitive rivalry in the market for electronic systems. The presence of the merchants had the dynamic effect of enhancing the pace of IC innovation and diffusion across the domestic economy as a whole.

The merchant segment of the industry which fully blossomed in the period 1966–1972 has been a shining example of two venerated features of competitive capitalism: the success of entrepreneurship backed by venture capital, and the triumph of the technological innovativeness of the small firm. However, to this day, perhaps the single most important contribution of the merchant producers has been their dynamic role in fostering increased competition in and proliferation of electronic systems markets. Indeed, as the United States confronts a chang-

[2]Semiconductor Industry Association, *The International Microelectronic Challenge* (Cupertino, Calif.: 1981), p. 35.

ing environment in the world market for microelectronics, it is this competitive dynamism, which is unique to its domestic industrial structure, that policy should seek to promote. For it is competition across this structure that has produced technological progress and market diffusion in the United States and sustained the international competitiveness of the American electronics industry as a whole.

A third stage of the industry's development may be loosely associated with the development of large-scale integrated circuits in the early 1970s. Large-scale integration involved a change in the character of the product that integrated circuit firms produced; increasingly, as device geometries were reduced and packing densities increased, "components" began to incorporate basic features of what were previously regarded as entire electronic "systems." The most salient example of this was the introduction by Intel of the microprocessor in 1971. With the development of these more complex, system-like devices, the third stage in the evolution of the industry's structure began. On the one hand, merchant producers began to integrate vertically into one or more of a variety of final electronic systems markets in order to capture the high value-added of their more complex devices. On the other hand, both to assure supply for their final product demand and to give their final system products a competitive edge through custom circuit design, an increasing number of electronic systems/producers began to integrate backward, either by establishing "captive" integrated circuit design and fabrication capacities or by acquiring existing integrated circuit houses in the United States. In turn, beneath these different segments of "component" and "systems" producers there grew up a developed infrastructure of materials suppliers and manufacturers of fabrication and test equipment.

The current structure of the U.S. industry can be understood, then, as a composite of these three relatively distinct stages of its development. The structure has four tiers: (1) small IC merchant producers, such as Siliconix and Monolithic Memories; (2) large IC merchants such as Texas Instruments, Motorola, Intel, and National Semiconductor; (3) electronic systems manufacturers such as Hewlett Packard and Hughes; and (4) the two dominant vertically integrated systems manufacturers, IBM and ATT. The uniqueness of this industrial structure lies precisely in its broad technological base and in the diversity of both firm capacities and market strategies which this structured segmentation implies; its strength rests upon the competitive dynamism this structure has spawned. Thus foreign industrial policies or coordinated foreign firm strategies which threaten the dynamic operation of competition in the American market must be regarded as more than a threat to a particular set of U.S. firms in particular product markets;

they must be seen as a threat to the dynamism of the American electronics industry as a whole. Leaving an evaluation of these matters for our second and third main sections, we shall describe here the historical development of the American industry and the structural underpinnings of its unique technological and competitive dynamism. This outline of the industry's development and structure will serve as a basis for describing how the current trade and development policy conflict between the United States and Japan has been generated by the structural differences between each nation's domestic sector.

Military Markets and Merchant Producers, 1958–1965

The specific technological direction of the U.S. industry was in large measure influenced by its early relationship with the U.S. military. The demand of the defense and aerospace markets pulled the industry along a specific technological trajectory and helped prod the domestic sector into a position of market dominance and technological leadership. During the 1950s, while Europe and Japan pursued the development and mass production of *germanium* transistor-based consumer electronic systems, the United States industry, prodded by U.S. military demands for miniaturization and devices of higher performance and reliability, became pre-eminent in *silicon* -based technology.[3] As a recent Department of Commerce study of the industry notes: "Initial U.S. Government endorsement of basic semiconductor research and product procurement for defense and space needs made possible the advanced silicon technology that laid the foundation of today's modern semiconductor industry.[4]

Perhaps the most important consequence of early defense sponsorship of silicon-based devices was its impact on the structure of the electronics component industry. Before the invention of transistors, the dominant electronic component technology was the electron tube, and component production tended to be dominated by major multidivisional electronic systems producers. The shift to the transistor and ultimately to the integrated circuit reshuffled the composition of the

---

[3]For a more detailed discussion of the impact of the Department of Defense on the development of the civilian electronics industry in the United States, see Norman Asher and Leland Strom, *The Role of the Department of Defense in the Development of Integrated Circuits* (Institute for Defense Analyses, Arlington, Virginia, 1977); and James Utterback and Albert Murray, *The Influence of Defense Procurement and Sponsorship of Research and Development on the Development of Civilian Electronics Industry* (Center for Policy Alternatives, M.I.T., 1977).

[4]U.S. Department of Commerce, *A Report on the U.S. Semiconductor Industry* (Washington, D.C.: Government Printing Office, 1979), p. 1. Hereafter cited as Commerce Dept., *Report.*

leading component manufacturers. Few of the leading producers of the electron tube managed to retain their component market positions in the new technologies.[5] In this reshuffling process, defense and aerospace procurement created a market incentive for entrepreneurial, technological risk-taking and thereby helped create an independent sector of semiconductor component manufacturers. As Utterback and Murray conclude: "Defense procurement and support for research and development stimulated the entry of new firms in the electronics industry in several ways, primarily through direct purchases. By providing an initial market at premium prices for major advances, defense purchasers speeded their introduction into use."[6]

The early development of the integrated circuit is most noteworthy in this regard. The first integrated circuit was demonstrated by Texas Instruments in 1958. Although it was developed without direct research and development funding from the U.S. government, in mid-1959 the Air Force awarded the company a $1.15 million, two and a half year contract to develop various integrated circuit devices. In December 1960 the Air Force followed its original award with a $2.1 million contract for the development of production processes and special equipment needed for the fabrication of integrated circuits in bulk quantities.[7] Asher and Strom report: "As late as 1961, the industrial and scientific communities still voiced doubts as to the worth of integrated circuits from an equipment and systems viewpoint. To alleviate these doubts . . . the Air Force proposed the building of a representative piece of electronic equipment using integrated circuits. Under Air Force sponsorship, the building of a digital computer was introduced into the Texas Instruments production program. Two identical computers were built: one with 9,000 individual components and one containing only 587 integrated circuits."[8]

Meanwhile at Fairchild, without any government research and development funding, the development of the planar process moved the integrated circuit out of the laboratory and into production. For both Fairchild and Texas Instruments, the initial market in 1963 for integrated circuits consisted of two major government procurement programs: for Texas Instruments it was the Minuteman II missile guidance system, and for Fairchild it was the Apollo spacecraft guidance computer. Between 1963 and 1965 the industry was awarded at least twelve other military and space electronic systems contracts calling for

[5]Ian Mackintosh, *Microelectronics in the 1980s* (London: Mackintosh Publication Ltd., 1979), p. 66, Table II.
[6]Utterback and Murray, *The Influence of Defense Procurement*, p. 3.
[7]Asher and Strom, *The Role of the Department of Defense*, pp. 4, 17.
[8]*Ibid.*, p. 17.

the incorporation of monolithic integrated circuits. In 1963, government procurement constituted 95 percent of the market for monolithic ICs, which had an average selling price of $50. In 1965, government procurement constituted only 75 percent of demand but the price per IC had dropped below $9. Over the three-year period, total IC production grew rapidly, from $4 million in 1963 to $80 million in 1965.[9] During this period new companies such as Signetics, Siliconix, General Microelectronics, and Molectro were founded primarily to manufacture integrated circuits. In turn, older electronics systems producers such as RCA, Sylvania, Motorola, Westinghouse, and Raytheon began to move, albeit more slowly, into volume production.

In the early development of integrated circuit production in the United States, the Department of Defense and the National Aeronautics and Space Administration played the role of "creative first users." Pursuing their respective strategic objectives, their support had two effects: the first was the intended effect of encouraging and accelerating the pace of technological advance; the second was the unintended effect of fostering the development of a unique segment of merchant producers. This latter result could not have been predicted, but in terms of the long-run impact of early government support, it was perhaps the more significant of the two, for the merchant producers kept the pace of technological innovation and diffusion alive and thriving in commercial markets long after the strategic objectives of the military had been realized.

Dynamic Competition: The Computer Market and Merchant Competition, 1966–1972

After its auspicious beginnings under government sponsorship in the early 1960s, U.S. production of integrated circuits more than doubled between 1966 and 1972.[10] The rapid rate of growth in integrated circuit production during this period reflected, in large measure, a fast acceleration in demand from computer and industrial equipment manufacturers during the late 1960s. Whereas in 1965 military sales still constituted more than 55 percent of the total value of domestic IC sales, by 1972 some 65 percent of all IC sales in the United States went to the computer and industrial markets, and military sales fell to less than 25 percent of the market.[11] The age of data processing had ar-

---

[9]*Ibid.*, p. 45.

[10]U.S. Federal Trade Commission, *Staff Report on the Semiconductor Industry* (Washington, D.C.: Government Printing Office, 1977), p. 11, Table II-3. Hereafter cited as FTC, *Staff Report.*

[11]Commerce Dept., *Report*, p. 46, Table 3.5.

rived and the integrated circuit industry, formerly under military tutelage, broke away to supply the more prodigious demands of the computer and industrial markets.

The relationship between the integrated circuit and computer industries has been characterized by Ian Mackintosh as a classic example of "industrial synergism." He writes: "Just as the American computer industry growth has been critically dependent on the availability of ever-increasing numbers of improved ICs, so has the spectacular growth of the American IC industry depended to a very high degree on having a large, innovative, and 'local' computer market avid to make use of its rapidly developing semiconductor capabilities."[12] Together, the demand from the computer and telecommunications markets helped the United States rapidly achieve a dominant international position in the design and production of the integrated circuit.

The infant computer industry in the 1950s had been an early market for discrete semiconductor devices. Because of the relative unreliability of tubes, transistors were rapidly assimilated into computer hardware design. In 1960 a large computer could easily contain over 100,000 diodes and 25,000 transistors.[13] Nonetheless, the shift to discrete semiconductor devices in the design of complex large circuits, though it offered the advantage of greater reliability and speed, still entailed high assembly and connection costs.

In 1964 IBM introduced the first computer line not based on discrete semiconductor technology. The IBM System 360 used a hybrid design in which several transistors and other devices formed an operating circuit. This hybrid design helped reduce the cost of producing a computer, reduced its power consumption, and increased its speed and capacity. With the introduction of user software that could be used on all models in the 360 line, the commercial computer market began to expand rapidly.

IBM's competitors reacted to the System 360 with computer hardware based on the integrated circuit. The integrated circuit allowed for the design and production of an entire logic circuit on a monolithic chip of silicon. By packing fifty or more transistors on a single chip of silicon, transistor interconnection distances were dramatically reduced, with the result that speed, power consumption, and reliability were all vastly improved. In turn, the integrated circuit eliminated many of the costs of producing discrete and hybrid devices. As IC prices declined rapidly during the late 1960s and the functional complexity of the IC increased (both were results of merchant competition), companies such

---

[12]Mackintosh, *Microelectronics in the 1980s*, p. 65.
[13]An excellent study of the evolution of the industry is John T. Sima, *The Computer Industry* (Lexington, Ky.: Lexington Books, 1975).

as RCA and Burroughs turned to IC designs to lower their computer prices in the uphill battle for market share against IBM. On the basis of this new price competition, the domestic computer market entered a period of rapid sales growth.

In turn, advances in IC technology and their availability in volume from the merchant sector helped form a new segment in the computer market: in 1965, Digital Equipment Corporation introduced the world's first minicomputer, the PDP-8. The availability of relatively low-cost integrated circuit logic chips from companies such as Texas Instruments and Fairchild helped to lower the capital and technological barriers to entry in the computer manufacturing industry. As a consequence, by the early 1970s minicomputers had become a high-growth and fiercely competitive market. The merchant integrated circuit industry also became highly competitive, as the firms tried through cost-reduction and product innovation to pre-empt their competitors in the race for minicomputer designs that used their respective "families" of IC devices. During the 1960s, as Mackintosh writes, "the computer industry's spectacular growth had been due mainly to its ability to produce equipment which would compute at ever-increasing speeds and reliability levels, and ever-decreasing costs and size, and essentially *all* of these attributes stemmed from advances in silicon technology."[14]

The evolution of integrated circuit design and fabrication started with the implementation of the basic logic gate and proceeded to the miniaturization of a complete computer subsystem, the microprocessor. The evolution is shown in Table 1. This trajectory reveals a first principle of component-system interaction: as a component, the technological evolution of the integrated circuit has made it increasingly capable of implementing on a single chip basic features of what had previously been regarded as entire electronic *systems*. In the 1960s, digital integrated circuit designs incorporated fewer than 50 transistors per silicon chip, and therefore had to be connected to one another to perform computing functions. As a consequence, "to sell digital ICs, semiconductor houses in the 1960s and early 1970s had to provide computer equipment makers with a complete 'kit' of electrically compatible parts that could be interconnected into a computer configuration. As a consequence, digital IC products came to be grouped into 'families' such as Resistor-Transistor Logic (RTL), Diode Transistor Logic (DTL), and the durable Transistor-Transistor Logic (TTL)."[15] (For definitions of technical terms and abbreviations, see the Glossary, at the end of this

[14]Mackintosh, *Microelectronics in the 1980s.* p.65.

[15]Charles River Associates, *Innovation, Competition, and Government Policy in the Semiconductor Industry* (Boston, 1980), p. 2–3; this book offers a more detailed analysis of the product "races" discussed below. Hereafter cited as Charles River study.

Table 1. Value of total U.S. sales of integrated circuit devices, 1962–1978

Markets	1962	1965	1969	1974	1978
Government	100%	55%	36%	20%	10.0%
Computer	0	35	44	36	37.5
Industrial	0	9	16	30	37.5
Consumer	0	1	4	15	15.0
Total U.S. domestic shipments (millions of dollars)	$4	$79	$413	$1,204	$2,080

SOURCES: Figures for 1962 are derived from John Tilton, *International Diffusion of Technology: The Case of Semiconductors* (Washington, D.C.: Brookings Institution, 1971). Figures for 1965, and 1969, and 974 from U.S. Department of Commerce, *A Report on the U.S. Semiconductor Industry* (Washington, D.C.: Government Printing Office, 1979), p. 102. Figures for 1978 are rough estimates based on figures in U.S. International Trade Commission, *Competitive Factors Influencing World Trade in Integrated Circuits*, Publication no. 1013 (Washington, D.C.: 1979), p. 102; *Business Week*, December 3, 1979, p. 68; and "1980 Semiconductor Forum," *Rosen Electronics Letter*, July 14, 1980; p. 150.

chapter.) The early computer market was dominated by competition between these different bipolar design families (see Table 2).

The first proprietary ICs were introduced by Fairchild and Texas Instruments; Fairchild offered circuits based on Resistor Capacitor Transistor Logic (RCTL) and Texas Instruments offered circuits based on Direct Coupled Transistor Logic (DCTL). These early product "families," though used in the Apollo guidance computer and the Minuteman II missile system, had design weaknesses and were quickly supplanted by DTL and RTL. Fairchild's 930 series DTL emerged as the industry leader in the period from 1965 to 1967. Its share of the then emerging commercial IC market, with demand from computer manufacturers the driving force, grew quickly from 18 percent in 1964 to 24 percent in 1967.[16] Texas Instruments, which had been the industry's leading producer of integrated circuits with more than 32 percent of the market in 1964, watched its market share drop almost in half by 1967 during a period in which total industry sales of integrated circuits almost doubled.[17] Innovative circuit design and aggressive price-cutting enabled Fairchild to grow rapidly and lead an increasing number of IC merchant producers in the early penetration of the computer and industrial markets.

Texas Instruments soon regained its market momentum with the introduction of a family of proprietary TTL circuits, whose fast-switch-

[16]FTC, *Staff Report*, p. 26, Table II-9.
[17]*Ibid.*, p. 11, Table II-3.

Table 2. Key digital integrated circuit product families, 1961–1975

Project family	Approximate introduction date	Originating firm
RTL (Resistor-Transistor Logic)	1961	Fairchild
DTL (Diode-Transistor Logic)	1962	Signetics
ECL (Emitter-Coupled Logic)	1963	Motorola
TTL (Transistor-Transistor Logic)	1964	Sylvania/TI
CMOS	1968	RCA
Schottky TTL	1970	TI
1K MOS RAMs	1970	AMS/Intel
Bipolar RAMs	1972	Fairchild
4K MOS RAMs	1973	Intel/Mostek/TI
Microprocessor	1973	Intel
16K MOS RAMs	1976	Intel/Mostek

Source: Charles River Associates, Inc., *Innovation, Competition, and Government Policy in the Semiconductor Industry,* March 1980.

ing speeds proved to be more appealing to the computer market than Fairchild's earlier family of DTL circuits. Again, innovation in integrated circuit design, the introduction by Texas of a set of TTL chips which individually implemented complete computer functions (adders, coders, decoders, and 4-bit serial memories), and aggressive price-cutting by Texas's second source—National Semiconductors, a recent entry in the merchant market—enabled the TTL bipolar logic family to regain a dominant position in computer hardware design by 1969. (A "second source" refers in the industry to a firm that produces a product originally introduced by someone else. Most users of components require a "second source" to assure a secure supply. The second source refers to a specific role in the market.) Building on that base, in 1970 Texas introduced Schottky TTL, which greatly improved the speed and packing density of its earlier TTL family and sustained Texas's leadership in the merchant bipolar logic market through the early 1970s.

The success of Texas Instruments in the bipolar logic market illustrates what we have spoken of earlier as the first principle of component-system interaction: that increasingly, components are technically able to implement basic features of what previously had been regarded as an electronic system. The introduction by Texas Instruments of single-chip adders, coders, decoders, and memories in the late 1960s is a classic example of the component-system relationship. By designing computer hardware subsystems on single component chips, Texas reduced the cost of these subsystems to the computer market and put itself in a dominant position in the rapidly growing computer market for digital ICs. Component manufacturers did not, however, proceed to develop a "chip version" of every electronic system and subsystem in existence, for two reasons. The first reason is that the costs of designing such chip systems are very large. The second is that in order to amortize the design costs and attain low production costs, large production runs are necessary. These large production runs are simply not possible for the many electronic system products that have small markets.

As the industry approached the era of large scale integration (LSI), these economic considerations influenced the strategic planning of IC manufacturers and came to be characterized as the "custom versus standard" debate. As neatly summarized by the Charles River Associates:

> Although not universally held, the general semiconductor industry consensus in the late 1960s was that the future of digital integrated circuits lay in custom LSI. The need for standard parts was expected to be small (*Electronics*, 2/20/67). The principal reason LSI was expected to be dominated by custom rather than standard products was that most semiconductor experts believed that the innovating equipment maker would not want to find that the complex integrated circuits, which determined the performance of its product, were readily available to its competitors. With early bipolar logic the equipment maker could differentiate itself from competitors by cleverly interconnecting standard ICs. In a design where LSI was to be used, most of the logic needed was now packed into a few ICs and therefore [fewer] performance differentiating options were open to the equipment manufacturer, unless the LSI used were circuits custom designed to optimize system performance.[18]

A number of strategies were developed to meet the expected demand for custom circuits. Both Texas and Fairchild planned to build wafers for inventory containing different standard logic-gate designs, which could then be pulled and processed through final masking to connect the logic gates on the wafer into the customer's unique circuit requirements. Texas called its approach Discretionary Wiring and Fairchild called its system Micromatrix.[19]

The custom market, however, never really emerged as conventional wisdom in the mid-1960s had anticipated. The "pull" of newly emerging mass markets in special calculator chips and semiconductor memories and the "push" of a newly developed technology—metal oxide on silicon (MOS)—conjoined to render the custom versus standard debate relatively moot and served to smooth the industry's entry into the era of large scale integration (LSI). Two choices then came to dominate the competitive strategies of IC manufacturers: on the one hand, LSI pro-

[18]Charles River study, pp. 4–16, 4–17.
[19]*Ibid.*, pp. 4–18.

ducts were designed which implemented *widely used components;* on the other, LSI products were designed with sufficient *flexibility* that they could be used to implement a variety of system functions.

The calculator market posed the custom versus standard LSI conflict most starkly. Mostek, founded in 1969, was the first company to produce a single chip calculator, a chip that included four functions: add, subtract, multiply, and divide. Intel, founded in 1969, working with the same calculator manufacturer as Mostek, was faced with the task of having to design a custom chip for a family of calculators. The key issue the company faced was whether the custom circuit could command a sufficient market both to justify the investment in design and production costs, and to get far enough down the learning curve in production to permit low prices. Intel's solution, the microprocessor, was a pioneering advance in *flexible* product design which gave the industry a new way out of the custom versus standard battle: by programming the on-chip memory, the microprocessor could be customized for each application.

The custom versus standard conflict, therefore, was resolved from two directions. On the one hand, what appeared to be "custom" markets rapidly proved to be mass markets for relatively low-cost MOS integrated circuits in calculators, watches, and semiconductor memories. On the other hand, the microprocessor, a standard single-chip central processing unit whose add-on memory could be programmed for customized functions, allowed integrated circuit manufacturers to break out of the vicious cycle (greater complexity leading to higher costs leading to smaller markets) and enter a wide field of new applications markets.

Between 1966 and 1972, thirty new merchant companies entered the U.S. integrated circuit industry. As Table 3 suggests, most of the new entrants were founded by management and technical personnel from existing companies. The mobility of technical personnel in the industry derived from two factors. First, at least until the 1969 changes in the capital gains tax, the venture capital market had been a ready source for start-up capital; and second, the domestic integrated circuit market was growing so rapidly and the number of potential product technologies becoming so diverse that one of the major merchant companies could exploit and develop the full potential of its existing technological resources. The capital constraints which rapid growth placed on company resources meant that firms often had to choose between expanding capacity and developing new products. There can be little doubt that frustration with the pace of product development as well as a market growth environment favoring entrepreneurial risk contributed to the number of new entrants which emerged during the period.

By the early 1970s the wave of new entrants was creating a highly competitive industry structure. One indication of this was that in 1965 the four largest merchant firms accounted for 69 percent of the industry's total shipments, but by 1972 their share had dropped to 53 percent. Likewise, the largest eight firms in 1965 accounted for 91 percent of the total, but by 1972 their share had dropped dramatically to 67 percent.[20] Another indication was increased price competition across the merchant sectors as a whole: "From 1966 through 1971, a period of rapid expansion in both output and the number of firms entering the industry, net earnings as a percent of sales declined from 5.3 percent to 2.7 percent. In each of these years, they were well below the all-manufacturing industries average. Due primarily to vigorous price competition, profits per unit of sales decreased even though sales volume increased."[21] While industrial concentration registered a decline during this period, the relative market-share positions of the leading firms also changed as consequence of new merchant entry. In 1967 the leading firms were, in descending order: Fairchild, Texas Instruments, Motorola, Signetics, Sylvania, RCA, and Westinghouse. By 1973, the entire order had been reshuffled with Texas Instruments regaining its early leadership followed by Motorola, National Semiconductor, Fairchild, Signetics, Intel, American Microsystems, and Mostek.[22] Since 1973, the fast fluctuation of competitive position has continued: in 1980 Texas Instruments and Motorola remained the number one and number two producers, and Intel had moved into the number three spot.

The Era of Large Scale Integration: Strategy and Structure, 1972–1978

The third stage of the industry's development rested upon a succession of technological advances which allowed ever greater numbers of transistors to be built into a single silicon chip. The generic technology—metal oxide on silicon (MOS)—proved to have technical advantages, in both production cost and density, over the bipolar techniques that had dominated early IC design and fabrication. Bipolar devices offered enhanced speed of circuit operation, but the fewer masking steps and higher yields associated with MOS design and fabrication offered the advantage of lower cost per electronic function. Thus, in tandem with enhanced circuit complexity, MOS facilitated progressive reductions in the cost of complex electronic functions, and thereby opened new growth opportunities in old and new markets.

As we noted earlier, between 1966 and 1972 thirty new companies

[20]Semiconductor Industry Association, *The International Microelectronic Challenge*, p. 35.
[21]Commerce Dept., *Report*, p. 56.
[22]FTC, *Staff Report*, p. 26, Table II-9.

Table 3. U.S. semiconductor companies founded between 1966 and 1976 and previous employment of founders, by year

Year and company	City[a]	Previous employment of founders (number of founders)
1966		
American Microsystems	Cupertino	Philco-Ford (4)
National Semiconductor	Santa Clara	Fairchild (3)
1967		
Electronic Arrays	Mt. View	Philco-Ford (4). Bunker-Ramo (2)
1968		
Intersil	Sunnyvale	Union Carbide (3)
Avantek	Santa Clara	Applied Technology (4)
Integrated Systems Technology		Philco-Ford (3)
Nortec Electronics Corp.	Santa Clara	Philco-Ford (2)
Intel	Santa Clara	Fairchild (3)
Computer Microtechnology		Fairchild (3)
Qualidyne	Sunnyvale	Intersil (1), Fairchild (2), Leher (1)
Advanced Memory Systems	Sunnyvale	Fairchild (1), IBM (2), Motorola (1), Collins (1)
1969		
Communications Transistor Corp.	San Carlos	National Semiconductor (3)
Precision Monolithic	Santa Clara	Fairchild (3)
Monolithic Memories	Santa Clara	IBM (1)
Advanced LSI Systems		Nortec (1)
Mostek	Carrollton, Tex.	Texas Instruments
Signetics Memory Systems	Sunnyvale	Signetics (2), IBM (2), HP (1)
Advanced Micro Devices	Sunnyvale	Fairchild (8)
Spectronics	Richardson, Tex.	Texas Instruments
Four Phase	Cupertino	Fairchild (6). General Instruments (2). Mellonics (1), other (1)
1970		
Litronix	Cupertino	Monsanto (1)
Integrated Electronics	Mountain View	Fairchild (2)
Varadyne		

1971		
Caltex	Sunnyvale	Texas Instruments (2), Nortec (4)
Exar	Santa Clara	Signetics (3)
Micropower		Intersil (2)
Standard Microsystems	Hauppauge, N.Y.	Four Phase (1), Electro-Nuclear Labs (1), Nitron (1)
Antex		
LSI Systems		
1972		
Nitron	Cupertino	Caltex (1)
Frontier	Newport Beach	Signetics (1)
Interdesign	Sunnyvale	
1974		
Synertek	Santa Clara	CMI (3), AMI (4), Fairchild (1)
Zilog	Cupertino	Intel (2)
1975		
Maruman (1975)	Sunnyvale	National Semiconductor (2)
1976		
Supertex (1976)	Sunnyvale	Fairchild (1)

[a]California unless otherwise noted.

SOURCE: U.S. Senate, Committee on Commerce, Science, and Transportation, *Industrial Technology* (Washington, D.C.: Government Printing Office, 1978), p. 91.

had entered the U.S. integrated circuit industry. These new companies made their entry on the back of MOS technology. By 1973 approximately 85 percent of the sales of these newly established IC firms were concentrated in MOS technology, whereas among those firms established before 1966 only 35 percent of sales were in MOS devices.[23] Spurred by its use in hand-held calculators, digital watches, and computer main memory, sales of MOS IC products rapidly expanded between 1970 and 1975. Sales of digital MOS integrated circuits in 1970 were only some $45 million; by 1975, however, MOS sales had reached $428 million and had surpassed the total value of digital bipolar IC sales.[24] Having risked all on the development of MOS circuits, the second generation of merchant producers both developed and profited from the rapid expansion of market demand that followed the diffusion of MOS technology. The surge in market demand for MOS circuits came largely from three market segments: consumer products, computer main memory devices, and microprocessors.

Between 1969 and 1974 the consumer products market for digital integrated circuits grew rapidly. From approximately $30 million in 1969, sales of integrated circuits in the consumer product market grew to over $300 million by 1975, the bulk of which was constituted by sales of special chips for calculators and watches. The consumer market's share of total integrated circuit production rose from a mere 4 percent in 1969 to over 15 percent in 1974.[25] During this time more than a dozen of the U.S. merchant firms founded in the period between 1966 and 1972 decided to integrate forward into the marketing and sale of their own calculators and watches for the consumer market. The moves into final consumer product markets had three primary rationales: (1) sales of consumer products would presumably allow the merchant IC producers to insulate themselves to some degree from the cyclical swings in the component market; (2) the consumer market offered the potential of a new mass market for integrated circuits; and (3) by integrating forward, the merchant firm would capture the higher margins available to system producers. Of these rationales, only the second was substantiated in the marketplace: the consumer market did prove to be a mass market for special calculator and watch ICs, but intense price competition and the vagaries of consumer product marketing forced many of the merchant firms to abandon their consumer product lines by 1977.[26]

[23]Charles River study, p. 2–9.
[24]U.S. House of Representatives, Ways and Means Committee, Subcommittee on Trade, *Competitive Factors Influencing World Trade in Semiconductors* (Washington D.C.: Government Printing Office, 1980), p. 64, Table 1.
[25]Commerce Dept., *Report*, pp. 46, 50.
[26]"The Mess in Consumer Electronics," *Dun's Review* (June 1977), p. 72; and "The Great Digital Watch Shakeout," *Business Week*, May 2, 1977, p. 78.

The use of the new MOS circuits in computer main memories spawned the growth of a new mass market for integrated circuit devices. Between 1971 and 1979 the U.S. market for digital semiconductor memories grew at an extraordinary pace: from a base of $60 million in 1971, sales of semiconductor memories were over $500 million in 1976 and reached $1.290 billion in 1979.[27] The first major breakthrough was the introduction of the 1,000-bit random access memory (1K RAM) by Intel in 1970. The rapid sales growth in RAM devices since then has been a function of increasing memory device densities and decreasing chip costs. First, storage capacity per integrated circuit advanced from 1K in 1970 to 4K in 1973 to 16K in 1976 to 64K in 1979. Second, the price per bit of storage has fallen from about 1 cent per bit in 1970 to .05 in 1979.[28] Progressive increases in storage density per chip have led the industry into the "virtuous cycle" of increased production volume leading to lower cost per bit leading to further increases in production volume. This cycle has come to be known as the "learning curve": for each doubling of cumulative output, the cost per electronic function has declined on the average by 28 percent. With the cost per electronic function declining at such a rapid and regular pace, there has been strong economic stimulus underwriting the rapid growth of memory device sales. But we must not forget that competition between the merchant producers on both circuit price and performance was the driving force behind the rapid diffusion of MOS-based circuits in the computer memory market.

Finally, the introduction of the microprocessor by Intel in 1971 offered "as big a step forward in digital systems as did the original integrated circuit."[29] The microprocessor launched "a virtual revolution" in the application of microelectronics to a variety of products and processes.[30] In essence, a microprocessor is a single-chip version of a computer's central processing unit. But its flexibility, a consequence of its capacity to be programmed for a variety of applications, introduced a new set of marketing challenges and strategic choices into the dynamic of market competition and product development. The fact that the specifics of the microprocessor's operation could be customized in its programmable memory meant that it could be tailored by users to meet a variety of specific requirements. However, while the relatively low-cost "intelligence" embodied in microprocessor hardware encouraged diffusion into new applications markets, the

[27]Charles River study, p. 4–23.
[28]*Ibid.*, pp. 4–22 to 4–28.
[29]Mackintosh, *Microelectronics in the 1980s*, p. 65.
[30]Marvin Sirb and James Utterback, *Microprocessor Applications: Cases and Observations* (Center for Policy Alternatives, M.I.T., 1979), p. 1.

cost of developing application programs or instruction sets for specific applications emerged as the new barrier to penetration and development of those applications markets.[31]

Competition between merchant producers of microprocessors, nevertheless, has rapidly brought the hardware cost of the device down and led to successive generations of increasingly sophisticated 4-bit, 8-bit, 16-bit, and, recently, 32-bit devices.[32] But of equal significance has been the shift in market strategies that has characterized the competition. Two general directions can be identified. First, in order to expand and penetrate the new applications markets which the relatively low cost of microprocessor hardware has made possible, a number of the merchant firms have established "learning centers" and offered "development systems" which allow the microprocessor user to program in high-level computer language an instruction set for its specific application. Second, in order to capture the higher value-added associated with the microprocessor, a number of merchant firms have integrated forward into the microcomputer and minicomputer markets, and one has moved into the plug-compatible mainframe market. Both strategies imply that microprocessor manufacturers have increasingly taken on the appearance and characteristics of systems-product houses in order to maximize sales of their new systems products. By 1977, sales of peripheral and input-output devices exceeded sales of the microprocessor itself, and the market for memory chips associated with the use of the microprocessor—RAM, ROM, PROM, and EPROM—was twice the value of microprocessor sales.[33] The total value of the market for the microprocessor and its family of peripheral and memory devices has grown rapidly, from $25 million in sales in 1974 to over $550 million in sales in 1979.[34]

In effect, the introduction and development of the microprocessor altered both merchant firm strategies and the structure of the merchant market. The microprocessor, along with semiconductor memory devices, has proved to be, in essence, a third generation—following mainframes and minicomputers—of *computer* technology. Each generation has been fathered by advances in semiconductor technology, and each has had the effect of further diffusing computational power

---

[31]Two excellent studies should be consulted for greater detail on the development of microprocessor applications: Sirb and Utterback, *Microprocessor Applications;* Economic Intelligence Unit, Ltd., *Chips in the 1980s: The Application of Microelectronic Technology in Products for Consumer and Business Markets* (London, June 1979).

[32]The Charles River study's account of the technology race in the microprocessors market provides an overview to the price wars and product development competition during the period 1971–1979. See Charles River study, pp. 4–30ff.

[33]Based on statistics from industry sources.

[34]Based on statistics from industry sources.

throughout society. The uniqueness of the microprocessor for the merchant firm lay in the fact that it was more of a "systems" product than any component the merchant sectors had produced before. Though both mainframe and minicomputer manufacturers have made ample use of the device in their own systems (to enhance performance and lower cost), the microprocessor provided the foundation upon which merchant firms began gradually to evolve into marketing vehicles for the third wave of diffusion of computer technology.

Finan's comment that the current phase of the U.S. industry's growth may be characterized as "the marketing era" gains new significance in this context.[35] As manufacturers of a complex, system-like component, the merchant firms have faced the primary strategic task of penetrating those markets in which electronic "intelligence" had yet to be applied because its cost had been prohibitive. Unlike the case with the previous generation of intelligent machines—the computer and minicomputer—the application of the microprocessor to new products and process equipment was not limited by size, complexity, or power consumption. Moreover, in the 1970s, as competition in the microprocessor field began to accelerate, prices began to fall rapidly; by 1980 standard 8-bit single-chip microcomputers (a microprocessor chip that incorporates a main control program in ROM, a clock oscillator, some input-output capability and some RAM capacity) were selling in the $8 to $5 range. Thus, hardware cost rapidly became marginal in a whole variety of application fields, and applications software emerged as the major barrier to diffusion and as a major marketing challenge to the merchant firms.

In the early 1970s the least expensive way of solving a problem that required software flexibility was to use a minicomputer. This solution was too expensive for many problems. The introduction of the microprocessor, however, changed this radically. For a few hundred dollars digital hardware could be purchased which was powerful enough to solve many problems and which was software programmable. Although the cost of microcomputer hardware decreased, the cost of developing the software necessary to the application often increased. This increase in software costs is attributable to the increasing complexity of applications software and a general increase in the cost of software development.

Software is generally of three types.[36] *Systems software* is the means by

---

[35]William Finan, *The International Transfer of Semiconductor Technology through U.S.-Based Firms* (National Science Foundation, 1975), p. 23. Hereafter cited as *International Transfer of Technology.*

[36]"1980 Semiconductors Forum," *The Rosen Electronics Letter* (Rosen Research Inc, New York, July 14, 1980), p. 80–10ff.

which a computer is given coordination. It includes such packages as compilers and operating systems. It is very costly to write, but once written it can be used for any application. *Software tools* include editors, debuggers, and other programs likely to be of general use to the programmer writing applications software. Software tools, like systems software, can be used for any application. *Applications software* consumes well over two-thirds of all programming resources. Typically, applications software is written in a high-level language such as COBOL in order to reduce the number of man-hours necessary to develop a specific application.

Early microprocessors forced programmers to program in the lowest of computer languages, machine language. For very short, simple programs this presented no problem, but as applications expanded so did the length of the programs, causing software development costs to soar. A partial solution was the introduction of microprocessor development systems. These systems provided programmers with software tools, but they did not yet allow the programmer to program in a high-level language.

The advent of the 16-bit microcomputer exacerbated the situation. A software application for a 16-bit microcomputer now costs more than 5 million dollars and accounts for 50 to 90 percent of total design cost, depending on the application. The IC manufacturers reacted to this problem in two ways: by providing most 16-bit microcomputers with facilities for high-level language, like PASCAL, and by implementing in hardware operations that had previously been done in software. This mix of hardware and software to yield "firmware" or standard applications "solid state software" has helped the microprocessor firms solve some of the more basic marketing challenges of their new product, and it has brought them, through hardware, into a rapidly growing new market for standard software. Most important, however, it has transformed the leading IC firms from simple component houses into the latest generation of computer systems companies.

To summarize, large scale integration implied that the integrated circuit was able to implement on a single chip what previously would have been regarded as an entire electronic system. As a flexible or programmable device, the microprocessor is only the most pervasive example of this characteristic feature of LSI products. The change in product complexity, however, was accompanied by a change in company strategies, as many of the merchants began to follow the complexity of their system-like products into the final products in which they were used. From the calculator market to the microcomputer market, the leading U.S. merchant firms—Texas Instruments, Fairchild, Intel, National Semiconductor, and Motorola—are developing into the next generation of diversified electronic systems manufactures, while the next tier of merchants find secure niches in markets that others will most likely dominate.

As integrated circuit components gradually took on the character of complete electronic systems during the evolution of large scale integrated circuit design, the strategic importance of integrated circuit design capability to final electronic system producers, both in the United States and abroad, became more acute. As a consequence, during the period 1972–1979, systems producers began to integrate backwards into integrated circuit design and production, either by creating their own IC capacity or by acquiring existing merchant producers. Since 1975 at least fourteen independent merchant houses, including Fairchild and Signetics, have been acquired by foreign companies (see Table 4). With the notable exception of Fairchild, many of these merchant companies welcomed acquisition as a means of financing further growth or of establishing financial solidity in a period of financial crisis. The financial constraints imposed on smaller firms by the highly competitive and rapidly growing integrated circuit market in the 1970s made acquisition by a financially more secure parent an attractive option. For, unlike the major integrated circuit manufacturers in Europe and Japan, for which high debt to equity ratios are commonplace, merchant firms in the United States depend primarily on equity and internally generated funds to finance growth. Given the vicissitudes of the equity market and periodic downturns in the semiconductor business cycle, acquisition proved to be a viable avenue through which to finance a position in a market characterized by rapid growth and rapid technological change.

While foreign companies played a dominant part in the wave of merchant acquisitions over the period 1975–1979, major American users of integrated circuit devices began during the 1970s to set up captive IC production and design facilities. Among the increasing number of American firms involved in captive production are defense equipment companies such as Hughes, minicomputer companies such as DEC, and electronic instrumentation manufacturers such as Hewlett-Packard. Overall, systems producers appear to have set up captive facilities in order to give their final systems products an important competitive edge. This competitive edge may exist because the IC is custom-tailored to meet the requirements of system features, or because the company has invested in R&D or processes to produce higher performance or reliability than is typical for merchant products. Since these characteristics are of significant value to users, the R&D investment underlying development of chips that enable such characteristics may earn a high rate of return. Such returns are a fundame l explanation of the advantages of vertical integration to systems producers.

Table 4. International corporate investments in U.S. semiconductor companies, 1978–1980, by company

Company	Corporate investor	Percent ownership[a]	National base
Advanced Micro Devices	Siemens	20.0	West Germany
American Microsystems	Robert Bosch	12.5	West Germany
	Borg Warner	12.5	United States
Analog Devices	Standard Oil of Indiana		United States
Electronic Arrays	Nippon Electric		Japan
Exar	Toyo	53.0	Japan
Fairchild Camera	Schlumberger		Netherlands Antilles
Frontier	Commodore International		Bahamas
Inmos	National Enterprise Board		United Kingdom
Interdesign	Ferranti		United Kingdom
Intersil	Northern Telecom	24.0	Canada
Litronix	Siemens		West Germany
Maruman IC	Toshiba[b]		Japan
Micropower Systems	Seiko		Japan
Monolithic Memories	Northern Telecom		Canada
MOS Technology	Commodore International	12.4	Bahamas
Mostek	United Technologies		United States
Precision Monolithics	Bourns		United States
SEMI, Inc.	General Tel. & Elec.		United States
Semtech	Signal Companies		United States
Signetics	Phillips	Merger	Netherlands
Siliconix	Electronic Engr. of Calif.		United States
	Lucas Industries	24.0	United Kingdom
Solid State Scientific	VDO Adolf Schindling	25.0	West Germany
Spectronics	Honeywell		United States
Supertex	Investment Group		Hong Kong
Synertek	Honeywell		United States
Unitrode	Signal Companies		United States
Western Digital	Emerson Electric		United States
Zilog	Exxon		United States

[a]No percentage indicates 100 percent (wholly owned), or presumed to be wholly owned, in the absence of data.

[b]Purchased in 1980 from Mansei KK, pending litigation.

SOURCES: *Morgan Stanley Electronics Letter,* December 31, 1979; Dataquest, Inc., January 1979, for percent of ownership; RA Asia Ltd., 1980, for Maruman IC data.

The International Character of the American Industry, 1960–1980

The United States integrated circuit industry is composed of firms that are multinational in their operations. Direct foreign investment by U.S. merchant firms has been an integral aspect of their penetration of foreign markets and of their competitive position in the world market. Foreign investment has been primarily of two types: investment in offshore assembly facilities, and point-of-sale affiliates.[37] Offshore assembly affiliates have been established largely in Southeast Asia and Latin America to take advantage of low-cost foreign labor to assemble U.S.-manufactured subassemblies for export back to the United States and to third markets. Point-of-sale affiliates, on the other hand, have been established primarily in Europe, both to mitigate the impact of the relatively high European Economic Community tariff and to better coordinate integrated circuit designs with European buyer demands.

The shift to offshore assembly by U.S. integrated circuit firms during the period 1964–1972 was primarily an aggressive move by which to reduce labor costs in the most labor-intensive stages of integrated circuit manufacture. It began with Fairchild's opening in Hong Kong. The natural division in integrated circuit production between wafer fabrication, assembly, and testing allows the assembly stage of production to be located at a different facility from the fabrication and testing stages without any significant impact on learning economies. In turn, the substantial difference between wage costs in Southeast Asian developing countries and the United States offers a substantial economic incentive to shift assembly offshore. Finan estimates that the lower wage rates available in Southeast Asia and Latin America could yield up to a 50 percent decline in total IC manufacturing costs. "For example, the total manufacturing cost for an MOS integrated circuit in 1973 was approximately $1.45 per device with assembly done in Singapore. If the same device was assembled in the U.S., the total manufacturing cost would be about $3.00."[38]

The timing and location of offshore assembly investment, however, suggests an additional set of economic incentives. On the one hand, the Tariff Schedules of the United States were amended in 1963; under items 807.00 and 806.30, imported articles assembled in whole or in part of U.S. fabricated components became dutiable only to the extent of the value added abroad. "Reductions in the duties achieved through use of Items 806.30 and 807 act to offset the transportation expenses incurred

---

[37]This terminology is borrowed from Finan's study, *International Transfer of Technolog* Finan adds a third category, "complete manufacturing facilities," which we shall trea. under the discussion of "point-of-sale affiliates."

[38]Finan, *International Transfer of Technology*, p. 60.

in using offshore facilities," thereby enhancing the final cost competitiveness of U.S. firm imports into the United States against foreign imports which do not receive similar tariff treatment.[39] On the other hand, beginning in 1967, the governments of Mexico, Taiwan, Singapore, Malaysia, and Korea established "export platforms" to encourage direct foreign investment in manufacturing for export. While the packages of economic incentives differ among developing countries, most involve duty-free export and import, property tax reductions, and some form of income tax holiday. While far from determinative, these various inducements were found in at least one survey to have ranked second behind the availability of low-cost labor among the reasons cited by industry executives for the shift to offshore production.[40]

The first great wave of offshore assembly affiliates was established between 1964 and 1972, with Mexico, Hong Kong, Malaysia, Singapore, and Korea the leading offshore locations.[41] By 1974, the number of offshore assembly facilities in low-wage developing countries had risen to 69.[42] By 1978, the top nine U.S. integrated circuit manufacturers together had 35 offshore assembly facilities in ten developing countries in Southeast Asia and Latin America.[43]

The second type of direct foreign investment has been the establishment of point-of-sale affiliates, primarily in Europe, to enhance the ability of U.S. firms to penetrate the foreign market for integrated circuits. Finan lists five general functions that influenced the decision by U.S. firms to initiate assembly in the European market: (1) the size of the European market; (2) the relatively high European Economic Community tariff (17 percent of value); (3) the competitive advantage over other U.S. firms which early investors, such as Texas Instruments, had derived from their European operations; (4) British and French government pressure on U.S. firms, particularly those serving the European military market, to take on more of the character of domestic producers; and (5) the fact that, as integrated circuit devices began to implement entire systems on a single chip, greater coordination in chip design between buyer and seller became a crucial factor influencing sales.[44]

---

[39]*Ibid.*, p. 69.

[40]For a more detailed discussion of the factors influencing offshore assembly activity, see two works by Richard W. Moxan: "Offshore Production in Less-Developed Countries: A Case Study of Multinationality in the Electronics Industry," *The Bulletin*, Nos. 98–99, July 1974; and "Effects of Offshore and Onshore Foreign Direct Investment in Electronics: A Survey" (Report for the Office of Technology Assessment, Washington, D. C., 1980).

[41]Finan, *International Transfer of Technology*, p. 56.

[42]Commerce Dept., *Report*, p. 86.

[43]Moxan, "Effects of Offshore and Onshore Foreign Direct Investment on Electronics," p. 24.

[44]Finan, *International Transfer of Technology*, p. 74.

The major period of direct foreign investment by U.S. integrated circuit firms in Europe occurred between 1969 and 1974. By 1974, U.S. firms had established over 46 point-of-sale affiliates within the European Economic Community, of which at least 18 were engaged in complete manufacturing activities.[45] The early U.S. leaders in integrated circuit technology—Texas Instruments, Fairchild, and Motorola—also led the move to European direct investment. However, with the softening of IC demand in the United States during the recession of 1979–1980, the more aggressive of the post-1966 companies also moved to capture sales volume in Europe, where demand for integrated circuits was still strong.

The same factors which led U.S. firms to invest in point-of-sale affiliates in Europe also encouraged U.S. firms to invest in Japan, though with much less success. Only Texas Instruments with its strong patent position was able to extract from the Japanese government permission to establish a wholly owned manufacturing subsidiary in Japan in the period prior to 1978. To circumvent the Japanese 12 percent ad valorem tariff on imports of integrated circuits from the United States, Finan suggests that other U.S. firms in the period prior to 1974 used offshore assembly affiliates in the developing countries of Southeast Asia as export platforms to the Japanese market. Imports into Japan from an affiliate located in a less developed country were duty free.[46] However, prior to 1975, integrated circuits that contained more than 200 circuit elements could not enter Japan, from any point of origin, without the permission of the Japanese government.[47] As a consequence, U.S. firms had little success in translating their superior technological capabilities and production experience into a strong position in the Japanese market. Whereas in 1975 U.S. firms held 98 percent of the U.S. market for integrated circuits and 78 percent of the Western European market, their share of the Japanese market for monolithic ICs was a mere 20 percent. The Japanese "liberalization" that began in 1976, while eliminating the import quota system on advanced ICs, left the 12 percent ad valorem tariff in place. Moreover, though the evidence is scanty, it appears that, at about the same time, Japanese customs officials began, for tariff purposes, to treat imports from U.S. affiliates in less developed countries as coming directly from the United States if more than 50 percent of an item's value-added originated in the United States.[48] Obviously, this nullified the tariff advantages to U.S. firms of exporting to Japan from Southeast Asian assembly affiliates.

[45]Commerce Dept., *Report*, pp. 84, 85.
[46]Finan, *International Transfer of Technology*, p. 75.
[47]*Ibid.*, p. 95.
[48]Commerce Dept., *Report*, p. 96, n.2.

This political structure governing market access and trade in integrated circuits has therefore influenced the pattern of exchange in which U.S. firms have engaged. In order to exploit their lead in IC technology and production experience, U.S. firms have been compelled by tariffs to invest in point-of-sale affiliates in Europe; and a variety of trade restrictions in Japan (investment controls, quotas, and tariffs) have led them to license their technology to Japanese firms as a means of generating residual earnings in a market to which access has been difficult at best. The implication of these technology transfers for the continued international competitiveness of U.S. firms will be considered in greater detail in the third section. For the moment, it is important to recognize the manner in which the political structure of international trade shapes the type of exchanges in which firms engage across national boundaries.

In order to generate residual earnings in the relatively "closed" Japanese market, U.S.-based firms have licensed technology to Japanese firms. There are two basic types of license: (1) a patent license, in which the licensee is given the right to use specific patents of the licenses; and (2) a second source or know-how license, in which the licensee in addition to receiving the legal right to use patents of the licenser also receives some form of technical assistance in putting the patent into production. Given the strong patent positions of U.S.-based firms—a product of their leadership in technological innovation—and the relative backwardness of Japanese technology, particularly in digital bipolar and MOS technologies, licensing arrangements have generated considerable returns to U.S. firms. Annual Japanese patent royalty payments between 1964 and 1970 for semiconductor and integrated circuit licenses went from 2.6 million dollars to over 25 million dollars in 1970.[49] As the Japanese shifted their IC production mix toward digital MOS integrated circuits in the mid-1970s, royalty payments to U.S. firms for integrated circuit technology alone have begun to exceed 20 million dollars per year, or almost 2 percent of the value of Japanese integrated circuit production.[50] Not all licensing agreements involve royalty payments, however. Indeed, the most characteristic form of technology transfer is the "cross-license" in which patents or know-how are exchanged. Nonetheless, where royalty payments are involved, it appears that payments from Japanese firms constitute the bulk of foreign receipts by U.S. firms. The fact that the Japanese market remains the only major world market that U.S. firms have failed to penetrate significantly seems to have enhanced technol-

---

[49]Finan, *International Transfer of Technology*, p. 41.

[50]Estimated on the basis of statistics in various issues of *Electronics News* and industry sources.

ogy licensing as a means of generating some modest residual return from the Japanese market.

By 1971 virtually every U.S. semiconductor firm had at least one offshore assembly affiliate. This international location of the U.S. industry has fundamentally influenced both the *composition* and the *level* of U.S. exports and imports. According to statistics compiled by the U.S. Department of Commerce, the last year in which the United States ran a trade surplus in integrated circuits was 1970.[51] Beginning in 1971, the Commerce statistics indicate that the U.S. trade deficit grew steadily from 3 million dollars to 672 million dollars in 1977.

Measuring the U.S. trade balance in terms of *finished integrated circuits,* however, obscures the real strengths of the U.S. integrated circuit industry and the significance of its international offshore assembly activities. In this respect, both the International Trade Commission study and the recent report of the Commerce Department are flawed. Throughout the 1970s the largest single category of U.S. semiconductor exports has been semiconductor "parts and accessories." This category is primarily composed of chips, dice, and wafers destined for U.S. offshore assembly facilities in Europe, Latin America, and Southeast Asia; when assembled and tested, these become "integrated circuits."[52] Although exports of finished integrated circuits from the United States were only some 348 million dollars by value in 1977, exports of chips, dice, and wafers were over 958 million dollars in 1977. In turn, U.S. imports of finished integrated circuits amounted to some 1.020 billion dollars in 1977. Imports of chips, dice, and wafers amounted, however, only to some 60 million dollars.[53] Thus, before adjusting for 806–807 imports, the U.S. trade balance in finished integrated circuits and chips, dice, and wafers shows in fact a surplus of 126 million dollars. Adjusting U.S. total imports in 1977 for imports entered under TSUS items 806.30 and 807 helps clarify the pattern of trade and the international division of labor by which U.S. firms serve both their domestic and foreign market positions. Of the 958 million dollars of chip, dice, and wafers that the U.S. exported in 1977, some 513 million dollars' worth was re-imported back to the United States under TSUS items 806.30 and 807 after having been assembled by U.S. offshore affiliates primarily in Malaysia, Singapore, Hong Kong, and the Philippines. The remaining 445 million dollars' worth of dice, chips, and wafers shipped to and assembled by U.S. offshore assembly affiliates appears to serve U.S. firms in their foreign markets.

[51]Commerce Dept., *Report,* p. 60.
[52]The Tariff Schedules of the United States have been changed since the early 1970s and these integrated circuit parts now can be found in TSUS 7768960.
[53]Commerce Dept., *Report,* p. 70, Table 4.10.

The pattern of trade described by these figures suggests the following conclusions. First, most U.S. exports of *finished integrated circuits* serve four markets: Britain, France, West Germany, and Japan. Second, U.S. exports of *unfinished* ICs (chips, dice, and wafers) go primarily to five countries: Malaysia, Singapore, Hong Kong, Korea, and the Philippines, for final assembly and packaging by U.S. affiliates located there. Third, the re-export of finished integrated circuits out of Malaysia, Singapore, Hong Kong, Korea, and the Philippines primarily serves five markets: the United States, Great Britain, France, West Germany, and Japan. Thus, U.S.-based integrated circuit manufacturers maximize both scale economies and learning-curve efficiencies on wafer fabrication operations in the United States, and they minimize labor costs by assembling finished integrated circuits primarily in Latin America and Southeast Asia for export and final sale to the five major industrial nations.

In terms of the international division of labor characteristic of the organization of production by U.S. firms, it seems that no less than 80 percent of all U.S.-based wafer fabrication operations are performed in the United States. Wafer fabrication is both the most technically difficult and the highest value-added stage of integrated circuit production. Of the remaining 20 percent, it seems reasonable to assume that most, if not all, of it occurs under the auspices of U.S. manufacturing affiliates in Europe and Japan. The situation for assembly operations appears to be just the reverse: it is likely that no more than 20 percent of total assembly operations occurs in the United States, and that 80 percent of it is conducted under the auspices of U.S. affiliates in Latin America, Southeast Asia, and to a much lesser extent in Europe. Assembly is both the most labor-intensive stage of production and the lowest value-added stage. It should be noted, however, that more stringent quality requirements and an increasing level of automation in assembly and packaging operations seem, in the current competitive environment, to imply a trend back toward assembly in the United States. Nonetheless, the existing international division of labor characteristic of U.S.-based integrated circuit producers, while taking labor-intensive assembly operations offshore, has left concentrated in the United States the highest value-added stage of production—wafer fabrication—and the highest skilled labor phases of production, research and development, and fabrication. This organization of production is therefore advantageous to both U.S.-based firms and to the U.S. domestic economy. A brief review of the pattern of growth and investment by the U.S. integrated circuit industry over the period 1974–1978 will further clarify this point.

Between 1974 and 1978, U.S.-based shipments of integrated circuits grew at an annual rate of 17.7 percent, from $1.056 billion in 1974 to $3.950 billion in 1978. If we exclude the recession of 1975, the annual growth rate over the period 1976–1979 is even more dramatic: shipments in 1976 were some $2.5 billion and by 1979 exceeded 5.0 billion—an annual average growth rate of 26 percent.[54] Investment in production equipment worldwide was over $355 million in 1974 and exceeded $662 million by 1978, with more than 75 percent of that investment being made in the United States.[55] Investment in plant and plant improvements was over $188 million in 1974 and exceeded $234 million in 1978, with more than 71 percent of that investment being made in the United States.[56] Expenditures in IC research and development by U.S. firms were $329 million in 1974 and exceeded $529 million in 1978.[57] Although little detailed information is available, it appears that no more than 10 percent of these research and development sums was invested outside the United States.

To put things in some perspective, industry sources suggest that more than half of total integrated circuit research and development by U.S.-based firms is done under the auspices of IBM and ATT. Together, then, these two firms appear to have invested more in integrated circuit research and development in 1978 than the entire Japanese IC industry combined. In turn, while Japanese integrated circuit production has grown rapidly, at an annual average rate of 30 percent between 1974 and 1978, it has been expanding from a much smaller base. In 1978, Japanese IC shipments still had not exceeded 30 percent of the value of total U.S. shipments of ICs.

Summary

This section has sought to outline the stages of the U.S. integrated circuit industry's development in terms of the shifting composition of the markets the industry has served and the changed character of the products it has produced. In the earliest period, from the invention of transistors through the commercial introduction of the integrated circuit, the U.S. military played the role of "creative first user." Military research and development programs, emphasizing miniaturization,

[54]U.S. Department of Commerce, *1980 U.S. Industrial Outlook* (Washington, D.C.: Government Printing Office, 1980), p. 268.
[55]U.S. International Trade Commission, *Competitive Factors Influencing World Trade in Integrated Circuits*, U.S.I.T.C. Publication No. 1013 (Washington, D.C., 1979), p. 105.
[56]*Ibid.*, p. 104.
[57]*Ibid.*, p. 102.

high performance, and reliability set the direction for early product design, and military and space agency procurement provided an initial market for the integrated circuit. The existence of strong government demand contributed to the entry of new firms and accelerated the pace of diffusion of the integrated circuit into nonmilitary markets.

The second stage of the industry's development rested upon its synergistic relationship to the computer and telecommunications industries. Advanced integrated circuit design moved from the implementation of basic logic circuits to the implementation of entire computer subsystems on a single chip of silicon. The growth of the mainframe and minicomputer markets was fueled by and also contributed to the rapid expansion of domestic digital integrated circuit production.

The third stage of the industry's development rested upon the shift to MOS technology, the emergence of large scale integrated circuit designs, and the appearance of the microprocessor. This stage saw a wave of new merchant entries and a broadening of the final systems markets that the integrated circuit producer served. Large scale integration brought with it new markets in semiconductor memories, in consumer products, in telecommunications, and most importantly in a wide variety of applications markets for the microprocessor and microcomputer. The strategies of firms changed as the markets for the more complex LSI ICs became more segmented, and as the microprocessor, the third generation of computation equipment, offered new market development opportunities and challenges.

As the industry has moved through large scale integration, the nature of the products it produces has changed and therefore so has its status as a "components" industry. Increasingly, the major merchant firms in the industry appear to be consolidating their strengths in integrated circuit technology and emerging as a new generation of diversified electronics "systems" manufacturers. At the same time, the smaller merchant firms are increasingly establishing themselves within niches of the rapidly segmenting markets for integrated circuit components. Also, "captive" production—either through acquisition or in-house start-ups—has apparently increased steadily as a variety of final electronic systems producers have recognized the strategic nature of the integrated circuit to their future product development and market growth.

Although the industry's evolution has certainly been shaped by changes and by growth in the final product markets for semiconductor devices, it is important to recognize that these market opportunities were a direct result of successive innovations in semiconductor technology. In the early years, semiconductors were simply replacements for vacuum tubes: they performed the same functions more effectively, but they did not fundamentally change the products into which they were incorporated. In the second stage of the industry's development, advances in semiconductor technology made possible the substitution of electronic circuits for many types of electrical mechanical functions. In the third phase of the industry's development, the advent of the microprocessor opened up new market opportunities beyond those substitution uses for which semiconductor technologies had proven cost-effective and performance-enhancing. In essence, the microprocessor and the growing range of complex large-scale integrated circuits opened the development phase of the industry.

The character of the current U.S. semiconductor industry remains diverse and dynamic. The existence of a set of merchant firms whose primary business is the design, manufacture, and open-market sale of advanced integrated circuit devices has been complemented by the emergence of a rapidly increasing number of systems firms engaged in custom IC fabrication and design. Together with the addition of the two giants of the domestic electronics industry—IBM and ATT—the structure of the domestic sector exhibits a technological breadth and dynamism unique in the world community. As we have argued, the existence of the merchant segment of the industry has been the critical stimulus to commercial market diffusion of integrated circuits: by making the most advanced integrated circuits available at low cost on the open market, merchants have lowered technological and capital barriers to entry in existing electronic systems markets and have helped develop new markets for the application of microelectronics technology. This competitive dynamism has spurred technological advance and until recently has sustained the international competitiveness of the American electronics industry as a whole.

JAPAN: MARKET POWER AND GOVERNMENT PROMOTION

On July 15, 1975, the Ministry of International Trade and Industry (MITI) and Japan's public telecommunications (Nippon Telephone and Telegraph, or NTT) agreed to unite parts of their separate, ongoing LSI development research projects into a joint program aimed at the development of very large scale integration technology (VLSI). The four-year project began in 1976 and was funded at some $250–350 million (72 billion *yen*). The funding was by public subsidies through MITI and NTT of some $150 million (30 billion *yen*). Contributions to

funding were also made by the program's private company participants, five of the six largest Japanese IC producers.[58]

Perhaps a quarter to a third of the project's funding was spent in the
United States to purchase the most advanced semiconductor manufacturing and test equipment from U.S. equipment manufacturers.[59]
These purchases inferentially support what U.S. industry observers
looking at the VLSI program have suggested: that a significant part of
the VLSI program was aimed at catching up with the U.S. industry's
production capability in advanced integrated circuits. The program
thus provided an assured direction and subsidy to the Japanese industry for the development of process technology and advanced research
and development. It thereby freed Japanese firms to apply resources to
the development of advanced, high value-added ICs, aimed at the competitive penetration of the U.S. merchant semiconductor market.

The latter strategy had, in fact, coalesced with the domestic reorganization in 1971 of the Japanese semiconductor-computer-telecom-
munications industry.[60] From the mid-1970s on, the major Japanese
firms expanded their semiconductor production capacity to meet growing demand in their domestic end-markets. They moved gradually
from a semiconductor capability significantly slanted toward more mature, less complex devices for consumer electronic products toward an
advanced integrated circuit capability that could serve domestic computer and telecommunications demand.

Also from the mid-1970s on, the major Japanese semiconductor

---

[58]The five are Nippon Electric Co. (NEC), Hitachi, Tokyo Shibaura (Toshiba), Fujitsu,
and Mitsubishi. The non-direct participant was Matsushita, Japans's largest consumer
electronics company, whose autonomous research capacities and relative independence
from the government's "administrative guidance" have been much heralded. The VLSI
participants were roughly aligned during the project in two groups which mirrored
formal working arrangements developed during the early 1970s. These were NEC and
Toshiba, with their joint NEC-Toshiba Information Systems, Co. (NTIS), and Fujitsu-
Hitachi-Mitsubishi, with their Computer Development Lab, Ltd. (CDL). The subsidies for
the VLSI program have been characterized by different sources as either direct subsidies
or loan guarantees. As with trade statistics, present publicly available sources of information are simply inadequate to determine the true situation. Implications remain roughly
unchanged, however. The public subsidy represents perhaps 10 percent of the value of
these companies' combined production of digital MOS ICs during the years of the VLSI
project. This is a very rough estimate based on MITI's figures for digital MOS IC
production in Japan and our estimate of the percentage of that production which is
accounted for by these five firms. Since most of the VLSI program's thrust involved
development of digital MOS ICs, the percentage given here should be a reasonable
representation of the impact of public spending in the VLSI program.

[59]Figures vary, but purchases in the first two years were at least some $42 million
worth. Purchases in the last two years were expected to be larger. See, for example,
Electronics News, July 19, 1976; September 27, 1976; and January 31, 1977.

[60]The linked characterization of the industry is suggested by Julian Gresser, *High
Technology and Japanese Industrial Policy: A Strategy for U.S. Policy Makers* (Washington,
D.C., June 26, 1980).

firms developed a solid marketing and distribution base in the United States—the essential requirement for penetration of a U.S. market completely dominated by U.S. firms. After 1977, demand in the United States for 16K RAMs greatly exceeded supply. Excess demand meshed perfectly with the Japanese strategy for penetration. After entering the U.S. market for 16K RAMs in 1977, by the end of 1979 Japanese firms—led by Nippon Electric Co. (NEC), Hitachi, and Fujitsu—had captured over 40 percent of the market. Simultaneously, the Japanese VLSI project wound down with an output of 600–700 patents, and left the participating Japanese firms seemingly well aimed toward VLSI capability. At the start of the new decade, then, the once unchallengeable U.S. domination of the world integrated circuit market seemed to be in some doubt.

The VLSI program and Japanese penetration of the U.S. integrated circuit market are part of a conscious national strategy of establishing comparative advantage in the technology-intensive and knowledge-intensive industries. MITI has been explicit about its goal: "[The] spirit of basing national development on technology should be our aim in the 1980s. . . . The basic course of knowledge intensification during the 1980s should be to increase the value added of products through technology intensification. . . . International specialization between Japan and advanced countries will also become possible as a result of the growth of industries where Japan has unique, creative technologies. . . . Possession of her own technology will help Japan *to maintain and develop her industries' international superiority* and to form a foundation for the long-term development of the economy and society."[61]

The emergence of Japanese competitiveness in world integrated circuit markets, like the more general national goal of creating comparative advantage, rests on a conscious government and industry strategy of controlling access to the domestic Japanese market, structuring the terms of domestic competition, making available stable sources of cheap capital, and using the controlled and structured domestic market as a secure base from which to gain entry and competitiveness in international markets. The purposes of this section are to describe these systemic features that give the Japanese semiconductor-electronics industry its advantage in international competition and to detail the industry's evolution and operation since the late 1960s. The reader will notice the structure and detail here differ markedly from those of the preceding section. The story of the Japanese semiconductor industry's growth is told differently because in fact, as in available detail, it is strikingly different from the U.S. industry's development.

[61]*MITI Policies*, pp. 136, 199, 200.

The following sub-section describes briefly the distinctive strategic character of the Japanese system as it was developed after World War II, and then examines the structure of the Japanese semiconductor-electronics industry as it exists today. We emphasize those features of Japanese business, finance, and state policy that have assisted the rapid competitive growth of Japanese firms. The second and much longer sub-section traces the evolution of the Japanese semiconductor industry during the 1970s, and emphasizes the manner in which Japanese government policies altered and assisted the strategies and capacities of the domestic Japanese firms. Our focus throughout will be on how *domestic* Japanese industrial structure, government policies, and company capacities intertwine to promote the *international* competitiveness of the Japanese semiconductor-electronics firms.

The Systemic Advantages of Domestic Structure and Market Power

In order to grasp fully the nature and strengths of the Japanese semiconductor industry, it is necessary to characterize briefly the domestic economic system within which the industry operates.

Since the end of the Second World War, the Japanese have been committed to rapid economic development as a systematic priority. "Macro-level economic growth has been the central political goal to which all other Japanese policies have been subordinated during the postwar period."[62] The conscious theme of policy has been to create comparative advantage in high value-added industries as an alternative to remaining dependent on the labor-intensive industries that might seem appropriate to an economy short on resources and capital. As a "resource-poor nation"—dependent even today on the export of manufactures to pay for the importation of almost 90 percent of its energy needs, over half of its food, and the greater part of its chief resources—the Japanese chose to develop domestic industries that could serve to expand overseas sales.[63] The state aggressively promoted the shift out of agriculture into industry and out of low-wage into high-wage industrial sectors. Government policy served to channel resources into those industries for which there was growing domestic demand and potential economies of scale to facilitate export. The targets were machinery, metals, chemicals, and ships in the 1950s, then automobiles and heavy machinery, and by the 1970s atomic power and computers. The state played a crucial role both in manipulating the access of foreign com-

---

[62]T. J. Pempel, "Japanese Foreign Economic Policy: The Domestic Bases for International Behavior," in Peter J. Katzenstein, ed., *Between Power and Plenty* (Madison: University of Wisconsin Press, 1978), p. 157.
[63]Import percentages are from *MITI Policies*, p. 30.

petitors to the domestic Japanese market and in restructuring the key domestic industries to promote their export competitiveness. As we shall see in the next sub-section, both of these tactics were an integral part of the development of the Japanese semiconductor-electronic industry.

The theory underlying both control over access and the restructuring of domestic industry was "to place undeveloped domestic industries with little competitive power under the government's active interference . . . to build up a large scale production system, while limiting entry into the domestic market of foreign enterprise with already established mass production systems and restricting the competition of foreign manufacturers in the domestic market."[64]

In the role of controlling access, the Japanese government has been characterized as an "official doorman [between domestic Japanese society and the international arena] determining what, and under what conditions, capital, technology, and manufactured products enter and leave Japan."[65] Selective control over internal foreign investment discouraged foreign efforts to control Japanese firms and to manufacture in Japan. Imports were limited through tariff and nontariff barriers to ensure that domestic firms would capture most of the explosive growth in domestic demand. Technology imports were controlled by MITI in order to force foreign firms, whenever possible, to sell technology and to be content with royalty payments rather than product sales in Japan. Thus, a closed market gave Japanese firms a stable base of demand on which to build competitive production and distribution networks.

In its companion role as promoter of industry restructuring, the state followed policies "which emphasized efficiency and rationalization." It encouraged competition through extensive support for expanding firms. The state organized a stable availability of cheap capital; it provided tax breaks to assure cash flow liquidity, gave research and development support, and helped to promote exports. Winners were encouraged, losers weeded out. In most sectors, a few large vertically integrated firms emerged and carved up the domestic market as a matter of company strategy and state policy. Markets were rationalized, and in MITI's words "intra-industrial specialization" was encouraged as a means of building efficient scale economies in market segments.[66] Capacity expansion was often planned with state help, and official or informal "recession cartels" were organized to manage periods of over-

[64]Edward F. Denison and William K. Chung, "Economic Growth and Its Sources," in Hugh Patrick and Henry Rosovsky, eds., *Asia's New Giant* (Washington, D.C.: Brookings Institution, 1976), p. 67.
[65]Pempel, "Japanese Foreign Economic Policy," p. 139.
[66]Quoted phrases from *MITI Policies*, pp. 31, 196.

capacity. In these many ways, "disruptive" competition was avoided. Thus vertical integration, "rationalization, oligopolization, and cartelization [were] an integral part of the sectoral development policy."[67]

Deeply contrasting images characterize the dominant analytic descriptions of the resulting Japanese economic system. At one extreme lies the image of "Japan Inc.," in which at every level of relations, businessmen and government promoters collaborate to further the development and international competitiveness of Japanese business. At the other extreme is "Japan the Land of Fierce Competition," in which cut-throat competition is assumed to characterize domestic Japanese markets. The available evidence in a range of economic sectors—and as the following will show, in the semiconductor electronics sector in particular—suggests that the extreme images are partial truths. Especially in the face of foreign economic and political power, there is a collaborative unity within the conservative coalition of business and state actors that rules Japan. Such collaboration can be expressed through formal, state-sanctioned market-sharing arrangements (like the recession cartels) or through less formal arrangements among economic actors (such as the strong preference to "Buy Japanese"). Simultaneously, among members of the ruling coalition—that is, among corporations and bureaucratic actors (such as MITI and NTT), as well as between business and the state—there exists strong and flourishing competition. Japanese firms do compete with each other in domestic and international markets. Japanese firms disagree about strategy; they can act independently of state strategies; and they often ignore the government pressures for market rationalization to compete fiercely and directly in segments of growing markets.

In contrast to the extreme images, we would characterize the Japanese economic system as one of "controlled competition" in which the intensity of competition between firms in key industrial sectors is directed and limited both by state actions and by the formal and informal collaborative efforts of industrial and financial enterprises. It is difficult to define in a neat way where the precise limits of competitive behavior lie. Our best guess is that, as a general rule, Japanese firms within market segments tend to tolerate existing market shares while engaging in intense competition over expanding shares of growing markets. Such competition would then tend *to shade into* collaboration in the face of *foreign* penetration of domestic Japanese markets. Since outsiders will compete over existing market shares and will probably not share common Japanese goals and interests (such as national economic development), there would be a reasonable tendency among

---

[67]Pempel, "Japanese Foreign Economic Policy," p. 159.

Japanese firms and the state to act in formal or informal concert against the outsiders.

Thus firms compete but they also collaborate. State bureaucrats, in turn, ride with the pressures of the market. They do not administer the market, but they do consciously contribute to the rapid growth of particular sectors. In its dual role of doorman and promoter, the state has helped in a detailed way to establish conditions of investment, risk, and collaboration that promote the long-term development and international competitiveness of favored industries. In this way, state initiative has mixed with private arrangements and domestic market competition to create extremely competitive domestic sectors. In automobiles, for example, the domestic market was closed to foreign producers, a competitive components industry was established under government leadership, and the infrastructure was laid down by public investment to permit a rapid increase in auto usage. In 1960 Japan produced 160,000 autos; by 1970, the figure was 3.1 million cars; by 1980, Japan was producing over 8 million cars a year. The consequent Japanese success in the U.S. auto market needs no recounting here. The story is similar in steel. State intervention closed the domestic market to preserve it for Japanese firms, provided cheap investment capital, staged investment through a series of rationalization plans to avoid overcapacity, and helped to manage excess capacity when it occurred. Firms did not always follow state policy, however, and by risking competitive expansion in the face of state (and sometimes industry) opposition, some firms prospered. In 1950 Japan produced about 5 million net tons of steel, by 1960 some 24 million net tons, and by 1970 over 100 million net tons per year. It was also, and remains, the lowest-cost volume steel producer in the world. A full 40 percent of that production is exported every year.

Control over access on the one hand, and vertical integration, market rationalization, and oligopolization on the other hand, have thus created certain commonalities in Japanese business strategies across a range of sectors. Initial production volume is built on a tacitly closed domestic market with different firms achieving large-scale economies in part through "intra-industrial specialization" in sub-segments of each market. Intense competition between firms appears to be centered on the expanding share of the market, while existing market shares are generally tolerated. Volume production is steadily expanded through selective exploitation of market niches abroad. Those niches provide an initial penetration of foreign markets and are followed by full-scale export drives. Steadily increasing production volumes at home generate the production economies that have often made Japanese producers the low-cost international competitors. In essence, the Japanese have used a secured and controlled domestic market as the base from which to launch large-scale penetration of foreign markets.

As we shall demonstrate, the characteristic features of Japan's high-velocity growth system, and the company strategies it encourages and sustains, have been an integral part of the development of Japan's international competitiveness in semiconductors. In pursuit of MITI's goal of creating comparative advantage in the knowledge-intensive and technology-intensive industries, the Japanese had to turn a relatively backward semiconductor industry into a world-class competitor. During the 1970s, the Japanese industry moved from a consumer-product orientation and a position of relative technological inferiority in components toward a state-of-the-art capability in components, telecommunications, and computers. Before we examine that successful development in detail, let us look at what it has produced: the Japanese semiconductor-electronics industry as it acts today.

Domestic Structure and Market Power

The six major Japanese producers of semiconductors are large multi-divisional vertically integrated firms which manufacture electronics systems products serving end markets primarily in consumer electronics, computers, and communications. The six firms, roughly in order of their share of the domestic Japanese IC market, are NEC, Hitachi, Toshiba, Fujitsu, Mitsubishi, and Matsushita. These six firms dominate the Japanese domestic semiconductor market, and accounted for approximately 79 percent of domestic sales in 1979.[68] For these firms, the percentage of total sales in 1979 accounted for by semiconductor sales, in comparison with a sample of representative U.S. merchant firms, is as follows.[69]

Japanese Firms		U.S. Firms	
NEC	17.8%	AMD	89%
Fujitsu	6.7	Fairchild	69
Toshiba	5.5	Intel	75
Hitachi	4.1	Mostek	93
Mitsubishi	3.8	Motorola	31
Matsushita	2.3	National	85
		Texas Inst.	36

These figures suggest the extent to which it is misleading to label the Japanese companies simply as semiconductor producers. Gresser's char-

---

[68]The Consulting Group, BA Asia Ltd., *The Japanese Semiconductor Industry 1980*, p. 145, for greater detail. Hereafter cited as BA 1980.

[69]Chase Econometrics, *U.S. and Japanese Semiconductor Industries: A Financial Comparison* (1980), pp. 1.5, 1.6. Hereafter cited as Chase study.

acterization of the industry as a unitary semiconductor-computer-tele-
communications industry captures its systems character and the slant
of its growth, but it understates the industry's continued heavy involvement in consumer electronics (which consumes roughly 50 percent of
ICs).[70] In order to emphasize the systems orientation of the industry,
the major firms must be briefly profiled.

NEC is Japan's leading communication systems equipment producer,
a strong computer manufacturer, and the largest producer of integrated
circuits. It is a domestic leader in MOS LSI, and especially in memory
semiconductor technology. Fujitsu is Japan's largest mainframe computer manufacturer and a leader in advanced MOS memory and digital
bipolar (ECL) semiconductor production. Hitachi is Japan's largest diversified electronic systems producer serving computer, communications, and consumer markets, and is a major producer of heavy industrial equipment and electrical machinery. It is strong in MOS memories
and is Japan's largest producer of TTL and ECL logic circuits. Toshiba
is also a large conglomerate that produces heavy electrical equipment,
instrumentation, appliances, and electronic systems. It is a leader in
standard and custom CMOS MSI-LSI and consumer linear semiconductor devices. Mitsubishi is a large diversified producer of electronic systems, Japan's largest manufacturer of small business computers, and a
manufacturer of industrial and heavy electrical machinery and appliances. It has adequate capability in MOS and digital bipolar and good
capability in industrial and consumer linear devices. Matsushita is Japan's largest consumer electronics and home appliance producer. It
derives most of its IC income from consumer linear ICs and is not a
factor in the domestic MOS LSI and bipolar markets.[71] All of these six
large firms are multi-billion-dollar companies, with sales in 1979 ranging
from Fujitsu's $1.8 billion to Hitachi's $10.7 billion. Most of this information is summarized in Table 5.

As these profiles suggest, the Japanese have rationalized the major
final electronics system markets among the major domestic firms. "Intra-industrial specialization" has enabled each firm to exercise a degree
of control over different product segments of the overlapping systems
markets they serve. As we have seen in the general discussion of the
Japanese system, such specialization characteristically enables these
Japanese firms to maximize economies of scale, thereby optimizing the
production-cost efficiencies of their systems products. Again, this is not
to suggest a lack of serious competition among some Japanese firms in

[70]BA 1980, p. 113.
[71]Descriptions are culled from The Consulting Group, BA Asia Ltd., *The Japanese
Semiconductor Industry: An Overview* (April 1979), hereafter cited as BA 1979, pp. 160–
178; BA 1980, pp. 134–135, 184–204; and Gresser, *High Technology*, pp. 1–3.

Table 5. Sales and strengths of dominant firms in Japanese semiconductor industry, 1979 and 1980, by firm

Firm	Total sales (billions of dollars)		Semiconductor sales (millions of dollars)		Percent of SC sales, 1979	SC strength	Systems market
	1979	1980	1979	1980			
NEC	3.2	3.7	100	928	17.8%	MOS-LSI (NMOS, CMOS) Memory (16K strong, 64K redesign strong) MPUs (4-bit) Linear	Leading IC firms Leader in telecommunications computers
Hitachi	10.7	9.2	553	702	4.1	MOS-LSI (CMOS, NMOS) memory (16K,64K very large scale integration) Bipolar logic–ECL Schottky-TTL; MPU (Motorola)	Leader in diversified systems computers, producer in communications, consumer, heavy industrial, electrical machinery
Fujitsu	1.8	2.5	240	383	6.7	MOS memory (NMOS) (64K strong) Bipolar logic–ECL	Leader in computers
Toshiba	7.0	7.0	426	638	5.5	CMOS, MSI-LSI (16K static, 64K) Consumer linear CMOS-MPU SOS (recent investment)	Diversified systems, especially consumer and business systems, instrumentation, appliances, electrical equipment
Mitsubishi	3.9	5.2	187	260	3.8	Industrial consumer linear 64K RAM entrant some ECL	Diversified systems, small business computers, industrial and heavy electrical equipment, medium appliances
Matsushita	9.8		213	340	2.3	Consumer linear New 64K static RAM (strategy shift)	Leader in consumer appliances, home computers

SOURCE: Constructed from Bank of America data in BA Asia Report, *The Japanese Semiconductor Industry, 1980.*

major final systems products; for example, NEC and Hitachi are currently engaged in a battle for the number two spot in large-scale computers behind Fujitsu. Rather, it appears that final systems markets have been rationalized, and that individual firms do specialize within market segments (Table 5, right column), but that markets are growing fast enough to permit serious competition over increasing shares in segments where the systems product strengths of the major firms overlap. Moreover, as the profiles above also suggest, the major Japanese firms slant their semiconductor production mix to meet the needs of the different markets which their systems products serve. This suggests that the Japanese firms have also rationalized their semiconductor device production as a logical outgrowth of specialization in final systems markets. Such component-product rationalization among Japanese firms mirrors the market segmentation that can be found among merchant U.S. firms serving different systems markets in the United States. Thus, the three leading Japanese exporters of semiconductors to the world merchant market—NEC, Fujitsu, and Hitachi—are the firms whose systems capability in computers and communications use technologically advanced MOS LSI and bipolar devices.

However, while production mix correlates strongly with system product markets, *internal consumption* by the largest firms of their captive production is relatively *low*.[72] Approximately 21 percent of the value of semiconductor production is consumed internally by the ten largest producers. (The figure varies among firms. NEC, for example, internally consumes only 16 percent of total sales, while Fujitsu's internal consumption rate rises to perhaps 50 percent, which suggests a primary orientation toward computer sales.) Moreover, internal consumption is particularly low in MOS devices, averaging 10 percent among the top four firms in 1979.[73] Such low internal consumption figures might seem peculiar because these same producers are also the largest *consumers* of domestic semiconductor devices. Indeed, the top ten firms consumed at least 60 percent of *total* Japanese domestic production, and the percentage of their consumption of the most advanced IC devices is undoubtedly even higher.[74] This juxtaposition of low internal with high overall consumption suggests that Japanese firms engage in a significant amount of *trade* themselves.

The implications of such inter-company trade are important and mesh neatly with the observation that component specialization occurs among Japanese firms. As we have seen, the systems strengths of each firm rest in overlapping final markets. A more sophisticated specializa-

[72]Figures that follow are from BA 1979, pp. 80 and 115.
[73]BA 1980, p. 148.
[74]BA 1980, p. 129.

tion in certain devices and technologies may occur among Japanese firms in which they supply each other with semiconductor devices to meet the component needs of their overlapping systems products. Such specialization would enable sophisticated rationalization of device production among the different firms. Indeed, one Fujitsu executive admitted that Japanese semiconductor firms have engaged in this kind of specialization in certain components: "In a small market like Japan's, it is the only way to attain scales of production."[75] As the quote suggests, the effect of such rationalization would be to enable each firm to maximize scale economies and move further down the learning curve in each of its devices than would be possible in the absence of rationalization and inter-company trade. It should be noted, however, that such inter-company trade in components, which is necessary for specific final systems products, may occur only minimally among the few direct competitors in those specific final market sub-segments. Thus NEC may be more likely to buy bipolar logic circuits from Fujitsu than from Hitachi, which is a more direct competitor in computer market sub-segments. However, the result of rationalization, wherever it occurs, is cheaper devices and cheaper systems that use these devices.

There is a crucial point to be made from the fact that the largest firms control over 60 percent of Japanese semiconductor consumption (and a higher percentage of advanced IC consumption). Such dominant power over demand in the domestic market for semiconductors enables the largest firms to control the pace and direction of growth in that market. By altering the composition of their production and demand, these firms can control the share and compositon of *imports* entering their domestic market. During the 1970s, U.S. firms succeeded in penetrating the domestic Japanese market primarily with advanced product innovations that Japanese firms were not yet producing. As Japanese firms became competent in the production of such devices, there was a characteristic experience for exporting U.S. firms. Their shares of the Japanese market in such devices leveled off or declined—even though domestic Japanese demand was growing explosively—as the major Japanese firms replaced U.S. imports with devices produced internally or by other Japanese firms.[76] This pattern could be no more than the straightforward result of successful import substitution. But at the very least, rationalized control over both production and consumption among the major Japanese firms gives them the potential to control the composition and share of fully competitive U.S.

[75]Quoted in Leslie Donald Helm, "The Japanese Computer Industry: A Case Study in Industrial Policy" (University of California, unpublished MA thesis in Asian Studies, June 1981), p. 34.
[76]Based on conversations with industry sources.

imports that enter their domestic market. The figures in Table 6 are consistent with the view that this potential may have been used to keep the import-consumption share from increasing during a period of rapid consumption growth. This hypothesis will be elaborated on in our third section, along with the story of a particular device, the 16K RAM (which largely accounts for the 1978–1980 pattern shown in Table 6). In short, we suggest that collaborative actions of the major Japanese firms may now enable them to take over the role of *doorman*, played so effectively by the state in other industries and in their own industry's early development.

The ability of the largest Japanese firms to use their domestic market to increase their competitiveness is enhanced by certain features of the overall domestic Japanese industrial and financial structure.[77] Each of the top six Japanese semiconductor companies is tied to a Keiretsu, a conglomerate industrial grouping of companies arranged around either a single large bank or large industrial firm (or several firms).[78] The Keiretsu's form ranges from groups with close inter-company ties to looser, basically financial arrangements. Keiretsu members are bound by equity cross-ownership and interlocking management, financing, and buying-selling arrangements. Another set of inter-company ties that tend to assist company stability is provided by equity cross-ownership outside of the Keiretsu structure, for a majority of company stock in Japan is held by other companies or banks.[79] The Keiretsu structure itself provides important advantages for the Japanese electronics firm that can draw on its resources. First, the Keiretsu members provide an important market for the firm's products (as, for example, when the Dai-ichi Bank replaced its IBM banking system with a Fujitsu product). Second, each Keiretsu usually includes a large trading company which is frequently used by Japanese firms to perform overseas sales, distribution, and financing. The trading company thus provides increased access to international semiconductor markets.

Although the infrastructural features described above are important,

[77]For an elaboration of the remainder of this paragraph, see Gresser, *High Technology*, pp. 4–7; and BA 1979, pp. 15–19.

[78]The companies and their Keiretsu are as follows (from Chase study, p. 8.2): Fujitsu Ltd., Hitachi Ltd., Matsushita Elec. Industrial, Mitsubishi Electric Corp., Nippon Electric Co., Ltd., Toshiba Corporation, Dai-Ichi Kangyo Bank (DKB) Group, Hitachi Group, Matsushita Group, Mitsubishi Group, Sumitomo Group, Toshiba-IHI Group. Hitachi, Matsushita, and Toshiba are the dominant members of their own independent industrial groupings. Mitsubishi and Nippon Electric are former Zaitbatsu (family-dominated industrial and banking combinations formally broken up after World War II, and restructured). See the Chase study for the structure and membership of each Keiretsu.

[79]S. Miyaski, "Japanese-Type Structure of Big Business," and Yusaku Futatsugi, "The Measurement of Interfirm Relationships," in Kazus Sato, *Industry and Business in Japan* (White Plains, N.Y.: M. E. Sharp, 1980).

Table 6. Value of domestic and imported integrated circuits consumed in Japan, 1975–1980

Year	Domestic consumption (billions of yen)	Imports (billions of yen)	Imports as percent of domestic consumption	Percent change in imports from previous year	Percent change in consumption from previous year
1975	Y160	Y50	31%		
1976	252	74	29	48%	57.5%
1977	272	64	26	-13.8	-0.4
1978	306	68	22	6.0	26.4
1979	403	111	27	63.0	31.7
1980	527	118	22	6.0	30.8

SOURCE: Figures for 1975–1978 based on data from BA Asia Ltd., 1980; figure for 1978–1980 based on MITI, Ministry of Finance, reported in BA Asia Ltd., 1981 (unpublished).

the most significant advantage offered by the Japanese industrial and financial structure compared to its U.S. counterpart is a *stable availability of capital* for continued growth—a basic need for semiconductor companies whose markets are expanding and whose products are changing rapidly. The point requires detailed elaboration because stable access to capital would seem to be an odd attribute, given the financing structure of the Japanese industry: as every observer has noted, the Japanese semiconductor companies, with the exception of Matsushita, have debt-to-equity ratios of 150 to 400 percent, compared with U.S. firm ratios of 5 to 25 percent. In an industry as volatile as semiconductors, where innovation can easily upset the plans of corporate investment, such high debt-equity ratios, with their attendant fixed costs, would normally imply instability rather than stability in the availability of capital. The more volatile an industry, the riskier it is for the lender and the less willing he will normally be to lend. What, then, are the infrastructural advantages that mitigate the risk of carrying debt in Japan and that provide Japanese firms stable access to debt capital?

It should first be noted that Japan's remarkably rapid postwar development was of necessity debt-financed. Such rapid expansion could not be sustained from internal profits alone, and the state could control the allocation of debt in a way that it would not control equity. The state indirectly influenced capital allocation toward favored industries, and as Ueno has shown, private lending followed shifts in public lending. "Broadly speaking, the total supply of funds in Japan was controlled by the Bank of Japan, the level and structure of interest rates were artificially regulated by the Ministry of Finance, and private funds were allocated, under the guidance of public financial institutions, by city banks which competed for market shares."[80] Corporate debt was shared by the banks, which diffused the risk to each. But collapse of a highly levered firm could threaten the banks as well as the company and its suppliers. Since a bank collapse could spread throughout the economy, company troubles became a matter of public policy. At bottom, then, despite the risks of high leverage, the resulting system is stable because government concern with the well-being of firms in favored sectors, like semiconductors, is taken as an implicit guarantee of loans made to them.[81]

The long-term risk born by lenders is thus reduced by the structural participation of the Japanese government, working through the bank of Japan, in assisting financially troubled firms. In particular, close

[80]H. Ueno, "The Conception and Evolution of Industrial Policy," in Sato, *Industry and Business in Japan,* pp. 400–407.

[81]Richard Caves, "Industrial Organization," in Patrick and Rosowsky, eds., *Asia's New Giant,* p. 488.

cooperation and financial assistance from lending banks and the government enables financially troubled Japanese firms to restructure their finances and operations without the threat of loan foreclosure to financial collapse. Lending risk is further reduced by a number of additional structural features. As the Chase study noted: "To the extent that a Keiretsu bank directly or indirectly owns a significant interest in the shares of a borrower, it has a continuing voice in establishing corporate policy and direction. This control, coupled with the assurance of financial assistance or loan guarantees from the borrower's Keiretsu reduces the risk taken by lenders."[82]

The huge relative size and product-line diversification of the Japanese electronics firms also make them a more secure investment risk. Indeed, the structure of market rationalization and oligopolization may also mitigate risk, because firms are less exposed to competitive failure in the market segments they dominate. Also, these Japanese firms normally hold relatively large portfolios of cash, time deposits, and securities. Large time deposits held in lender banks act as compensating balances for the loan exposure of these banks. Large security holdings of relatively liquid assets mitigate investment risk. In sum, low risk for investors means greater willingness to lend, and that translates into relatively stable access to debt capital for Japanese semiconductor firms. Note, too, that these infrastructural features which make Japanese firms low-risk investments also appeal to U.S. investors. U.S. banks which lend to Japan understand that the Japanese government and the Bank of Japan are the ultimate sources of security for U.S. bank loans.[83] Here, the Japanese *domestic* structure provides important advantages for Japanese firms that compete with U.S. firms for *international* debt captial from "American" multinational banks.

Finally, of course, the large diversified operations of the Japanese electronics companies add to the stability of capital. Funding of electronics projects may be generated by other operations of the corporation. Profits earned in older, declining sectors may be used to finance expansion of the growing operations. The money may be used directly or to make interest payments on debt incurred in financing expansion.

From the perspective of the firm, the stable availability of capital provides crucial advantages for growth and competitive development. The stability of their capital allows Japanese managers to use a longer planning horizon. They can make commitments to projects that may yield returns only after many years. Such projects may of course range from research and development to capacity expansions to market-share

[82]Chase study, p. 23.
[83]For elaboration of what follows, see the Chase study, Chap. 6.

battles. In that regard, the extensive use of bank financed debt provides additional freedom to Japanese managers. The banks can give them commitments for a series of loans over many years. The funds which the corporation will have available are not dependent on the immediate earnings of its operation or the price of its stock, as in the United States. Short-term fluctuations in the companies' operations will also be more easily explained and communicated to a small group of cooperative bankers than to participants in an impersonal capital market.

By contrast, the availability of capital is much less stable for U.S. firms, who raise most of their capital through retained earnings and equity investment (as their debt-equity ratios suggest). Since U.S. merchant firms lack those infrastructural advantages that mitigate the risk of carrying debt in Japan, they simply cannot achieve comparable debt levels: lenders would see the risk as so extreme that they would simply refuse to provide capital. Furthermore, U.S. firms operate with certain disadvantages compared to the Japanese industry. The financing of projects from current earnings could well force a firm to forego promising projects, which would ultimately yield market share and profits, because of a current slump in sales. Long-term planning becomes much more difficult. Moreover, a return to the equity markets might not provide a meaningful choice much of the time. New equity issues must be timed to coincide with variable evaluation of the stock in the market. High stock prices may be poorly correlated with a firm's internal requirement for capital. U.S. firms must also be sensitive to the demands of shareholders, who want quarterly improvements in earnings to raise the price of shares and generate higher dividends. The firm may be unwilling or unable to inform the public of its long-term projects and thus unable to prevent a fall in the price of shares when current earnings falter. A reduction in the value of the stock decreases the ability of the firms to raise not only equity but also additional debt. At the extreme, a sustained decline in the price of the stock may even lead to a takeover of the company by unfriendly outsiders.

Aside from the advantages provided by stable access to debt capital, Japanese firms may also enjoy access to *cheaper* capital. This, of course, is the central claim of the Chase study.[84] In general, capital

[84]Several of the assumptions of the Chase study, which are crucial to the size of the capital cost differential it asserts, are questionable. Most significantly, Chase uses the historical growth rate of stock prices as the measure of the *firm's* cost of equity. This ignores the relatively light demand on current cash flow made by equity holders who expect returns on uncertain, future earnings (hence a limited drain on current funds). Other questionable assumptions include (1) the very low differential used to compensate for exchange rate changes between dollar and *yen*, and (2) the use of current (extremely *high*) costs of debt in the U.S. instead of the historical rates actually paid by U.S. semiconductor firms. There are, finally, other technical problems in the study—for example, use

would be cheaper for Japanese firms if, discounting inflation, debt in Japan is cheaper than equity in the United States—that is, if interest rates in Japan on long-term debt (the "cost" to the firm of debt) are lower than the return on investment demanded by U.S. equity investors (the "cost" to the firm of equity). In fact, the cost of capital may be cheaper for Japanese firms given their respective debt-equity ratios, because under U.S. tax law, as in Japan, returns to equity investors come out of taxed income whereas interest payments on debt are deductible as current expenses. Moreover, given the size and diversity of the Japanese electronics firms and the structural advantages underlying capital stability, the cost of debt to them should also be lower than to U.S. firms. Since large size, diversification, and a tacit government guarantee against failure reduce the likelihood that Japanese firms will be unable to repay a loan, lower interest costs should result. Indeed, the size discrepancy alone between most Japanese firms and U.S. merchant firms suggests that capital will be cheaper for the Japanese firm. The risk to lenders is generally perceived to be smaller when financing a $100 million expansion for a corporation with $2 billion in assets than when financing the same expansion for a corporation with only $100 million in assets.

Cheap and available capital is a special advantage in an industry like semiconductors. As that industry has matured, the contribution to total device cost that comes from capital equipment has increased. The cost of capital has also become a much more significant component of final product cost. For example, in the early 1970s the ratio of capital investment to annual revenues for wafer fabrication was on the order of approximately 1:15. That ratio for the latest generation 64K devices is now on the order of 1:2.5.[85] To the extent that available capital is cheaper for Japanese firms, the increasing contribution of capital equipment to cost puts those firms in a superior competitive position, given their longer planning horizons and relatively lesser need to generate short-term earnings. Simply stated, they can afford to compete directly through product pricing. If their capital is cheaper, their final product will also be cheaper. And this result will be increasingly true as the contribution of capital to cost continues to increase. We should note here that this trend is generally true of most technology-intensive industries. Indeed, the Japanese may well have recognized that point

---

of the entire integrated Japanese firm instead of the semiconductor division. While, as we suggest, the Chase study's conclusion is plausible, a more careful study would be required to prove that capital is actually cheaper for Japanese firms.

[85]These ratios are based on information supplied by industry sources.

when they reconstructed their financial system in the postwar period to generate more cheap capital for favored growth industries.

Whether or not capital is cheaper, the fact of relatively stable supply gives Japanese semiconductor firms an advantage in their international competition with U.S. firms. (If capital is indeed significantly cheaper, the Japanese advantage would of course be enhanced.) Japanese firms can finance research and development and capacity expansion, can engage in price competition to expand market share, and can finance penetration of foreign markets with relative unconcern for current earnings, even in a recessionary environment. By contrast, growth, development, and the ability to compete over market share are all less stable for U.S. firms because they are subject to the vicissitudes of the business cycle. In relative terms, U.S. firms must be very profitable to attract or generate sufficient capital to grow and compete, because they lack the infrastructural advantages of a stable capital supply.

We may now infer the implications of the *domestic* Japanese market, industry, and financial structures for the *international* competitiveness of the Japanese semiconductor-electronics industry. As in numerous other Japanese industrial sectors, vertical integration, oligopolization, and rationalization stabilize the domestic market environment and permit the Japanese firms in this industry to build massive production volumes in devices and systems destined for export. Control over access further stabilizes the domestic market and prevents U.S. firms from consolidating their innovations and victories in the international marketplace into long-term advantage in the Japanese market. The domestic market thus serves as a stable mass-production base from which to launch penetration of foreign markets, particularly U.S. markets. Stability of capital secures the domestic base and underwrites the Japanese ability to bear short-run adjustment costs in order to gain increasing shares of foreign markets over the long run. In brief, domestic Japanese systemic strengths have helped create a formidable international competitor in semiconductor markets.

The competitive advantages which the industry's structure and the structure of Japanese business and finance offer Japanese semiconductor-electronics firms mesh neatly with Japanese government policies aimed at assisting the industry's development. During the last decade, Japanese government *promotional* policies aimed at restructuring the domestic industry, along with *protectionist* trade policies aimed at limiting foreign access to the domestic market, have nurtured the international competitiveness of the domestic industry. The next sub-section examines the character of this interaction between the industry and the state during the 1970s.

State Action and the Promotion of International Competitiveness

By 1968 the Japanese semiconductor-electronics industry was almost completely dominated by production for consumer products. The industry was weak in IC capability, and IC production accounted for only about $24 million out of a semiconductor production of some $252 million, and a total component production of some $1.4 billion.[86] By 1978, roughly half of Japanese semiconductor consumption was still in the consumer area, but production for computer and telecommunications needs had brought Japanese firms near international state-of-the-art capability in IC, and especially LSI MOS memory production. IC production accounted for some $1.2 billion out of a semiconductor production of some $2.4 billion and a total components production of some $8.75 billion.[87] Here we shall examine the role played by the Japanese government as doorman and promoter in this rise of the domestic semiconductor-electronics industry to international competitive prominence.

Recall that we have characterized the U.S. semiconductor industry's development as dynamically driven by the interaction between technological innovation and market development. The attractive growth potential of new markets opened up by diffusion of technological innovations—generated to meet the needs first of the military and then of the computer and consumer markets—has been a central dynamic. By contrast, the relative weakness of Japanese markets in computers and telecommunications, and the complete lack of military demand, meant that the domestic semiconductor industry's development was not pulled toward innovation except in consumer products. This situation posed a central dilemma for Japanese policy-makers. Under conditions of free trade and open market access, they faced a risk that U.S. firms might dominate domestic Japanese markets in semiconductors, computers, and telecommunications. If they protected their markets and denied U.S. firms open access, they risked severe technological backwardness in those sectors. The solution the policy-makers chose was characteristic of postwar Japanese development strategy. They used trade policy to limit foreign penetration of the domestic market while deploying a range of financial and promotional policies to assist the industry's growth. Simultaneously, Japanese firms purchased huge amounts of foreign technology, mostly from the United States, and used their strength in consumer products to subsidize a limited price competition with U.S. firms in international semiconductor markets. Only after 1975, when Japanese

---

[86]Figures are from Japan Electronics Industry Development Association (the predecessor to the present Japan EIA).

[87]BA 1979, pp. 83 and 48; *yen* conversion at 212:1 for 1978.

firms had grown in their technological competence and domestic market dominance, did the government begin to move toward a partial dismantling of the restrictions on foreign penetration.

In 1968 the estimated percentage share of Japanese firms in their domestic semiconductor market was as follows.[88]

Hitachi	23%	Kobe Kogyo	3%
Toshiba	21	Mitsubishi	3
Matsushita	15	Sony	2
Sanyo	13	Fujitsu	1
NEC	7	Other, including imports	12

This list suggests the extreme degree to which Japanese production was dominated by a consumer-electronics orientation. Note in particular that NEC, the industry's largest producer of semiconductors and integrated circuits at the end of the 1970s, had only a 7 percent market share in 1968. At that time also, NEC was the Japanese industry's largest producer of ICs, which suggests the degree to which IC production was a relatively insignificant segment of total semiconductor production. Note also that Fujitsu, Japan's largest computer manufacturer in 1980, accounted for only 1 percent of semiconductor production in 1968. Fujitsu did not produce semiconductors for consumer-product markets until its merger in 1968 with Kobe Kogyo, which again suggests that firms which did not produce semiconductors for consumer products could not grow effectively in the 1960s.[89] In 1968, consumer products dominated the industry's electronic systems sales, accounting for at least 60 percent of production. The significance of this domination for Japanese semiconductor production cannot be overemphasized. NEC began limited commercial production of the integrated circuit and the MOS transistor only one year after their commercial introduction by Texas Instruments and Fairchild in the United States. However, with no significant military or computer demand to stimulate the production and innovation of those devices, they remained a relatively insignificant part of Japanese semiconductor production. Thus, by 1968, with a limited IC production worth only $24 million, Japanese semiconductor production was serving its consumer systems strength, and its capability in advanced ICs was weak. It has been estimated that by the end of the 1960s Japanese firms had achieved only rough technological parity with U.S. firms in producing ICs with under 100

[88]Source is John E. Tilton, reprinted in FTC, *Staff Report*, p. 33. Kobe Kogyo and Fujitsu merged in 1968.

[89]On NEC and Fujitsu's orientation, see John E. Tilton, *International Diffusion of Technology* (Washington, D.C.: Brookings Institution, 1971), pp. 143, 145.

gates.[90] Japanese firms lagged in basic LSI research and capabilities, and they were simply not an important factor in international competition.

The Japanese developmental strategy of creating comparative advantage in advanced technology sectors centered in this period on promoting the domestic computer industry.[91] Earlier attempts at promotion had been relatively unsuccessful, and innovation by U.S. firms in integrated circuit technology threatened to increase the U.S. advantage in computers. If the Japanese development strategy was to succeed, Japan needed a competitive semiconductor sector. Thus, during the 1960s and the early to mid-1970s the Japanese government, principally through MITI, sought to build a competitive semiconductor industry by limiting foreign competition in the domestic market and acquiring foreign technology and know-how. Foreign investment laws created after the war required the Japanese government to review for approval all applications for direct foreign investment in Japan. The government consistently rejected all applications for wholly owned subsidiaries and for joint ventures in which foreign firms would hold majority ownership. It also restricted foreign purchases of equity in Japanese semiconductor firms. Simultaneously, the government limited foreign import penetration of the home market through high tariffs and restrictive quotas and through approval-registration requirements on advanced IC devices in particular. For example, until 1974, ICs that contained more than 200 circuit elements simply could not be imported without special permission. Penetration was also managed by exclusionary customs procedures and "Buy Japanese" procurement and "jawboning" policies.[92]

The price that U.S. firms paid to gain limited access to the Japanese market was to allow licensing of their advanced technology and know-how. This, too, was regulated closely by the Japanese government, whose approval was required on all patent and technical-assistance licensing agreements. Since MITI controlled access to the Japanese market and its approval was required for the implementation of licensing deals, it was in the powerful monopsonist's position of being able to dictate the terms of exchange. Its general policy was simple and effective. It required foreign firms to license all Japanese firms requesting access to a particular technology. It limited royalty payments by Japanese firms to a single rate on each deal, thereby pre-empting the competitive bidding-up of royalty rates among Japanese firms. In line with the characteristic emphasis on export strategy, MITI often linked the

[90]Estimate from industry sources.
[91]Helm, "The Japanese Computer Industry," documents this strategy.
[92]On the above points, see Tilton in FTC, *Staff Report*, p. 146; Gresser, *High Technology*, pp. 15, 45, 93 (n.42), 95 (n.46); and Finan, *International Transfer of Technology*, p. 95.

import of particular technologies to the acquiring firm's ability to develop export products using that technology.[93] MITI also conditioned approval of certain deals on the willingness of the involved Japanese firms to diffuse their own technical developments, through sub-license agreements, to other Japanese firms. The total result of these policies was a controlled diffusion of advanced technology throughout the Japanese semiconductor industry. Tilton gives a convincing measure of the extent to which Japanese firms depended on the acquisition of U.S. technology: by the end of the 1960s, Japanese IC producers were paying at least 10 percent of their semiconductor sales revenues as royalties to U.S. firms—2 percent to Western Electric, 4.5 percent to Fairchild, and 3.5 percent to Texas Instruments.[94]

Royalty income may have been substantial for a number of U.S. firms, but market access (with one notable exception) was ephemeral indeed. Diffusion of advanced technology meant an on-going Japanese catch-up, during the 1960s and 1970s, to successive generations of technological innovation by U.S. firms. As this occurred, domestic Japanese production displaced U.S. imports, and U.S. firms maintained Japanese market share only by shifting the composition of their imports toward products that Japanese firms were not yet producing themselves. (The implications of this will be discussed later.)

The one successful entry into the Japanese market by a U.S. firm came when Texas Instruments (TI) reached agreement with Sony on a joint venture in 1968. In fact, TI's entry strategy was really a replication of IBM's earlier success at establishing a wholly owned subsidiary in Japan in 1960 by giving the subsidiary the use of its industry-leading technology. Indeed, government's system of control over technology was developed in response to IBM's success at penetrating and then dominating the Japanese computer market. The Japanese did not want to allow IBM's success to be repeated by other foreign firms in other sectors—especially a sector as crucial as semiconductors. In that light, the Texas Instruments story is significant for what it reveals about Japanese government policies, attitudes, and strategy in this period.

Texas Instruments petitioned the Japanese government for a wholly owned subsidiary in the early 1960s, and was offered a minority-share joint venture, which it rejected. Its chief bargaining chip during these negotiations was its continuing refusal to license its critical IC patents to Japanese firms without gaining in return a substantial production subsidiary in Japan. NEC and the other firms sub-licensed to it were in fact producing ICs based on technology developed by TI and Fairchild,

[93]Helm, "The Japanese Computer Industry," p. 76.
[94]Tilton in FTC, *Staff Report*, p. 148.

through an NEC-Fairchild licensing agreement. However, because the TI-Fairchild patent accord explicitly excluded Japan, those Japanese firms were not protected, as Fairchild licensees were in Europe, against patent-infringement suits brought by TI. The Japanese government stalled approval of TI's patent application in Japan, and this enabled NEC and the other firms to play domestic technology catch-up, thereby forcing TI to negotiate for quicker access. The Japanese government then held up Japanese exports of IC-based systems to the United States because TI threatened infringement action. A compromise was finally reached in which TI got a 50 percent share of a joint venture with Sony. In return, it agreed to license its IC patents to NEC, Hitachi, Mitsubishi, Toshiba, and Sony, and agreed further to limit its future share of the Japanese semiconductor market to not more than 10 percent. TI bought Sony's share of the joint venture in 1972, and through 1980 remained the only U.S. merchant firm with a wholly owned manufacturing subsidiary in Japan.[95]

The strategy of technological diffusion and limited market access, implied in the TI story and elaborated before, enabled Japanese firms roughly to mimic technological developments in the United States. However, the pace of semiconductor innovation in the United States was accelerating, driven by the computer market, and Japanese semiconductor-computer firms were lagging far behind. This was occurring, moreover, despite a decade or more of Japanese government promotional policies aimed at the development of a domestic computer sector that could pull semiconductor capability into rapid growth. These policies included the creation of a specialized infrastructure of advisory bureaus, promotional institutions and laboratories, preferential government procurement, credit allocation and tax incentives, and direct and indirect research and development subsidization.[96] As Gresser summarizes: "By 1969 it was obvious that the six major computer and semiconductor manufacturers were operating inefficiently. MITI well understood that if the Japanese firms continued to produce similar systems for a domestic market a fraction of the size of the U.S. market, the Japanese industry would not be able to compete internationally despite the most generous government asistance. MITI therefore decided to expedite the development of core technologies and to realign the industry."[97]

Through 1970, direct Japanese government subsidization of advanced IC and production-technology research and development by

[95]Based on Tilton, *International Diffusion of Technology*, pp. 146–147.
[96]These policies are elaborated in Gresser, *High Technolgoy*, pp. 22–23 and 88–91 and notes 27–41.
[97]Gresser, *High Technology*, p. 16.

Japanese firms was not significant, although significant basic research was carried out in government and NTT laboratories. Moreover, private company funding of research and development was not at all competitive with U.S. company spending. Indeed, in the early 1970s, combined spending by Fujitsu, Hitachi, and NEC on semiconductor *and* computer research and development was less than that of Texas Instruments.[98] It was, then, toward greater subsidization and coordination of research and development in computer, LSI, and production technology that the government turned in order to pull Japanese firms toward greater international competitiveness.

In 1971 the Japanese government introduced a national policy for the promotion of certain industries, which targeted the development of advanced technologies. This Law for Provisional Measures to Promote Specific Electronic and Machinery Industries designated three strategic categories: (1) advanced technologies needing direct R&D support— especially technologies like LSI, where Japanese firms lagged considerably behind U.S. firms; (2) production technologies, like those demanded in LSI production, which were intimately linked to device-system cost, quality, and performance; and (3) high-volume production technologies. MITI was given responsibility for financing research and development and rationalizing production. By 1977 over sixty different projects had received total financial support in the several hundred-million-dollar range, in such areas as E-beam exposure and LSI production equipment, high performance discrete devices, basic materials research, low power-high performance ICs, and VLSI.

MITI's attempt at restructuring the domestic Japanese industry was centered on promoting internationally competitive computer production. The target of the reorganization attempt was IBM's 370, which dominated world mainframe computer sales and used IC but not LSI technology. Significant entry into world computer markets could be gained by leapfrogging and introducing an LSI-based computer system. Semiconductor research and development funding was aimed, therefore, at final usage in next-generation computers. It was hoped that once a growing and competitive computer sector took off, its needs would stimulate semiconductor development. The six major semiconductor-computer manufacturers were accordingly the focus of MITI's attempt at structural realignment.[99]

In 1971 the six semiconductor-computer firms formed three paired groups: Fujitsu-Hitachi, NEC-Toshiba, and Mitsubishi-Oki. Through

[98]Thomas Hout and Ira Magaziner, *Japanese Industrial Policy* (Berkeley: Institute for International Studies, 1981), p. 83.
[99]Based on Gresser, *High Technology*, pp. 16–17, and Mackintosh, *Microelectronics in the 1980s*, p. 18.

205

these pairings MITI hoped to force a specialization of development efforts and long-term competitive segmentation of the computer market. Toward that end, each group received subsidies totaling some 200 million dollars between 1972 and 1976. Also in 1971, MITI and Japan's Electronics Industry Association formed an LSI cartel among the ten major semiconductor producers. Its purposes were to standardize LSI basic structures and packages, to streamline and standardize manufacturing processes, and to develop LSI test equipment.[100] This cartel may indeed have been the seedbed for the device specialization among the major Japanese firms that we discussed earlier.

These efforts to shift semiconductor production and development to meet the needs of Japan's fledgling computer industry must be located within the context of a continuing demand pull from consumer electronic markets. Through 1979 discrete semiconductor devices and linear integrated circuits, both used in consumer products, accounted for well over 50 percent of the value of Japanese domestic semiconductor production. Moreover, all of the major producers except Fujitsu were heavily involved in calculators and consumer linear ICs.[101] During the late 1960s, the move abroad of major U.S. semiconductor and consumer electronic companies undercut part of the Japanese comparative advantage in electronic consumer products. As LSI technology penetrated consumer product markets in the early 1970s, particularly in calculators and watches, the U.S. shift abroad and the relative technological weakness of Japanese producers presented a serious challenge to their strength in international consumer markets. The case of calculators is suggestive. In 1971 Japanese firms held approximately 85 percent of the domestic U.S. market for calculators. By 1974, under severe price competition from U.S. producers, that share fell to 25 percent. At the beginning of the period, Japanese firms like Sharp, Sanyo, Canon, and Casio entered into long-term contracts with Rockwell, GI, Texas Instruments, and Fairchild for calculator chips and technical assistance to close the technology gap. Also during that period, the largest Japanese semiconductor producers capitalized on their emerging, MITI-coordinated, LSI capability to produce competitive calculator chips. After 1974, when semiconductor-calculator technology stabilized and production costs equalized, the Japanese share of the U.S. market began to rise again.[102]

By the end of 1975, the cooperative computer efforts, MITI's subsidization and coordination of research and development for LSI, and

---

[100]Gresser, *High Technology*, p. 19; Hout and Magaziner, *Japanese Industrial Policy*, p. 84; and Helm, "The Japanese Computer Industry," p. 34.

[101]BA 1979, pp. 96, 110, 128.

[102]The calculator data are largely from CRT, pp. 4–36 to 4–39.

shifting demand in the consumer-product market had succeeded in raising the value of the industry's IC portion of domestic semiconductor production from 27 percent in 1971 to about 42 percent.[103] While MITI's promotion of LSI capability had worked well, its attempt to consolidate the computer operations of the six semiconductor-computer companies had largely failed. The attempt at consolidation did produce joint *marketing* ventures, notably (in 1974) NEC–Toshiba Information Systems (NTIS) and Fujitsu-Hitachi's ACOM-HITAC; and coordinated research and development had benefited each of the participating firms. However, there was continuing strong competition in computer systems products between the three groups and between each group's members, and the six firms remained largely independent. More important, by mid-1975 it was clear that the MITI-industry effort to leapfrog into an internationally competitive position in computers had fallen victim to changes in the international computer market.

The most significant market development was the introduction by U.S. computer companies of low-cost, LSI-based plug-compatible mainframes (PCM). PCMs were made economically possible by advances in LSI technology and the continuing decline in cost per function generated by them. They offered superior performance per dollar and generally used IBM's software. PCMs thereby reinforced IBM's international dominance in software, and consolidated for U.S. firms the LSI-based international computer market-segment toward which *Japanese* efforts had been aimed. Innovation in the market thereby rendered Japanese goals obsolete. This point is important, for it reveals a potential competitive weakness amid this Japanese industry's high-volume production strategy (discussed earlier). Quite simply, competitive innovations in the market can lay waste to massive sunk investment in the production of devices and systems based on an older technology. Of course, the ability of Japanese firms to recuperate in their controlled domestic market and to draw on stable sources of capital can mitigate the long-term impact of competitive innovations from abroad (as we shall explain in the next section). In any case, if Japanese computer companies wanted to break into the international market for computers in a big way, they were going to have to do so on the basis of the next generation of semiconductor-computer technology—VLSI. (Note that a complementary response would be acquisition of a growing PCM firm, which Fujitsu did with Amdahl in 1976.)

It is within the context of these events that MITI's liberalization of some of the restrictions on foreign access to the Japanese market in semiconductors and computers, announced on December 24, 1975,

---

[103]Percentages are estimated from figures in Commerce Dept., *Report*, p. 82.

must be understood. During the previous four years of market protection and industry promotion, Japanese semiconductor-computer firms had developed a significant LSI capability, and by 1976 they dominated their domestic market in all but the most advanced IC devices. They had also succeeded in raising their share of the domestic installed base of general-purpose digital computers to over 60 percent. They were thus in a dominant position in their domestic market at a time when the issue of a protected domestic base from which to enter international competition in LSI-based mainframes had been rendered moot by international market developments. Liberalization of trade in components and computers, with continued structural control over the character and composition of penetration, thus made sense—especially when combined with a program of promotion aimed at VLSI. Moreover, liberalization also made great political sense because the industrialized West was in the midst of a mid-decade cycle of recession and recovery, and Japan was exporting excess domestic capacity in several economic sectors (such as steel and consumer electronics). The beginning clamor in the United States and Europe for domestic protection against Japanese imports could be best countered by liberalizing access to the Japanese market. In preparation for liberalization and the push toward advanced LSI, the Japanese semiconductor-computer industry regrouped in late 1975.[104] Fujitsu, Hitachi, and Mitsubishi formed a joint venture, called Computer Development Industries, Ltd., to develop VLSI and the next generation of computer prototypes. Mitsubishi also joined with Hitachi and Fujitsu in their MITI-sponsored research, and Oki, no longer among the elect, split off to specialize in terminals. Also in 1975, NTT formed an LSI group with Hitachi, Fujitsu, and NEC to develop advanced communications systems. Just after liberalization, the corporate articles of NEC-Toshiba Information Systems were amended to emphasize VLSI development, and a VLSI lab was established within NTIS. Finally, of course, MITI, NTT, and the five major semiconductor-computer firms organized the VLSI project, and in March 1976 they formed the VLSI Technology Research Association.

We should note here that the movement toward trade liberalization in Japan, quite apart from the debt it owes to pressure from the United States, marks a divergence between the strategies of Japanese businesses and the Japanese government. The movement toward trade liberalization should be seen in part as the result of Japanese business opposition to MITI's continuing protection. As Japanese firms grow in

---

[104] The following is from Gresser, pp. 7, 17–18, 20. Gresser does not, of course, situate either the regrouping of the industry or his description of liberalization within the domestic and international market context that we have eleaborated above.

international competitive power, they view MITI's protectionist policies, which can generate retaliation, as a probable limitation on their ability to expand competitively abroad. How far formal liberalization goes will depend in part upon the extent to which such pressure from Japanese business prevails.[105] We remain skeptical about the extent and impact of liberalization, however, especially given the collaborative ability of some Japanese firms to play the role of doorman. To the extent that an industry like semiconductors, through its successful development, begins in this way to slip away from state control, state *promotional* policies provide a continuing opportunity to re-assert the government presence.

In this context, the trade liberalization of 1976—contemporaneous with the Japanese industry's regrouping—was ambiguous. Gresser summarizes:

> Foreign capital investment was greatly expedited and the burdensome import quota system was eliminated. Trade and investment in computers was completely liberalized on schedule by April 1976. . . . The Cabinet released the following statement . . . "the Government . . . will keep an eye on movements in the computer market so that liberalization will not adversely affect domestic producers nor produce confusion."
>
> To mitigate liberalization, the government expanded its support for research and development of "core" technologies; foreign penetration of the Japanese market was checked, principally by limiting foreign procurement opportunities and by other administrative means.[106]

Such policies for mitigating the impact of liberalization have generally continued in force. Moreover, as suggested earlier, the ability of the largest Japanese semiconductor firms to collaborate in playing the role of doorman acts structurally to mitigate the impact of liberalization on the domestic market. In the late 1970s, then, both trade policy and industry structure combined to regulate access to the domestic market for semiconductors.

The VLSI program was the major *promotional* vehicle to assist the competitiveness of the Japanese semiconductor-computer firms during the late 1970s. As suggested before, the program was aimed at developing semiconductor technology for the next generation of computers. This meant developing state-of-the-art capability in the production of both memory devices and logic circuits. Figure 1 gives a rough organizational picture of the project.[107] The stated aims of the project were:

---

[105] The preceding is based on correspondence with T. J. Pempel.
[106] Gresser, *High Technology,* p. 20.
[107] Hout and Magaziner, *Japanese Industrial Policy,* p. 104.

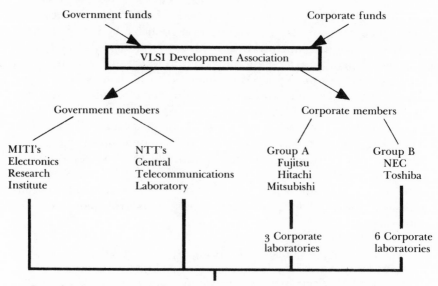

Central Laboratory at MITI's Institute (in close co-operation with respective supporting laboratories)

Figure 1: Very large scale integration project. Redrawn from Thomas Hout and Ira Magaziner, *Japanese Industrial Policy* (Berkeley: Institute for International Studies, 1981), p. 104.

(1) development of micro-fabrication methods to handle sub-micron lithography, especially electron-beam lithography; (2) development of low-defect large-diameter silicon wafer substrates; (3) development of improved computer-aided design technology; (4) development of improved LSI micro-fabrication processing techniques and equipment: (5) development of VLSI evaluation and testing techniques and equipment; and (6) definition of logic and memory devices that could utilize 1–5.

As this list suggests, much of the VLSI program was aimed at catching up to the U.S. industry's capabilities in advanced IC process technology. Toward that end, as described at the beginning of this chapter, a significant portion of the program's funding was spent in the United States to purchase production and test equipment. Such purchases were not surprising, for in the first years of the VLSI program, imports of foreign (mostly U.S.) production equipment accounted for an estimated 70 to 80 percent share of the domestic Japanese market. Japan's indigenous capital equipment industry for semiconductor manufacture is still relatively small, but its fastest growing segment appears to be controlled by the major Japanese semiconductor producers. Since the import share of production equipment fell to about 50 percent in 1980, one result of the VLSI program was a strengthening of the domestic

Japanese infrastructure in production and test capabilities.[108] Indeed, the general manager of NEC's VLSI development division admitted, for example, that his firm would have had to spend five times as much on the development of electron-beam technology without the VLSI program.[109]

An equally important impact of public subsidies and nonduplicative research coordination in the VLSI program was the release of company funds for capacity expansion (and eventual penetration of the U.S. market). In 1977, the top six Japanese semiconductor producers spent a total of some $116 million on new plant and equipment. That figure rose to an estimated $212 million in 1978, with NEC accounting for $66 million and Fujitsu for $42 million.[110] Most of the investment made by NEC and Fujitsu went to build IC and especially MOS RAM production capacity. In 1979, investment spending by the top ten semiconductor producers in Japan climbed to an estimated $420 million dollars. This pattern of heavy spending was a response to increasing demand in the domestic Japanese market and to rapidly growing export opportunities, which were carefully nourished by Japanese companies.

The exploitation of export opportunities was particularly apparent in the domestic U.S. market. During the first two years of the VLSI program, the major Japanese firms (led by NEC and Fujitsu) rapidly built up a distribution system in the United States. Prior to 1976, major U.S. distributors had been hesitant to serve Japanese producers who could not meet commitments for large volumes and continuous supplies of high-margin memory and MPU devices. This situation changed as the Japanese rapidly expanded production capacity and advanced their technology. By the middle of 1977, NEC, Fujitsu, Hitachi, and Toshiba were all moving toward broad-based distribution channels, which were frequently managed by marketing experts recruited from U.S. companies. NEC, Fujitsu, and Hitachi each set up wholly owned domestic U.S. subsidiaries for marketing LSI products. Toshiba sold its LSI devices through a sales group of original equipment manufacturers attached to Toshiba America Corporation. NEC and Fujitsu each developed extensive ties to a large number of U.S. distributors, which gave them access to most regions of the country. By the beginning of 1978, when MOS memory demand jumped in the United States, Japanese firms were well placed to take advantage of the situation.[111]

[108] BA 1979, p. 122; BA 1980, p. 137.

[109] *The Economist*, April 5, 1980, p. 75.

[110] BA 1979, p. 133, and BA 1980, pp. 136–138, 153. *Yen*/dollar conversions are 274:1 for 1977, 212:1 for 1978, and 250:1 for 1979.

[111] *Electronics News*, December 6, 1976, p. II–33; April 18, 1977, pp. 1, 4; October 17, 1977, p. 56; January 30, 1970, p. 58.

Japanese firms could take advantage of export opportunities in the U.S. market because the growth of production for their own domestic market had brought them toward international state-of-the-art capability by the late 1970s. Tables 7, 8, and 9 compare the composition of domestic Japanese IC *production,* by units and value, in 1974 and 1978; the composition of Japanese IC *consumption,* by units and value, in 1979; and the percentage of Japanese IC consumption in 1979 by major market segments.

These three tables reveal important shifts in the growth and composition of Japanese production. The quantity and value of Japanese IC production almost tripled from 1974 to 1978. Linear ICs as a percentage of unit production rose to 53 percent. Note that linear ICs are relatively low value-added devices. Since most linear ICs are consumer devices, the growth in their production suggests the continued demand pull of the *consumer* electronics market on the composition of Japanese IC production. Indeed, as Table 9 suggests, consumer electronics, calculators, and watches consumed approximately 50 percent of the ICs that entered the domestic market. The continuing importance of consumer IC consumption and the associated high percentage of linear ICs in the Japanese production mix have important implications for the international competitiveness of Japanese firms. As W. E. Steinmueller has noted, "ICs are not in the forefront of technical advance or potential. . . . [They] do not provide the basis for building Japanese technological parity or advantage in world IC markets. Linear IC production may [however] be an important testing ground for automated assembly or other 'post-fabrication' operations. [Moreover], capacity in linear production is not easily retooled to produce digital ICs."[112] To the extent that the consumer sector continues to influence the mix of Japanese IC production, Japanese firms will be forced to allocate their resources to lower value-added production for consumer markets. Moreover, since 69 percent of consumer electronics production is exported, and international demand fluctuates over time, the inability to retool production capacity may have a cyclical impact on the earnings of Japanese firms.

The consumer market in Japan has centered on the consumption of television sets, stereo components, tape recorders, and recently videotape recorders. The video disc is the next big consumer growth item for both the domestic and the export markets. The 1980 Bank of America study estimates that the domestic production value of video discs in 1982 could be worth about $800 million. This would imply a

---

[112] W. E. Steinmueller, "Studies of U.S. and Japanese Semiconductor Producers—An Overview" (Stanford University, April 1980), pp. 12–13.

Table 7. Volume and value of domestic Japanese production of integrated circuits (ICs), 1974 and 1979, by type of IC

Type of IC	1974				1979			
	Units (millions)	Value Percent of units	(millions of dollars)[a]	Percent of value	Units (millions)	Value Percent of units	(millions of dollars)[b]	Percent of value
Linear	154	45.0%	$110	25.2%	561	53%	$ 363	29.0%
Digital	152	45.0	273	62.3	450	42	769	61.0
Bipolar	106	32.5	109	25.0	222	21	183	14.6
MOS	46	13.5	163	37.0	228	21	585	46.4
Hybrid	34	10.0	54	12.4	52	5	126	10.0
All ICs	340	100.0%	$439	100.0%	1,063	100%	$1,260	100.0%

NOTE: Figures may not add to totals given because of rounding.
[a]Yen/dollar conversion at 286:1 in 1974.
[b]Yen/dollar conversion at 212:1 in 1978.
SOURCE: BA Asia Ltd., 1979, pp. 89–94.

Table 8. Volume and value of domestic Japanese consumption of integrated circuits (ICs), 1979, by type of IC

Type of IC	Units (millions)	Percent of units	Value (millions of dollars)	Percent of value
Consumer linear	700	34%	$ 300	19%
Other linear	150	7	80	5
Digital bipolar	550	27	304	19
Digital MOS	576	28	760	47
Hybrid ICs	80	4	160	10
All ICs	2,056	100%	$1,604	100%

NOTE: Yen/dollar conversion at 250:1.
SOURCE: BA Asia Ltd., 1980, p. 113.

semiconductor content of some $40 million. With additional continued demand from the calculator and watch markets, it is likely that consumer product markets will continue to exert a strong influence on Japanese semiconductor production, thereby slanting it in the directions suggested above.

The continuing importance of consumer production must be viewed in the context of the rapid growth of digital IC capability between 1974 and 1978. As Table 7 suggests, those years witnessed a rapid changeover from concentration on digital bipolar production to concentration on MOS. (Recall that a comparable changeover occurred by 1975 in the United States.) The relative de-emphasis of bipolar production suggests a strategic evaluation of where the best prospects lie for rapid growth and international competitiveness of Japanese production. The most important market factor in the growth of MOS production was Japan's burgeoning computer industry, which by 1979 accounted for 35 percent of domestic Japanese IC consumption. MOS production is the fastest growing and highest value-added segment of the IC production mix. Moreover, unlike linear ICs, MOS memory ICs are complex circuits that require technically sophisticated design and production capabilities. Technical sophistication here is transferable to the design and production of other complex products, and thereby posed problems for the international competitiveness of Japanese firms. Thus, while the consumer market pulls Japanese producers toward technological complacency, the computer market pulls them toward technological advance. Indeed, the rapid growth of MOS LSI capability to serve domestic computer demand increasingly displaced complex MOS imports to the Japanese market, and forced U.S. firms to shift the composition mix of their exports to supply devices not yet produced in quantity in Japan. Equally important, by 1978 that growth had enabled Japanese firms to enter the U.S. markets for MOS memory and microprocessor devices.

Table 9. Domestic Japanese IC consumption, 1979, by major market segment

Market segment	Percent of consumption
Consumer	29%
Computer	35
Communications	6
Test and measurement	2
Calculators	11
Other (including watches, automotive)	17
Total	100%

SOURCE: BA Asia Ltd., 1980, p. 113.

The domestic computer market in 1978 and 1979, by sales value of the major producers, is given in Table 10. The increasing market share taken by domestic firms will probably continue through the 1980s, with a resulting favorable impact on the technological competitiveness of these Japanese semiconductor firms.

Demand from the growing telecommunications sector also stimulated Japanese LSI capability during the middle to late 1970s, and this growth was intimately tied to the policies of Nippon Telephone and Telegraph (NTT). NTT buys almost all of its equipment from NEC, Hitachi, Fujitsu, and Oki (the Big Four) and has also played the characteristic role of doorman for telecommunications. Until the very end of the 1970s, NTT's procurement was completely closed to foreign firms; moreover, it did not allow the Big Four to use imported semiconductors in the equipment they supplied to them. Hout and Magaziner describe the promotional character of NTT's impact on technological development and market rationalization: "NTT makes all decisions on technical specifications, and engineers of the Big Four manufacturers are invited to develop new equipment partly after basic research is completed by NTT's own engineers. Therefore, all research and development expenses incurred by manufacturers are mostly application and production related. . . . NTT assigns actual production and supply to each manufacturer, depending upon availability of technical capacity and actual performance of the company on past assignments."[113] Under such guidance, the production value of communication equipment rose steadily from under $2 billion in 1973 to over $2.6 billion in 1977.[114] The Bank of America study estimates that communication equipment consumed approximately $235 million worth of semiconductors in 1978,

[113] Hout and Magaziner, *Japanese Industrial Policy*, p. 108.
[114] BA 1979, p. 57, and for the following figures, p. 35.

Table 10. Japanese domestic computer sales, 1978 and 1979, by company (in billions of yen and millions of dollars)

Company	1978		1979	
	Yen	Dollars	Yen	Dollars
Fujitsu	Y303	$1,420	Y340	$1,360
Hitachi	190	896	220	880
NEC	167	787	200	800
Mitsubishi	45	212	53	212
Oki	48	226	50	200
Toshiba	60	283	55	226
IBM Japan	315	1,480	324	1,290

SOURCE: BA Asia Ltd., 1980, p. 47.

NOTE: Yen/dollar conversions are 274:1 for 1977, 212:1 for 1978, and 250:1 for 1979. The fall of the yen versus the dollar in 1979 accounts for the rise in yen value and the decline in dollar value between 1978 and 1979.

with NEC and Fujitsu combined accounting for about 35 percent of that total.

Apart from financing and directing research and development, NTT also helps indirectly to finance exports. Since NTT negotiates its equipment purchases on a cost plus basis, it acts to provide "monopoly-like" prices somewhat as U.S. military purchases do. The exclusion of foreign procurement stabilizes prices and production volumes. NTT also advances part of the purchase price, thereby providing interest-free loans to the manufacturer. The result is great flexibility in export pricing. As Hout and Magaziner describe the resulting export growth during the 1970s: "Japanese companies got off to a late start in telecommunications exports, in large part because of their undistinguished technology. However, the boom in the OPEC and developing Asian markets in the middle and late 1970s, combined with lower growth at home, brought them into export markets. Exports, only 8 percent of sales in the early 1970s, are now 18–20 percent."[115] The international markets developed during the 1970s can be expected to grow significantly during the 1980s, with a resulting favorable impact on the technological sophistication of the largest semiconductor producers.

The separate but rapid growth during the 1970s of the three markets discussed above—the consumer, computer, and telecommunications markets—produced conflicting demands on the major Japanese semiconductor-electronic firms. In conjunction with the MITI and NTT promotional policy actions, the various demands of rapid growth have

[115] This paragraph and the quotation are from Hout and Magaziner, *Japanese Industrial Policy,* p. 108.

also been responsible for the specialization of product and semiconductor technology among Japanese firms described at the beginning of this section.

Through most of the 1970s, Japanese government policies limited foreign access to the domestic market and ensured that the advantages of rapid domestic growth would accrue mostly to domestic Japanese firms. Growth was underwritten partly through public subsidies but mostly through the stable access to capital delivered by the structure of domestic Japanese business and finance.

By 1978, a decade of Japanese government assistance and protectionist policies had finally coalesced with the growth of domestic IC markets to create a strong domestic semiconductor sector. Moreover, the industry was rapidly expanding its export penetration of important and growing international electronics markets, which further strengthened its semiconductor capability. Through its industry structure and market power, the Japanese semiconductor industry dominated its domestic market, and achieved near state-of-the-art capability in the fastest growing segments of the international IC market. For the first time in history, major Japanese IC firms were positioned to enter world MOS LSI memory markets on a roughly equal technological footing with their U.S. merchant competitors. In the next section we shall analyze the ways in which the entry has altered the character of competition in the international market for semiconductors.

INTERNATIONAL COMPETITION IN INTEGRATED CIRCUITS: U.S. AND JAPANESE STRATEGY AND STRUCTURE

As we have seen, the U.S. and Japanese semiconductor industries proceeded along separate lines of market development in relative isolation from one another during the period 1960–1976. To oversimplify slightly, the Japanese were not capable of penetrating the U.S. market in any significant way, and Japanese state policy permitted U.S. firms neither direct investment nor significant market share in Japan. By the late 1970s, however, the Japanese had successfully established a thriving domestic IC sector to serve growing domestic computer and telecommunications needs. These needs could only be met by producing more sophisticated IC devices like those which dominated IC markets in the United States and Europe, and in which, of course, U.S. producers were pre-eminent. This growing convergence in demand for advanced ICs between international and Japanese markets provided the basis upon which international competition between U.S. and Japanese IC producers accelerated in the late 1970s.

217

Japanese Entry and Systemic Strengths in International Competition

From their secured domestic base, the leading Japanese firms entered those international markets at the leading edge of IC memory devices whose standardized commodity-product character had been developed and dominated by U.S. merchant firms. The value of Japanese IC exports to the United States rose from about $50 million in 1977 to just under $300 million in 1980.[116] The value of Japanese IC exports to Europe rose from $12 million in 1976 to about $165 million in 1980.[117] Although Japanese IC firms had clearly matured enough to expand competitively in international markets, they apparently chose not to accept the full brunt of competition in their domestic market. The *characteristic* pattern of organized import substitution continued to limit the domestic Japanese market opportunities of U.S. firms. The available evidence suggests that as Japanese demand for even the most advanced IC devices began to increase, the domestic Japanese market share held by U.S. firms tended to decline.[118] U.S. competitive advantages could not be consolidated into enduring market positions in Japan. Figure 2 gives a rough indication of the pattern of domestic Japanese IC consumption accounted for by imports from U.S.-controlled sources (domestic and offshore facilities combined).

If U.S. firms were consolidating their product innovation advantages into enduring market positions, we would expect the percentage of consumption accounted for by a progressively higher value-added mix of U.S. exports into Japan to increase. As Figure 2 indicates, this has not been the case; rather, a pattern of organized import substitution seems to exist. The rise in 1979 in the U.S.-controlled import share of Japanese IC consumption is accounted for, in particular, by an increase in 16K RAM sales (to be discussed below).[119] The decline in 1980 again seems to verify the general Japanese strategy discussed above.[120]

Given the controlled nature of access to the Japanese market, the competitive interaction of the U.S. and Japanese semiconductor industries in the late 1970s centered most crucially on Japanese entry to the domestic U.S. market for ICs. The most significant international market battle took place in the MOS memory market, and centered on the domestic U.S. market for 16K MOS RAMs. The price per bit equiva-

---

[116] Estimated from figures in *Fortune*, March 23, 1981, p. 116.
[117] *Business Week*, March 30, 1981, pp. 86–87.
[118] Based on conversations with industry sources.
[119] BA 1980, pp. xix–xx.
[120] The nature of the Japanese competitive challenge depends, as we have emphasized, on a judgment about the existence of a system of conscious and organized import substitution. The available evidence is consistent with our position, but the generation of data to test the proposition formally should be an objective of policy.

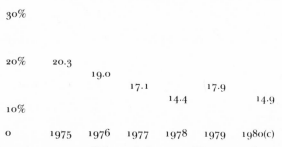

Figure 2: Estimated percentage of domestic Japanese IC consumption accounted for by U.S.-controlled imports into Japan, by value. Source: Author's estimates based on data in The Consulting Group, BA Asia Ltd., *The Japanese Semiconductor Industry 1980*, pp. 117, 123. Estimated percentages for 1975 and 1976 assume that the U.S.-controlled percentage of total Japanese imports remained roughly the same as in 1978 and 1979. The 1980 figure is an estimate based on industry sources. Actual numbers would have to be radically different to alter the general pattern described in the figure.

lency between 4K and 16K dynamic RAMs occurred in 1978 and with it came a significant and accelerating demand for 16K RAMs. On top of the demand generated by this crossover, IBM entered the merchant market with a huge demand for 16K RAMs to meet the memory needs created by the rapid market acceptance of its new series 4300 computer. The increasing demand for 16Ks was paired in the U.S. market with a significant production capacity shortfall. This stemmed largely from the failure or inability of merchant IC firms to invest in capacity expansion during the 1975 recession, and from their cautious investment policies following the recession. Here, of course, reliance on internal funds and equity markets constrained the business strategy choices of U.S. firms. By contrast, the stable availability of capital for Japanese firms permitted them to engage in a rapid capacity build-up that could support their export strategy. Indeed, in 1978 and 1979, the major Japanese firms strode, in force, into the market gap created by significant undersupply in the domestic U.S. memory market. By the end of 1979, they had taken 43 percent of the domestic U.S. 16K RAM market. Table 11 summarizes 16K RAM production in 1979, by major producer.

The 16K RAM story offers important insights into the ways in which the Japanese industry's *domestic* market structure and power give Japanese firms an advantage in international competition. First, in the ways described in the previous section, Japanese firms were better able than U.S. firms to add production capacity and pursue a high-volume production strategy because capital was available and Japanese firms could be relatively unconcerned with current earnings. Second, their characteristic rationalization of production apparently enabled the major

Table 11. World 16K RAM production, 1979, by firm (in thousands of units)

Leading firm	Units produced	Other firm	Units produced
Mostek	16,800	Fairchild	1,900
NEC[a]	11,300	ITT	1,700
TI	9,000	Mitsubishi[a]	1,250
Hitachi[a]	7,100	Siemens	875
Fujitsu[a]	6,500	Zilog	190
Motorola	4,700	Signetics	175
Toshiba[a]	3,475	AMD	65
Intel	3,250	Intersil	10
National	3,200	SGS-ATES	3

[a]Japanese firm.
SOURCE: Dataquest, Inc., January 1979.

Japanese firms to concentrate capacity expansion of the high-volume production of a single memory product—16K RAMs—destined for the U.S. market, while meeting their other product needs through specialization and trade between domestic firms. Third, since they exercised dominant market power over consumption in their domestic market, the major Japanese firms could play the role of doorman and control the growth and composition of imports entering their market. This meant two things. First, until late 1978 Japanese producers apparently used a two-tier pricing strategy. They kept RAM prices high in their controlled domestic market, thereby subsidizing their ability to offer lower prices in the U.S. market. (Prices only came down in response to the ITC's "dumping" investigation, initiated by SIA lobbying in the United States.)[121] More important, as domestic Japanese demand for 16K RAMs rose in 1978 and 1979, Japanese IC firms chose to let *imports* (mostly from U.S. firms) meet domestic Japanese demand—and by implication, to meet a part of their own consumption needs. This enabled Japanese producers to divert their own production to the United States in order to increase their share of the U.S. market. Thus, as we have seen, exports by U.S. firms of 16K RAMs to Japan actually *rose* in 1979.[122] Since the major Japanese producers of 16K RAMs have also dominated 16K RAM *consumption* in Japan, they have been able to limit and displace future U.S. imports; as we have suggested, this appears to have occurred in 1980. Since a parallel market power is not held by merchant U.S. firms in the domestic U.S. market, Japanese penetration in the United States will not be comparably limited and displaced. Thus, the cost to U.S. firms of temporarily increased access

[121] On pricing, see BA 1980, pp. xix–xx.
[122] *The Economist,* April 26, 1980, pp. 54–55; see also *Rosen Electronics Letter,* July 7, 1980, p. 59.

to the Japanese market is a significant and perhaps enduring Japanese presence in the domestic U.S. market. The Japanese firms also used the issue of higher quality as an extremely effective technique to help penetrate the U.S. RAM market. A number of U.S. consumers of Japanese 16K RAMs, notably Hewlett Packard and NCR, have suggested that the failure rates of the Japanese product were significantly lower than those of U.S. devices. Though U.S. devices met the quality standards of U.S. purchasers, there was an unexploited market demand for devices of even higher quality. Japanese producers correctly appraised the U.S. market and used a higher-quality penetration strategy to capture additional market share. On the one hand, consistently higher quality is generally more expensive to produce. Since, as described in the previous section, Japanese firms were relatively less constrained by a concern for current earnings than U.S. firms, they could afford to spend more on quality without increasing the prices they charged. The effect could be to penetrate the U.S. market through "dumping" high quality (because not reflected in component price), thereby evading the problem of price-triggered dumping accusations. On the other hand, quality is built into the production process. U.S. manufacturers, until the advent of Japanese competition over quality, had made a tacit decision that fast volume output, with component testing only to cover imperfections in the manufacturing process, was more important than high quality. The Japanese instead concentrated on perfecting their production process to deliver higher quality devices. As U.S. firms retool and expand capacity, they have apparently been "tweaking" their production process to meet higher quality standards.[123] It may well be, then, that the Japanese ability to use quality as a penetration strategy will not carry over to the next round of competition.

In sum, the 16K RAM market was the most significant battleground for U.S. and Japanese IC competition in the late 1970s. As we would expect the earlier discussion, the Japanese firms systematically used their controlled domestic market as a secure base from which to gain significant penetration of the U.S. market. Although the 16K RAM was a U.S. innovation, and U.S. merchant firms were the first volume producers of it, Japanese firms used their control over access to this domestic market to prevent U.S. firms from consolidating an initial lead in 16K RAMs into long-term advantage in the Japanese market. Instead, Japanese firms followed their characteristic strategy of exporting from a large-scale production base built in their secured home market, and thereby captured over 40 percent of the U.S. 16K RAM market. Stable availability of capital at home secured the Japanese domestic

---

[123] Based on conversations with industry sources.

base and underwrote the ability of Japanese firms to compete on price in the U.S. market. Thus by exploiting their systemic strengths the Japanese emerged from the 16K RAM battle, at the end of the 1970s, as formidable international competitors at the leading edge of commodity IC memories.

Structural Adjustment in an Age of International Competition

Japanese entry into the United States 16K RAM market only strengthened a set of more generic challenges confronting U.S.-based integrated circuit producers in the late 1970s. The fact that Japanese entry occurred in the high-volume memory market, which had historically delivered the margins upon which U.S. merchant firms had in part financed their continued growth, only served to heighten the severe capital constraints which the U.S. industry faced in the late 1970s. These constraints can be broken down into two separate but related strategic areas: first, financing the expansion of capacity to meet rapid growth in world demand across the range of integrated circuit devices; and second, financing the development of the next generation of IC products associated with the advent of VLSI (very large scale integration). In the context of rapidly escalating capital equipment and design application costs, Japanese entry exacerbated the cash flow problems which the industry confronted in trying to finance both growth and new product development.

U.S. firms responded to these interrelated market and financial challenges in two ways: politically, and through new market arrangements. The major political response was the formation of the Semiconductor Industry Association, which coordinated intensive lobbying of the U.S. government. Through political action the industry sought both to sensitize the government to the nature of the Japanese "threat" and to generate policies that would facilitate the industry's future growth.[124] Responses in the market, although they differed among firms, were all calculated to generate the capital necessary for continued competitive growth and to spread the costs of new product development and market penetration. This was accomplished through several kinds of arrangements: cross-licensing and technology-exchange agreements, acquisitions and equity investments, product-development contracts with electronic systems manufacturers, integration forward into systems markets by merchant producers, and integration backward into captive

---

[124] The *political* response will be considered in our "Conclusions" section. It is not described here because it is widely known and has generated both the recent policy studies on the industry and the policy debate which this essay joins.

production by a variety of systems producers. Each of these new market arrangements between firms helped to facilitate a rapid expansion of capacity for existing products, and also helped to sustain the level of research and development across the industry as a whole. Together, these political and market responses effectively enable U.S. firms, at least over the short term, to meet the challenges of increased international competition under conditions of rapid market growth.

Cross-Licensing

Cross-licensing, technology exchanges, and less formal second-source arrangements were a major way in which U.S. firms spread the risks of systems development and market penetration in the late 1970s. For example, by developing and cross-licensing different components of a systems product, U.S. firms were able to spread the risks and share the costs of development and production. U.S. firms also were able to enter systems markets with assured second sources tied together through cross-licensing arrangements. The assurance of supply and support which these actions represented enabled easier market access and more rapid customer acceptance. Moreover, cross-licensing and technology exchanges dispersed technical know-how among the partners and thereby enhanced the technology position of each. The different deals struck during the late 1970s captured different aspects of the opportunities described above. The particular characteristics of each deal depended upon the strengths, needs, and strategies of the partner firms.

The advantages and opportunities of exchange can be best seen in the proliferating deals which centered on the rapidly expanding markets for microprocessors (MPU) and related devices. Market penetration required not only that MPUs be supported with a supply of memory and peripheral chips, which would in effect create an MPU-based systems product, and that true-mask second sources be available. The costliness of developing and adding peripherals and the need for second sources resulted in a number of mask exchanges and cross-licensing agreements during 1977, 1978, and 1979. Major MPU peripheral deals involved the proprietary 8-bit and 16-bit MPU families of such U.S. firms as Intel, Texas Instruments, Motorola, Rockwell, and Zilog.[125] For example, Motorola licensed its 8-bit 6800 MPU to Hitachi in exchange for three controller chips, and has entered into similar

---

[125] See, for example, stories in *Electronics News*, May 29, 1978, p. 110; August 8, 1978, p. 1; April 25, 1977, p. 33; March 27, 1978, p. 1; June 4, 1977, p. 1; September 14, 1978, p. 58; June 27, 1977, p. 1; August 27, 1978, p. 12; April 17, 1978, p. 34. See also *The Economist*, August 2, 1980, pp. 63–64. See *Electronics*, July 5, 1979, p. 39, for the AMD-Zilog story.

exchange agreements with Hitachi, Rockwell, and Thomson-CSF for its 16-bit 6800 MPU. Rockwell reached deals with MOS Technology and Synertek for its 8-bit 6500 family MPU, and Texas Instruments reached deals with AMI and Standard Microsystems for its TMS 9900 MPU. The advantages of such agreements are perhaps best illustrated by the case of a deal between two smaller merchant firms, Zilog and AMD, which was built around Zilog's 16-bit Z8000 MPU. AMD is second-sourcing the Z8000, and developed three peripheral chips for it; Zilog, in turn, will second-source the three chips, and has developed four additional peripheral chips that AMD will second-source. Through these actions, the total systems development cost has been spread and the complete system is second-sourced, which will make market penetration easier. Thus, the challenges of high development cost and market entry, which might have overtaxed each firm acting alone, were successfully met through cross-licensing.

Another pattern of cross-licensing involved the exchange of differing proprietary technologies. Intel was a notable participant in this area. For example, Intel licensed the MPU-peripheral architectures of its MSC-48 and UPI-41 families to IBM in exchange for IBM's current bubble memory patents. Intel also exchanged certain 8-bit MPU masks and process technologies with Phillips for charge-transfer devices and Locos (local oxidation of silicon) technologies used in MOS VLSI. Similarly, Texas Instruments licensed masks for its 16-bit MPU to AMI in exchange for AMI's proprietary V-MOS technology.[126] These and similar deals broadened the potential markets for product and process technology, spread the cost of technology development, and broadened each firm's technology base.

The participants in the majority of these cross-licensing arrangements were the largest merchant firms (those with IC sales above $100 million in 1979). Unlike smaller firms, these companies had both the productive resources and the complementary proprietary technologies necessary to strike mutually beneficial bargains. For them, opportunities for growth lay in all the major markets—especially the computer, industrial, and consumer markets—served by the range of their IC products. Through cross-licensing, they could take advantage of each other's competitive strengths to build market position and simultaneously reduce the risks and costs of product development. Cross-licensing and related arrangements thereby served to help meet the problems of rapid market growth and technology development which dominated the industry's agenda in the late 1970s.

[126] *Electronics News,* June 27, 1977, p. 1; August 8, 1977, p. 46; and May 1, 1978, p. 12.

Acquisitions

Acquisitions and major equity purchases of merchant U.S. semiconductor firms were another competitive response to the challenges of rapid growth.[127] For the smaller U.S. firm, faced with costly problems of growth, development, and competition, acquisition often delivered a number of advantages. First, it provided an infusion of capital to meet the demanding requirements of capacity expansion and continued technology development. It also held out the promise of future access to cheap debt capital for continued expansion. Second, acquisition often meant access to new geographic and product markets through the marketing resources and systems products of the parent. Third, acquisition also offered access to the parent firm's technological and production resources, which meant the ability to acquire technology and to move forward into production of more complex systems devices. In many cases, of course, acquisition held out the notable long-run disadvantage of the loss of corporate autonomy or identity. For the parent firm, however, acquisition offered several obvious advantages. First, for foreign electronics firms, acquisition meant instant access to the U.S. market in both semiconductors and electronic systems. Equally important, acquisition meant access to the world's most advanced semiconductor technology. Finally, for original equipment manufacturers (OEMs) integrating backward into semiconductors, acquisition provided a cheap, rapid way of "installing" a captive semiconductor division. The different acquisitions and equity investments listed earlier in Table 4 each express different aspects of the above advantages, and it will be instructive to examine some particular cases.

The AMD-Siemens linkage is an ideal case of a mutually beneficial competitive response to market challenges. It increased AMD's access to cheaper capital and gave AMD entry to some of Siemens's markets. This kind of mutually advantageous arrangement is also indicated in the Phillips-Signetics merger, and in the United Technologies–Mostek and Schlumberger-Fairchild acquisitions. All of these semiconductor firms are large producers who have the financial muscle for capacity expansion and product development. These firms have, moreover, broadened their systems capability and enhanced their opportunities in the parent's markets.

Competitive enhancement for the parent firm similar to the AMD-Siemens deal can be seen in the equity acquisitions by Bosch and VDO to feed their automotive systems requirements, by Lucas to meet

---

[127] For foreign firms, the timing of the acquisition wave seems to be related to a cheap U.S. dollar relative to the acquiring firm's home currency.

its automotive and aerospace market needs, and by Northern Telecom for its telecommunication needs. In each case, rapidly expanding market demand for advanced electronic systems required the acquisition of the advanced LSI capabilities upon which those systems rest. The acquired firms in these cases—AMI, Solid State Scientific, Siliconix, and Intersil—were each significantly smaller firms than AMD. The effect has been to stabilize their growth by infusing capital and providing systems markets for their products. With the possible exception of AMI, these and similar *smaller* firms will coalesce around the systems market segments served by their parent companies. In this way, competitive adjustment has been achieved by tying the more limited capacities of the smaller firms to the IC requirements of particular fast-growing final market segments.

A slightly different competitive response can be seen in the complete acquisitions of smaller firms by OEMs like Honeywell, GTE, and Commodore International. Here, the *small* acquired firms have mostly lost their independent character and have become essentially captive component divisions of the parent firm (although Synertek and SEMI still sell MOS ICs on the open market—a function of the advanced LSI MOS needs they meet for their parents). The parent firms have thereby developed an assured supply and advanced technology base to meet the demands of the expanding final markets they serve. The future implications of such backward integration (here, through acquisition) will be dealt with in the upcoming sub-section on vertical integration.

In almost all of the acquisitions, then, the acquiring firms acted to procure advanced technology, to establish market position, or to ensure supply for their own needs. For the *larger* acquired firms, their "parents" provided the capital needed for expansion and development, and often provided new or expanded market opportunities as well. For the *smaller* merchant firms, acquisition meant the ability to consolidate their resources around particular market opportunities for growth. Finally, the independence of some smaller firms was sacrificed to the needs of their parents for captive production in expanding electronics end-markets.

Technology-Development Contracts

The infusion of IC technology into rapidly growing *new* or changing markets required significant development and applications expenditures. The costs of such development were sometimes picked up through technology-development contracts with the equipment manufacturer whose specific needs had to be met. The competitive benefits to U.S. IC firms were obvious: they developed new technologies at minimal cost to themselves, and often gained market access for their resulting products. Though such contracts were given in most major market segments, the example most notable for its size and impact was the series of development contracts given by GM to develop IC-based automotive electronics systems. The automotive operating environment and range of applications posed flexibility and reliability requirements seldom demanded of IC systems. Moreover, GM imposed quality-failure rate targets "literally orders of magnitude lower from one generally associated with . . . large-scale integrated circuits."[128] The results for IC vendors who participated in GM's program (and similar programs by Ford and others) were a significant leap in product and process development technology and the promise of a share in GM's huge procurement program. That program now finds sources of circuits worldwide to support GM's overseas activity, and for GM's IC vendors like Fairchild, Hitachi, Motorola, National, Signetics, and Texas Instruments, it represents significant new market demand. As one indication, Table 12 gives the percent of existing world capacity (at the end of 1979) that GM-Delco will consume in 1981 for selected ICs. Note, of course, that the major participants in this rapidly growing market are the largest merchant U.S. producers and the larger foreign IC firms.

Vertical Integration

Perhaps the most significant response by U.S. firms to the challenges of market growth in the late 1970s was the continued forward integration into systems by the largest merchant U.S. firms and the exceptionally rapid backward integration into semiconductor production by a wide range of OEMs.

Backward Integration. From 1977 through 1980 there was a literal explosion of backward integration by OEMs into semiconductor production, and the pace is accelerating. By 1980, at least 45 major OEMs at some 80 locations had established captive semiconductor operations ranging from R&D labs to full production lines. These companies spanned all of the major semiconductor markets: computers, data-processing, telecommunications, industrial, consumer, and military.[129] There were three major competitive reasons for the growth in backward integration. First, as microelectronic products increasingly infiltrated new systems markets, OEMs integrated backward to ensure themselves a competitive position in those markets. Second, the serious supply shortages in the merchant market during the late 1970s forced OEMs into captive production to ensure supply for their needs and to

[128] See remarks by GM-Delco's Frank E. Jaumot, in *Rosen Electronics Letter,* July 15, 1980, pp. 133–143. See also *Business Week,* October 8, 1979, pp. 440–443; *Electronics News,* April 4, 1977, p. 40.
[129] ICE, *Status,* 1980, "A Report on the Integrated Circuit Industry," pp. 57–66.

Table 12. Consumption 'of ICs by
General Motors–Delco as percentage
of world consumption, by device

Device	Percent of consumption
8K/PROM	56%
MOS ROM	17
Low Power Schottky	6
MOS Logic	10
Data Conversion	40

SOURCE: *Rosen Electronics Letter,* July
15, 1980, p. 143.

supplement purchased inventories. Third, most OEMs have relatively low-volume custom circuit requirements, which merchant firms have been unwilling to meet. Moreover, even where custom volumes have been large enough to attract merchant production capacity, captive production has remained an attractive secondary source of supply. A representative list of large-sized captive and mostly captive suppliers is given in Table 13. The large number of U.S. firms now engaged in or entering into integrated circuit design or production, including some of the largest U.S. manufacturing enterprises, suggests a broadening of the technological base in the United States that should enhance the pace of both innovation and diffusion in microelectronics.

It is important to note that the growth in captive facilities was made possible in part by the emergence in the later 1970s of a sophisticated infrastructure of independent firms—manufacturers of materials and equipment for testing and production, and suppliers of analysis, consulting, and design services to both captive and merchant semiconductor producers. This infrastructure had developed during the 1970s to support merchant firms, but its capacities were ideally suited to the needs of backwardly integrating OEMs. The flexibility and capacities of this segment of the U.S. industry are a major competitive strength. Through a combination of meeting user requirements and carrying on independent research into semiconductor manufacturing processes, the equipment producers have become increasingly important to the technical progress and competitive position of the U.S. integrated circuit industry.

Forward Integration. The forward integration of the largest merchant U.S. semiconductor firms during the LSI period (described in the first section) continued apace in the late 1970s. As development and design costs rose with the complexity of IC devices, these firms moved forward into systems production to recapture the higher value-added that

Table 13. U.S. captive suppliers of semiconductors

Company	R&D lab	Prototype lab	Pilot production	Full production
Aerojet Electro Systems	X			
Amdahl Corporation	X	X		
Ampex Corporation				X
Bell Telephone Labs				
Boeing Company	X	X		
Burroughs	X	X	X	X
Chrysler Corp.	X	X		
Control Data Corporation	X	X	X	X
Cutler-Hammer/Eaton	X			
Data General	X	X	X	X
Datel Systems		X		
Delco Electronics Division	X	X	X	X
Digital Equipment Corp.				
Eastman Kodak	X	X	X	X
E-Systems, Inc.	X	X		
Essex Group, Inc.				X
Fluke Automatic Systems Division				
Ford Aerospace Communications	X			
Foxboro Company				
Four-Phase System, Inc.	X	X		
General Dynamics			X	
General Electric				
SSAO	X	X	X	
Corporate R&D	X	X		
Aerospace Electronics Systems	X	X	X	X
Gould, Inc.	X	X		
GTE Laboratories	X	X	X	
Honeywell				
Solid State Electronics Center	X	X	X	
SSEC Center				X
IBM				
Corporate	X			
General Systems Division		X		
Data Systems Division				
General Technology Division				
System Development Division	X	X		
Data Products Division			X	X
General Systems Division			X	X
Federal Systems Division			X	X
Lockheed Missiles and Space	X	X	X	
Magnavox	X		X	
Martin Marietta Aerospace	X	X		
McDonnell-Douglas				
Astronautics	X			
Micro-Rel	X	X		
NCR				
Northern Telecom				
Northrop	X			
Rosemount	X			
Sandia Labs	X	X	X	

Sperry					
Storage Technology Corp.					X
Microtechnology	X	X	X		
Stromberg-Carlson	X	X	X		
Tektronix	X	X	X	X	
Western Electric					
Teletype Corp.		X	X	X	
Westinghouse	X	X	X	X	
Friendship Solid State Research	X				
Xerox	X	X	X		
PARC	X	X			

SOURCE: ICE, *Status*, 1980, pp. 59–61.

systems represented. The move forward was also aimed at meeting the applications needs of users in systems markets, and thereby served to enhance and establish positions in expanding markets. We have already described some of the move forward in terms of cross-licensing arrangements, acquisitions, and development contracts. In addition, the largest firms integrated forward by establishing systems subsidiaries and through forward mergers.

Once again, the movements forward by different firms spanned the major markets for semiconductor devices. Texas Instruments continued to expand into a broad range of consumer systems markets, as did Fairchild (electronic games) and Motorola (automotive entertainment) in discrete consumer-product segments. Motorola continued to expand its telecommunications capability, notably through acquisitions of two small communication chip producers, Codex and Universal Data Systems. National moved further forward into plug-compatible machines (PCM) through merger with its formerly independent marketer, Itel. All of the major MPU manufacturers moved forward into microcomputer systems, into MPU-based industrial control systems, and toward distributed processing systems. These moves included further refinement of microprocessor development systems and entry into software support, notably by Texas Instruments, Motorola, and Intel, in the form of ROM-based "firmware." The notable purchase in the software-distributed processing area was Intel's acquisition of MRI Systems Corp., a Texas vendor of data-base management software.[130]

---

[130] As advances in semiconductor hardware technology speed the "computerization" of society, yet another new industry is being fostered, the independent software business. Lack of software capability at both the systems level ("teaching" the machine to function as a computer) and the applications level (enabling the computer to perform specific tasks) is the major structural block to the spread of computer technology. For a good introduction to the emerging software industry and the problems of software development, see "Missing Computer Software," *Business Week*, September 1, 1980, pp. 46–56.

The Impact of Integration

In the late 1970s, vertical integration both backward and forward expressed most dramatically the impact of rapid growth of the different markets served by IC-based electronic system products. The fact that moves toward vertical integration are being pulled so dramatically by the market suggests that the most recent wave of integration is different in kind from those that may have preceded it. For OEMs, captive capacity is no longer merely the source of *potential* competitive advantage. Rather, because it serves the strategic needs we have described under "backward integration," it appears to be absolutely essential merely to *remain* internationally competitive. For large IC firms, integration forward is no longer merely a potentially lucrative market opportunity. Rather, it appears to be the primary way that enough invested value can be recaptured to underwrite continued internationally competitive growth and development at the levels achieved in the past.

Market Outcomes and Industrial Restructuring

The market challenges and competitive responses in the U.S. IC industry during the late 1970s were dominated by the fact of rapid growth throughout the spectrum of markets served by IC firms. Rapidly expanding markets helped make possible Japanese penetration, stimulated captive production, and required capacity expansion. In conjunction with rapidly escalating development and applications costs, rapid growth was the main impetus behind the patterns of cross-licensing, acquisition, vertical integration, competition, and consequent market concentration described above. Moreover, the requirements of rapid growth also spurred a proliferating and flexible infrastructure of independent semiconductor firms providing materials, production and test equipment, and services. Taken as a whole, the actions described here constitute a process of ongoing industrial adjustment to increased international competition under conditions of rapid market growth. This outcome, in terms of world IC production and market share, is summarized in Tables 14 and 15. As these figures suggest, the decline in U.S. (and merchant) world market share between 1974 and 1978 was arrested during 1978–1980 by the flexible structural adjustments we have been describing. Total U.S. world market share, both merchant and captive, has stabilized since 1980 and may even have risen.

What is concealed by the aggregate figures in Tables 14 and 15 is the degree to which the industry's adjustment at the end of the 1970s has altered the industry's organization. As demonstrated in the first section of this chapter, expanding markets, competitive challenges, company

Table 14. World IC production (million of dollars)

Producing Region	1978	1979	1980 (estimated)	1981 (projected)
United States				
IC Merchant	3,238	4,620	5,636	7,330
IC Captive	1,344	1,940	2,580	3,400
All United States	4,582	6,560	8,216	10,730
Western Europe	453	570	680	750
Japan	1,195	1,470	1,850	2,220
Rest of world	782	673	728	943
All world	67,212	9,273	11,474	14,643

SOURCE: ICE, Status, 1980, p. 4.

responses, and market outcomes have historically interacted in different periods to *restructure* the semiconductor industry. Indeed, what the process of adjustment described in this section suggests is an emergent competitive restructuring of the U.S. industry. This emerging structure is best understood as a process of market *segmentation*.

By segmentation, we mean the emergence of large and rapidly growing market segments for electronics systems within the overall markets for computers and data processing, telecommunications, and industrial, consumer, automotive, and military applications; each segment is served primarily by a number of the largest merchant firms who will overlap from segment to segment, and secondarily by a few of the smaller firms (among which, from segment to segment, there will be little or no overlap). Because markets are growing so rapidly and are producing such varied and costly demands on IC technology, however, a merchant "components" sector cannot economically serve all markets and meet all demands. Therefore, coexisting with merchant firms will be significant captive production firms, which will fill the segment gaps inadequately served by merchant production. Thus the pattern of OEM backward integration described above is, in fact, an expression of the occurrence of market segmentation. Similarly, the patterns of cross-licensing, acquisition, and forward integration have positioned the participating firms to take advantage of growth opportunities in different market segments.

This process of segmentation is likely to produce discrete tiers of merchant firms differentiated on the basis of size, growth, profitability, systems capability, and the degree of their formal ties to OEMs. The largest merchant firms will expand rapidly, become more and more like systems houses, and be very profitable. Since the systems required to serve different segments will overlap, these firms will appear to be relatively full-line systems houses. Comparatively smaller firms are likely to be locked into one or two major market segments where they

Table 15. World IC market share, United States and Japan

Country	1978	1979	1980 (estimated)	(projected)
United States				
Merchant	48%	50%	49%	50%
Captive	20	21	23	23
All United States	68%	71%	72%	73%
Japan	18%	16%	16%	15%

SOURCE: Based on ICE, *Status*, 1980, p. 4; percentages rounded.

will be significant participants, but their growth will be slower and they will be less profitable. The smallest firms are likely to coalesce as secondary suppliers around the distinct market segments served by the largest merchant firms or served by OEM captive production. However, these smallest firms will also serve non-captive market segments that demand low-volume custom chips.

Market segmentation and its generation of growth opportunities within market niches are likely to foster a spate of new merchant entries. Since capital gains taxes were relaxed in 1978, venture capital has been flowing at an increasing rate into start-ups in the different sectors of the U.S. economy. Venture capital financed an estimated $250 million in new enterprises in 1980, up from just $20 million in 1975.[131] A share of that capital has indeed found its way into the semiconductor industry. The explosive growth potential of IC markets and the new availability of venture capital have attracted entrepreneurs away from established IC firms into new ventures. For example, five engineers left Intel in January 1981 to start Seeq Inc., which will compete in Intel's markets. National Semiconductor lost four top employees in July 1981 to a new venture that will produce linear ICs for the instrumentation and telecommunications markets.[132]

New ventures are also being fostered to meet some OEM demand for custom chips, because backward integration to produce low-volume custom chips in a range of new market segments is likely to be too costly for those OEMs. Such entry could well take the form of the "silicon foundry," which would run off a batch of chips based on custom masks designed and delivered by the customer. As the infrastructure of semiconductor service firms proliferates, the ability to design and produce custom masks will also grow. At least one silicon foundry venture was started in 1980, VLSI Technology. To the extent that the foundry proves economical, the larger merchant IC firms are also likely to open divisions that perform foundry services. If that occurs,

[131] *Business Week*, August 24, 1981, p. 112.
[132] *Ibid.*

the largest firms will profit by serving custom market segments they now ignore.

The restructuring of the U.S. industry in the ways outlined above may be seen as the obvious result of rapid market growth in a situation where the industry's firms are disparately positioned, on the basis of capacities, to capitalize on market opportunities. In that sense, the projected changes in the U.S. industry represent an intensification of structural tendencies not fully realized during adjustment throughout the era of LSI in the 1970s. What is fundamentally new, however, is the presence of Japanese competitors well positioned to challenge U.S. firms across a range of market segments. Benefits from responding to growing market opportunities that used to redound almost automatically to unchallenged U.S.-based firms may very well be denied them by Japanese competitors.

Structure and Strategy in International Trade

By 1980 the Japanese integrated circuit industry had arrived as a market force in international competition. American industry, however, has by no means lost its own market momentum. Though Japanese firms have captured more than 40 percent of the world 16K RAM market, over the entire range of integrated circuit production U.S. firms have managed to absorb that loss and sustain their overall world market-share position. Indeed, were the full extent of U.S. captive production known, it is likely that the percentage of world production accounted for by U.S.-based firms has actually increased in the last several years.

Some ominous clouds, nonetheless, have appeared on the U.S. horizon. Japanese firms have led their U.S. competitors in introducing and moving more quickly into production the latest generation of random access memories—the 64K RAM. As noted earlier, the Japanese have proved quite competent as market followers but as yet have failed to lead American firms in new product and market development. For this reason, early Japanese entry into the 64K RAM market caught many observers by surprise. Nevertheless, this attempt to establish an early market position remains no more than an attempt; sustaining a leadership position will be fraught with difficulty.

Both Japanese and American firms have apparently been preparing for a major market battle in the 64K RAM. The ten largest Japanese firms spent more than $500 million in 1979 and more than $775 million in 1980 on semiconductor plant and equipment—that is, between 17 and 18 percent of sales. The ten largest U.S. merchant producers, having learned their lesson in the 16K RAM market—where a failure to keep investment levels high during the 1975 recession led to a loss of market shares in the period 1978–1980—have more than matched the Japanese in adding new capacity. As a group, these ten producers spent more than $910 million in 1979 and more than $1.2 billion in 1980, or more than 20 percent of sales during each of the two years. Given the relatively depressed conditions of IC sales since the fourth quarter of 1980, the willingness of the U.S. industry to spend during a recession suggests a heightened awareness of the role that capacity and scale play in Japanese strategy.

Although the leading U.S. merchants are no strangers to the strategy of gaining a market-share position on the basis of scale economies and learning-curve efficiencies, historically it has been process innovation and new product development that have supported U.S. international competitiveness. In this respect, even during the boom in capital investment U.S. firms have maintained research and development expenditures at around 10 percent of sales. Indeed, it appears that the early Japanese position in the 64K RAM market could be made vulnerable by an innovative effort on the part of several leading U.S. producers.

One reason for the early Japanese lead in the introduction and production of 64K RAMs was that they adopted a relatively conventional approach in their design, which enabled them to apply their experience in the 16K RAM design very quickly to the task of producing the 64K device. Early U.S. designs, first announced by the leading U.S. captive producers (IBM in 1978 and Bell Labs in 1979), called for the incorporation of "redundancy" as "fault tolerance" in the layout of the 64K device. As a matter of design, a chip incorporating "redundancy" has an extra set of spare cell rows and columns. After wafer fabrication and processing, computer-controlled testing equipment can be used to locate defective cells in the individual chips on each wafer and permanently inactivate them. The extra set of spare cells is then used, and the otherwise defective chip can thereby be made to function properly. The use of redundancy, then, can dramatically boost yields—the number of usable chips per wafer manufactured—because the design and process allow the additional cells to be substituted for the defective ones to create a functional device. Thus, the use of a redundant design and the associated improvement in yields should lead to lower unit costs and also should reduce the investment in plant and equipment required to meet the volume demand expected to emerge for the 64K RAM device.

Although the first 64K RAM offered in limited sample quantities by U.S. merchant firms (Texas Instruments and Motorola) did not incorporate the use of redundancy, considerable momentum behind the redundancy design has been generated with the announcement by In-

235

tel late in 1980 of its redundancy device; following Intel, both Mostek and Inmos have announced a commitment to it. The Japanese firms, with the exception of Fujitsu, apparently have not anticipated the need for redundancy in 64K RAM devices, thinking that could wait for production of a 256K device. This may reflect an expectation that yields on their conventional device, combined with a massive increase in production capacity, will leave them cost-competitive with U.S. firms in any event.

The outcome of the 64K RAM market competition between Japanese and American firms is still uncertain, but the competition to date illuminates the relative strengths and weaknesses of the two industries. It appears that the early leadership of Japanese firms has been based on a build-up of 64K RAM capacity for "captive" demand in the domestic market, which would enable them, through price competition, to gain a dominant international merchant market position. Indeed, although most industry analysts had not expected 64K RAM prices to fall below $10 per chip until 1982, Japanese firms had begun to quote a $4 price by late 1981 in an effort to pre-empt American market competition.

In the coming battle in the 64K RAM market (as in the 16K RAM before it), it is possible that the Japanese, by applying their unique production strengths and domestic market power, will become a particular kind of competitor in the international merchant market. The stable availability of debt capital underwrites their growth, development, and ability to compete abroad. Rationalization and oligopolization of the domestic market among the major Japanese firms help create a stable environment, and they may be used instrumentally to achieve scale economies and, by freeing individual firm resources, to encourage production for export. Control over access to the domestic market limits the ability of U.S. firms to turn the competitive advantages from product innovation and market position abroad into long-term market share in Japan. Ongoing government promotion of cooperative research and development further compensates the Japanese firms for their relative international weaknesses in technological innovation. In short, the large and vertically integrated Japanese electronic firms use their controlled domestic market as a stable, high-volume production base from which to achieve penetration and potential competitive domination of foreign markets. Unlike their U.S. merchant competitors, the strength of the Japanese semiconductor firms lies in a production strategy rather than in an innovation strategy.

In its traditional role of promoter, following MITI's basic strategy of creating comparative advantage in the knowledge-intensive industries, the Japanese government appears intent on further assisting the international competitiveness of its IC-electronics firms. Thus, for example, the major IC-computer firms, with MITI funding, have created the Electronics Computer Basic Technology Development Association to continue the computer development efforts that emerged from the VLSI program. The Association's major focus over the short term is to overcome Japan's seriously uncompetitive position in computer software development.[133] Table 16 gives a rough indication of ongoing major Japanese government support to the Japanese electronics industry.

Such massive support will fit neatly with the Japanese firms' long-term strategy in integrated circuit and systems markets. Indeed, the current ability of the Japanese to be competitive in international RAM markets apparently foreshadows an attempt to dominate a broad range of both commodity IC and electronics systems markets. RAMs are among the few large-volume products that can provide Japanese firms with the manufacturing and technological know-how to continue to move forward along the path of innovation established by U.S. firms.[134]

In semiconductors, however, U.S. firms still dominate microprocessor, peripheral, logic-circuit, and custom-circuit development and production. The Japanese firms, on the other hand, are aiming for the lucrative computer and telecommunication markets. Indeed, since the end of the 1970s, Fujitsu has developed joint venture links with TRW and Sumers. These give Fujitsu a strong new toehold for distributing and improving its computer system in both the U.S. and the European markets. The Japanese are also strong players in the growing automotive electronics markets.

The long-range competitiveness of the Japanese industry in commodity IC and systems production may be further enhanced by an unwillingness to license proprietary production technologies that emerge from either government-coordinated or individual-firm research and development. Indeed, it appears that U.S. firms—as a result of MITI policy or industry choice—are being denied access to proprietary production technologies that emerged from the VLSI project and are being made available to Japanese firms.[135] This should not be surprising, since the source of Japanese competitive advantage lies in production strategy; it suggests, however, that the Japanese are determined to remain formidable international competitors by controlling access to the fruits of "controlled competition" as well as access to the market.

By contrast, the U.S. merchant firms against which the Japanese industry has taken aim continue to generate a technological and com-

---

[133] BA 1980, p. 29; and *Datamation*, February 28, 1980, pp. 52–58.
[134] See testimony of AMD Vice President George Scalise in hearings of the U.S. Congress, Joint Economic Committee, Subcommitttee, on International Trade, Finance, and Security Economics, July 9, 1981. (Advance copy, p. 48.)
[135] Based on conversations with industry sources.

Table 16. Value of Japanese government support to information industry, 1970–1991, by type of support (in millions of dollars)

Type of support	Years	Value
Hardware		
Pattern information process	1971–1980	$ 104
3.75 Series computer	1972–1970	290
Peripheral development		
IC development	1973–1974	17
VLSI development	1970–1979	139
Base technology for new-era computer	1970–1979	350
Scientific processor (super)	1981–1988	112
5th generation computer system (planned)	1981–1990	500
Opto electronic applied measurement and control	1979–1986	86
Opto-IC development (planned)	1981–1991	
Software		
Software module development	1973–1975	14
Software product technology	1976–1981	32
IPA agency (program development)	1971–1980	52
Software maintenance technology development	1981–1985	24
Loans		
Japan Development Bank to IECC	1971–1980	1,900
Bank loans to software companies	1971–1980	487

ªProjected.
SOURCE: IECC Computer Note.

petitive dynamism unique to the American industrial structure. Dynamic technological advance has underwritten the international competitiveness of the American industry. In this process the merchant firms have played a critical role, both as innovators and as diffusers and have shown no interest in withholding their technological advances from the market. Indeed, the ability of merchant firms to innovate and fuel the process of diffusion has depended upon their achieving as wide a market as possible for their new products. Commodity positions in a high-volume market have enabled them to finance the risks of new product development and thereby to act as an independent catalyst to the process of technological innovation across the electronics industry as a whole.

The immediate Japanese threat is directed toward this merchant sector of the U.S. industry. By bringing their high-volume strengths to bear in merchant competition, Japanese firms could come to dominate U.S. microelectronic commodity markets to an extent that would deny U.S. firms the margins that have historically underwritten their capacity to create new products and develop new markets. Significant Japanese domination of merchant commodity markets—if it occurs—could rob the U.S. electronics industry of the competitive dynamism that has been its hallmark. The pace and character of innovation and diffusion throughout the U.S. electronics industry could be slowed. In other words, the Japanese could come to dominate systems markets over the very long term.

We do not mean to overstate the nature of the competitive challenge from Japan. In 1982, these threats to the long-run development of the U.S. industry and economy are no more than possibilities, and U.S. policy should not be formulated primarily to confront them. But it is clear that the Japanese will continue to develop an internationally competitive IC-electronics industry to underpin the knowledge-intensive development of their own economy. How the U.S. government should respond to these Japanese ambitions is the subject of our final section.

CONCLUSIONS

The semiconductor industry is transforming industrial life around the world. Its applications to data processing, automated production, robotics, communications, and military systems are changing the products we use, the way we make them, and the means by which we communicate with each other. In trade between the advanced countries, competitive position is being gained by product differentiation and the management of sophisticated production systems, both of which will be shaped by the possibilities offered by integrated circuits. Consequently, we believe that the relative strength of the several advanced industrial countries in the next few decades will be significantly affected by differing national capacities to develop and apply these electronic component technologies.

The United States must reconcile its desire to maintain its position of leadership in this industry with similar Japanese and European desires to ride the wave of electronics into the future. The story told here of marketplace competition is also a tale of conflict between nations over the role of government in promoting and shaping growth sectors. In the 1980s, arguments about tariffs and quotas will give way to trade debates about government policies of procurement and promotion. The integrated circuit case, where government policies are vital, may prove to be a prototype for the trade conflicts of the next decade and beyond. The real danger is that each nation's pursuit of its own advantage will fragment this worldwide industry into a series of national markets insulated by policies of government procurement and subsidies. In this regard, we must not forget that American-Japanese conflicts cannot be resolved without attention to the European position.

American electronics producers dominated world markets for semi-conductor components—from which advanced electronic systems are built—from the time of the industry's inception until 1979, when Japanese producers captured 43 percent of the American market for 16K RAMs. That surge signaled the beginning of a challenge to American pre-eminence in advanced electronics. Success with a sophisticated product in an advanced-technology industry dramatized the economic and technological competitiveness of the Japanese electronics industry. At the end of World War II Japan still depended heavily on agricultural production, and Japanese-manufactured goods sold in world markets were primarily labor-intensive. The government, specifically the Ministry of International Trade and Industry, sought to advance the Japanese position in the world economy and took concerted action to promote rapid industrial development and the expansion of capital-intensive production. Domestic markets were insulated from foreign direct investment and imports. Foreign firms sold their technology to Japanese companies because they were not permitted to enter the Japanese market. Importantly, the Japanese government chose to sponsor those sectors in which rising Japanese incomes would mean an expanding market, and in which Japanese firms competing for home demand would gain the economies of scale they needed in order to export. By the middle 1970s Japanese firms had become a force in the international markets for steel, ships, automobiles, and consumer electronics. The first shift away from labor-intensive production to capital-intensive production was achieved.

In the 1980s the Japanese government, as a matter of national economic policy, has been actively promoting the development of knowledge-intensive industries—of which a prime example is the industry that produces integrated circuits and the systems built from those circuits, which include computers, telecomunications, and automated production equipment. The direct influence of the Japanese government in industrial affairs has dwindled, and intergovernmental rivalries—such as the one between MITI and NTT—are important to understanding both the formulation and the implementation of government policy. Nonetheless, the high-growth techniques first applied in the 1950s and 1960s in industrial catch-up have been used since then to create an advanced Japanese position in markets for electronics. Japanese government policies and private industrial arrangements create advantages in international competition for Japanese companies that place otherwise competitive American firms under intense market pressure. Those advantages encourage longer-term corporate planning horizons by lifting constraints that force a shorter-term perspective on American firms. More concretely, they permit Japanese firms distinct production strategies not open to most American companies. An internationally competitive Japanese electronics industry has been built up, like other priority industries before it, with active government assistance; and within protected markets, direct government aid has gone not only to promote the advance of integrated circuit technology but also to support the development of the final systems, such as computers and telecommunications, in which semiconductors are used.

Trade policy has been as important as direct promotion in the evolution of the Japanese industry. The main challenge posed by Japanese policy over the years has been to manipulate access to its domestic market as a means of neutralizing the strength of American firms. At least until 1978, the government forced American firms to sell their patents and know-how to Japanese firms rather than allowing them to sell and produce in Japan. Although many of the formal restrictions on sales and direct investment in Japan by foreign companies have been eliminated since 1978, access to the Japanese market remains very difficult for foreign producers. The inter-company ties built up during the years of formally closed markets cannot be severed at a stroke because the government announces a more open policy. For example, the market for integrated circuits is dominated by six large captive producers, and each is part of an integrated electronics systems house that incorporates integrated circuits into its final products. The final systems product speciality of each electronics firm is reflected in the type of semiconductor devices it produces, which is not surprising. Yet on the average less than a quarter of each firm's production is for its own use; because these firms account for over 70 percent of production and 60 percent of consumption, there is extensive trade between them. The evidence suggests that the extensive trade between the major firms represents a pattern of convenient specialization which more readily permits each company the volumes it needs to achieve competitive costs in certain products. Since the major producers are integrated electronics manufacturers, they are also in a position to subsidize semiconductor development and production capacity with income from the final products.

Such structured markets are available to other Japanese industries. Intense competition does exist in Japan, but it is also controlled or structured to assure conditions for the growth of the electronics industry as a whole. The structures and controls assure more stable demand and permit capacity to be expanded more rapidly than would be possible in an entirely open market. Until very recently, Japanese firms have been able to expand capacity and innovate in production techniques because they could follow technological developments abroad and sell into a closed home market. Their production-oriented strategies in

241

commodity products were facilitated by the substantial financial resources that their size and extensive use of debt provided.

Even in an industry evolving as rapidly as electronics, Japanese strategies have at least until now hinged on finding the efficiencies and advantages that become possible when products stabilize and price competition proves essential. Japanese electronic component companies are not the only ones that have adopted a strategy of following the technological and market leaders by entering production in force and selling into already established market segments. Some American firms have also been technological followers, or commodity sellers hovering closely behind the technological leaders. But the Japanese firms seem to have been a special type of follower. The evidence suggests that until very recently they have not tried to establish any of their own products as world industy standards; by saving themselves years of heavy investment in development, they have been able to concentrate on production refinements. They are now on a par with American companies in many technologies, and have entered in force the race toward very large scale integrated memory circuits (VLSI). Although the technical advance in memory circuits remains extraordinary, that market segment is now established and open to volume production. By contrast, the Japanese have not yet established their own proprietary microprocessor designs as industry standards, and this is a segment in which rapid adjustment to market needs is more important. In essence, the Japanese have tended to wait for a clear market to emerge before entering volume production. This is a production bias that requires predictable demand and easily available capital. The scale of the Japanese firms and the arrangements of the Japanese financial system assure the financing. A set of integrated companies, each with a captive internal market and each collectively engaged in convenient specialization, creates the structural conditions for the stable demand that production strategies require. Demand is all the more stable if foreign—chiefly American—penetration into domestic markets is limited.

A pattern of import substitution, originally forced by government policy, apparently still continues. Several explanations for this have been offered. The first is that when the Japanese begin to produce a product—any product—they immediately have a production advantage over American producers; but the economies of scale and learning-curve economies that characterize the electronics industry make this explanation implausible. The second is that the Japanese have mastered manufacturing techniques that assure significantly higher yields than are being achieved in the United States, techniques which therefore give them dramatically lower costs. A third is that American companies do not actively pursue an advantage in the Japanese market; but this does not account for the aggressive expansion of American-controlled multinational semiconductor companies around the world.

The fourth explanation—and the one we have argued for—is that the secure position of Japanese firms over the last two decades has been the result of a clear and forceful government policy of restricting access to domestic markets. That position is now maintained by the pattern of inter-company specialization noted above. In our view, the Japanese could not have played this production game so effectively if their home markets had been truly open. To elaborate the consequences these Japanese arrangements have had for the American electronics industry, we must consider the workings of the American semiconductor sector. Competition in the American industry has centered on continuous product innovation and on the constant diffusion of semiconductors into new markets. Each new generation of technology has rapidly undermined the production advantages gained in the standard circuits of the previous generation. The structure of the American semiconductor industry has encouraged competition by diffusion and innovation of new products, rather than simply by the reduction of production costs in existing goods.

That structure consists of a few giant integrated firms, a number of smaller integrated systems firms, and a vibrant merchant sector. In the United States, in sharp contrast with Japan, the largest giant integrated firms (ATT and IBM), by court decree and by corporate choice, have not been sellers of semiconductor components to other users. The market position of the American giants is therefore fundamentally different from that of the integrated Japanese firms. If ATT was allowed to sell on the merchant component markets, then the situations would be parallel. As it is, Japanese firms, through cross-subsidization, can use their privileged position as telecommunications suppliers to gain special advantages in commercial semiconductor markets.

It is important, then, that ATT and IBM are not merchants who sell their products to others; they enter the merchant marketplace only to buy in order to supplement their captive production. Because they are not sellers in this merchant market, they tend to diffuse their technology by development contracts and the exchange of patents and know-how with the smaller producers. The giants produce in such a large volume that they can capture internally adequate benefits from a broadly based research program. As a result, they provide the industry at large with the "public good" of basic research. In part because the giant producers do not use their production muscle in the merchant sector, competition between integrated circuit companies has been in the area of product innovation and diffusion. The merchant sector of the market—firms whose primary business is to manufacture and sell

243

component products to systems users—has been a potent stimulant to competition in all electronics goods. Electronic systems producers depend on semiconductor companies to gain advantage in their final markets, whereas component producers depend on systems customers to achieve the volumes that justify their investment in product development and capacity expansion. The relative advantage in world competition of these semiconductor merchants lies in product innovation and the development of new markets. The American industry, and the merchant sector in particular, has had a relative advantage in "making" new markets by innovating in applications and by advancing the product technology; but they face a powerful challenge from the Japanese in the volume production of commodity products. A loss of high-volume markets, where Japanese advantages weigh most heavily, could prevent the American firms from using their strengths in entrepreneurial innovation.

It is here that the special policy and market arrangements of the Japanese pose the most serious problem. The Japanese companies have displayed remarkable technological and marketing prowess, but the arrangements in their domestic market have given them important advantages when competing in commodity semiconductor products in the United States market. So long as the Japanese market is closed off from the outside competition, the terms of competition in world markets will be biased toward Japanese strengths and against American strengths.

There are four main reasons for this. First, the Japanese producers are not simply merchants of semiconductor products but competitors in a range of final systems that depend on integrated circuits. Second, individual firms in the insulated and segmented domestic market face more stable patterns of demand than they would if there were foreign competitors or less domestic specialization. This stable demand permits more rapid expansion of capacity and probably also offers more opportunities to automate production lines. Third, any excess capacity that results from an overestimation of the domestic market can be directed toward export markets, including the U.S. market. If, by contrast, American producers expand capacity too rapidly to position themselves for a future upswing, formal and informal barriers to the Japanese market will prevent them from directing their excess capacity to that market. Consequently, they must dispose of increased products entirely in their own markets or permit the extra capacity to lie idle. Thus, rapid Japanese expansion in closed domestic markets may turn foreign markets into residual or secondary markets for excess Japanese capacity; this does not imply "dumping" or predatory pricing, but it is a logical consequence of a secure home market base. Even a partially insulated domestic market will therefore give production advantages to Japanese firms and also tend to insulate them from the consequences of any downturn in demand. Fourth, if domestic arrangements encourage Japanese firms to buy from local producers regardless of cost-quality advantages, American firms will not be able to consolidate a competitive position in the Japanese market.

The immediate problem for the United States is that Japanese government policies which sponsor the development of a competitive electronics sector slant the terms of worldwide semiconductor competition toward the Japanese relative advantage in production and away from relative advantage of American firms in market development and innovation. The broader policy question is how the United States should respond to foreign efforts to create a comparative advantage in the advanced technology sectors on which our industrial future must rest.

GLOSSARY

A/D converter	Analog-to-digital converter. A device to convert variable or **analog** signals to digital representation. Also called ADC.
Access time	The time interval between the instant that data is called from or delivered to a storage device (memory) and the instant the requested retrieval or storage is complete.
Algorithm	A prescribed set of well-defined rules for the solution of a problem. Algorithms are implemented on a computer by a stored sequence of instructions.
Alignment	The arranging of the **mask** and **wafer** in correct positions, one with respect to the other. Special alignment patterns are normally part of the mask.
Analog	Indicates continuous, non-digital representation of phenomena. An analog voltage, for example, may take any value.
Binary	A system of numbers using 2 as a base, in contrast to the decimal system which uses 10 as a base. The binary system requires only two symbols, 0 and 1.
Bipolar	Refers to transistors formed with two semiconductor types (the N and P types).
Bit	A **binary** digit. A bit is the smallest unit of storage in a digital computer and is used to represent one of the two digits in the **binary** number system.
Bus	A circuit or group of circuits that provides a communication path between two or more devices.
Byte	A set of contiguous **binary bits,** usually eight, which are operated on as a unit. A byte can also be a sub-set of a computer **word.**
Chip	A single square or rectangular piece of **semiconductor** material into which a specific electrical circuit has been fabricated.
CMOS	Complementary Metal Oxide Semiconductor. A logic family made by combining N-channel and P-channel **MOS** transistors.

CPU	Central Processor Unit. The part of a computer that fetches, decodes, and executes program instructions and maintains status of results.
D/A converter	A device to convert **digital** representation into an **analog** voltage or current level. Also called DAC.
Data	A general term used to denote any or all facts, numbers, letters, and symbols. It connotes basic elements of information that can be processed or produced by a computer.
Depletion device	A type of **MOSFET** that is "on" when no input signal is present. See **MOS, MOSFET.**
Development system	**Microcomputer** system complete with peripherals, memory, and software, used to write, compile, run, and debug application programs for one or more target **microprocessors.**
Die	Plural, **dice.** Another name for **chip.**
Diffusion	A method of **doping** or modifying the characteristics of semiconductor material by "baking" wafers of the base semiconductor material in furnaces with controlled atmospheres.
Discrete	Containing only one active device; a **transistor** or a diode is a discrete device.
Dynamic RAM	A Random Access Memory in which the presence or absence of a capacitive charge represents the state of a **binary** storage element. The charge must be periodically refreshed. See **RAM.**
ECL	Emitter Coupled Logic. A form of current-mode logic in which the output is available from an emitter-follower output stage.
EPROM	Erasable Programmable Read Only Memory. Similar to **ROM,** but enables the user to erase stored information and replace it with new information when necessary. Most EPROMs are erased through exposure to ultraviolet light.
EAROM	Electrically Alterable Read Only Memory. A read-only memory whose contents may be altered on rare occasions through electrical stimuli.
EAPROM	Electrically Erasable·**PROM.**
Enhancement device	A type of **MOSFET** that requires a control signal input to turn on the device. The device is "off" when no input signal is present.
FET	Field Effect **Transistor.**
FPLA	Field Programmable Logic Array. Field means capable of being programmed by the user.
Firmware	Software in hardware form. Refers specifically to computer microcode in Read Only Memory.
HMOS	High performance **MOS.**
Hybrid circuit	Any combination of two or more of the following in one package: Active substrate integrated circuit; Passive substrate integrated circuit; Discrete component.
Input/output	Relating to the equipment or method used for transmitting information into and out of a computer.
Integrated circuit (IC)	A semiconductor **chip** or **die** containing multiple elements that act together to form the complete device circuit.
LED	Light Emitting Diode. A semiconductor device that emits light whenever current passes through it.
LSI	Large Scale Integration. LSI devices contain 100 or more **gate equivalents** or other circuitry of similar complexity.

LS TTL	Low-power Schottky Transistor = Transistor Logic. The power dissipation of LS TTL is typically one-fifth that of conventional **TTL.** See Schottky TTL.
Linear IC	An **analog** integrated circuit, as opposed to a digital integrated circuit.
MESFET	Metallic Schottky Field Effect Transistor. A field effect transistor whose gate structure consists of a metallic Schottky barrier.
Microprocessor	Computer central processing unit on a single chip.
MOS	Metal Oxide Semiconductor. Devices using **FETs** in which current flow through a channel of N-type or P-type semiconductor material is controlled by the electric field around a gate structure. MOSFETs are **unipolar** devices characterized by extremely high input resistance.
MOSFET	A type of Field Effect **Transistor.** See **MOS.**
MPU	See **Microprocessor.**
MSI	Medium Scale Integration. ICs containing between 10 and 100 gate equivalents.
Mask	A patterned screen, usually of glass, used to expose selected areas of a semiconductor (that has been covered with a **photoresist**) to a light source that causes polymerization.
Microcomputer	A **microprocessor** complete with stored program memory (**ROM**), random access memory (**RAM**), and input/output (**I/O**) logic. If all functions are on the same **chip,** this is sometimes called a **microcontroller.** Microcomputers are capable of performing useful work without additional supporting logic.
Microcontroller	See **Microcomputer.**
Microelectronics	Microscopically small components or circuits made by means of photolithography techniques.
Micron	Synonymous with micrometer: one millionth of a meter.
Microprocessor	The basic arithmetic logic of a computer. See **CPU.**
Monolithic device	A device whose circuitry is completely contained on a single **chip** or die.
PLA	Programmable Logic Array. A general purpose logic circuit containing an array of logic **gates** that can be connected (programmed) to perform various functions.
PROM	Programmable Read Only Memory. A read-only memory that can be programmed after manufacture by external equipment. Typically, PROMs utilize fusible links that may be burned open to produce a logic **bit** in a specific location.
RAM	Random Access Memory, which stores digital information temporarily and can be changed by the user. It constitutes the basic storage element in a computer. Also called a read-write memory.
ROM	Read Only Memory, which permanently stores information that is used repeatedly, such as microcode or characters for electronic display. Unlike **RAM,** ROM cannot be altered.
SOS	Silicon on Sapphire. A faster **MOS** technology in which the silicon is grown on a sapphire **wafer** only where needed.
SSI	Small Scale Integration. Integrated circuits containing fewer than 10 logic **gates.**
Schottky TTL	A form of TTL logic in which Schottky diodes are used to clamp the transistors out of saturation, effectively eliminating the storage of charge within the transistor, allowing increased switching speeds.
Semiconductor	A material with properties of both a conductor and an insulator. Common semiconductors include silicon and germanium.

247

Static RAM	A type of **RAM** that does not require periodic refresh cycles, as the **Dynamic RAM** does.
Transistor	The basic solid-state device used to amplify or switch electrical current.
VLSI	Very Large Scale Integration. VLSI devices are integrated circuits that contain 1,000 or more **gate equivalents.**
Wafer	A thin disk of semiconducting material (usually silicon) on which many separate **chips** can be fabricated and then cut into individual integrated circuits. Also called a slice.
Word	A set of **binary bits** processed by the computer as the primary unit of information.

CHAPTER FIVE

The Politics of Protection in the U.S. Textile and Apparel Industries

VINOD K. AGGARWAL, WITH
STEPHAN HAGGARD

The textile, apparel, and footwear industries in the rich industrial nations have all been hit hard by competition from the newly industrializing countries. In these industries, in which easily available and standard production technologies can be combined with inexpensive labor, newly industrializing countries can often undersell producers in the richer nations. There are, however, several potentially successful adjustment strategies that remain open to producers in the advanced countries. In some products, more sophisticated machinery not easily available to the developing countries can be deployed to cut costs. In fashion-oriented sectors, high-price producers can compete in style and speed of delivery to the market. In addition, some large-scale producers have diversified their production locations to give themselves a mix of price and delivery-time options. In essence, advanced country producers big enough to diversify products and production locations while modernizing equipment appear able to survive. The same is true of small fashion houses or secondary suppliers whose market advantages depend on speed or style. Nonetheless, the emergence of newly developing countries as producers has brought a long-term loss of production and employment in the textile, apparel, and footwear industries. In the United States the global shift in the division of industrial production has been accompanied by a domestic regional shift: production has moved from the Northeast toward the Southeast in search of inexpensive, non-union labor. Many of the disruptions caused by these domestic shifts have been attributed to imports.

Protection against imports has been the only important policy adopted to help American firms in these industries adjust to changing market conditions. The following chapter traces the domestic politics of protection in the textile and apparel industries. The coalition for protection began in the early 1950s, when imports represented only a tiny fraction of domestic production. It continued to provide political support for protection twenty years later, when American firms had become exporters. Part of the competitive strength came from American oil prices that were kept well below world market levels, but the export boom was substantial and extended across a wide range of products. That export advantage appears in part to have been created by modernization of equipment forced in response to health and safety regulations. What is important in this story is that the politics of protection do not in any automatic way correspond to the economics of decline. France, for example, has insisted on protecting the textile and clothing industries, while the German government has refused to do so.

In the United States, the story is of a protectionist snowball growing in size as the years pass. Cotton producers were given price supports in the domestic market, which raised the cost of cotton for American textile manufacturers. Textile manufacturers then sought protection to compensate for this increased cost which imposed higher costs on the manfacturers of cotton clothing. Instead of resisting, the apparel manufacturers jumped on the protectionist bandwagon themselves. The coalition that solidified by the early 1960s has been able to win significant restrictions on imports. Some would argue that protection simply raised costs to consumers without halting the inevitable decline of domestic production in textiles and apparel. Others would argue that the time bought by protection in fact permitted more jobs and production to survive than would otherwise have been the case. This debate is not resolved here. The point we wish to make is that the only important policy adopted in response to the decline of two of our largest industries has been protection. There have been no significant policies to facilitate adjustment within these industries or to aid in the shift of resources out of them.

THE AMERICAN textile and apparel industries are usually thought of as "mature" if not declining industries. In some ways, this picture is accurate. Facing conditions of excess capacity and steadily tightening markets, these industries have suffered plant closings and job losses. As predicted by product cycle theories, domestic firms have faced stiff competition from countries seeking to develop their industrial bases. Not only must firms compete with foreign producers in home markets, but export-oriented firms are challenged in third markets and by tariffs in foreign producer countries.

In some ways, however, such a picture is static and ignores the marketing and production strategies of firms. Certain segments in both industries have done quite well; in fact, the textile industry as a whole has been running overall trade surpluses in recent years (see Table 1). From 1970 to 1979 textile exports have grown faster than any major

Table 1. U.S. imports, exports, and trade balance of textiles and apparel, 1967–1981 (in millions of dollars)

Year	Imports (customs value)			Exports			Trade balance		
	Textiles	Apparel	Total	Textiles	Apparel	Total	Textiles	Apparel	Total
1967	$ 803.9	$ 595.2	$1,399.1	$ 509.4	$ 118.6	$ 628.0	$ −294.5	$ −476.6	$ −771.1
1968	949.1	786.0	1,735.1	501.1	130.8	631.9	−448.0	−655.2	−1,103.2
1969	1,006.9	1,012.8	2,019.7	549.5	163.8	713.3	−457.4	−849.0	−1,306.4
1970	1,121.9	1,152.8	2,274.7	578.2	154.5	732.7	−543.7	−998.3	−1,542.0
1971	1,359.0	1,401.5	2,760.5	607.1	164.1	771.2	−751.9	−1,237.4	−1,989.3
1972	1,496.7	1,718.3	3,215.0	774.6	198.0	942.6	−752.1	−1,520.3	−2,272.4
1973	1,541.1	1,955.5	3,496.6	1,163.5	229.3	1,392.8	−377.6	−1,726.2	−2,103.8
1974	1,597.1	2,095.4	3,692.5	1,703.8	332.7	2,036.5	+106.7	−1,762.7	−1,656.0
1975	1,211.9	2,318.1	3,530.0	1,532.7	340.6	1,873.3	+320.8	−1,977.5	−1,656.7
1976	1,626.3	3,256.5	4,882.8	1,855.2	434.2	2,289.4	+228.9	−2,822.3	−2,493.4
1977	1,764.8	3,649.7	5,414.5	1,857.3	524.1	2,381.4	+92.5	−3,125.6	−3,033.1
1978	2,212.0	4,833.3	7,045.3	2,073.4	551.0	2,624.4	−138.6	−4,282.3	−4,420.9
1979	2,213.8	5,015.0	7,228.8	3,028.9	772.1	3,801.0	+815.1	−4,242.9	−3,427.8
1980	2,474.6	5,702.8	8,177.4	3,457.6	1,000.6	4,458.2	+983.0	−4,702.2	−3,719.2
1981	3,014.7	6,756.1	9,770.8	3,474.2	1,032.1	4,506.3	+459.5	−5,724.0	−5,264.5

SOURCE: Market Expansion Division, OTEXA, ITA, U.S. Department of Commerce.

manufactured product. Through technological innovation, shifting production from low to higher value-added segments, merging, and specializing, a number of firms—both large and small—have survived. Of course, some of this success may also be due to protection.

A key characteristic of advanced industrial societies in the postwar period has been the politicization of the adjustment process. Firms not only "adjust" by increasing competitiveness; through industry organizations they also enter the political arena. In principle, states may adopt several strategies to manage industrial decline, beyond simply letting market forces operate. They may act to promote *exit* from the industry by aiding labor and capital in making the transition out of declining sectors. States may also adopt *positive adjustment* policies aimed at reestablishing competitive position. The success of these strategies depends on a whole range of factors, including the structure of the industry, the policy instruments available to government, the organization of labor, and the character of the markets.

The purpose of this chapter is to explore the economic and political dynamics behind a third policy option: *protection.* The case of the textile and apparel industries illustrates the conditions under which "mature" industries will pursue protection as well as market strategies of adjustment. Recent debates over the automobile industry suggest that the problem posed by the emergence of protectionist coalitions is not unique. As foreign producers enter more and more sectors, government will be faced increasingly with the choice of directly supporting failing firms, restricting trade, pursuing positive adjustment strategies, or allowing market forces to operate.

Over the last twenty-five years, industry and labor groups in the textile and apparel industries have responded to global market changes by attempting to insulate the domestic market from international competition. Arguing that low profits, unemployment, and plant closings are due to imports, they have insisted that the government impose quotas. Their efforts have been successful. In 1955, under pressure from the United States, Japan restricted its exports of a few cotton textile and apparel products. By 1982, the United States was severely restricting imports of cotton, wool, and man-made fiber textiles and apparel under the global Multifiber Arrangement, which controlled virtually all world trade in textiles and apparel.

Imports have undoubtedly been a key factor in the restructuring of both industries. But both industries, and particularly the cotton textile manufacturers, had already been deeply affected by a series of domestic market and technological changes as early as the mid-1950s. These changes affected the market position at various segments differently.

While some were capable of adjusting, others faced intense competitive pressures that influenced their political strategies.

Strong pressure from imports and rapid job losses in a large, well-organized segment—cotton textile manufacturers—provided the political basis around which a protectionist coalition could form. Once protection was secured for cotton textiles, market conditions in other segments were altered. The result was that the *least* competitive segment of the two industries became the spokesman for both of them, and defined the character of their problems in terms of imports. The geographic dispersal of both industries made alternative, more directly interventionist adjustment policies virtually impossible to implement. Protection provided a common denominator, uniting various types of firms and industry segments around a common political program.

The relative weakness of the state vis-à-vis business interests contributed to the success of the protectionist coalition. The American bureaucracy, in contrast to the bureaucracies in France and Japan, lacked an independent vision of industrial policy, independent sources of information, and policy tools to implement disaggregated, industry-specific policies. Government weakness was also reflected in a high degree of institutional fragmentation, which increased the number of arenas in which business could exert pressure. Industry organizations were able to exploit access to Congress and competition between government bureaucracies to achieve their aims. A number of policy actions, particularly in the spheres of agriculture and foreign policy, contributed to the plight of firms in these sectors. Once industry groups could argue that government was responsible for industry performance, they could justify calls for exceptional measures.

The victory of the protectionist coalition in the United States, the world's dominant consumer of textiles and apparel, restructured world trade in both, and contributed to the gradual spread of protectionism and "managed trade." The reasons for this lie in the character of the protective instruments themselves: they are quantitative restrictions. Bilateral restraint agreements with the United States in cotton products encouraged the migration of production facilities to other low-wage countries. U.S. attempts to coordinate these bilateral accords and make them consistent with GATT norms through the formation of an international textile regime appeared successful initially. Gradually, however, foreign producers adjusted to the trade restrictions. Their diversification into new products, particularly man-made fibers, led to new accords between the U.S. and Far East producers. In response to new American restrictions, exporters adjusted by diverting products to Europe. The European textile and apparel industries came under new competitive pressures. The result was a further expansion of the scope of the regime and a gradual increase in its restrictiveness through the 1970s.

This chapter is divided into three sections. In the first, we look briefly at the pressures facing the two industries in the mid-1950s—a baseline period during which imports had a negligible impact. It will be shown that both industries were facing serious domestic difficulties that were spurring structural changes *prior* to the import boom. In the second, we examine the formation of the protectionist coalition, its political triumph, and the international repercussions of American trade restrictions. In the third, we examine the current state of the industries and the limitations on adjustment policy in mature sectors. We will argue that the government response to political pressures must itself be a *political* strategy that seeks to counter protectionist alliances.

INDUSTRIAL CHANGE IN TEXTILES AND APPAREL: THE "PRE-POLITICAL" PHASE

The textile and apparel industries in the United States have been considered problem industries for many years. In the early 1950s, when imports were still unimportant, many problems that were later connected to imports were already afflicting them. These included the closure of mills, unemployment, and low profits on sales. This section explores some of the sources of industrial transformation in these two industries.

Three points will emerge. First, in the early postwar period, both industries faced a set of changing market and technological conditions that adversely affected the competitive position of many firms. These changes were under way prior to any dramatic increases in imports.

Second, certain government policies adversely affected industry performance. These government policies were politically important because they served to justify calls for special relief.

Finally, the impact of imports, domestic changes, and government policy was not uniform across segments and firms. The picture of a uniformly declining sector is inaccurate. Once firms are disaggregated into types—by product, or size, or strategy—a different picture emerges. Some firms and segments are challenged by imports; others are pressed by domestic and government policies; still others are innovating, diversifying, expanding, and making profits. This disaggregation becomes of importance in understanding how and where protectionist pressures originate.

254

Changes in the Market

A number of market changes had begun to affect both apparel and textile manufacturers by the mid-1950s. These included changes in consumption patterns, fashion shifts, substitution by other products, competition from man-made fiber goods, and rising wages in the North. Textile and apparel firms responded in part by increasing capital intensity of production, merging, and relocating in the South.

One key factor in both industries was the failure of domestic consumption to keep pace with the growth of overall domestic demand for manufactures. These trends in demand were partly a function of income elasticities for these products. In 1950, clothing—a major consumer of textile products—represented 10.2 percent of overall consumer expenditures. By 1960 this share had dropped to 8.2 percent, and had fallen to 6.75 percent in 1977 (see Table 2).

Firms in the apparel industry have faced another problem. In order to compete successfully, they have had to respond rapidly to changes in fashion. This response has taken two forms. Large firms, with long production runs on fairly standardized products, have exploited brand-name recognition through advertising. Two types of small firms, one occupying high fashion or speciality niches in the market, and the other subcontracting for surplus demand, have remained competitive by exploiting the secondary labor market. These small firms are subject to high rates of failure, even though as *groups* they survive.[1] For both industries, but particularly for small firms, changes in the pattern of demand contributed to increasingly competitive domestic markets throughout the 1950s.

Textile manufacturers have also faced the problem of substitution. The cotton and wool textile industries confronted declining demand for their products because of an increase in the use of plastic and paper products which began in the 1950s. Substitution has also affected the man-made fiber sector of the textile industry, but since the production of man-made fiber products was often part of a larger diversified chemical industry complex that also produced plastics, the direct impact on these producers was not as dramatic. Firm size is again central. Small firms which concentrate on only a few lines of production tend to be more severely affected by substitution than broadly diversified firms.

The main problem of substitution is not between textiles and other

[1] For more on the industrial structure of the apparel industry, see Chap. 3 in José de la Torre *et al.*, *Corporate Responses to Import Competition in the U.S. Apparel Industry* (Atlanta: Georgia State University, 1978).

Table 2. Personal expenditures for clothing and shoes and overall personal consumption expenditures, 1950–1977 (in billions of dollars)

Year	Overall	Clothing and shoes	Percent of overall expenditures
1950	$ 192.0	$19.6	10.2%
1955	253.6	23.1	9.1
1960	324.9	26.7	7.1
1965	430.2	33.5	7.8
1970	681.8	46.6	6.8
1975	979.1	70.1	7.2
1977	1,206.5	81.5	6.8

SOURCE: *Economic Profile of the Apparel Industry* (Arlington, Va.: American Apparel Manufacturers Association, 1979), constructed from Table 26, p. 47.

products, however, but between *types* of textiles.[2] The international trend toward increasing production of synthetic fibers marks a technological revolution that has had a profound effect on the structure of the industry (see Figure 1). It also demonstrates the difficulty of characterizing an entire industry as being "in decline." Production of synthetics has boomed since the middle and late 1950s. In the United States in 1947, cotton accounted for 72.2 percent of apparent domestic consumption of fiber; by 1955, its share had shrunk to 64.5 percent. At the same time, rayon, acetates, and synthetic fibers had increased their share of the market from about 16 percent in 1947 to 27.9 percent in 1955 (see Table 3). This inter-fiber competition had crucial effects on the structure of the industry. Cotton and wool textile producers who did not retool to handle man-made fibers and smaller firms that would not adjust rapidly to technological change became uncompetitive.

Wage differentials and variations in union strength within the United States resulted in changes in the geographic location of production. Even before production was globally diffused and imports became a threat, increased competition had contributed to a major shift toward the South and West in both industries, with attendant plant closings elsewhere. In 1950, six states in the Northeast accounted for 40.5 percent of textile employment; by 1970, they accounted for only 21.7 percent. The tale is similar in apparel. In 1950, New York and Pennsylvania alone accounted for 47 percent of the jobs in the apparel industry. By 1970, the percentages had dropped to 31 percent, and by 1975

[2]For details on types of substitution, see U.S. Congress, House of Representatives, Subcommittee on Foreign Trade Policy of the House Ways and Means Committee, *Compendium of Papers on U.S. Foreign Trade Policy*, 1957 (hereafter cited as *Compendium*), pp. 856–861.

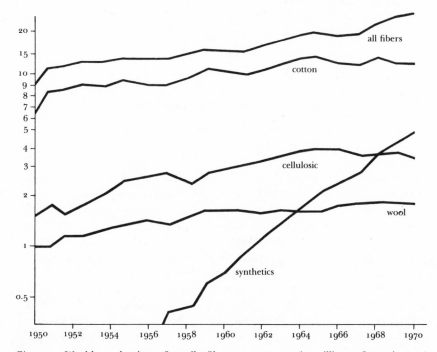

Figure 1: World production of textile fibers, 1950–1970 (in millions of metric tons). Redrawn, by permission of the Business Publishing Division, Georgia State University, from J. de la Torre *et al., Corporate Responses to Import Competition in the U.S. Apparel Industry* (Atlanta: Georgia State University, 1978), p. 31.

it was only 24 percent. South Carolina, Georgia, Tennessee, and Alabama increased their share of total apparel employment from 7.4 percent in 1950 to 22.0 percent in 1970.[3]

With modern equipment and non-unionized workers, firms in the South were able to sell at lower cost, further undermining the competitive position of Northern firms. In many cases, the capital for new textile plants came from Northern investors. Mill closures in New England were often followed by the development of new and more modern plants in the South, a trend of significance in mobilizing labor into the protectionist coalition.

One effect of these technological and market changes has been a trend beginning in the 1950s toward greater capital investment. From 1955 to 1977, the index of industrial production rose from 64.4 to

[3]U.S. Department of Labor, Bureau of Labor Statistics, *Employment and Earnings, States and Areas, 1939–1957* (Washington, D.C.: Government Printing Office, 1976).

Table 3. Domestic consumption of fibers, 1947–1977, by type (in percent)

Year	Cotton	Wool	Rayon, acetates	Synthetics
1947	72.7%	10.9%	15.4%	0.6%
1955	64.5	7.5	21.4	6.5
1965	53.5	6.0	17.8	22.6
1977	27.3	1.7	6.9	64.1

SOURCE: *Economic Profile of the Apparel Industry* (Arlington, Va.: American Apparel Manufacturers Association, 1979). Percentages calculated from data in Table 6, p. 22.

137.1, with 1967 as 100.[4] In that period employment dropped by 22 percent. Although this trend in increasing labor productivity was recognized early, little has been done to ease the transition process for labor. Even Senator Pastore's Subcommittee on Textiles of the Interstate and Foreign Commerce Committee (which always emphasized imports in its policy recommendations) noted in 1962: "A corollary of improved efficiency, however, is that labor requirements will be reduced. *It is our hope that management and labor can work cooperatively to minimize the impact of reduced labor which will accompany modernization.*"[5] "Hoping" was hardly a sufficient policy proposal. In contrast to strong recommendations for a broad scheme to regulate the inflow of imports on a worldwide basis, the vital problem of technological change was not given serious thought. From a political standpoint, this stance made sense: large firms investing in new capital and equipment would hardly welcome the additional burden of concerning themselves with the disposition of surplus labor.

Changing market conditions have also forced concentration in both industries. Although numerous studies have found the textile industry to be among the least concentrated in the United States, concern over mergers in this industry arose early in the postwar period. In 1955, for example, the Senate Committee on the Judiciary produced a major study entitled "Merger Movement in the Textile Industry," in which the role of mergers in leading to unemployment was emphasized.[6] The number of firms in the textile industry has steadily declined since World War II. This has been of major concern to labor groups. Moreover, large

[4]Bureau of Labor Statistics, *Employment and Earnings*, March 1978, and *Employment and Earnings, United States, 1909–1975.*

[5]Hearings by the Subcommittee on Interstate and Foreign Commerce of the United States Senate, 85th Congress, 2nd Session, chaired by Senator Pastore, were held at various times from 1958 to 1963 (hereafter cited as *Pastore Hearings*). *Pastore Hearings*, 1962, 2nd Supp. Report, p. 15.

[6]U.S. Congress, Senate, Antitrust Subcommittee on the Judiciary, *The Merger Movement in the Textile Industry*, August 1, 1955.

firms showed higher profit margins than small firms, on the average. (See Tables 4 and 5.) In 1956, small firms (with assets of less than 1 million dollars) earned 6 percent of industry profits and comprised 11 percent of industry assets. On the other hand, large firms (with assets over 50 million dollars) earned 41 percent of industry profits while holding only 34 percent of industry assets. These figures reflect the ability of larger firms to pursue a more diversified response to market changes, including the ability to move toward capital intensification.

The purpose of this brief overview has been to establish that the textile and apparel industries were subject to a set of changes that characterize "mature" industries: tightening markets, increased competition, company failures, and plant closings. These trends were under way prior to the import boom. Total imports accounted for less than 2 percent of consumption in 1955—at a time when complaints about imports being the critical source of trouble abounded.

Government Policy

Government policy affecting textiles and apparel in the 1950s not only had an important impact on the structure and performance of these sectors: it also had a crucial role in shaping industry's *political* response to changing market conditions. Although government policy is often chastised for its incoherence, these inconsistencies spring from genuine conflicts of interests and goals. Two types of policy conflicts have been important in the textile-apparel story: one between competing domestic aims, the other between foreign and domestic policies. While the U.S. government in the 1950s had no sector-specific policies for industry, it did have an agricultural policy that adversely affected cotton textile and apparel manufacturers. A number of other policies, including taxation and minimum-wage policies, also affected the competitive position of the firms. The second conflict—between domestic and foreign policies—was often in fact a conflict of interest between inward-looking and international business. Sometimes, however, the conflict stemmed from ideological and strategic concerns, reflecting a commitment to anticommunism and free trade, even at significant material costs to some sectors.

Domestically, U.S. policy toward agriculture has tended to encourage the replacement of natural fibers by synthetics, increasing the pressure on cotton manufacturers. A price support system for cotton was instituted in 1933 in response to depressed cotton prices resulting from overproduction. The price-support system had two crucial effects on the cotton textile and apparel industries. First, American textile producers were faced with cotton prices that were often higher than the

Table 4. Number of mills and employees in U.S. textile industry, 1956–1977, by industry segment

Industry segment	1956	1962	1966	1970	1977
All textile industry					
Mills	8,231	7,441	7,035	7,009	6,702
Mills with 500+ employees	482	387	397	440	418
Employees	1,061,868	874,677	927,492	947,734	883,161
Cotton weaving					
Mills	n.a.	494	468	453	310
Mills with 500+ employees	n.a.	147	139	121	75
Employees	n.a.	224.042	216,395	179,363	112,749
Synthetic weaving					
Mills	777	344	379	385	442
Mills with 500+ employees	47	38	57	71	116
Employees	114,240	72,024	95,749	119,801	160,141
Wool weaving					
Mills	n.a.	463	336	284	152
Mills with 500+ employees	n.a.	25	18	16	8
Employees	n.a.	60,103	45,091	36,912	16,578
Narrow fabric					
Mills	n.a.	496	399	394	323
Mills with 500+ employees	n.a.	3	6	5	4
Employees	n.a.	26,702	26,393	27,982	22,092
Knitting					
Mills	2,939	2,701	2,688	2,615	2,328
Mills with 500+ employees	67	66	70	86	76
Employees	229,659	215,098	233,221	248,490	228,881

NOTE: n.a. = not available.

SOURCE: Bureau of the Census, U.S. Department of Commerce, *County Business Patterns,* various issues.

world market price; but they were unable to buy foreign cotton because the price-support system was supplemented by a highly restrictive quota on cotton imports. This situation was crucial in forcing the shift to man-made fibers. Second, declining exports of raw cotton owing to high U.S. consumption led to the imposition of a two-price cotton system under the 1956 Agricultural Act. This policy added insult to injury: exports of cotton and cotton products were subsidized, which enabled foreign producers to buy U.S. cotton at the world price! The net cost difference was about 25 percent, a substantial amount given the value-added in cotton textile manufacturing.[7] In response to continuous protests from cotton textile producers, the two-price system

[7] J. L. Juvet, "The Cotton Industry and World Trade," *Journal of World Trade Law,* September-October 1967, p. 553.

Table 5. Number, assets, and profits of U.S. textile firms as percentage of textile industry totals, 1956, by size of assets

Assets	Number of firms as percentage of total	Assets of firms as percentage of total industry assets	Net profits of firms as percentage of total industry profits
Less than $1 million	78%	11%	6%
$1–10 million	19	32	28
$10–50 million	2	23	25
$50 million and over	1	34	41
Total	100%	100%	100%

SOURCE: U.S. Congress, Senate, Committee on Interstate and Foreign Commerce, *Problems of the Domestic Textile Industry*, 85th Cong., 2 sess. (1958), p. 1665.

was finally eliminated in 1964 by government subsidization of the entire cotton crop, allowing American textile producers to buy cotton at the world price. As will be seen, however, the political damage had been done.

The most significant effect of government policy in apparel has concerned labor. Although minimum wage legislation is not specific to the apparel industry, the dependence of apparel manufacturers on the secondary labor market leads to a greater de facto impact of wages on this industry. In some cases, the minimum wage may prevent marginal firms from competing with imports.

U.S. foreign policy goals during the 1950s were also an important element in the loss of foreign markets. Aid policies encouraged foreign indigenous textile production, and the promotion of a liberal order opened foreign markets to Japanese exporters. These policies, pursued for strategic and ideological reasons, also reinforced the textile industry's incentive to seek "recompense" for U.S. government action.

To respond to the perceived threat of communist expansionism, a number of aid programs, in addition to the Marshall Plan, were implemented in the 1950s and 1960s. Four programs in particular affected textile production in foreign countries. These were: (1) sales and grants of raw materials (cotton) under Public Law 480 and aid through the Community Credit Corporation (CCA); (2) aid for machinery requirements under loans from the Export-Import Bank, the International Cooperation Administration (ICA), and the Development Loan Fund; (3) procurement of textiles and apparel from foreign countries by the ICA as part of the mutual security program; and (4) technical assistance to the industry under the Mutual Security Act.[8]

[8]*Pastore Hearings*, 1958, p. 1768.

These programs represented an ideological commitment to less developed countries to help resist the threat of communism through the slogan "trade, not aid." Japan was by far the major source of ICA procurement of textile goods. In 1968, for example, $42.3 million (out of $68 million) worth of textiles was obtained from Japan; as Leonard Saccio, Deputy Director of the ICA noted, this aid had "helped Japan to ward off economic penetration from Red China."[9] This objective was widely accepted by other government officials. For example, Deputy Assistant Secretary of State for Economic Affairs Beale pointed to a "Soviet threat" and noted that "the Soviet bloc started on its economic offensive in 1954, and as of the middle of 1958, it has offered 17 textile plants to eight different countries and additional textile machinery to four countries."[10] He also made a claim which was to come under increasing industry scrutiny: "In safeguarding our national security, through the mutual security program, we are also pursuing the best long-range interests of the American business community."

The conflicts of interest between various segments of the American economy became most evident with respect to U.S. efforts to promote an open trading system. With a clear overall trading surplus, U.S. policy-makers saw free trade as being in the American interest—even if it was at the expense of the textile industry. Under questioning from Senators at a Senate hearing, Secretary Beale admitted that in aiding foreign textile industries "it was recognized that the expansion of textile production abroad might reduce the potential market for U.S. textile exports."[11] Yet he countered that U.S. exports as a whole were expected to rise with economic development and reconstruction abroad.

Although the growth of foreign textile production and competition from countries internationally (both in displacing U.S. export markets and in subsequent exports to the United States) can hardly be attributed to these government policies, they did have a significant political impact. In conjunction with the government price support program in cotton (which led to higher raw material costs), these policies of aid to foreign textile industries provided a target for textile groups in arguing that their problems should be treated *sui generis*. Since government policies were adversely affecting the textile industry (and particularly the cotton textile industry), it was a natural step for them to ask that exceptions to U.S. policy be made on their behalf. Exceptionalism became the key to snowballing protection.

[9]*Ibid.*, p. 1845.
[10]*Ibid.*, p. 1777.
[11]*Ibid.*

Differences in Performance of Firms

An undifferentiated picture of an industry in decline is not accurate, however. Once firms are disaggregated by size and product line, it is clear that not all have suffered. The cotton and wool textile manufacturers and many small firms in the apparel industry have faced problems of increased competition and technological change. Cotton product producers were adversely affected by government agricultural policies. Beginning in the late 1950s, the man-made fiber segment of the textile industry began to grow rapidly, aggravating the difficulties of the natural fiber producers.

In both the textile and the apparel industries, large firms pursuing a diversified strategy (which may include relocation, merger, capital intensification, and establishment of brand names through advertising) have survived and prospered. Small firms, particularly in the apparel industry, have also been able to survive because of their flexibility; as individual firms they are subject to the continual threat of failure, but as a group they occupy an important structural position in the apparel industry, and are likely to hold this position. Medium-sized firms suffered the most: they were too small to invest heavily and too large to be flexible and take advantage of the secondary labor market.

These differences in performance suggest that a blunt instrument like protection would not be appropriate for the delicate operation of increasing the competitive position of a diverse set of enterprises. This was particularly true because the problems facing the industry arose before the influx of imports, and because government policy itself was in part responsible for industry performance. To understand how trade restriction emerged as the chosen aim of the industry, we must examine how a protectionist coalition emerged under the leadership of the largest, but declining, segment—cotton textile producers.

THE POLITICS OF PROTECTION

In the previous section we described how industrial structure has changed as a result of company-level strategies to adapt to changing market conditions. We treated government policies as external forces affecting the terms of competition. It is clear, however, that firms do not simply accept government policy as a given. Rather, they seek to force certain policy outcomes. In nations where government does not have autonomous sources of information or the policy instruments to intervene selectively, or where industry has multiple channels of access to decision-making centers, government action will be significantly shaped by the interests of industry, as represented by politically experienced industry associations. To understand policy outcomes, we must therefore examine the *interests* and *strategies* adopted by the sectors that are pressing for protection.

First, what interests did textile and apparel groups have in pushing for restriction of imports as a response to their problem? It is far from clear that the apparel industry had an interest in forming an alliance for the purpose of raising the prices of its key input. But on closer examination, it is precisely the market links between the two sectors that make such an alliance likely. Once it became clear to the apparel industry that textiles would receive some import protection, they were forced to go along. With one side of the market—the sellers—organized, it became incumbent on the buyers to organize as well. This was only the first of a series of snowballing effects that led to calls for wider and wider protection.

Industry structure and company-level interest in maintaining decision-making autonomy limited the range of policy options. Imports were only one among several problems these two industries faced. But the instrument of import protection, which is intervention at the level of *trade*, leaves the decision-making autonomy of the firm intact. Were the government to seek to address a series of other key problems in the industry through positive adjustment policies—labor displacement, mergers, relocation, technological change, or inter-fiber competition— it would be drawn into forms of intervention at the level of *production*. The fragmented character of the industries, and the limited tools of the government, would have made such intervention difficult in any case; but all positive adjustment proposals discussed within the government were carefully sidestepped by industry.

The very fragmentation of these industries posed a key strategic question to industry representatives. How were industry interests to be aggregated? In highly concentrated sectors, such as autos or steel, a small group of large firms can simultaneously represent their particular interests and speak with authority about the shape of the industry as a whole. As we have seen, however, the market positions of various segments of the textile and apparel industries diverge widely. This fragmentation made import restriction a lowest common denominator to which everyone could agree—although, as will be seen, the *motivation* for controlling imports in the case of some segments did not come from import pressure at all.

The industry strategy—to form specific textile-apparel coalitions— also illustrates the importance of the arena in which certain issues are decided, and the importance of the ability to pit competing segments of the bureaucracy against one another. Using access to Congress, and pressing the issue of jobs, to which elected politicians are so sensitive, the coalition was able to hold hostage the trade acts that empowered the President to negotiate tariff reductions.

Once a coalition for a restrictive trade policy had been built and succeeded in serving its initial aims, the most important element in the political dynamics of increasing protection was the market impact of protection itself. Protection that is *limited*—either by country or by product line—tends to generate pressure for more protection by affecting the terms of competition that domestic producers face. This snowballing effect is strikingly illustrated by the textile-apparel story. Each form of protection came to entail the next one.

The first problem created by import restrictions concerned the shift in the *composition* of imports. After 1961, when the U.S. government moved to control cotton products, foreign countries adjusted accordingly, concentrating on the export of wool and man-made fiber products to the U.S. market. Since the only real objective of the government was to minimize the severity of trade controls, administrative officials resisted the industry attempts to extend the quota system to other non-cotton fiber-based products in the early 1960s; but as imports of other fiber-based products grew rapidly, the government was eventually forced to conclude restrictions on these fiber-based products as well.

This process of foreign adjustment was not limited to product lines, but manifested itself in the spread of textile and apparel manufacturing to other countries as well. This posed a second problem. Under the international arrangements which the United States negotiated, bilateral agreements were concluded with major exporters. As these countries faced growing restrictions, other countries whose exports were not controlled began to move into the production and export of textile and apparel products to the U.S. market. This problem arose as early as 1957, when the United States first concluded a bilateral agreement that regulated the export of Japanese cotton textile and apparel goods to America: Hong Kong moved quickly to fill the gap created by Japanese restraints. This meant that Orderly Marketing Agreements had to be extended to new producers.

The third problem that resulted from import restrictions concerned consumers, not producers. As the United States closed its market, exports of textile and apparel goods from less developed countries were directed to the European market. This diversion led to increasing international tension between the United States and Europe, as both competitively juggled restrictions to avoid diversion. Ironically, however, it also enabled the United States to secure a Multifiber Arrangement in 1973. By negotiating bilateral agreements with major Far East exporters in 1971, the United States altered the incentives of reluctant European countries and encouraged them to jump on the bandwagon for an *international* protectionist arrangement.

We have now identified three factors which have determined the political outcomes in the textile-apparel area: the interests and strategies of domestic producers, the character of their interaction with the government, and the international market repercussions of limited protection. In this section, we examine the politics of protection in three distinct periods.

During the first period, lasting from 1955 to 1961, government policy evolved from a relatively free-trade position, with only tariffs in effect, to a bilateral system of import control on cotton textile and apparel goods from Japan. Subsequently a multilateral pact, the Short-Term Arrangement, was concluded in 1961 to regulate national restrictions on the import of cotton textile and apparel products. It was during this first period that the industry strategy emerged to focus on *imports* as the preferred area for government intervention. The strategy that textile groups used in securing their objectives was to block various trade bills. They thus alerted the administration that they were a political power to be reckoned with. The conclusion of a bilateral agreement with Japan had important market and political effects. It encouraged apparel producers to join the protectionist coalition as Japan expanded apparel exports to the United States. It also led to a spread of textile production to other countries, which then focused their exports on the U.S. market.

During the second period, from 1961 to 1973, other groups pressed for and succeeded in securing an expansion of the Short-Term Arrangement in cotton to cover products made of other fibers. President Kennedy's intervention scheme clearly illustrates some of the difficulties associated with a *domestic* intervention plan that is not properly integrated with policies at the international level. The "snowball effect" became evident during this phase. Foreign countries whose cotton-based exports were controlled moved into the production of woolen and man-made fiber-based products. Countries whose exports were not controlled increasingly entered into textile and apparel production for the American market. When the United States concluded bilateral agreements covering man-made and wool-based products, exporting countries redirected a large portion of their exports to the European market. This shift to the European market encouraged the Europeans to go along with U.S. demands for a multifiber arrangement. The United States was able to internationalize its own domestic adjustment problems.

During the third and final period, 1974 to 1980, the situation was reversed, as actions taken by the European Economic Community (EEC) directly affected U.S. policy on textiles and apparel. Because the EEC was slow to negotiate its bilateral agreements under the Multifiber Arrangement, exports by less developed countries (LDCs) to the Europeans grew rapidly. The EEC's response was to press for a major modification of the international agreement in 1977. The modifications incorporated into the Multifiber Arrangement allowed the EEC to conclude bilateral arrangements with LDC producers that were more protectionist. The response of U.S. textile and apparel groups was to press the U.S. government for more restrictive bilateral agreements because they feared a diversion of exports back to the American market. Following their old strategy, they threatened to disrupt the negotiations taking place under the Tokyo Round. This threat proved to be credible. The government agreed to renegotiate its bilaterals with Far East suppliers in the beginning of 1980, to further restrict their access to the American market. The interdependence of national policies and international market intervention is the most noticeable feature of this period. It also demonstrates the enduring ability of the textile and apparel coalition to remain united around the protection issue, and to use its political power in a potent fashion, even at a time when the textile industry had a large trade surplus and the apparel industry a large deficit.

From Free Trade to the STA, 1955–1961

Despite the problems which were to emerge, the textile and apparel industries in the United States experienced high profits and a remarkably favorable export position immediately after World War II. Yet this situation was a distinct *anomaly* when considered in historical perspective.[12] The cotton and wool segments of these industries had been protected by relatively high tariffs in the 1920s and 1930s. By 1937, import penetration in cotton fabrics reached 1.5 percent of U.S. production. Although seemingly insignificant, this level of imports was sufficient to stimulate demands to restrict the imports of Japanese textile goods. After the unilateral restraint exercised by Japanese exporters in December of 1935 failed to satisfy domestic producers, a private voluntary agreement was concluded between the American and Japanese cotton textile industries in 1937. This action proved to be

[12] After 1911, although U.S. production increased considerably, the United States remained a net importer of textiles and apparel to the present (except during World War I and immediately after World War II). See the chart in *Pastore Hearings*, 1958, p. 1786.

satisfactory to U.S. textile interests: imports as a percentage of U.S. production declined in subsequent years.[13]

Almost twenty years passed before the import levels of textile and apparel products once again rose to the 1937 level: in 1956, cotton textile imports were 1.7 percent of domestic production.[14] Yet a call for government action to restrict imports was made in July 1955, and a strategy to restrain imports was discussed even earlier.[15]

The Motivation to Focus on Imports

A brief examination of the market positions of key actors shows that there was much to be gained from focusing on imports as the basic problem. Turning first to the cotton textile industry, it appears that both large competitive firms and smaller marginal ones perceived that direct benefits would result from import restrictions. As we have seen, large firms were facing competition from man-made textile producers and sought to adjust by moving to the southern part of the United States to improve their competitive position. Moreover, large textile firms were increasingly replacing their labor with automated facilities.

In this situation of ongoing industrial change, imports provided a ready scapegoat for internal problems. Labor recognized the inadequacy of the import argument. For example, Solomon Barkin, Director of Research for the United Textile Workers of America, noted in the 1958 Pastore hearings on the textile industry that the Senate committee should "focus on the basic domestic problem. The fact is that in 1948 and 1949, we were not threatened by imports; we were not threatened and we were still concerned with domestic problems." The clear split between the views of labor and management, and the industry's desire to divert government attention from the domestic issues, was made clear when Barkin noted: "If we stopped all imports we will not have solved our problem. This industry would still continue to shrink . . . if you read carefully the presentation of ACMI (the cotton textile industry association) you would see that they begged you not to investigate and study the problems of the industry."[16] Due to the organizationally weak position of labor, it was unable to press for major changes in U.S. policy that would treat the fundamental problems of the industry. As a result, labor agreed to endorse a policy of protection—the only policy acceptable to business interests.

[13]*Compendium,* p. 1014.

[14]Hunsberger notes that imports declined with a recession in the United States and a boycott movement against Japanese aggression in China. See Warren Hunsberger, *Japan and the United States in World Trade* (New York: Harper & Row, 1964), p. 317.

[15]Minutes, American Cotton Manufacturers Institute (hereafter cited as Minutes, ACMI), November 18, 1953; on the 1955 request, see *Compendium,* p. 1014.

[16]*Pastore Hearings,* July 1958, pp. 331, 333.

Marginal producers of cotton textiles also stood to gain from the import focus. These producers were in fact most susceptible to import competition, and thus shared a common tactical interest with the larger firms. Since the government was reluctant to involve itself in a struggle among domestic producers, policy-makers were more willing to consider demands for import restraints.

The producers of man-made fiber textiles were in a very strong market position during the 1950s and faced almost no competition from low-priced imports. Man-made fibers represented the growth segment of the industry. Yet they also went along with cotton textile demands for import restrictions. Three factors appear salient in their decision. First, they wished to restrict tariff cutting on their products to keep out *European*-produced man-made fiber textile products. It was important for them from a political standpoint to go along. Second, and most important, they wished to keep attention focused on imports rather than the much more critical problem of inter-fiber competition. They hardly expected stiff competition from foreign producers in the near future, because their technology was at the leading edge and they were successful in exporting goods. In fact, controls on cotton textile imports accelerated the substitution process and eventually led to an import "threat" to these producers. Third, the possibility of short-run gain also tempted man-made fiber textile producers. Restrictions on low-priced cotton textile imports preserved part of the market for American textile producers to compete for the consumer's dollar. Although part of the market share would go to domestic cotton textile producers, man-made textile producers could also compete for part of the insulated market. This would not have been the case if low-priced imports were allowed into the United States, because consumers might favor foreign cotton products over higher-priced, domestic man-made fiber products.

By and large, apparel producers were less than enthusiastic about import restrictions in textiles. From an economic standpoint, this made sense. Low-priced textile imports served two functions: they allowed domestic apparel manufacturers to procure inexpensive material for garments, and they kept downward pressure on domestic prices of textiles. Yet apparel producers also joined the coalition to restrict textile and apparel imports. What was their motivation? Ideally, of course, apparel producers would have preferred to have control only on apparel imports. *Politically*, however, this was not feasible. The high degree of fragmentation in the industry, and the high turnover of firms due to the intensity of competition, made it extremely difficult for this industry to develop a politically unified voice. Apparel producers were thus more than happy to follow the political lead provided by the cotton textile manufacturers association. In addition, there lurked the powerful threat of facing a textile industry, on which the apparel industry depended, unilaterally organizing its domestic market. The market made political goodwill out of necessity.

Apparel producers had also experienced changes in their competitive position due to government policies. Cotton blouse producers had experienced intense import competition, but other apparel manufacturers were not threatened by imports.[17] Restrictions on Japanese cotton products (mainly of velveteens, ginghams, and blouses) led to an important diversion process, however. As Hong Kong entered the American market in cotton textiles, it began to use its foothold to export massive amounts of apparel as well. The ease with which apparel products could be produced and exported in less developed countries led to grave reservations on the part of apparel producers. Higher imports of apparel products, particularly between 1957 and 1960, led to a change in strategy on the part of apparel producers. They decided to ally themselves with textile producers around protection. This decision was greeted with glee by textile manufacturers. In a statement made at the 1961 Senate hearings on the textile industry, textile producers noted that apparel producers were having problems: "The men's clothing industry, a leading customer of the U.S. woolen and worsted industry, as recently as 1957 opposed efforts of wool mills to obtain adequate tariff protection." They then went on to quote an advertisement by the clothing industry committee which illustrated the shift in attitude: "Let us admit that when Government permitted a flood of fabrics from low-wage countries to engulf American mills, many apparel manufacturers rushed to buy the imports, to the detriment of our own textile industry and ultimately ourselves."[18]

The Strategy to Secure Import Controls

Although the *incentives* to seek government intervention to insulate the domestic market from imports was present in the 1950s, a *strategy* to press the administration to institute protective measures had to be developed.

The leading organization in the battle for protection was undoubtedly the American Cotton Manufacturers Institute (ACMI). As early as 1953—when imports were insignificant—the ACMI had begun to plan for the battle against imports. It clearly recognized that the favorable post-World War II export position of the textile industry was due to destruction of foreign textile industries in World War II and would not

---

[17]Hunsberger, *Japan and the United States in World Trade*, p. 305.
[18]*Pastore Hearings,* July 1961, p. 112.

be enjoyed forever. For example, the chairman of the Foreign Trade Committee of the Cotton Manufacturers Association, in commenting on a public relations proposal, noted that "it was but one of the strategic moves planned by the industry in its campaign to combat the deluge of free trade propaganda flooding the country." He urged that in the struggle ahead, the industry be careful to avoid pitfalls and not allow misguided zeal to jeopardize the industry's position.[19]

The path chosen by the ACMI was to use the reciprocal trade act agreements as a hostage to secure their objectives. By gathering congressional support, textile manufacturers threatened to block bills that would allow the United States to negotiate tariff reductions. Given the strong U.S. desire to promote free trade for economic and strategic reasons, this was clearly a potent threat. Various administrations were always willing to buy off the textile and apparel industries by giving them quotas on imports.

The strategy of focusing on the use of an international instrument—import restriction—had another important political dimension: it sidestepped domestic opposition. Rather than confronting other interest groups head-on through an attack on governmental programs that were detrimental to textile interests (such as the cotton support program and wool tariffs), the ACMI simply argued for quotas as "compensation." This had the effect of passing the cost on to actors who had no political clout: consumers, and producers in less developed countries.

The actual struggle to secure import restrictions during the first phase came in three steps. First, attempts to have quotas imposed to restrict Japanese imports were sought. Second, after a bilateral agreement was worked out with the Japanese in 1957, Hong Kong started its export drive and textile producers once again sought global quotas. They argued (correctly, though perhaps in bad faith) that bilateral agreements would never succeed in insulating the American market, because new suppliers would continue to appear. When the U.S. government sought to restrict Hong Kong exports rather than imposing a global quota, and Hong Kong refused, pressure on the government mounted. Third, the U.S. government promoted a global agreement to regulate the development of bilateral agreements with exporting countries. The outcome of this process was the Short-Term Arrangement on cotton textiles and apparel. This was seen as a way of controlling imports without destroying the GATT. Moreover, it helped to take pressure off of the American market by forcing European countries to take more imports from less developed countries.

[19]Minutes, ACMI, November 18, 1953.

Japanese Restrictions. The year 1954 was a key one in the development of the struggle to obtain import quotas for the textile and apparel industries. In the latter half of 1954, textile imports from Japan grew rapidly just as textile profits were experiencing a cyclical downturn, though the import penetration ratio in cotton textiles in 1956 was only 1.7 percent. The industry experienced the worst profit performance in the postwar period.[20] With some exceptions, apparel firms fared better and were not yet facing growing imports. The ACMI decided to focus its political resources on resisting HR 1, a bill to extend the Reciprocal Trade Agreement Act for a period of three years beginning in 1955.

To develop a coalition to block the bill, the ACMI appealed to other textile organizations and to apparel and raw material producers of cotton and wool. The apparel producers, with the exception of the National Association of Blouse Manufacturers, however, were not actively interested. Raw cotton producers, with interests in foreign markets, chose to support the tariff bill. Labor unions in the textile industry, however, were willing to go along with opposition to HR 1.

In testimony at hearings for HR 1, members of the ACMI emphasized the unity of textile and apparel interests and the employment issue. Claudia Murchison, Economic Adviser for the ACMI, testified that "this giant activity—and I combine these two great industrial divisions because they are so closely related—employs roughly two and a quarter million people." Labor also stressed the issue of jobs. Congressmen even testified on industry's behalf after a vigorous letter-writing campaign led by the ACMI. Some Congressmen indicated that quotas might be needed to cope with "low-wage imports."[21] In the end, HR 1 passed with great difficulty, an important achievement by House majority leader Sam Rayburn, particularly since pressures to reject the bill had grown rapidly after it was announced on June 8, 1955, that tariffs on textile products were to be cut considerably.[22]

Though the battle against HR 1 was lost, the war was just beginning. The ACMI and other textile groups pursued action in a number of different arenas. The bill to set up the Organization for Trade Cooperation to replace the GATT (HR 5550) was opposed by textile groups before the House Ways and Means Committee. It soon became clear to the administration that the bill would not be passed by the House, and

[20]SEC-FTC Quarterly Financial Reports for Manufacturing, Mining, and Trade Corporations. Federal Trade Commission, U.S. Government, various issues.

[21]U.S. Congress, House, Hearings, Committee on Ways and Means, *Trade Agreements Extension*, 84th Congress, 1st Session, 1955, pp. 1612, 1596–1827.

[22]R. Bauer, I. de Sola Poole, and L. Dexter, *American Business and Public Policy* (Chicago: Aldine, 1963, 1972), p. 64.

it was never brought up for a vote. Opposition to this bill served to further unify various textile groups.[23]

Textile producers also sought restraints on imports through the escape clause provision of the 1951 Trade Agreements Extension Act. This act directed the Tariff Commission to determine if products were being imported into the United States as a result of trade concessions in quantities that would harm American producers. Although the Commission was unanimous in recommending that tariff concessions on velveteen be modified on October 24, 1956, President Eisenhower decided that this action was not warranted because by that time (as we shall see below) the Japanese had agreed to restrict their exports of this product.[24] Other petitions on blouses and ginghams were withdrawn in light of Japanese restraints, and an application for relief on cotton pillowcases was found unwarranted. Although restraints were not actually imposed, these actions were critical in persuading the Japanese to restrain their exports voluntarily.

The third avenue pursued by textile interests in December 1955 focused on possible restrictions through Section 22 of the Agricultural Adjustment Act. This act was intended to prevent the import of commodities that would undermine the agricultural support system—in this case, the cotton support program. But action on this petition was not forthcoming. After reviewing the facts, the acting Secretary of Agriculture, True D. Morse, rejected the industry appeal, noting that imports of cotton products were less than 1 percent of the American cotton crop and were equivalent to less than 1.5 percent of domestic mill consumption.[25] He also pointed out that Japan was the best consumer for U.S. cotton, and thus concluded that restrictions on the import of cotton textiles were not warranted.

The fourth element of the ACMI's strategy—trying to secure a negotiated agreement with the Japanese—illustrates the significance of multiple channels of institutional access to decision-making. While the other administrative and legislative efforts were not bearing fruit, this tack proved to be more successful. In April 1955, President Smith of ACMI argued that tariffs would not suffice to control imports and advocated the use of quotas. Harkening back to 1937, he hinted that although such an agreement was no longer possible, because the U.S. Justice Department argued that private agreements were a restraint of free trade, it demonstrated "the willingness of the Japanese to accept

[23]See J. Lynch, *Toward an Orderly Market* (Tokyo: Sophia University Press, 1968), for a discussion of the defeat of this bill; on the unifying effect, see p. 87.
[24]*Congressional Record*, August 29, 1966, p. 20967.
[25]*Pastore Hearings*, 1958, p. 917.

the principle of quota limitation whenever such a principle is sound."
Efforts by the ACMI to convince the U.S. government that bilaterally
negotiated quotas would be "sound" were not initially successful. But the
Japanese took a pragmatic attitude, fearing that U.S. industry interests
might prevail. On December 21, 1955, they announced that they would
unilaterally restrain the export of cotton fabrics, blouses, velveteens, and
ginghams.[26] This measure did not, however, satisfy American producers, who were now confident that they could insulate the domestic
market more securely. They continued to advocate a government-spon-
sored bilateral arrangement that would give them greater control over
market access. In spite of opposition to quotas by the State Department,
producers enlisted the aid of the Commerce Department in negotiating
quotas. Considering the pressure coming from congressmen and the
ability of textile interests to block legislation, the government's policy
options were not particularly appealing.[27] Given the alternatives, having
the Japanese restrict their own exports was a solution that appeared to
do the least damage to the government's other objectives. After numerous meetings, the Japanese sent a note to the State Department on
September 27, 1956, in which they proposed restrictions on exports. On
January 16, 1957, the U.S. government announced that a five-year program to restrain Japanese exports would take effect.[28]

The Coalition Expands. Whereas these first attempts to secure governmental action had seen the ACMI leading a loose coalition of interests,
during the second period the coalition began to solidify. Apparel
manufacturers began to feel the pressure of imports, particularly from
Hong Kong. The Japanese "voluntary" export restraint had merely
resulted in a shift in sources of supply and the development of textile
and apparel exports from other countries (see Table 6). Rayon producers also began to feel competition from imports, and were willing to
throw their hat into the ring with the other producers.

The ACMI had decided on a strategy after the 1957 Japanese limitations. Their basic objectives were as follows:

1. Restore effective congressional control.
2. Change the basic purpose of trade policy from stimulation of exports
to maintenance of growing domestic production.

[26]Lynch, *Toward an Orderly Market*, pp. 92, 102.
[27]As Assistant Secretary Beale pointed out in Senate hearings: "Our feeling has been
that if the U.S. were to abandon its policy of opposing quotas and were instead to favor a
policy of imposing quotas, we would find ourselves confronted throughout the world
with retaliatory action of some kind or another" (*Pastore Hearings*, 1958, p. 1743).
[28]The agreement called for an overall ceiling, with the total divided into a number of
categories and subcategories, with provisions for shifting exports between categories. For
details, see Lynch, *Toward an Orderly Market*, pp. 109–113.

Table 6. U.S. imports of cotton manufactures, 1956–1961, by source (in millions of dollars)

Source	1956	1957	1958	1959	1960	1961
All sources	$154.3	$136.2	$150.0	$201.3	$248.3	$203.3
Japan	84.1	65.8	71.7	76.7	74.1	69.4
Hong Kong	0.7	5.8	17.4	45.8	63.5	47.0
Other Asian countries	15.3	13.0	14.3	24.0	34.0	25.0
Egypt	0.4	0.5	0.3	0.3	5.9	1.0
Spain	0.3	0.3	0.4	1.6	7.2	3.2
Portugal	0.0	0.1	0.3	1.0	5.2	2.3

SOURCE: Warren Hunsberger, *Japan and the United States in World Trade* (New York: Harper and Row, 1964), p. 325.

3. In order to avoid discriminatory treatment with respect to imports from high-cost as opposed to low-cost countries, quota limitations—both physical limitations and tariff quotas—should be recognized as an instrument to assure that both high-cost and low-cost countries of supply shall have equality of access to the American market.

4. Discontinue the present system of the Interdepartmental Trade Agreement Committee so as to eliminate State Department domination of trade policy.[29]

These objectives, which reflect an understanding of the importance of shifting the decision-making arena as well as a grasp of the subtleties of foreign trade policy, were emphasized in Senator Pastore's subcommittee hearings. The industry faced a sympathetic audience: almost without exception, the Senators looked upon the demands of the industry with favor.

The strategy of the textile industrial groups was to admit that many problems of an internal nature were facing the industry while emphasizing that imports, a factor "beyond their control," were markedly aggravating those problems. Most of the other problems fell by the wayside, as the problem of imports was continually underlined. The Senators agreed that quotas were definitely needed. In the best American tradition, Senator Pastore commented with regard to the Japanese voluntary export restraint: "I say this. If we are going to have a quota in America, it ought to be an American-made quota. We ought not to allow other countries to institute our quotas."[30] This statement was not mere flag-waving. Since the State Department was reluctant to force severe restrictions on the Japanese for strategic reasons, the bilateral agreements which had been concluded allowed a high degree of flexibility for Japanese exporters. Naturally, this frustrated American pro-

[29]Minutes, ACMI, November 14, 1957.
[30]*Pastore Hearings*, 1958, p. 1744.

ducers, who were trying to effectively control access to the U.S. market. An "American" quota would allow the United States to impose stiffer restrictions by controlling the monitoring of violations. Moreover, the United States would not have to bother with negotiations, since it could impose restrictions unilaterally.

On February 4, 1959, the committee announced its recommendations. Noticeably *absent* from the recommendations were the two proposals made by the Textile Workers Union of America: (1) establishment of a permanent textile development agency to engage in research and development, to administer a short work week, and to finance the movement of workers and retraining and retirement benefits; and (2) creation of a specialized board to administer the Federal Labor Relations Act.[31] Opposition to a textile development agency by industrial groups was especially strong. Management officials argued that this agency would be superfluous and stifle research. They did not want government directly involved in plans that could affect production decisions. Industry saw that the proposed agency and board might have the effect of promoting greater unionization of the workforce, an issue of continual conflict between management and labor. On other matters, however, such as the elimination of the two-price cotton system, International Cooperation Administration procurement, and so on, labor strongly sided with management. They got little in return.

Rather than accepting the Pastore committee recommendations on quotas, the government attempted to restrict growing Hong Kong imports to the United States with an agreement similar to the Japanese bilateral pact. After concerted efforts, Hong Kong offered to limit exports of apparel but suggested high rates of growth for their voluntary quotas. U.S. textile and apparel producers rejected the offer in strong terms, noting that with such high growth rates, there would hardly be any restriction of imports. This rejection of Hong Kong's offer provided the basis for a new and more powerful alliance of producer and labor interests. The growth of apparel imports had made apparel producers eager to see restrictions imposed. They had become more vulnerable. Raw cotton producers were also beginning to believe that their fate lay with domestic producers, since other countries were becoming important producers.[32]

At approximately the same time, the Interagency Textile Committee,

---

[31]*New York Times*, December 29, 1959, p. 433.

[32]Eisenhower told the Tariff Commission only to investigate the effect of imports on the cotton *export* subsidy program, a narrow interpretation. Relief was given under the escape clause to producers of cotton typewriter ribbon in 1960. See Hunsberger, *Japan and the United States in World Trade*, p. 312 (*Congressional Record*, August 29, 1966, pp. 20967–68).

established in response to the Pastore committee recommendation, was resisting the call for quotas, reflecting intragovernmental conflict: "The Interagency Textile Committee is not proposing the regulation of textile imports by quotas. The imposition of textile quotas would be a far-reaching departure from our foreign policy of the last 25 years."[33] This proved to be a major sore point with domestic producers, as they demonstrated at the February 1961 Pastore hearings.

The breadth of interests represented at the 1961 hearings is indicative of the growth in the base of support which had developed to restrain imports. Aside from the usual representatives of the cotton and wool textile industry, representatives of man-made fibers, cotton growers, wool growers, and various unions in both the textile and apparel industries testified. The apparel producers were also well represented. Evidence on the unity of interests abounds. For example, man-made fiber producers argued that "increased imports of man-made fibers will cause serious injury to the directly competitive domestic industries of cotton and wool."[34] This linkage was ironic, unmasking the specificity of the quota coalition. Throughout the 1950s, competition from man-made fibers had led to the displacement of cotton and wool consumption. Though the importance of inter-fiber competition as a problem for the domestic cotton and wool industry was often discounted, that same importance was used as a "selling point" for the imposition of quotas on imports of man-made fiber products!

Multilateral Arrangements. As pressure from the unified fiber-textile-apparel coalition increased, it became apparent to government policymakers that something needed to be done on a comprehensive basis for the textile and apparel industries. Although the multilateral arrangement on cotton textiles and apparel came into being under the Kennedy administration in 1961, initial steps had been taken in 1959 under the Eisenhower administration. At the start of tariff-cutting negotiations, the Under Secretary of State, Douglas Dillon, sought to have GATT participants develop a program to cope with low-priced imports.[35] Three interrelated objectives stimulated this request. First, the fiber-textile-apparel coalition was increasingly pressuring the U.S. government to impose global quotas on imports, an action that ran counter to U.S. economic and strategic objectives. Second, the United States hoped to open the European market to a wide range of products to take pressure off the U.S. market; it saw restrictions on "low-priced" imports as a way of alleviating European fears of a rapid increase in

[33]*Pastore Hearings,* 1961, p. 526.
[34]*Ibid.,* p. 451.
[35]*New York Times,* November 1, 1959, and June 1, 1960.

imports. Finally, the United States wished to have the Europeans re-move their trade restrictions against American exports. Since the Euro-peans were using restrictions on Japanese exports illegally, GATT was being undermined. It was hoped by U.S. policy-makers that an *organized* deviation from GATT on the issue of "disruption" from low-priced imports would allow the United States to convince the Europeans to follow GATT rules across the board.[36]

On November 20, 1960, the GATT decided on a procedure for dealing with the problem of low-priced imports.[37] The first case of "market disruption" was not long in coming: the United States decided to base the Short-Term Arrangement on cotton textiles and apparel on this concept.

As one of the first objectives of his administration, President Ken-nedy wished to have a new trade act passed which would allow for major tariff cuts. Yet as a former Senator from Massachusetts, a major textile state, Kennedy also recognized that he would face strong opposi-tion from the textile and apparel industries if he sought to reduce tariffs across the board. Moreover, he had promised "a comprehensive industry-wide remedy" for these industries before the 1960 election.[38] Kennedy followed what has been called "a strategy of satisfying in advance the demands of enough injured industries to neutralize them."[39] Although the plan developed by Kennedy to assist the textile and apparel industry was quite elaborate, it failed to provide import "relief" for the wool and man-made fiber based sections of the indus-try, and focused instead on the cotton textile and apparel manufactur-ers. Although the man-made fiber based sector of the textile industry was not very distressed by this, since they hardly expected a rapid and massive diversion to exports of these products, the wool textile industry was up in arms. As we shall see, Kennedy at various times promised to implement import restrictions for the man-made fiber and wool sectors of the textile industry as well. Although he reneged on this promise,

[36]In Dillon's words, the objective of raising the idea of studying market disruption "was to facilitate an olderly expansion of trade." He added that the United States "hoped that the development of safeguards will enable the member countries still refusing the bene-fits of the GATT to Japan to remove this barrier to imports of Japanese goods" (*New York Times*, June 1, 1960). Charles Adair, Jr., Deputy Assistant Secretary of State for Economic Affairs (the U.S. delegate in Geneva) noted that the market disruption negotiations provided "an opportunity for the importing countries to share equitably the increase in imports among themselves" so as to ensure that "the impact on any one market would become much less" (*New York Times*, June 1, 1960).

[37]*New York Times*, November 20, 1960, p. 9.

[38]Letter from Senator Kennedy to Governor Ernest F. Hollings of South Carolina, cited in "Textile Import Quotas: A Short History," by R. Buford Brandis, American Textile Manufacturers Institute, May 1979.

[39]Bauer, de Sola Poole, and Dexter, *American Business and Public Policy*, p. 78.

there was little that the textile and apparel industries could do in the short run. The Trade Act of 1962 was passed with the explicit support of the cotton textile industry. Since the cotton textile sector was the major segment of the industry as this time, with 80 percent of production, Kennedy's assistance measures were clearly in its interests. Thus the interests of a specific segment triumphed over the interest of the whole. From an industry-wide perspective, the growth segment was not cotton but man-made fiber products.

Summary

From 1955 to 1961, the textile and apparel industries coalesced around the issue of protection. Although internal changes and prior government policies were in part responsible for industry performance, there were also important market and political reasons for pressing for a broad, relatively undifferentiated government response, such as quotas. The lack of a coordinated government policy allowed the industry to pursue lines of influence in Congress, and to pit competing policy interests in the bureaucracy against one another.

Protection of the cotton textile and apparel industries had an important unintended consequence. The cotton textile and apparel quota system encouraged imports in precisely the type of products in which the United States was competitive—man-made fiber based products. At the same time, it helped to maintain a relatively inefficient and internationally uncompetitive industry. Thus, Kennedy's victory in securing passage of the Trade Act of 1962 was also a victory for the senescent— but politically powerful—cotton textile and apparel industries. The precedent did not go unnoticed.

From the STA to the Multifiber Arrangement, 1961–1973

The period from 1961 to 1973 illustrates two important and closely connected developments. First, the Short-Term Arrangement on cotton textiles and apparel (STA) gave rise to a diversion of production to man-made fibers and wool products. Protectionist sentiment spread from cotton to other segments, resulting finally in the Multifiber Arrangement. Second, an ill-conceived domestic adjustment program failed to provide relief, and demonstrated the power of the industry to keep government attention focused on the international dimensions of the problem. Together, these two factors led to greater industry pressure for restraints. This created international political problems, as other producers resisted American unilateralism. Trade policy came into conflict with wider foreign policy goals, not only with the less developed countries but across the Atlantic as well.

279

The diversion into man-made fiber and wool products resulted directly from the Short-Term Arrangement on cotton textiles and apparel. While insulating the domestic American market from imported cotton products, it actually encouraged a number of countries to switch their exports to *uncontrolled* man-made and wool-based products. Though this process had been anticipated by domestic textile producers, the predominance of the cotton industry in the protectionist coalition led the government to focus on what was the wrong industry from the standpoint of comparative advantage. Since the government lacked a positive industrial policy, its only objective was to "get away" with as little protection as possible. With Kennedy Round negotiations under way until 1967, the textile and apparel industries had little leverage on the government; as a result, some import controls were imposed but nothing was done for the man-made fiber based textile industry, which began to face increasing competition from imports. These imports were in large part a result of the closure of the American market in cottons. When the textile and apparel industries had the opportunity to block a trade act, as in the late 1960s, they did so with a vengeance. This had wider implications for U.S. trade policy, for it impaired the ability of the United States to conclude agreements on imports that were not severely restrictive and politically disruptive internationally.

Nor did adjustment policy seem to work. Kennedy's domestic aid plan was a good idea in principle. In practice, however, the kinds of adjustment that were promoted were inappropriate and failed to treat the real problems of the industry, such as relocation from North to South within the United States, overcapacity in the cotton textile industry, and fragmentation in the apparel industry. Since the government was not sure what the real problems of the industry were, it was a simple matter for textile and apparel groups to emphasize the import-control aspects of Kennedy's plan.

Toward a Long-Term Arrangement

Kennedy's plan to aid the textile and apparel industries was announced on May 2, 1962. It consisted of seven measures:

1. An expanded program of research covering new products, processes, and markets to be carried out by the Commerce Department in cooperation with union and management groups.
2. A proposal to change the depreciation allowances on textile machinery.
3. Assistance from the Small Business Administration to "assist the cotton textile industry to obtain . . . financing for modernization of its equipment."

4. A directive to the Department of Agriculture to recommend ways to offset the differential arising from the two-price cotton system.

5. An assistance program for industries experiencing or being threatened by injury because of growing imports.

6. A conference between exporters and importers of textile products to seek an understanding which will provide a basis for trade that will avoid undue disruption of established industries.

7. An advisement that any application by the textile industry under the escape clause or national security provisions of the Trade Agreements Extension will be carefully considered on its merits.[40]

The key provision of the plan with regard to international trade was the sixth point, which called for an international conference of exporters and importers of textile and apparel products. The first step was a meeting of key developed countries called by Under Secretary of State George Ball on June 21, 1961. Representatives of these countries requested the GATT to convene a meeting of importers and exporters on July 17, 1961. After discussions with exporting countries, a temporary one-year agreement—the Short-Term Arrangement (STA)—was signed, to become effective October 1, 1961.[41]

The negotiations leading up to the STA were straightforward. Exporting countries had an unenviable choice between unilaterally imposed restraints, which the Europeans were already employing, and a multilateral arrangement that would govern the imposition of controls on trade. The STA contained provisions to negotiate a Long-Term Arrangement (LTA), which went into effect on October 1, 1962, for five years. It also contained procedures for handling market disruption.[42] If such disruption arose, importing countries could request that specific categories of imports be restricted for the period of the STA at levels not lower than imports in the period of July 1960 to June 1961 (the "base level"). Unless exporters exercised a unilateral restraint within 30 days of such a request, importing countries could impose their own restraints on exports. The effect of the STA was a rapid reduction in exports of cotton goods to the United States—apparently because exporters feared that restrictions might be imposed by the United States. The total value of textile and apparel imports declined from $268.7 million in 1960 to $214.5 in 1961.[43]

The LTA that followed was signed by nineteen countries and was

[40]See United States International Trade Commission, *The History and Current Status of the Multifiber Arrangement* (Washington, D.C., January 1978), p. 7. Hereafter cited as *Status of MFA.*
[41]*Ibid.*, pp. 7–8.
[42]See *ibid.*, pp. A-4 through A-20, for the text of the STA and the LTA.
[43]*Congressional Record,* August 29, 1966, p. 20970.

similar to the STA. Since it was to be in force for five years, a growth provision of 5 percent per year in restricted categories was permitted. But two articles in the LTA undermined its ostensibly multilateral character. Article 3 allowed the imposition of unilateral restraints by importing countries. The second restrictive clause was Article 4, which stated: "Nothing in this Arrangement shall prevent the application of mutually acceptable arrangements on other terms not inconsistent with the basic objectives of this Arrangement."[44] This opened the door for the United States to negotiate a series of bilateral agreements with producers. A Japanese bilateral was signed before the LTA even came into effect, and was renewed several times. After unilateral action was taken against Hong Kong in March 1962, for its refusal to restrict imports, a bilateral agreement was reached.[45] Because it was not necessary to demonstrate market disruption in order to conclude a bilateral agreement (in contrast to Article 3 unilateral restraints), bilateral agreements became the preferred form of import restraints. By 1966 the United States had negotiated eighteen bilateral agreements under the LTA.[46] The LTA sanctioned bilateralism; the *character* of the U.S. bilaterals was in turn determined by the textile-apparel coalition.

Domestic Adjustment Fails

Additional provisions in the seven-point Kennedy plan were also carried out rapidly. The Textile and Clothing Division of the Department of Commerce had expanded its research program after the first Pastore subcommittee report was issued. Most of the research, however, was of a fact-gathering and statistical nature. No direct aid was provided to the industry. The second point of Kennedy's plan—a change in the depreciation period for textile equipment—was also implemented rapidly, and was later extended to industry in general.[47] The net result, however, was to increase unemployment in the textile industry while raising domestic production capacity. When demand for textile products fell, this increased production capacity became idle, encouraging producers to press for greater restrictions on the import of textile and apparel products.

The provision that affected production most directly was the directive to gradually eliminate the two-price cotton system. After the Department of Agriculture failed to institute an import equalization fee in 1964, Congress proceeded to approve a one-price system by subsidizing

[44]*Status of MFA*, p. A-14.
[45]Nigel Ruscoe, "Tragedy of Errors," *Far Eastern Economic Review*, March 29, 1962, p. 702.
[46]*Congressional Record*, August 29, 1966, p. 20973.
[47]*Pastore Hearings*, 2nd Supp. Report, p. 8.

the entire U.S. cotton crop. This removed the price differential between the world price and domestic prices for U.S. textile producers, contributing to improved textile mill profitability (see Table 7).

In accord with point seven of Kennedy's plan, the Wilton and velvet carpet industry sought and received escape-clause relief from the Tariff Commission.[48] But this was the only escape-clause action sought by the industries at this time. Instead of using the escape clause, the textile and apparel industries unified to file for relief under the national security provision of the Trade Extension Act of 1958. An investigation by the government, initiated under this provision to determine if imports were entering the country in quantities that would "impair the national security," remained open for several years. In the end, no action was taken, but the participation of cotton textile and apparel manufacturers in this petition is noteworthy.[49] Even though they were being granted protection from imports through the STA and LTA, for the sake of unity, and possibly in the hope of more stringent restrictions, they joined with other disgruntled manufacturers whose products were based on different fibers.

Diversion Leads to Pressure for Further Restraints

The LTA satisfied cotton textile and apparel producers to some extent, but it did not deal with products of other fibers, a fact that greatly annoyed producers of wool and man-made fibers. Although in retrospect it appears that President Kennedy did not intend to negotiate multilateral arrangements for these producers immediately, the industry appears to have been misled on this point. For example, on February 26, 1962, Kennedy wrote a letter to the Chairman of the House Informal Textile Committee, Congressman Vinson, saying: "I have also requested the departments involved to implement my program for the wool, man-made fiber, and silk divisions of the industry. Almost all of the points in the program announced on May 2, 1961, apply equally to each of these."[50] The whole textile and apparel story of the 1960s is one of continual efforts to make the words "almost all" include the wool and man-made fiber sectors of the industry in an international agreement. There were several reasons for the delay. First, man-made fibers enjoyed a trade surplus until 1967. In fact, the entire industry was experiencing high demand and high profits, largely because of the Vietnam war. Second, although wool textile and apparel producers

---

[48]*Ibid.*, p. 9.

[49]See Hunsberger, *Japan and the United States in World Trade*, p. 336, note 95, for a list of participants in the application for relief under the national security clause (Sec. 8) of the Trade Extension Act of 1958.

[50]*Pastore Hearings*, 1963, p. 22.

Table 7. Profits of textile and apparel industries before and after one-price cotton, 1963–1965, by quarter

Industry	Before one-price cotton						After one-price cotton					
	1963				1964		1964		1965			
	1	2	3	4	1	2	3	4	1	2	3	4
Textiles												
Profits after taxes (millions of dollars)	$64	$90	$97	$103	$85	$108	$155	$159	$151	$166	$176	$201
Profits after taxes as percentage of equity	4.4%	6.2%	6.6%	7.0%	5.8%	7.2%	10.2%	10.6%	9.9%	10.5%	12.0%	9.4%
Profits after taxes as percentage of sales	1.8%	2.4%	2.5%	2.5%	2.3%	2.7%	3.7%	3.7%	3.7%	3.8%	3.8%	4.1%
Apparel												
Profits after taxes (millions of dollars)	$39	$40	$54	$56	$57	$56	$117	$88	$68	$80	$115	$114
Profits after taxes as percentage of equity	6.4%	6.7%	8.7%	8.9%	8.6%	8.5%	17.2%	12.4]	9.5%	10.8%	15.3%	15.0%
Profits after taxes as percentage of sales	1.2%	1.2%	1.5%	1.6%	1.7%	1.6%	2.8%	2.1%	1.9%	2.0%	2.7%	2.5%

SOURCE: *FTC Quarterly Financial Report for Manufacturing, Mining, and Trade Corporations*, various issues.

were experiencing a deficit in their trade, they were also the weakest segment of the industry, both industrially and politically; and in any case, wool tariffs were high. Third, the United States was attempting to pursue a free trade policy to its limits. Kennedy Round negotiations were taking place until 1967, which made the setting of quotas difficult. In addition, the Europeans were important exporters of man-made fiber products and could not be pressured in the same fashion as less developed countries. These factors had only a delaying effect, however, as business and labor groups pursued demands for the widening of controls. Many groups joined the fray, but the now unprotected wool segment became a key actor.

After it became clear that a multilateral arrangement was not immediately forthcoming in other fibers, representatives of the wool growers argued on behalf of wool manufacturers that "quotas on wool products, from tops to apparel, by countries and by category, are urgently needed in the best interest of the growers, the mills, and the nation." The wool industry felt that the levels at which imports are restricted should be a "ceiling" and not a "floor" from which imports could gradually increase. The market disruption clause also disturbed the industry; it argued that this provision would be difficult to enforce, and noted that textile imports might gradually take over more and more of the domestic market without becoming "disruptive" in the technical sense. Isolating the impact of imports was always difficult. Moreover, the industry argued that tariffs were not enough, and that quotas were essential.[51]

Man-made fiber producers argued that the administration had failed to pursue a multilateral solution to the import "problem." But although they submitted a statement to the Pastore hearings, they did not directly testify. It appears that changes in the depreciation allowance and the economic boom in their products were initially sufficient to satisfy man-made fiber producers.[52]

Apparel producers also urged that more be done to curb imports. In a statement representing the view of most of the apparel industry, Lawrence Phillips noted that apparel producers expected the President to implement his sixth point by the "establishment of quotas in textile mill products, on garments and apparel, and on man-made fiber, staple, filaments, and filament yarn by country and by category of product." In what was to become a familiar linkage between industries, he said: "I hope it will be clear that the Apparel Industry Committee on Imports is in thorough accord and complete agreement with the

[51]*Ibid.*, 1962, pp. 4, 5–13.
[52]*Ibid.*, pp. 164–170.

position taken before you by other segments of the domestic textile-apparel-fiber industry."[53]

The unity of the protectionist coalition extended to labor groups as well. Although they continued to press for creation of a textile development agency instead of temporary groups to promote research, the importance of maintaining a united front was uppermost in their minds. In calling for a single committee to address the problems of the textile industry, a spokesman for the Textile Workers Union pointed out that the wool segment remained dissatisfied. Labor groups in the textile and apparel industries not only managed to have the AFL-CIO come out in support of the LTA agreement; they also succeeded in getting them to press for a broader agreement, even though the benefits to be gained were not clear.[54]

Wool Conflict. The Kennedy administration followed delaying tactics with the most affected segment, which was wool. Promises of action proved disingenuous. Repeated promises of import "relief" were made by the President, his Special Assistant, and numerous Secretaries and Assistant Secretaries of various departments.[55] Yet at the same time, Edwin Martin, Assistant Secretary of State for Economic Affairs, testified with regard to a possible multilateral arrangement in wool that the industry had received substantial increases in tariffs toward the end of 1960, and that the effect of tariff action had to be assessed before deciding whether to embark on new international negotiations.[56] The gap between these promises and the immediate intentions of the State Department became a conflict between the Commerce Department and the administration, with the administration being represented by both the Special Trade Representative's Office and the State Department. These differences came into the open after attempts to negotiate a multilateral wool agreement proved to be difficult. Only four major countries were involved in wool exports: the United Kingdom, Italy, Japan, and Hong Kong.[57] As in the negotiations leading up to the LTA, the United States discussed the possibility of a long-term arrangement for wool textiles in December 1963. But in 1963, the lines

[53]*Ibid.*, p. 158.
[54]*Ibid.*, pp. 55, 56, 59.
[55]*Ibid.*, 1963, p. 22.
[56]*Ibid.*, p. 82.
[57]In 1963, these four provided 77 percent of total U.S. imports of wool products (in square yard equivalent); by 1979, they still accounted for 73 percent of total imports of these goods. Yet during this period, Japan and Hong Kong's share of this four-country total rose from 41 percent to 67.5 percent. (Author's calculations based on tables prepared by Office of Textiles, Department of Commerce, March 1972, entitled *Cotton, Wool, and Man-made Fiber Textiles. Tables Depicting U.S. Foreign Trade.*)

were not conveniently drawn, as they had been in the case of cotton products, between low-wage developing countries as exporters and developed countries as importers. The same types of pressure were simply inappropriate. Intergovernmental meetings floundered. The U.S. government proceeded to call a conference on trade for the autumn of 1964, but the key suppliers declined to attend.[58] In June of 1965, the government decided to approach Japan on its own, but Japan proved unwilling to restrain its exports without a fight.

Negotiations with Japan had their start in talks between Prime Minister Sato and President Johnson in Washington at a summit meeting in early 1965: Johnson asked Sato whether he would be willing to receive a U.S. industry-government mission to discuss the wool issue, and Sato agreed "in principle" to such negotiations. Although industry leaders were pleased at this opportunity, the U.S. government's position was not fully resolved. There was still debate on the feasibility of an international agreement on wool products. Some thought it impossible, but others felt that approaching Japan first might lead to a successful agreement. The U.S. mission, led by Warren Christopher in his capacity as special representative of the Secretary of State, included five members and ten observers from the American wool industry. This rather unusual procedure of having industry representatives at an official intergovernmental negotiation led to a stormy meeting on June 7–8, 1965. One U.S. industry official, from the National Association of Wool Manufacturers, stated sharply: "If we fail here to develop a solution with your cooperation, a solution will be developed without it." He then went on to threaten that "should we be forced to go home and report failure of this mission, the consequences would be tragic."[59] The Japanese representatives resisted American initiatives by arguing that the LTA did not allow extension to other fields. Under the LTA, Japan had lost part of its market share in cotton to other unrestrained suppliers. It was unwilling to repeat the mistake by restricting wool product exports.

The crisis that led to the breakdown in talks developed on the second day of the meeting. Warren Christopher bolstered the statement made by the National Wool Association official by threatening that "if relief from disruptive imports is not forthcoming, Congress may well take matters into its own hands." The exercise of this kind of market power was not at all unusual. The United States had applied it successfully in the negotiations leading up to the LTA in the 1950s and in the LTA

[58]The British Spinners' and Doublers' Association, "International Trading in Cotton Textiles: Agreements, Organizations, Controls, and Customs" (Manchester, November 1965), draft ms., p. 35.
[59]*Congressional Record*, August 29, 1966, p. 20982.

itself. What was unusual about the meetings was the presence of Japanese and American industrialists, which only served to raise the room temperature. The response from a Japanese textile spokesman made the American industry's statements look polite by comparison. After expressing shock at the American presentation, he said: "We, too, have means for our protection, including trade in textiles. Therefore, to avoid an ugly showdown, you should check the real facts and change your position. We are not easily frightened and our relationship will suffer. We do not like political threats. We are not North Vietnam. We hope you will make distinctions between your friends and your enemies."[60] The reference to Vietnam was badly received, and the meeting adjourned abruptly. Although an official from the Japanese Ministry of Trade and Industry apologized, the meeting quickly came to an end.

This incident illustrates the limitations of trying to negotiate international agreements. It is one thing to have less developed countries restrict the export of their goods to the U.S. market; it is quite another to have major developed countries do so. The less developed countries are much more dependent on the good will of the developed countries, and they have little to offer in return for concessions. The United States had no interest in antagonizing its major ally over a specific trade issue. Strategic considerations were still of paramount importance, and Japan was an important ally in the conflict in Southeast Asia. As we shall see, the emerging policy of seeking international detente—and the growth of pressure from the U.S. textile and apparel industries—led to a severe conflict with Japan. In the 1950s Japan had been a developing country. By the mid-1960s it expected to be treated more like a major ally, and was no longer totally dependent on U.S. markets.

Renewal of the Long-Term Arrangement. After the failure of the mission to Japan in 1965, the textile and apparel industries turned their attention to the forthcoming renewal of the Long-Term Arrangement (LTA). Their efforts were initially focused on enlarging the agreement to include products of other fibers. But it soon became evident to industry groups that attempts to broaden the LTA might instead lead to its termination, thereby ending the multilateral justification for the bilaterals previously negotiated by the United States. Hence, pressure for renewal of the LTA solely for cotton products was followed by renewed attempts to negotiate separate multilateral arrangements for wool and man-made fiber products.

The strategy followed by U.S. negotiators to renew the LTA was one

[60]*Daily News Record,* Fairchild Publications, September 30, 1965.

that was later used by European Economic Community negotiators, with equal success, in 1977. They secured arrangements with major supplying countries *before* the expiration of the LTA, thereby assuring that the LTA arrangement would continue as before. By August of 1966, through promises of favorable treatment, bilateral agreements with Japan, Hong Kong, Taiwan, and Korea had been negotiated.[61] A multifiber pact was out of the question as part of the LTA, however; in fact, the preamble of the LTA specifically forbade it. The American industry therefore adopted a two-step strategy: press first for the extension of the LTA beyond its expiration in 1967, and then work for a provision for future negotiations on other fibers.[62] Although the textile and apparel industries were not happy with the diversion of imports from cotton goods to other fibers and the increases in cotton product imports, they recognized that this formula offered "the only restraint" they had.

Although the United States had negotiated bilateral agreements in advance, the negotiations for the renewal of the LTA proved to be somewhat difficult because of strong resistance from less developed countries.[63] In spite of this opposition, the United States was able to make side payments—offering tariff cuts and agreeing to slightly larger quotas and a three-year instead of a five-year extension of the LTA. The quid pro quo was continued *control* of international trade in cotton textiles and apparel through an unchanged LTA. As a palliative to U.S. producers of wool products, only a 5 percent tariff cut was made on their products.[64]

Bilateral Agreements. Following the extension of the LTA, the textile and apparel interests turned their full attention to pressing for an accord on wool and man-made fiber products. Over the previous six years, imports of products had been growing rapidly. In 1968, apparel imports of these fibers exceeded cotton apparel imports for the first time. Moreover, in 1967, imports of man-made fiber textile products exceeded exports for the first time.[65] This trend was not totally unexpected. Since the LTA controlled cotton products, which were defined as being over 50 percent cotton fiber by weight, exporting countries shifted to synthetic-and-cotton mixes of 51 percent synthetic and 49

[61]*Ibid.*, various issues, 1961.

[62]*Ibid.*, September 23 and October 21, 1966.

[63]V. Aggarwal, "Hanging by a Thread: International Regime Change in the Textile/Apparel System, 1950–1979," Stanford University, unpublished Ph.D. dissertation, 1981.

[64]T. Curtis and J. Vastine, Jr., *The Kennedy Round and the Future of American Trade* (New York: Praeger, 1971), pp. 174–175.

[65]Office of Textiles, Department of Commerce, *U.S. Cotton, Wool, and Fiber Textiles: Tables Depicting U.S. Foreign Trade*, March 1972.

percent cotton. The most common statistic, which became a shibboleth for protectionist demands, was the tenfold increase in imports of man-made fiber products from 1962 to 1968. While the *motivation* to stop imports of these products had been present before, the conclusion of the Kennedy Round and the expiration of presidential authority under the Trade Act of 1962 provided a new *forum* in which to make these demands a reality. In 1967 the textile and apparel industries made major attempts to pressure Congress into blocking any extension of presidential tariff-cutting authority. Following the termination of the Kennedy Round, Wilbur Mills of the House Ways and Means Commit-tee asked the U.S. Tariff Commission to investigate the impact of im-ports on the textile and apparel industries. The report, issued in 1968, recognized that there had been an increase in imports of textile and apparel products, but pointed out that both industries were prosperous and were not being harmed by such imports.[66]

Nonetheless, the election year of 1968 was marked by statements in support of restrictions of some kind on textile and apparel imports, a practice which had become standard electoral rhetoric since 1960. Hu-bert Humphrey, Richard Nixon, and George Wallace all pledged to control trade in textiles. Nixon's pledge was explicit; he promised to "promptly take the steps necessary to extend the concept of interna-tional trade agreements to all other textile articles involving wool, man-made fibers, and blends."[67] Scholars have argued that the decision to pursue bilateral agreements with Far East suppliers can be attributed to Nixon's strategy for mustering electoral support in the South.[68] While the subsequent heavy-handed and often inept handling of the issue may be attributed to Nixon's victory, there is little doubt that restric-tions would have been sought even if Humphrey had been elected. Nixon's argument that textiles and apparel products should be con-sidered an exceptional case within a broader commitment to free trade was not a deviation from previous government policy. Through years of effort, the textile and apparel industries had firmly planted the idea in the minds of policy-makers that their case had to be treated *sui generis*.

A gradual change in the overall international competitive position of the United States also decreased the leeway of central decision-makers. Many industries were beginning to experience an adverse position in

[66]U.S. Tariff Commission, *Textiles and Apparel* (Washington, D.C.: TC Pub. 226, Janu-ary 1968).

[67]Telegram to Republican members of Congress who supported import control legisla-tion, August 21, 1968, cited in Brandis, "Textile Import Quotas: A Short History."

[68]I. M. Destler, H. Fukui, and H. Sato, *The Textile Wrangle* (Ithaca: Cornell University Press, 1979), p. 68.

their international trade, a trend which was to continue and worsen. These groups had little commitment to an open trading policy.[69] "Low" politics was becoming "high" politics. This made it difficult for decision-makers to construct a coalition that would support free trade. This point cannot be overemphasized. The inability to form a political counterweight to industry—through the courting of labor, for example—meant government capitulation. When textile and apparel groups pressed for restrictions on imports from Japan, the government had little choice but to comply. The result was a bitter struggle, because Japan decided to resist.

The international negotiations illustrate once again the ability of the textile and apparel industries to pressure Congress. Not only did the industry strongly press President Nixon in the early phases of the negotiations to ensure that he would fulfill his promises. It was also able, by threatening to force unilateral congressional action, to block compromises with the Japanese that would have settled the negotiations with less acrimony. At every turn, the negotiators were made to understand that no agreement would be reached without industry approval.

Nixon first sought to fulfill his campaign promise to negotiate a multilateral agreement by initiating discussions with the Europeans—a plan which, as we shall see, was doomed to failure. Although their importance had declined over time, Britain and Italy were still important suppliers of wool products, especially in yarn and fabrics. Hence the U.S. decision to pursue negotiations in Europe first was greeted with distrust by the Europeans. In fact, the United States initially wished to have the *Europeans* accept voluntary export quotas—a goal that would obviously be difficult to achieve, given the relative bargaining strengths involved. European opposition was met with a plan to call a world conference under the auspices of GATT. Although Secretary of Commerce Maurice Stans emphasized that the real objective of the discussions was to find a way to limit Far Eastern imports, the European view can be summarized by the British opinion that "if the source of Stans's problems was the Far East, then he needed to go there to work out the means of solving it."[70] The Europeans' lack of enthusiasm for trade restrictions was also based on their positive trade balance in textiles and apparel. Furthermore, they were already able to restrict imports from less developed countries on a bilateral basis.

---

[69]For a discussion of changing incentives for U.S. industrial groups with respect to international trade, see Stephen Krasner, "U.S. Commercial and Monetary Policy: Unraveling the Paradox of External Strength and Internal Weakness," in Peter Katzenstein ed., *Between Power and Plenty: Foreign Economic Policies of Advanced Industrial States* (Madison: University of Wisconsin Press, 1978).

[70]Destler, Fukui, and Sato, *The Textile Wrangle*, pp. 81–82.

Stans's strategy, after failing to secure European cooperation in setting up a multilateral system of control in textile and apparel trade, was to seek comprehensive bilateral agreements. This strategy would serve two purposes. It would create a diversion of goods to Europe and make Europeans more willing to accept a multilateral control arrangement; and it would also give less developed countries with whom the United States had bilaterals a vested interest in having the United States restrain uncontrolled suppliers. Stans flew to Tokyo on May 10, 1969, to discuss restraint agreements with the Japanese. The Japanese were no more cooperative than the Europeans. Japanese government officials were under strong pressure from their man-made fiber industry, which was one of the most dynamic sectors in Japan at the time.[71] The situation was further aggravated by U.S. demands for a comprehensive agreement on textiles and apparel, rather than selective restriction. Stans returned without the desired concessions from Japan.

Throughout the negotiations with the Japanese, industry groups maintained their pressure on the government for a comprehensive agreement. In November of 1969, Premier Sato met with President Nixon and secretly agreed to secure Japanese restraints on textile imports in exchange for a return of Okinawa without nuclear facilities.[72] After Sato failed to deliver on this agreement as promised, U.S. government pressure on the Japanese mounted, as government officials themselves were increasingly pressured by industry groups. To counter this increasing pressure from U.S. textile and apparel interests, who threatened to force a legislative solution that would restrain Japanese imports, Donald Kendall of the newly formed Emergency Committee for American Trade developed a compromise plan for a negotiated bilateral solution. Although this plan called for temporary restraints of all textile and apparel exports from Japan at 1969 levels, it contained a provision that restrictions would be continued only on items which the Tariff Commission had determined were being seriously injured by imports. The American Textile Manufacturers Institute and ten other textile and apparel organizations rejected the Kendall plan on March 30, 1970; their experience with the Tariff Commission on injury findings was not good. Since this plan had also failed to gain widespread acceptance in Japan, it was doomed to failure.

The U.S. textile and apparel industry was not particularly distressed by the failure to secure a bilateral understanding with the Japanese. In fact, on March 19, 1970, they had called for an end to negotiations with Japan. Their objective had already shifted to a legislative solution that

[71]*Ibid.*, p. 85.
[72]The discussion in this section is based in large part on Destler, Fukui, and Sato, *The Textile Wrangle.*

would lead to the imposition of stringent unilateral quotas. Congress had proved a more responsive channel of access. To increase pressure on Congress, the Amalgamated Clothing Workers Union demonstrated against imports from "low-wage" countries by staging a work stoppage. Ways and Means chairman Wilbur Mills was finally led to introduce a bill to restrict textile, apparel, and footwear imports through the use of quotas. Under the terms of this bill, textile and apparel imports for 1970 would have been limited to the 1967–1968 average. Growth in the quota would be keyed to changes in consumption in the U.S. market.

The previous alliance of fiber, textile, and apparel manufacturers with labor grew even larger when the footwear industry joined the protectionist ranks to press for the Mills bill. Although the textile-apparel coalition hoped to keep this bill from becoming a "Christmas tree" with multiple amendments to impose quotas on other products—a bill that Nixon would surely veto—they had great difficulty in securing this objective. The original bill included an amendment that automatically conferred quotas on industries which the Tariff Commission determined were being "injured." In addition, the injury determination procedure was specified in terms of the import-to-consumption ratio without regard to other factors. Although the bill as reported out of committee was more flexible with regard to the imposition of quotas, it still permitted their implementation without great difficulty. In an ironic twist, the textile-apparel alliance joined *anti-quota* forces in an attempt to make the bill adequately "liberal" to be passed by Congress and avoid a presidential veto!

While negotiations continued in stop-and-go fashion with the Japanese, the House of Representatives passed the Mills trade bill on November 19, 1970. The Senate Finance Committee began consideration of the bill and removed the provision to invoke quotas for other products while retaining the textile, apparel, and footwear quota provisions. The optimistic outlook for passage of the Mills bill put pressure on the Japanese government to come to an agreement.

The negotiations between Presidential Assistant Peter Flanigan and Ambassador Nobukhio Ushiba approached a successful conclusion. With only relatively minor differences remaining between the U.S. and Japanese positions, Flanigan initiated discussions with industry leaders at the White House. In a major show of power, they rejected the proposed American-Japanese accord. With a strong possibility of passage of the Mills bill, a moderate position was unnecessary. Their stand led to the collapse of the bilateral talks. At the same time, however, the Mills bill was encountering trouble with the Senate, and failed to come to a vote.

In early 1971, Mills decided to pursue an agreement with the Japanese on his own initiative. He hoped that a unilateral arrangement by the Japanese to restrict their imports might prove satisfactory to the textile and apparel industry. Although the Japanese decided to pursue such a unilateral restriction, political rivalry between Nixon and Mills, and the industries' dissatisfaction with the Japanese initiative, led to Nixon's rejection of the unilateral restraint.

In a rapid sequence of events that led eventually to an agreement with the Japanese, President Nixon announced his visit to China (July 15); imposed a 10 percent across-the-board import surcharge (August 15); and threatened to invoke the Trading with the Enemy Act to unilaterally restrain imports of textiles and apparel (September 21). With a new U.S. Ambassador (David Kennedy) to conduct "negotiations," an agreement was finally concluded on October 15, 1971, the day the Trading with the Enemy Act provision was to take effect. The agreement was comprehensive in nature, and set group and category ceilings on products as well. The Japanese were able to secure relatively high base levels for growth rates, which were set at 5 percent. In contrast to the five-year accords negotiated with Korea, Taiwan, and Hong Kong, the Japanese accord provided for controls for three years.[73] While the agreement was greeted with enthusiasm by U.S. textile producers, apparel interests were dismayed by the high base periods that were used.[74]

The Multifiber Arrangement

Almost immediately after the conclusion of bilateral agreements with Far East suppliers, U.S. textile and apparel manufacturers turned their attention to the negotiation of an all-fiber agreement. Whereas the Europeans had previously opposed such an agreement, textile and apparel producers in Europe were astute enough to recognize that U.S. bilateral agreements would increase pressure on the European market as the restrained exporters diverted their exports. The potential changes in the market forced a change in political interests: a multilateral accord became attractive.[75]

The need for the United States to conclude a multilateral arrangement had also become clear. On this point, U.S. producers and the restricted Far East suppliers actually found themselves in accord. Exporters recognized that unless other countries were also restrained, the

[73]*The Wall Street Journal*, October 18, 1971.
[74]*Daily News Record*, October 18, 1971.
[75]*Wall Street Journal*, October 18, 1971.

eventual result would be the total loss of their export markets. Hence the struggle to develop a multilateral arrangement was basically a problem of "convincing" less developed countries that were not already restrained and of getting the Europeans to agree on a common position.

An unexpected development in the U.S. bilateral with Japan was the trend of Japanese exports to the United States. In 1971, Japan exported 1.282 billion square yard equivalents (SYE) of man-made fiber products to the United States; by 1973, this had dropped to 650 million SYE.[76] This shift appears to have been due to a loss of Japanese comparative advantage (with respect to less developed countries) and the currency realignment of 1971. The result of this change—combined with an increase of Japanese imports from other countries—was to make Japan more amenable to some kind of multilateral agreement. In effect, the changed market conditions resulting from previous agreements were extending the protectionist coalition internationally. There was virtually no one left to resist.

The actual negotiations leading to the development of the Multifiber Arrangement were relatively smooth. U.S. textile and apparel manufacturers strongly supported the government's efforts. In Europe, the German government was somewhat reluctant to endorse the Multifiber Arrangement. Since policy-making authority on this issue had shifted mainly to the European Economic Community, Germany was constrained in its attempts to oppose the agreement. Moreover, Gesamttextil, the German textile manufacturers association, was being pressured by American producers and came out strongly in favor of an all-fiber agreement.[77] Other European countries also discussed the possibility of linking an all-fiber agreement to U.S. tariff reductions in textile and apparel products. But an issue of greater significance in their acceptance of the Multifiber Arrangement was the pressure they were under from Comitextil, the pan-European textile producers organization. As exports were diverted from the American market because of the American bilateral agreements, Comitextil was able to argue convincingly that the EEC Commission needed to participate in the development of a multilateral agreement (see Table 8).

The Japanese argued that they were opposed to an extension of the Long-Term Arrangement to other fibers, but this was only a tactic to develop a bargaining position. On June 9, 1973, they noted their reasons for opposing the Multifiber Arrangement but then pointed out

[76]Destler, Fukui, and Sato, *The Textile Wrangle*, p. 316.
[77]*Daily News Record*, January 31, 1973.

Table 8. EEC and U.S. imports from countries in Long-Term Arrangement and Multifiber Arrangements, 1970–1973 (in millions of dollars)

Region	Year	Textiles	Clothing
EEC	1970	$957[a]	$689[a]
	1973	1,831[a]	1,980[a]
Percent change		91%	187%
United States	1970	$1,086[b]	$1,099[b]
	1973	1,408[b]	1,751[b]
Percent change		30%	59%

[a]C.I.F.

[b]F.O.B.

SOURCE: General Agreement on Tariffs and Trade, *Production and Trade in Textiles and Clothing, 1974 to 1976*, Com. Tex/W/35, October 29, 1976 (restricted document). Import data from Table 8, p. 22. Percentages calculated by author.

that it would be acceptable under two conditions: if a surveillance body was set up to monitor bilateral agreements, and if safeguards were only used when the actual injury had taken place.[78] In the end, proposed conditions served as the basis for bargaining between exporting and importing countries. The issues were resolved by the creation of the Textile Surveillance Body, a weak organization which was given no enforcement powers, and a slightly more stringent definition of market disruption. The overall quota growth rate was increased from 5 to 6 percent per annum as a further concession to the demands of less developed countries. As with the Long-Term Arrangement, bilaterals were to be negotiated under the auspices of this agreement, and existing bilaterals, on which the United States had a head start, were to be brought into conformity with the terms of the Multifiber Arrangement.

Summary

Three important lessons can be drawn from this complicated history. The first concerns domestic intervention schemes; the second and third have to do with the international ramifications of certain forms of protection.

The first lesson is provided by the Kennedy plan, which did little to counter the protectionist trend, either economically or politically. The measures it prescribed actually had the result of strengthening protectionist demands. Without clear provisions to eliminate excess capacity or to force positive adjustment through the phase-out of inefficient equipment, government policy contributed to the pressures on the in-

[78]*Ibid.*, June 19, 1973.

dustry when demand softened in the late 1960s.[79] The Kennedy plan also illustrates the failure of government to formulate its own *political* strategy toward the textile-apparel coalition. As we have noted, the coalition was not an obvious one. Labor should have been a prime candidate for government attention, but little aid was provided under the Adjustment Assistance Act, part of the 1962 Trade Act, and the plan failed to give labor any guarantees, even though massive changes—mergers, technological development, and relocation—were responsible for high unemployment. If government policy had focused on the domestic troubles of the industry, and aided the transition for labor, a free-trade alliance might have been constructed. With more positive adjustment measures, large competitive firms and the financial community might also have been interested in maintaining free trade.

The second lesson concerns the economics and politics of protection in the international arena. As we have seen, the building of the protectionist coalition was not a foregone conclusion. A set of divergent interests demanded aggregation. With the conclusion of the multilateral control system on cotton products, however, and the subsequent diversion to man-made fiber and wool products, the political clout of the man-made fiber section of the industry was increased, and its interest in free trade was being diminished by the division process taking place.

The third lesson to be drawn from international negotiations consists of several points. We have already noted the snowballing effect whereby protection was gradually extended to new producers and consumers. But the negotiations illustrate the weaknesses as well as the strengths of the textile and apparel industries. The U.S. government effort to negotiate an international arrangement to regulate controls in the wool trade failed because Britain and Italy were important exporters of these products. Such conflicting policy imperatives—Atlantic harmony and industry demands—can sometimes be manipulated. But the textile and apparel industries did not have the ability to influence the government at this time, because negotiations were still being conducted under the 1962 Trade Act. In 1964, man-made fiber textile and apparel manufacturers had neither the interest nor the capability to press for restrictions, even though they were the major segment of the industry.

By 1969, the situation had changed. The man-made fiber producers were experiencing a trade deficit, domestic demand had weakened, and textile and apparel producers had excess capacity, due in part to Kennedy's plans for promoting capital investment. The relative cap-

[79]The elimination of the two-price cotton system, which had at first hurt cotton textile and apparel manufacturers, was largely irrelevant because the whole industry had become oriented to MMF textile and apparel products.

abilities of government and industry had also changed. The textile and apparel industries were able to block attempts to pass a new trade bill, and to secure a promise from President Nixon that he would conclude an international agreement on woolen and man-made fiber products in exchange for electoral support. The government found it easier to press for international concessions because Far Eastern suppliers had displaced Europeans as the major exporters of woolen and man-made fiber based products in the United States. Nor is it completely clear that all Far Eastern suppliers were hurt by a protectionist agreement. Although their exports were limited, the movement of their prices reflected effective cartelization. Japanese producers could also move into more expensive goods. Convincing the Europeans to go along was easy: by concluding bilateral agreements with major suppliers, the United States altered European incentives as Far Eastern exporters diverted their exports to the European market. In short, the result of government capitulation to industry was to aid in the internalization of the protectionist coalition, even though some of the partners had joined reluctantly.

Throughout the international negotiations, the U.S. textile and apparel industries demonstrated that they could block any concessions they considered unfavorable. Because the U.S. government had failed to develop an industrial policy—and equally important, a political coalition to support it—it was forced to follow industry's lead. Ironically, the only constraint on the demands of the domestic industry was international.

The EEC Takes Charge; the United States Takes Advantage

The renewal of the Multifiber Arrangement in 1977 marked an important change in the international politics of market intervention in the textile and apparel trade. Whereas the United States had always taken the lead in trying to develop and change international agreements in the textile and apparel trade, it was the European Economic Community (EEC) which sought to institute major changes when the Multifiber Arrangement came up for renewal. The reason was simple. The EEC had been slow to negotiate its bilateral agreements under the first Multifiber Arrangement (MFA). Since the United States had effectively controlled access to its market, the less developed countries began exporting to Europe. The rapid growth of imports of textile and apparel products into the EEC—imports diverted from U.S. markets—was pressuring European producers. The result was an even stricter accord. The amendment that was finally incorporated into the new MFA allowed "jointly agreed reasonable departures" from the 6 percent growth rate in quotas and "flexibility provisions" under the first MFA—an objective that the textile and apparel producers in the

United States had long been seeking. The battle had been won by changing the market conditions under which the Europeans had to negotiate.

As with the first MFA, bilaterals with exporting countries had to be negotiated. To ensure that "departures" would take place in the "correct" direction, U.S. textile and apparel producers applied their traditional strategy by attempting to remove textile and apparel products from the Tokyo Round tariff negotiations and by exploiting access to Congress. The result of this pressure was President Carter's White Paper, which called for the strict monitoring of imports and contained provisions to renegotiate important aspects of the bilateral agreements to make them more restrictive. It also contained a U.S. government pledge to unilaterally restrict imports if the MFA should collapse in 1981, the year in which it was to come up for renewal again.

U.S. policy toward the textile and apparel industries remained oriented toward the control of imports into the U.S. market. Some feeble attempts were made to encourage exports of textile and apparel products, but the fundamental problems of labor losses due to technological change, the movement of firms from North to South, and fragmentation and overcapacity of certain segments of the industry were not addressed.

Why was the United States not in the forefront of the effort to secure the final objective of the twenty-five-year industry struggle to control trade? There were two reasons: the different impact of the oil crisis of 1973 on the United States and the EEC, and the EEC's struggle to develop a unified policy on textiles. The recession of 1974 and 1975 substantially altered the demand for textile and apparel products. Whereas the MFA growth-rate provision had seemed reasonable in the boom year of 1973, it proved to be a major sore point for the EEC in the recessionary period that began a year later. Although employment showed a steep decline in the United States, the problem was even more severe in the EEC, and was aggravated by rising productivity (see Table 9). Moreover , in marked contrast to the EEC, where employment showed a secular decline in textiles and clothing from 1973 and 1977, U.S. textile and apparel employment recovered well. In fact, in May 1976 the Foreign Trade Committee of the American Textile Manufacturers Institute had decided that their primary purpose was not to amend the MFA to make it more stringent, but rather simply to extend it.[80]

The second politically significant factor in the development of pres-

[80]American Textile Manufacturers Institute, Minutes, May 18, 1976. Hereafter cited as TMI, Minutes.

Table 9. Index of production, employment, and productivity in textiles and clothing in EEC, Japan, and United States, 1974–1978 (1973 = 100)

	1974	1975	1976	1977	1978
EEC					
Textiles					
Production	96	88	87	94	92
Employment	95	89	86	84	81
Productivity	101	99	113	112	114
Clothing					
Production	96	95	100	98	94
Employment	94	89	86	87	n.a.
Productivity	102	107	116	117	n.a.
Japan					
Textiles					
Production	88	83	90	88	89
Employment	92	87	83	76	71
Productivity	96	95	108	116	125
Clothing					
Production	89	83	88	88	89
Employment	102	107	107	107	105
Productivity	87	78	82	82	85
United States					
Textiles					
Production	93	86	95	96	98
Employment	98	89	95	97	97
Productivity	95	97	100	99	101
Clothing					
Production	97	92	104	106	108
Employment	99	91	95	94	93
Productivity	98	101	109	113	116

SOURCE: General Agreement on Tariffs and Trade, "Textile and Clothing Production, Employment and Trade Statistics, 1973–1979," Com. Tex/W/63 (restricted document) (Geneva, October 1979), Tables 1 and 2.

sures for renewal was EEC policy. Whereas the United States had negotiated with major producers *before* the MFA was concluded, EEC negotiations with less developed countries were delayed by the lack of agreement over a "fair" allocation of imports *within* the EEC. In part, this delay was based on British demands that countries with high levels of imports be allowed lower quota allocations. The first bilateral agreement between the EEC and a less developed country (India) was signed on April 19, 1975. Agreements with major suppliers (Hong Kong, Korea, Singapore, and Japan) were concluded late in 1975—a full two years after the MFA was negotiated.[81] Another factor that delayed the

[81] European Economic Community, *The European Community and the Textile Arrangement* (Luxembourg: Office for Official Publications of the EEC, n.d.), p. 61. Hereafter cited as EEC, *Textile Arrangements.*

conclusion of bilateral agreements was the question whether the EEC should conclude comprehensive or selective agreements. The choice of selective agreements aggravated the import situation in the member countries of the EEC. Exporters branched out into other products; and trade was deflected between member countries because restrictions on specific products were often applied by each country within the EEC. Again, the character of the policy instrument forced the producers in less developed countries to adjust.

While attempts to eliminate trade barriers and to lower tariff barriers in the Tokyo Round negotiations were beginning in serious fashion, little attention was paid to problems that might arise from the political demands of the textile and apparel industries. The MFA stated that intervention in trade should be "accompanied by the pursuit of appropriate economic and social policies, in a manner consistent with national laws and systems, required by changes in the pattern of textiles and in the comparative advantage of participating countries, which policies would encourage businesses which are less competitive internationally to move progressively into more viable lines of production or into other sectors of the economy."[82] Though policies to completely phase out the textile and apparel industries were not considered politically or economically feasible by U.S. policy-makers, little attention was given to improving the competitive position of problem industries.

The Objectives of Textile Producers

Since the MFA had proved reasonably satisfactory to U.S. producers, they were at first willing to have it renewed as it stood rather than see it collapse. When it became clear that the EEC was pressing for major changes, the U.S. producers had little choice but to join the Europeans in their attempts to institute revisions. The protectionist coalition had become international. But the real opposition from domestic industry came *after* the MFA was renewed, when it was felt that the Europeans had managed to get a "better deal" in their negotiations. It is in the very nature of bilateral accords to stimulate competitive protection: each party comes to fear diversion from the other. The textile-apparel coalition again sought to obtain special concessions from the government by attempting to delay the conclusion of the multilateral trade negotiations.

Although management and labor showed a great deal of unity on the issue of the MFA, this was not the case with the provisions for "outward processing," which allow importers to pay duty on only the value added

[82]GATT, *Arrangement Regarding International Trade in Textiles* (Geneva: GATT, 1974). Text also in *Status of MFA*, p. A-23.

to a product if the materials which were used in its assembly came from the United States and were not "fundamentally altered." As might be expected, labor unions fought to repeal Section 807 of the tariff code, and have continued to do so. The issue of 807 imports was raised whenever labor unions had an opportunity to testify on problems in the apparel industry. The American Textile Manufacturers Institute, eager to avoid being caught up in a struggle that might destroy producer-labor unity on protection, has continued to preserve a neutral stance on the issue. The American Apparel Manufacturers Association has also tried to remain neutral since its membership is composed of different types of firms, only some of which engage in Section 807 operations. [83] As long as there is little danger of a repeal of Section 807, the peak associations will try to minimize their involvement.

As noted earlier, the American Textile Manufacturers Institute initially feared that the MFA might not be extended at all if amendments to the agreement were introduced. They did, however, decide on a "fallback" position if the MFA was "opened to amendment." On March 10, 1977, they specified their objectives. They argued that the "agreement should be extended for at least five years with the present 6 percent quota factor reduced to a level no greater than the domestic market growth"; and they noted the need for an exemption of textiles from the Multilateral Trade Negotiations and the need for a bilateral agreement with the People's Republic of China.[84] These very points were proposed by the informal House Textiles Committee in 1977, which went further in arguing that the bilaterals should not allow "growth in categories of products already heavily impacted by imports."[85]

The Negotiations over MFA Renewal

By March of 1977 in Geneva, it had become clear that the EEC was not planning to renew the MFA without changes to make it more restrictive. The European textile and apparel manufacturers were arguing that there was need for a "social clause" in the agreement stipulating that countries should only receive benefits if they followed the International Labor Organization's norm on the treatment of labor. They called for differentiation between "genuinely developing countries and the over-industrialized countries in the textile field"—the latter being a euphemism for Hong Kong, Korea, Taiwan, and other

---

[83]Interview with American Apparel Manufacturers Association.

[84]TMI, Minutes, March 10, 1977. For an earlier position, see Minutes for May 18, 1976.

[85]House of Representatives, Subcommittee on Trade of the Committee on Ways and Means, *Background Material on the Multifiber Agreement* (1979 edition), April 2, 1979, p. 3.

highly competitive exporters. The Europeans, facing import surges and slowing economics, were playing tough. On the other hand, the U.S. representatives to the fifth meeting of the GATT Textiles Committee in late 1976 argued that "the MFA represented the successful evolution of internationally agreed standards for the conduct of textile trade . . . [and] it should be renewed immediately."[86]

It quickly became clear to the United States, however, that the likelihood of the MFA being extended in its present form was slight. The EEC was now the largest market for less developed countries' textile and apparel exports, and unless it agreed to extend the arrangement, the MFA would be replaced by unilateral and bilateral agreements made without any concern for an international regime. This time, the EEC was unified. Member countries had resolved their differences *prior* to the start of renewal negotiations, so that their representative, the EEC Commission, was able to speak with a powerful voice. To prevent the demise of the MFA, the United States proposed to extend the MFA with the provision that the EEC be allowed to negotiate its bilateral agreements with exporting countries prior to the signing of the renewal of the MFA, with the "possibility of jointly agreed reasonable departures from particular elements in particular cases."[87] This amounted to the virtual abandonment of binding rules. The Commission invoked unilateral import restrictions in July of 1977 on a number of products.[88] The Commission also proceeded to rapidly negotiate bilateral agreements with major suppliers. To ensure compliance with the quota-level objectives, Tran van Thinh, Chief Negotiator on Textiles for the Commission, explained that he had a "limited pie" to share among the less developed countries (LDCs) and that the first countries to sign an agreement would receive the largest pieces.[89] Faced with this dismal prospect, unity among the LDC's rapidly dissipated. Tran's skill as a negotiator is suggested by Table 10, which illustrates the difference between the objectives and outcomes of the Commission's negotiations with the eight most "sensitive" textile and apparel products.

With restrictive bilaterals virtually concluded, the EEC signed the protocol extension proposed by the United States. The new clause referring to "reasonable departures" proved to be a major change in the MFA. No longer could the LDCs be assured of stable markets. The burden of adjustment had been effectively shifted to the LDCs: if they

[86]GATT, *Draft Report of the Fifth Meeting of the Textiles Committee,* November 30 to December 10, 1976, Document Com. Tex/W/39 (restricted), pp. 16–17.

[87]GATT, "Paper Circulated at the Request of the United States," Com Tex/4/44 (restricted), July 24, 1977, p. 2.

[88]*EEC, Textile Arrangements,* p. 29.

[89]Interviews with EEC officials and delegates (textile negotiators from LDCs).

Table 10. Volume of imports sought and achieved by EEC in renewal of 1977 Multifiber Arrangement, 1978, by category

Category	Description	Volume sought	Volume achieved
1	Cotton yarn, not for retail sale	220,449 tonnes[a]	227,716 tonnes[a]
2	Woven cotton fabrics	109,270 tonnes[a]	215,150 tonnes[a]
3	Woven fabric of man-made fibers (discontinuous or waste)	42,905 tonnes[a]	43,873 tonnes[a]
4	Undergarments, knitted or crocheted, not elasticized or rubberized	235.27 million pieces	234.87 million pieces
5	Outer garments and other articles, knitted or crocheted, not elasticized or rubberized	171.07 million pieces	160.54 million pieces
6	Men's, boys', women's, girls', and infants' outer garments	109.53 million pieces	116.88 million pieces
7	Outer garments and other articles, knitted or crocheted, not elasticized or rubberized, and women's, girls', and infants' outer garments	111.53 million pieces	105.42 million pieces
8	Men's and boys' undergarments, collars, shirt fronts, and cuffs	177.99 million pieces	173.09 million pieces

[a]Tonne (metric ton) = 1.1 tons.
SOURCE: *The European Community and the Textile Arrangements* (Brussels: Europe Information, n.d.), p. 43.

wished to maintain their exports of textiles and apparel, they would be forced to transfer production to "less sensitive" products. Even if they should find buyers for "sensitive" goods, the "basket extractor" mechanism (which leads to automatic quota negotiations when imports from a country reach a certain percentage of total EEC imports of a product) would effectively prevent rapid growth in a specific product.[90] The market position of producers in LDCs had been made difficult, if not impossible. Not only were they denied the certainty of market growth by the "reasonable departures" clause, but they were unable to profit from surges in demand in products on a discretionary list of "sensitive items."

[90]EEC, *Textile Arrangements*, p. 40.

More Concessions from the U.S. Government. The United States also negotiated agreements which were slated to expire in 1977, but many bilaterals ran into 1978 and thus were not immediately open to negotiations. When they were negotiated in 1978, agreements with major suppliers (Hong Kong, Korea, and Taiwan) were more restrictive. This did not, however, satisfy the textile and apparel industries. Noting that the European bilaterals were more stringent than comparable American agreements, part of the U.S. textile-apparel complex pressed for renegotiation of the bilaterals. The Tokyo Round gave industry an obvious point of leverage. The intent of U.S. negotiators to reduce textile and apparel tariffs had always been a *bête noir* of industry groups. A unified coalition emerged to wage the new campaign. Chairman Klopman of the American Textile Manufacturers Institute Foreign Trade Committee "emphasized the need for the Committee and the industry to stick together and not let the Government 'divide and conquer.' Stressing that the industry-approved policy was to keep all textile products off the tariff table, he warned that attempts to make cases for particular products would only play into the hands of Ambassador Strauss and others."[91]

With support in the House and Senate, a bill to exempt textile and apparel products from tariff reductions was passed in October 1978. The President was forced to veto this bill on November 11, 1978, to prevent EEC protests from sinking the multilateral trade negotiations altogether. But further pressure to ensure favorable treatment was being exerted. On behalf of the textile and apparel industries, several congressmen threatened to refuse to extend the President's authority to waive countervailing duties on a number of products that were being subsidized by the Europeans. It quickly became clear to President Carter that if he were to save the Tokyo Round, action would have to be taken to counter textile and apparel industry pressure.

The outcome of this conflict was an Administration Textile Program announced on February 15, 1979, known as the White Paper.[92] It promised careful monitoring of import quotas, a renegotiation of bilateral agreements to prevent "surges" of exports, and a "snap-back clause." This clause would allow tariffs to be restored if the MFA was not renewed and contained a pledge to restrict imports of textile products legislatively if the MFA was not extended.

To implement the portion of the program on surges, the United States proceeded to renegotiate portions of its bilateral agreements

[91]TMI, Minutes, April 28, 1978.
[92]Office of the Special Representative for Trade Negotiations, press release No. 302, March 22, 1979.

with Hong Kong, South Korea, and Taiwan. In new negotiations with China and Sri Lanka, a reduced degree of flexibility was offered. Similar changes were made in the agreements with other countries.

The 1981 renegotiation of the MFA marked a sharp turn toward increased protectionism. Numerous provisions in the renewal protocol leave developed countries virtually unhindered in negotiating bilateral agreements. While new bilaterals are currently being negotiated, the American strategy appears to be to tie import growth to growth in the domestic market, a long-standing aim of industry. This could require, however, an even lower growth provision for major suppliers, as the United States (and the EEC) treat LDC suppliers differently, according to their degree of "development." The politics of these developments were predictable.

The first step in this direction was taken by candidate Ronald Reagan in a letter to Senator Strom Thurmond on September 3, 1980: "The MFA expires at the end of 1981 and needs to be strengthened by relating import growth from all sources to domestic market growth. I shall work to achieve that goal." As negotiations for the MFA renewal proceeded after Reagan's election, the industry encouraged senators and congressmen to "remind" U.S. negotiators of Reagan's commitment. Senators Ernest Hollings and Strom Thurmond took the lead in lobbying U.S. officials. For example, Hollings, in a letter to William Brock, the U.S. Special Trade Representative, criticized a statement by the Chairman of the Council of Economic Advisors, Murray Weidenbaum, which stated that President Reagan had pledged to "explore the possibility" of global quotas.[93] Hollings tersely noted that the President had never used the word "explore," but had made a firm commitment to global quotas keyed to the domestic growth rate. In his letter, Hollings even called for *negative* growth rates for the Big Three in some categories!

The pressure increased with signs of success. The Congressional Textile Caucus of the U.S. House of Representatives wrote to Brock expressing their pleasure at his proposal to "isolate (the Big Three) and severely limit their exports" to the United States. Having secured victory on this issue they pressed a proposal to tackle problems created by "other large and potentially disruptive suppliers . . . such as China, India, etc."[94] Moreover, they pointed out the need to take a multi-country approach to the quotas, to adopt a lower growth rate keyed to the domestic market, and to eliminate *all* flexibility provisions. Senators

[93]Letter from Senator Ernest F. Hollings to William E. Brock, III, May 15, 1981.
[94]Letter from Congressional Textile Caucus, U.S. House of Representatives, to William E. Brock, III, May 22, 1981.

from the Committee on Finance supported similar ideas in a letter to Brock. Although there was opposition from such groups as the American Importers Association, they had little effect on the final American proposals for the MFA's renewal.

A number of departments in the U.S. government—such as the Council of Economic Advisers, the Treasury, the National Security Council, and the Department of Justice—pushed for a policy that would not simply toe the industry line. In various interagency discussions, some attempt was made by these departments to push Peter Murphy, the U.S. Chief Textile Negotiator, to resist global quotas and an import growth rate tied to domestic market growth. It was hoped that cutting back the Big Three might satisfy the industry—at least enough to prevent continued opposition. These departments and agencies had some success in pushing Murphy to take a more moderate position in negotiations than the industry desired. But events soon took a more protectionist turn.

In early December of 1981, a number of congressmen from North and South Carolina made it clear to the administration that the Foreign Aid Appropriations bill and other legislation under discussion would be opposed unless the President put pressure on Peter Murphy to "strengthen" the American proposal on the MFA. An Assistant to the President, James A. Baker, III, quickly responded that the President had instructed Murphy to strengthen the U.S. proposal. He emphasized the President's previous commitment: "This Administration will make every effort to satisfactorily conclude an MFA that will allow us to relate total import growth to the growth in the domestic textile and apparel market."[95]

The "strengthened" U.S. position brought it closer to the highly protectionist stance taken by the EEC. With the two key markets now in accord, the previously stalled negotiations came to a rapid conclusion. A weakened MFA was the result. Once again, the textile and apparel industries had prevailed.

POLICY CHOICES FOR THE UNITED STATES: CONSTRAINTS AND OPTIONS

This chapter has described the political dynamics that have shaped U.S. government policies in textiles and apparel. The policy process leading to protection can be explained by four factors. We began by

[95]Letter from James A. Baker, III, to Carroll A. Campbell, December 11, 1981.

noting that these industries faced economic problems typical of "mature" industries. In response to changing domestic market conditions as well as imports, a coalition-building process was initiated by the cotton textile industry and subsequently joined by other textile and apparel groups. This coalition proved successful against a U.S. government which lacked a coherent industrial vision; there was no effective resistance. The initial choice of limited trade protection as a favored policy instrument aggravated the problems facing the industries and led gradually to the spread of protection globally.

How are we to judge this protectionist outcome? On the one hand, it can be argued that protection has a viable adjustment strategy. Plant closings have been avoided, jobs have been saved, and textiles, at least, appears to have been transformed into a dynamic and internationally competitive industry. On the other hand, these benefits must be weighed against important political and economic costs. Consumers have paid higher prices for apparel, with those in the lower income brackets (who spend proportionately more on clothing) suffering the most. Protection has given false market signals, deceiving employers and workers into thinking that saved jobs reflect a growing strength of the industry rather than its weakness. Protecting segments of one industry has tended to create problems in other industries. Once upstream industries are protected, inputs to downstream industries are raised; these downstream industries (apparel, in this case) may then become uncompetitive and therefore seek protection as well. Protection has channeled labor and capital into industries in which the United States no longer has a comparative advantage, thereby undermining America's international competitive position. Finally, protection has also had international effects, both political and economic. Trade restraints have limited the ability of developing countries to pursue their comparative advantage. Unnecessary political conflicts between developed and developing countries and among allies have been created.

It is clear that a policy of protection can never succeed in freezing an industry in place. The question is really whether change will be directed or undirected, whether it will be undertaken with short-term or long-term considerations in mind. If positive adjustments are to take place, government objectives must change; they must embody an interest in increasing industry competitiveness and in minimizing the efficiency and welfare costs of protection. Such a shift involves developing a political strategy toward industry in general, and achieving an understanding of the different problems of various industry segments. Adjustment can be fostered largely through market signals, though positive intervention and compensatory measures are needed to ease the transition. Ultimately, however, such changes may involve institutional reforms in government itself, changes which may become the center of a new set of bureaucratic and political battles.

Some economists contend that the ideal industrial policy would simply be openness. Free trade claims a number of advantages, at least in theory. Most notably, it avoids the whole problem of elaborating a sectoral policy. Efficiency and competitiveness would be increased, though admittedly with short-term losses in employment. But resources would be freed for investment in more productive growth industries, which would absorb displaced labor. Adjustment assistance programs could be used to ease the transition. Finally, there would be overall gains in consumer welfare.

This idyllic picture has several flaws, however. The first concerns the problem of lags in adjustment. If protection is removed too rapidly, firms which are *potentially* competitive may be prematurely eliminated. The shock will force adjustment, but not necessarily an adjustment that will be most efficient in the longer term. Managerial response may not be adequate or rapid enough. In addition, as we have sought to stress, both protection and a free-trade policy do not address themselves to certain *domestic* changes that would occur even in the absence of imports.

Perhaps the most important flaw in the free-trade model is its political infeasibility. The very disruptiveness of the unhindered operation of market forces makes such a policy impossible, even if it were desirable from the standpoint of global welfare. When labor and business are vulnerable to rapidly changing market conditions, they will always use political power to protect themselves. The textile and apparel industries have succeeded in developing a unified stance on foreign economic policy which has been translated into U.S. government policy. This coalition, *if* it can remain unified, will retain the power to veto government initiatives. From a *political* standpoint, then, intervention should be aimed at regaining control over the policy process and over the definition of issues.

This overview allows us to distinguish three sorts of policy problems that must be solved. First, the political problems must be faced. Government must develop a vision of industrial change based on a differentiated view of the industry. It must then seek support for such a policy from groups that can be weaned from their protectionist position and encouraged to take an interest in positive adjustment. The second problem is to develop coherence between domestic and international policy. Trade policy can be a useful instrument, if it is used to channel market signals in a way that induces domestic adjustment. The third problem is to develop domestic instruments for promoting competitiveness, and where necessary, for easing the costs of exit and adjustment. As we have argued, any policy that does not address domestic changes cannot succeed. We may now suggest possible solutions to these three problems.

If a political coalition is responsible for protectionism, then a political coalition will have to be responsible for dismantling it. The U.S. government must act to break up the textile-apparel alliance, in part by distinguishing between the problems of the two industries. Several politically important groups could be mobilized around such a counter-coalitional effort: consumer groups, retailers, and other industrial sectors would welcome reduced protection. The financial community also has a potential interest in seeing an internationally competitive industry. A more important task, however, is to foster or create vested interests within the textile and apparel industries that will favor an open trading system.

Building such coalitions demands a view of industry structure that permits the formation of selective policy measures. Distinctions must be drawn between the textile industry and the apparel industry, between small and large firms, and between different segments of the industry. Policy can then be formulated with the dual purpose of increasing the competitiveness of particular segments while attracting allies. Some brief examples may help illustrate this process.

Although the apparel industry has joined the textile industry on the specific issue of protection, its problems and industrial characteristics are very different from those of the textile industry, and they require different policy responses. By all indicators the textile sector has made progress toward adustment. Production is up, capital investment is substantial, and exports have increased dramatically, tripling between 1970 and 1979.[96] Since exports appear to be a significant aspect of the adjustment process in textiles, government policy could be aimed at *dismantling* foreign restrictions and opening markets. It may be the case that some developing-country markets are overprotected, particularly in product lines in which there is no significant domestic production. If so, the liberalization of U.S. markets could be used as a lever for broader liberalization.

The apparel industry continues to face larger problems. As our analysis of "declining industries" has shown, policy-makers must learn to identify industrial segments and specific firms with growth potential. A recent study by a prominent consulting firm has outlined a set of marketing strategies that large firms could use in order to become

[96]P. Handel and M. P. Daniels, "Politics, Protection, and Domestic Industry," a position paper presented on behalf of the American Importers Association before the Subcommittee on Trade, July 21, 1980.

competitive with imports.[97] Nor must industrial contractions or consolidation necessarily take place entirely at the expense of small firms. In Japan, for example, assistance has been provided to small firms by the government's encouragement of large trading corporations that can market the products of small firms more effectively.

This brings us to the second policy problem: the coherence of international and domestic policy. As we have noted, U.S. policy during the postwar period has forced adjustment by foreign firms. By channeling international market forces in a selective way, potentially competitive segments of the U.S. industry may be induced to adjust on their own.

A look at three segments of the apparel industry will clarify the importance of combining a coherent view of international and domestic policy with a differentiated approach to industrial policy. First, segments with high market penetration ratios should have their quotas, if any, relaxed in order to promote the needed exit of less successful firms. Some companies in these areas of high market penetration may be prepared to cope with competition by developing their own strategies of adjustment. Other companies will be unable to compete, but aid might be provided in exchange for a relaxation of quotas. Second, firms or product lines with an intermediate degree of import competition could be protected with quotas in the first of a two-stage program. In the second stage, quotas should be gradually reduced to subject these firms to increasing competition in the international market place. Third, segments of the market that have very low import competition should be disaggregated into two sub-segments. If low import penetration is due to restrictive quotas, these products must be treated as in the first case of high import penetration. On the other hand, firms that are competing on their own, without high levels of import quotas, should be allowed freedom to respond to market conditions. In these cases, the government should institute an efficient mechanism to monitor the potential dumping or subsidization of products that enter the U.S. market. Government policies should legitimately be concerned with ensuring that foreign producers do not engage in unfair trade practices in order to gain a foothold in the U.S. market. This surveillance cannot become an excuse for protection, however. These brief examples show how a refined view of the industry can be used as a lever for forcing competitiveness and building political allies, while still relying on market forces.

The final and much more general policy need is to address changes in the industry that are domestically rooted. This must be the core of

[97]Kurt Salmon Associates, *Marketing Strategies for U.S. Apparel Firms to Compete More Effectively with Imports* (New York, 1980).

any real industrial policy. Here is where a more directly interventionist approach is required. Again, a few examples may be illustrative.

As was suggested in our first section, inattention to technological change and shifts in product preferences can lead to major problems. Although the U.S. government has subsidized research and development through a variety of mechanisms in high-technology areas for years, this policy has not been pursued in lower technology areas, such as the textile and apparel industries. Market research on new product development must go hand-in-hand with any kind of intervention policy.

Regional policy needs to be harmonized more closely with industrial adjustment strategies. In regions of the country that have been depressed by mill closings caused by company relocation, government policy must seek to promote new investment and ease the burden of transition. In cases where plants can remain competitive at their present location, through organizational and technological changes, incentives should be provided to keep them from moving. Equally important, however, regions hosting new industries should be supported and encouraged. In the past, U.S. policy has been slow to aid in the elimination of bottlenecks in the flow of resources to growing regions and industries.

Finally, industrial policy must be coordinated. Larger amounts should be given to labor, and labor should be brought into the decision-making process. Aid could be tied directly to the reduction of quotas, giving labor an interest in opening the domestic market. Aid can be aimed at retraining and increasing productivity, or at increasing mobility or encouraging early retirement. Consideration must also be given to the organizational interests of labor. Innovative solutions, such as cooperatives and worker purchase of closed mills, should be encouraged, perhaps through government loans or guarantees.

These comments are obviously not a set of concrete policy prescriptions. Rather, they outline the prerequisites for a coherent strategy that seeks to move beyond the sterile alternatives of protection and free trade. We have stressed both the economic and the political factors that affect the development of such a policy. A final caveat must be added, however. Ultimately, the success of an industrial policy rests on reducing the internal fragmentation of the relevant policy bureaucracies themselves. Without some institutional reform, the various fights and deadlocks we have outlined will continue to be replayed within existing institutions. While this speculation carries us beyond the scope of our concern here, it is clearly an important factor in considering the prospects for a coherent industrial strategy.

Chapter Six

Adjustment in the Footwear Industry: The Consequences of Orderly Marketing Agreements

David B. Yoffie

The following chapter on the footwear industry explores the consequences of the most popular American protectionist instrument, Orderly Marketing Agreements (OMAs). An Orderly Marketing Agreement amounts to a "voluntary" agreement by an exporting country to limit its shipments to the importer. For successive U.S. administrations, committed to international free trade as a principle but buffeted by intense domestic pressures for protection, OMAs have offered a means of maintaining the principle of free trade while achieving temporary protection in specific cases.

The pernicious consequences of OMAs are evident in every case in which they are discussed in this volume. When faced with quantitative limits on the volume of output that can be sold—which in this chapter means the number of pairs of shoes—foreign producers adjust their production and sales strategies. One common adjustment is to move production and sales toward higher-priced, more expensive items—from cheap sandals toward expensive hiking boots, for example. As a result, within the quantitative limits, the value of the units sold can rise. A second adjustment to OMA protection is to move foreign production to countries not bound by the quantitative limitations of the OMA.

The next chapter provides a detailed analysis of OMAs in the footwear industry. The author's conclusion is that OMAs do nothing to help the adjustment process in trade-impacted industries. They do not even buy time, because they create strong incentives for foreign competitors to make adjustments that leave them in even stronger positions in American markets. This conclusion strength-

A somewhat different version of this chapter appeared as an article entitled "Orderly Marketing Agreements as an Industrial Policy: The Case of the Footwear Industry," in *Public Policy* 39, no. 1 (Winter, 1981) pp. 93–119, published by John Wiley & Sons, Inc.

ens the one we offered in the first chapter: that protection by itself is not an effective adjustment strategy in either the short or the long run.

THE DILEMMAS of the U.S. footwear industry have relevance far beyond that sector's small share in the gross national product or its meager contribution to national defense. Government policy toward shoe manufacturing firms can illustrate the problems of the U.S. government's approach to industrial intervention. The political struggles of the industry exemplify the plight of many industrial sectors in American politics. And because automobile manufacturing and other sectors will face competitive pressures in the 1980s similar to those confronted by footwear producers in the 1970s, one can learn valuable lessons from the government's ill-fated attempt to foster industrial adjustment.

Footwear firms, like companies in other "import-sensitive" industries such as textiles, steel, and consumer electronics, see themselves as permanently disadvantaged by "cheap" foreign labor. For over a decade, footwear organizations have sought government protection as a remedy for their decline. After many failures, the footwear industry finally realized its wish: on April 1, 1977, President Carter rejected recommendations of the International Trade Commission to impose a tariff rate quota on "non-rubber footwear," but announced in its place a "special" footwear program to "revitalize the shoe industry."[1] The government stated its intention of negotiating Orderly Marketing Agreements (a form of export restraint) with the principal foreign producers, and of expanding and reorganizing trade adjustment assistance at the same time.

Between May and July of 1977, the Carter administration fulfilled its promise: it negotiated export restrictions with Taiwan and Korea, and established a Footwear Industry Team to foster domestic adjustment. Previous government programs for the shoe industry had been aimed exclusively at trade-impacted firms. In contrast, this combined domestic and international package seemed to give the industry some reason for hope. The government not only departed from the refusal of previous administrations to provide protection, but also initiated one of the first major attempts by the United States to confront the problems of industrial decline on an industry-wide basis. Fifty-six million dollars were allocated for a three-year domestic program; and policies such as promoting technological development were designed to help all firms in the sector, not just the ailing ones.

[1] Special Trade Representative (STR), Press Release No. 247, April 1, 1977. Except when noted otherwise, "footwear" will refer to the "nonrubber" segment of the industry.

Yet two years later, in 1979, footwear imports held an even larger share of the domestic market supply than before the Carter program. Although there has been a slowdown in the loss of domestic capacity, overall trends still point toward decline. The Carter administration had hoped to limit imports and increase or at least maintain American producers' share of the U.S. market. But the deterioration of the footwear industry has been so severe that the United States may soon be faced with a hard choice: either committing hundreds of millions of dollars to long-term subsidies, or allowing the continual loss of jobs and productive capacity. The apparent inability of government assistance to maintain or regenerate America's competitive position in this industry is a matter of serious concern.

Would a different set of policies have better served domestic adjustment? Or has the shoe industry's decline been the inevitable result of a shifting comparative advantage to low-cost labor countries? To answer these questions, we must rethink the relationship between foreign trade and domestic intervention. When imports capture half of a domestic market and are on the rise, as is the case in footwear, the domestic impact of international competition takes on great significance. An ineffective international policy in the footwear industry could undermine virtually all domestic adjustment efforts (a result that would not necessarily occur in sectors with lower import penetration, such as textiles, steel, and automobiles).

Most footwear firms have failed to become competitive with imports precisely because the government's approach to international policy has failed to meet the industry's essential needs. International policy can serve two interrelated functions for furthering domestic adjustment. First, it can furnish a necessary breathing spell for producers to adapt to import competition. Firms may require time to make changes, and the government can effectively reduce foreign market penetration either by levying a tax on imported goods (that is, applying a tariff) or by placing quantitative restrictions on total imports.[2] Second, producers in a declining industry demand some assurance of growing markets or increased profits before risking new investment for modernization. Limiting imports has traditionally been seen as a government guarantee to domestic producers that modernization is worthwhile. If foreign products are gathering increasing portions of a slow-growth market, import restraints are the obvious means of inspiring confidence.

The Orderly Marketing Agreements (OMAs) negotiated with Korea and Taiwan failed on both counts. Unlike unilateral, global protection,

---

[2]The danger of imposing quantitative restrictions is that they are politically difficult to remove; and if they remain intact for extended periods, there are few incentives for domestic producers to adjust.

OMAs are bargained, selective restraints that limit the quantity of exports of only a few dynamic producers. Such quantitative restrictions, by their very nature, tend to facilitate adjustment by foreign manufacturers rather than by domestic firms. To compensate for a potential loss in exports, Taiwan and Korea were forced to upgrade and diversify their product lines into the strength of the American producers' market. Furthermore, uncontrolled foreign exporters such as Italy and Brazil were free to extend their share of imports, and new producers in low-wage countries such as Hong Kong could easily enter the low-priced market. Finally, Taiwan and Korea obtained sufficient flexibility in the bargaining over the OMAs in 1977 that they, too, could maintain and in some cases increase their share of the U.S. shoe supply. The Orderly Marketing Agreements have led not to domestic adjustment but to increased import competition with the American footwear industry.

The special Footwear Industry Team (FIT), organized by the Commerce Department in 1977, has undertaken a series of new policies for the shoe industry.[3] But its efforts have been swamped by a counterproductive foreign economic policy. So long as international and domestic policies work toward different ends, the FIT efforts to create a competitive sector can have no more than a marginal impact. International and domestic action must be *coherent* if an industry is to adjust.

This chapter is organized in five sections. The first considers the theoretical arguments for and against Orderly Marketing Agreements and similar export restraints; the second outlines the specific economic dynamics of the footwear sector; and the third explores the politics of the industry and the reasons behind the government's decision to use OMAs. The fourth section reviews the implementation and impact of the OMAs, and the final section discusses their policy implications.

OMAs as an Industrial Policy for Imports

When the Carter administration opted for Orderly Marketing Agreements, imports from a variety of sources had been squeezing the domestic footwear industry for over a decade. The choice of an international policy was thus of critical importance, because the effectiveness of the domestic program was likely to depend on an appropriate foreign economic response. Under these circumstances, it is somewhat surprising that OMAs were chosen. Arrangements of the OMA type have predictable negative effects, especially in labor-intensive manufac-

---

[3]These policies include speeding up the process of certification for trade adjustment assistance, providing consulting services for shoe manufacturers, promoting exports, funding technological development, and urging retailers to buy American-made goods.

turing industries.[4] Yet for more than forty years, the American government has persisted in using them for a variety of industries, ranging from textiles and apparel to steel and consumer electronics.

Orderly Marketing Agreements and other export restraints have three basic characteristics. First, they are *bargained* accords between an importing country and an exporting country. The exporting partner "agrees" to restrict the shipment of a particular good to a level lower than it might otherwise expect in a competitive market. Second, OMAs are *quantitative* limits, usually based on type, not on price. And third, they are *selective,* meaning that they apply only to a few dynamic producers. The consequence of the bargaining and selectivity of OMAs is that they *do not work in the short run* and that the quantitative restrictions they apply *can accelerate competition in the long run.* OMAs potentially help foreign producers adjust and move into the strongest segments of an American market.

The Political Economy of OMAs

OMAs have a twofold purpose. Politically, they are supposed to appease a domestic industry that is fighting for protection. Economically, they are designed to give marginal producers a breathing spell for the short run—an opportunity to produce under conditions of restricted competition.[5] If surplus capacity exists domestically, the American manufacturers using this capacity should be able to fill the void left by the restrained exporters. Unfortunately for U.S. companies, this may not be an advantage for long. A fundamental characteristic of OMAs as opposed to global quantitative restrictions (QRs) is that they selectively single out a few foreign producers. Under an OMA, not only do American producers have the opportunity to recapture lost market shares, but unrestrained exporters may also be able to recoup their losses or extend their gains in the American market. In the footwear case, Italy, Brazil, and Spain, as well as those marginal producers which the OMA was designed to protect, could have gained at the expense of Taiwan and Korea; why they did not will be explained later.

A second related difficulty of OMAs in labor-intensive industries,

---

[4]OMAs have been known under many names. Bilateral Quotas, Voluntary Export Restraints, Voluntary Restraint Agreements, and OMAs are all virtually identical, except for their legal interpretation. Bilateral quotas and OMAs usually refer to legal contractual arrangements between governments. Voluntary restraints negotiated between industries, or between a government and an industry, have been judged by the American courts to be in restraint of trade and illegal.

[5]Comptroller General of the United States, *Assistance to the Non-rubber Footwear Industry* (1975), p. 16.

such as footwear, is the possibility that they will encourage the transfer of production to other locations. Footwear is a relatively homogeneous product with very low skill requirements, particularly in the low-priced end of the market. Manufacturing facilities can be quickly established in a less developed country that is unrestrained by an OMA. This is not a problem with a global policy—using either tariffs or QRs—because in that case all nations would be equally affected. With selective protection, however, importers as well as firms in restrained countries have an incentive to set up facilities in third countries whenever capital, technology, and labor-skill requirements are not too high.

Historically, this transfer of resources in response to selective protection has been the pattern in textiles and apparel. When the United States negotiated a "voluntary" restraint for textiles with Japan in 1956-1957, importers immediately sought other suppliers of low-cost goods. Production required only modest amounts of capital, unskilled labor, and simple technology. As a result, Hong Kong, for example, was able to increase its sales 3,000 times in the first three years of Japanese restraints. Instead of decreasing total imports, the voluntary restraint program with Japan increased foreign market penetration in cotton textiles. The footwear OMAs, as will be shown later, have produced similar results.

A third problem with OMAs and all quantitative restrictions is that prices usually increase because of forced or anticipated reductions in supply. The distributional effects of OMAs and QRs differ from other forms of protection, such as tariffs. Under a tariff, the importing country absorbs any scarcity gains. But with quantitative restrictions, foreign producers or importers are most likely to capture the windfall profits. The distributional effects of QRs and OMAs are well documented in the economic literature.[6] In formal terms, the windfall profits generated by a tariff are distributed to the importing government in the form of higher revenues. Three alternatives are possible for the distribution of the windfall profits generated by an equivalent quota or OMA. First, foreign producers may raise prices to absorb the windfall profits for themselves. Second, if the foreign producers fear a loss of market shares from other similar suppliers, the exporters may absorb little of the windfall gain; if the U.S. merchandisers are relatively concentrated, they will absorb the gain. And third, if both foreign producers and importers are worried about a loss of market shares from the possible entry of new domestic producers, prices will remain low despite the scarcity induced by the quota or OMA, and the windfall

[6]See, for example, Nicholas Chaocholiades, *International Trade Theory and Policy* (New York: McGraw-Hill, 1979).

profits will not be realized.[7] In general, who gains depends partly on the relative concentration of market power between exporters and importers.

Who captures the scarcity gains also depends on the absence of abnormal shifts in supply and demand and on the extent to which the foreign government controls or intervenes in the market. If a government, such as Japan or South Korea, takes an active role in fostering oligopolies or bargaining with importers, it will strengthen the supply side of the equation. This may transfer more of the windfall gains to the exporters, even in a highly concentrated importing market.

A fourth difficulty that arises from the use of OMAs is that despite the dominant position of the United States in world trade, an agreement must still be negotiated.[8] The restrictiveness and effectiveness of protection is likely to provide higher import levels, greater import growth, and more flexibility for the exporter in a bilateral arrangement than in a unilaterally fashioned protection program. This appears to be true regardless of the degree of compulsion in the bilateral accord. In this sense, an OMA is inherently less effective from the point of view of the importing state, because "some element of bargaining" is always present.[9]

Beyond the simple haggling over numbers, an agreement of this type is almost always loosely worded and poorly designed the first time it is negotiated within a given manufacturing sector. As is the case with domestic legislation negotiated to serve conflicting special interests, international trade agreements result from the pushes and pulls of different interests, both within governments and between them. Compromise and ambiguity will almost certainly be reflected in the first attempt at a new protectionist program. Ambiguity may cover up substantive disagreements between governments and may allow each government varying interpretations to help it legitimize the agreement with its respective domestic interest groups. Ambiguity usually benefits the weaker country, by providing loopholes that allow the exporter to achieve production goals despite aggregate restrictions.[10]

Another bargaining problem arises when exporters try to ship large quantities of goods before an agreement becomes operative. These

[7]William R. Cline, *Imports and Consumer Prices: A Survey Analysis*, published by the American Retail Federation and the National Merchants Association, 1979.

[8]See David Yoffie, "The Advantages of Adversity: Weak States and the Politics of Trade," Ph.D. dissertation, Stanford University, 1981.

[9]Remarks by Julius Katz, former Assistant Secretary of State for Economic Affairs, in *Proceedings of the 72nd Annual Meeting of the American Society of International Law* (Washington, D.C., April 27–29, 1979), p. 13.

[10]Conversely, if the lack of clarity increases uncertainty, it may lower the sales and production levels of the restrained exporters.

goods are not counted as part of a quota because a quota is usually based on the date of exports. If goods shipped in anticipation of agreements can be marketed during the restraint period, then the short-term gains normally captured by the domestic producer will be lost.

An exporting nation's government also requires the support of its domestic industry to make an OMA work; and the target product of the OMA is likely to be much more important in the exporting country than it is in the economy of the United States. This invariably gives the exporting government a relatively greater stake in the negotiations. The resulting asymmetry of motivation favoring the exporter tends to produce more concessions by the importer.[11] Here again, similar trading problems abound in textiles and apparel.

Related to the bargaining side of the OMA is the problem of implementation. International treaties of this sort rarely provide for effective sanctions. The problem becomes compounded because the monitoring of these accords is never perfect, especially in the early stages. Bargaining theorists have hypothesized that treaties in international trade should become more "objective" when quantitative measures are used, and thus easier to implement. Yet circumvention and cheating in such arrangements have been widespread since the 1930s.[12] Sometimes circumvention takes ingenious forms, ranging from simple transshipments to changing packaging, mixing products, and varying slightly the raw materials to change classifications. If the loss of quantity to individual producers is not outweighed by higher prices, and no immediate sanctions are likely, both importers and exporters have an incentive to evade regulations.

An OMA may also encourage foreign production and thereby increase exports from restricted countries. If a foreign government allocates quotas for export on the basis of previous export performance, an exporter is given an additional incentive to produce large quantities. In some cases, producers must fill their quota or at least notify their government within sufficient time to allow the auctioning off of the remaining quota allocations. If the producer fails in either of these tasks, he may face heavy fines.[13] This means that the *maximum* allowed under the bilateral agreement actually becomes a *minimum* for the individual manufacturer and the exporting country. Unless the importing country is very strict in regard to overshipments—which is rare—increased im-

[11]C. Fred Bergsten, "The Non-Equivalence of Import Quotas and 'Voluntary' Export Restraints," in *The Maidenhead Papers*, ed. C. Fred Bergsten (New York: D. C. Heath, 1975).

[12]Heinrich Heuser, *Control of International Trade* (Philadelphia: P. Blakiston's, 1939).

[13]John Lynch, *Toward an Orderly Market* (Tokyo: Sophia University Press, 1968).

ports may result. Because of the several characteristics discussed here OMAs tend to create specific problems in the trade of manufactures. These problems have not tended to develop in agricultural or commodity trade to the same extent, and OMAs regulating such trade have been successfully applied in some cases.

Historically, American protectionist policies have been implemented when one segment of the market becomes oversaturated, creating excess supply. Rarely will the whole market be simultaneously inundated with imports. In a small number of cases, like some items of cotton textiles and apparel in the 1950s, protection via voluntary export restraints was implemented only when a segment of the domestic market was virtually stagnant. If the OMA provides protection for the slow-growth market segments and simultaneously leaves open the dynamic parts of the market, the policy may have a doubly perverse impact: first, it may encourage domestic production in a slow-growth or no-growth segment of the market; and second, it may encourage the foreign producer to diversify and upgrade into new product lines. This second point is especially important. If a manfacturer is producing efficiently and profitably in certain product areas, he will normally continue production in that line until he has fully exploited the available productivity gains. As long as market access is maintained, and the line is profitable, there is no reason to change production in the short run. Exporters will continue to produce that product, taking advantage of new technologies, new capital equipment, and so on.

The calculus of profitability changes with protection. An OMA by its very nature encourages diversification and upgrading of product lines by foreign exporters. To avoid long-term losses in revenues due to restricted market access, foreign manufacturers will often move into more dynamic markets that are unrestrained and offer higher profit margins. Under an OMA, it is entirely possible that foreign manufacturers will diversify into the strongest segments of the American market.

In fact, the original purpose of bilateral quota arrangements was to force diversification. The use of voluntary export restraints with Japan in the 1930s and 1950s was not introduced because Japanese textile exports were capturing too large a portion of the domestic market supply. Rather the Japanese focused narrowly on a few low-priced products, which they exported in large quantities. Export restraints were sought specifically to protect this segment of the domestic market from annihilation and to help foster an upgrading of the Japanese product line. The United States was interested in promoting Japanese economic development as part of its broader foreign economic goals.

(Thus the term "orderly marketing" came into existence.) In addition, it was widely recognized that the cotton textile market was growing slowly in the 1960s, and the Long Term Agreement in Cotton Textiles forced all major exporters to diversify out of cotton into synthetics— the more dynamic part of the market—in order to maximize their gains from textile trade.[14]

It should be noted that foreign producers may seek to diversify and upgrade production even without the incentive of quantitative restrictions. In many historical cases, however, producers were sufficiently profitable in their production lines that the cost of moving into higher-grade products was not justified in the short run, without the threat to market access in existing products.[15] At a minimum, OMAs will always accelerate a foreign producer's adjustment process.

In summary, the overall performance of Orderly Marketing Agreements as adjustment policies has been rather dismal. These agreements are designed specifically for short-term purposes. Marginal producers are supposed to benefit from reduced competition, while the industry as a whole is supposed to gain the confidence and the profits needed to support *domestic investment*. On the other hand, however, these immediate benefits are almost certain to be lost in the early stages of an agreement: other exporters enter the market; new production centers can be quickly established in a labor-intensive industry; bargaining may permit the exporter to circumvent restrictions; and the agreement is almost impossible to implement. On the other hand, even if the short-run gains could be realized to greater extent, as they tend to be when the system becomes institutionalized for many years, little can be done to prevent long-run problems: for OMAs to be effective in the long run, they would have to be designed to inhibit the realization of foreign economic goals. Thus at best, OMAs always create more uncertainty in the marketplace and produce greater difficulties over time for both domestic industry and government. OMAs have a "boomerang" effect: on the surface they appear to satisfy immediate political and economic demands, but in the long run the problems of an OMA come back to haunt all those concerned.

We can now turn to the specific dilemmas of the footwear industry and see why Orderly Marketing Agreements were so ill suited to the requirements of this particular American sector.

---

[14] U.S. International Trade Commission, *The History and Current Status of the Multifiber Arrangement*, USITC Publication 850 (Washington, D.C., January 1978).

[15] This is true in almost all cases dealing with textiles, apparel, and footwear. One exception is that the Japanese government decided to diversify into synthetics before American restrictions were implemented.

THE FOOTWEAR INDUSTRY AND THE MARKET

The footwear industry has been in decline for over a decade. Even though Americans are spending 11 billion dollars a year on 750 to 800 million pairs of shoes, imports have continued to gather larger and larger portions of the American market. The general wisdom is that this decline is simply a loss in comparative advantage. Closer scrutiny, however, reveals that many factors have led to the industry's demise.[16] A brief review of these factors will point out this sector's market deficiencies as well as show that there was a competitive core in the domestic industry that could potentially hold its own with imports. This sector was especially vulnerable to the negative consequences of OMAs for two reasons: immediate relief was required, and it was critical that the solid segments of American production not be undercut.

The Decline

American producers supplied almost 100 percent of the domestic market in the years following World II. With low barriers to entry, domestic firms increasingly entered the market as demand grew. By the early 1960s there were over 700 footwear firms in the United States employing 240,000 workers. Domestic production reached a peak of 600 million pairs, making the United States the largest producer of shoes in the Western world. This pattern of growth, however, has been reversed in the last decade. Since 1966, over 350 firms have gone out of business, shutting down almost one-third of manufacturing capacity. Domestic production fell to 390 million pairs in 1977, and employment dropped to 160,000 workers.

This decline has had severe political and economic consequences. The first set of consequences stems from the regional character of the industry. Shoe factories tend to be concentrated in small towns, where they are often the principal employer: 30 percent are in localities with populations of less than 5,000, and an additional 40 percent are in towns with 5,000 to 20,000 inhabitants. Furthermore, 49 percent of footwear manufacturing in 1973 was located in the Northeast and the

---

[16]Government and private studies abound with explanations for the industry's overall decline. See, for example, the following: USITC Publication 758, February 1976, and USITC Publication 799, February 1977; GAO reports ID-76-36, *Assistance to the Non-rubber Footwear Industry;* ID-78-53, *Adjustment Assistance to Firms under the Trade Act of 1974—Income Maintenance or Successful Adjustment;* and LCD-79-102 (forthcoming), *The U.S. Footwear Industry—Is This the Future of U.S. Manufacturing;* U.S. Dept. of Commerce, January 1979, "Summary of the Reports from the Footwear Specialist Teams," and August 1978, "Strategies for Success in the Footwear Industry." Also *Trends in the Demand and the Supply of Non-rubber Footwear* (Brimmer and Company, 1977, 1978, 1979).

mid-Atlantic states. Within this area, New York and Massachusetts have been the most severely affected, as the figures in Table 1 indicate: losses have averaged over 50 percent in their footwear production and employment between 1968 and 1976. While the Northeast has the greatest problems, it is not alone. Though some manufacturers moved out of the Northeast in an attempt to reduce costs, Table 1 shows that production and employment have fallen in every major manufacturing center, with the minor exception of employment in Arkansas.

To further complicate footwear's predicament, its workers have many of the characteristics of a secondary labor market. Only 14 percent of the labor force are skilled workers, as compared to the 20 percent average in all manufacturing industry, and the average worker earns three and a half dollars less per hour than the average in other manufacturing industries. Workers are also relatively concentrated in the under-20 and over-60 age brackets, and women make up about 66 percent of the employment in footwear as compared to 29 percent in the total U.S. manufacturing industry.

Both its regional character and workforce characteristics have heightened political concern over the footwear industry. Regional strength in a pluralistic system can give an interest group influence beyond its numbers. In addition, if a business shuts down, an entire town can be affected and left with little hope of retraining or relocating the majority of the workers.

The gainers in the battle for the American market have been foreign producers. Over seventy nations export footwear to the United States, with the bulk of imports coming from Taiwan, Italy, Korea, Spain, and Brazil (see Figure 1). Between 1965 and 1977, imports increased from 12 percent of the U.S. market to 49 percent—and these five nations accounted for 86 percent of all imports. The Treasury Department has levied numerous countervailing duties on Korean, Taiwanese, Brazilian, and other shoes, but they have been unable to check growing import penetration. Today, imports represent more than 50 percent of the domestic market supply, accounting for over 390 million pairs of shoes annually.

REASONS FOR DECLINE

The impact of imports has varied in severity across market segments. But as Table 2 demonstrates, no segment has been invulnerable to import competition. All categories of U.S. footwear, except athletic shoes, have declined in absolute and relative terms during the last decade.

324

Table 1. U.S. production and employment in non-rubber footwear, by principal producing state, 1976

State	Production		Employment		Number of plants	
	Million pairs, 1976[a]	Percent change, 1968–76	Thousands employed, 1976	Percent change, 1968–76	1976	Total difference, 1968–76
Pennsylvania	57.9	−32.0	16.6	−33.9	88	−35
Missouri	43.0	−24.0	18.0	−25.0	57	−34
New York	40.5	−47.1	10.6	−48.3	94	−78
Massachusetts	37.1	−56.5	14.6	−51.8	77	−69
Tennessee	32.6	−20.2	13.5	− 7.0	40	− 1
Maine	29.4	−49.5	16.2	−39.8	67	−15
New Hampshire	22.5	−51.5	9.8	−45.5	40	−31
Arkansas	19.6	− 7.5	7.6	+ 1.4	27	+ 2
All principal producing states	282.6		106.9		490	
All United States	422.5		169.9		780	

[a]AFIA estimates.

Foreign competitiveness in the shoe industry derives from two factors. First, footwear production is a labor-intensive process, with low skill requirements. Between 50 and 250 separate operations may be required for the making of a single pair of shoes—and less than 1 percent of the average factory's yearly production is identical. This indicates that unlike many other manufacturing industries, footwear does not have much potential for production economies of scale. Machinery has been developed to duplicate a few specific tasks, but footwear production has remained largely the same over the past one hundred years.[17] Since labor costs account for up to 33 percent of the price of a pair of shoes, and no country appears to have a technological edge in present footwear manufacturing, nations with low labor costs have a classical comparative advantage in production. In the 1970s, Taiwan and Korea exploited their advantageous position and captured most of the low-priced shoe market. But since footwear production requires only modest amounts of capital, technology, and skilled labor, it is relatively easy for other developing countries to enter the market. American competitiveness would

[17]There has been very little increase in productivity or investment in research and development since World War II. Footwear manufacturing has registered among the lowest productivity gains of all American manufacturing sectors in the past twenty years. Technological innovation has been lacking in the industry largely because of the monopolistic practices of the major supplier of capital machinery to the industry. Between 1953 and the late 1960s, the footwear industry depended on the United States Shoe Machinery Corporation for over 90 percent of its machinery and equipment (GAO). U.S. Shoe was accused of numerous anticompetitive practices, including leasing out equipment and enforcing lease restrictions to freeze out potentially innovative competitors. In the past ten years, since the Justice Department changed U.S. Shoe's corporate structure, few companies have wanted to absorb the necessary risks to develop new technologies.

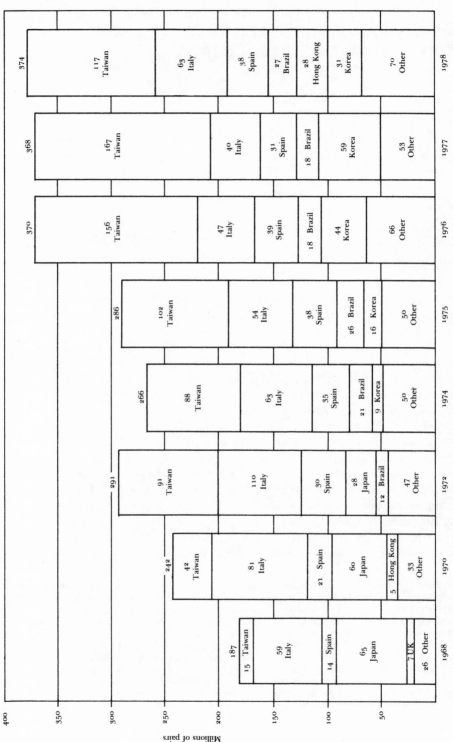

Figure 1: U.S. non-rubber footwear imports, top five countries, 1968–1978. Data supplied by the Department of Commerce and the American Footwear Industries Association. "Other" includes over 15 countries in 1968; a recent estimate suggests that over 70 countries supply footwear to the United States.

Table 2. Nonrubber footwear, by product category, 1968 and 1977 U.S. production, imports, and apparent consumption (millions of pairs)

Year and Shoe category	U.S. production	Imports	Apparent consumption[a]
1968			
Women's and misses'	317	133	450
Men's, youths', boys'	114	31	145
Children's, infants'	60	14	74
Athletic	8	2	10
Other[b]	143	2	143
All categories, 1968	642	182	822
1977			
Women's, misses'	154	204	358
Men's, youths', boys'	94	87	181
Children's, infants'	37	24	61
Athletic	10	51	62
Other[b]	90	2	86
All categories, 1977	385	368	748
Percent change, 1968–1977			
Women's, misses'	−51%	+53%	−20%
Men's, youths', boys'	−18	+181	+25
Children's, infants'	−38	−71	−18
Athletic	+25	+2540	+520
Other[b]	−37	0	−50

[a]Apparent consumption is the total of domestic production and imports less U.S. exports. Exports constitute less than 2 percent of domestic production.

[b]AFIA suggests that changes in "other" may be due to classification changes of slippers. "Other" includes primarily slippers and men's work shoes.

SOURCE: International Trade Commission, Department of Commerce, and American Footwear Industries Association.

seem to be limited until and unless more advanced capital-using, labor-saving technologies can be developed.

Second, footwear has become an increasingly fashion-conscious industry over time. Shoes are a complex product, varying across several product dimensions—style, price, material, size, width, and shape. Unfortunately, Americans have always lagged behind the Europeans in style leadership and shoe design. The United States has nothing similar to Italy's three educational institutions for training talented designers in the footwear field. In addition, traditional organizational relationships within the American industry impede the rapid creation of new styles: small manufacturers must go to one of a few suppliers and sometimes wait two to six months to obtain the sample of a new idea. This lack of flexibility prevents the average manufacturing firm from introducing style changes in the middle of a season and creates a bottleneck in going from "shoe concepts" to shoe designs.[18] Especially in recent years, styles have been changing rapidly. Hence the ability to set styles and adapt to changing market trends has often been as important as factor costs in determining the strength of producers, particularly in the higher-priced market segments. For over a decade, Italy, Spain, and Brazil have been capturing much of the fashion segment of the U.S. market. Until 1977, middle-priced footwear, where style is not so critical, was the only relatively secure portion of the American market in which U.S. producers could compete.

These aggregate trends, however, mask the success of certain individual firms. Despite import competition, a number of profitable firms in all regions of the country have maintained their market share and competitiveness. For analytical purposes, the 360 U.S. footwear firms can be divided into three categories: (1) a few small and medium-sized manufacturers that profitably produce less than four million pairs annually for specific market segments; (2) a few large firms that profitably produce more than four million pairs per year in many market segments; and (3) the vast majority of small and medium-sized firms that are unsuccessful because they lack either the economies of scale or the marketing skills that might offset their comparative disadvantage in labor costs relative to foreign producers.

The basic structure of the footwear industry requires that firms possess at least one of the following characteristics to be successful: market power (the ability to minimize a firm's vulnerability to its sources of supplies or outlets for goods); or a market niche (a specialized market segment). Market power, which is directly related to a firm's size, is perhaps the most important. Footwear's structure involves much more than a manufacturing operation. The many small manufacturers are critically dependent upon concentrated suppliers and retailers. Suppliers, on the one hand, provide manufacturers with a variety of services, ranging from cutting leather and making samples to supplying raw materials and equipment for footwear assembly. Independent retailers, on the other hand, provide the outlet for most goods; only 17 percent of domestic production is sold directly to company-owned stores. The interests of retailers may also be directly at odds with those of many domestic manufacturers, because retailers can search an international market to satisfy consumer demands and maximize profits.

Size can overcome these problems as well as some of the difficulties related to imports. Although production economies of scale may not be critical, there are administrative economies of scale which provide greater capacities to meet marketing and design needs. In fact, the

[18]Research Triangle Institute (1979), unpublished studies.

major distinction between small firms and large firms is that small companies tend to focus exclusively on manufacturing, while large ones vertically integrate. Most big firms run their own retail outlets and import to fill in their product lines; a few also operate their own tanneries and chemical plants. On the production side, bigger companies are more flexible, or less vulnerable to the structural rigidities of the footwear market than small companies: through backward integration, they either provide their own raw materials and supply operations, or they get higher priority and discounts from suppliers by placing larger orders.

Large firms have demonstrated the flexibility needed to meet fluctuating demand and the quality control needed to enter high-priced markets. Given the relatively high labor costs in U.S. production, these are critical factors in maintaining international competitiveness. Since footwear demand is subject to fads, retailers often want goods immediately. Foreign orders may take up to six months for delivery, at which time a fad may be over; and there are additional administrative and financial costs for imports when letters of credit are required. Large firms therefore *want* to maintain their domestic production in order to exploit shifting market demands quickly. Otherwise, they would move offshore, as multinational corporations in other industries, such as consumer electronics, have done. In addition, domestic production can serve other needs. Instead of competing directly with foreign footwear, some firms import low-priced Asian shoes and high-fashion European footwear to complement their own manufacturing in the medium-priced segments. Importing also allows the large firm to reduce its risk in initiating new production runs. These companies import new lines, test their competitiveness, and then start their own long-term production runs if the style proves popular.

On the marketing side, forward integration into retailing increases the profitability and market sensitivity of big firms. Wall Street has not looked favorably on the footwear industry for many years, which has posed a problem for the average manufacturer seeking funds for modernization. Large firms, however, have few problems raising capital: the higher profits derived from retailing provide for added financial stability. Retailing also heightens sensitivity to market shifts and has been one means of forcing domestic producers to manufacture more marketable goods.

The growing concentration of large firms with a secure hold on their share of domestic production is evidence of their relative health. As Table 3 suggests, there has been an increasing concentration of production in these larger firms since the late 1960s. Although the concentration is not of the same magnitude as in the steel and automobile

Table 3. Number of U.S. footwear producers and percentage of total output, by size of firm, 1967–1975

Producer size (number of pairs)	1967		1969		1974		1975		Net change 1967–1975	
	Number of firms	Percent of total output	Number of firms	Percent of total output	Number of firms	Percent of total output	Number of firms	Percent of total output	Number of firms	Percent of total output
Small										
Less than 200,000	226	2%	192	2%	139	2%	129	2%	−97	0%
200,000–499,999	170	10	146	8	105	8	92	7	−76	−3
500,000–999,999	121	14	113	14	05	10	71	12	−50	−2
Medium										
1,000,000–1,999,999	100	24	93	24	57	17	42	14	−58	−10
2,000,000–3,999,999	42	19	32	15	22	13	23	15	−19	−4
Large										
4,000,000 or more	16	31	21	37	21	50	21	50	+5	+19
Total	675	100	597	100	409	100	378	100	−297	

SOURCE: Compiled from data supplied by the U.S. Bureau of the Census.

industries, four of the largest companies have continually produced 30 percent of domestic production by value, and the top 21 firms presently account for 50 percent of the declining U.S. output. The remaining 50 percent of production is accounted for by the other 340 firms.

Even though imports hurt *everyone's* manufacturing operations in the 1970s, these top 21 firms were relatively competitive without government intervention. At a minimum, they could maintain profits through retailing. In addition, perhaps another 5 percent of American production was somewhat securely in the hands of small firms that found survival strategies by producing for specific market niches and exploiting brand names. With proper management, even small companies can be successful if they quickly and effectively capitalize on style changes or produce specialty items (cowboy boots, for example). In a series of studies commissioned by the Commerce Department, it was suggested that the profitable firms, regardless of size, "do not compete on the basis of price alone."[19] The key to successful competition against imports is to take the lead in meeting consumer preferences. By establishing brand names or using similar techniques, both large and small firms can "command a higher price for their product."[20]

The unsuccessful small firm lacks both market power and marketing skills. As noted earlier, domestic producers can remain profitable in this industry if they are more flexible and more responsive to domestic demand than foreign producers. Adaptability is a necessary condition for small-firm success. Unfortunately, the many "one-man shows" in the footwear industry do not have the "depth" and the entrepreneurial skill to capitalize on their closeness to the domestic market.[21] The managers of these firms tend to use inefficient manufacturing operations that increase costs relative to their competitors, and they compound their problem by using inadequate accounting systems that often lead to poor pricing decisions. Many manufacturers are also ignorant of changes in the marketplace. The prominence of production has meant that many less successful producers have no marketing "approach," no marketing research program, and seem to believe in selling any style at any price in order to fill factory demand.[22] These small firms have been very conservative and slow to enter new markets. In the 1950s this was an acceptable strategy because the retailers and domestic manufacturers had a symbiotic relationship: retailers would buy most anything

[19]U.S.Department of Commerce, *Footwear Industry Revitalization Program; First Annual Progress Report (1978)*, p. 22.
[20]U.S. Department of Commerce, *Summary of the Reports from the Footwear Specialist Teams* (1979), p. 10.
[21]*Ibid.*
[22]*Ibid.*

domestic producers made. Given the changes in the international market, and their basic disadvantage in factor costs, small and weak firms can no longer afford the luxury of inefficiency.

These companies face a Catch-22. They fear the costs of adjustment because import competition is so strong; but without either modernization or protection they have no hope for survival. Therefore, it is not surprising that some form of international protection, preferably global QRs, is what these firms favor most.

In the long run, the industry will be competitive only if there are changes in the production patterns and marketing strategies of these small firms. These companies must move into more profitable segments, become integrated with larger companies, or diversify into other industries. Otherwise, their continual decline is inevitable.

The Industry and OMAs

The footwear industry is in a precarious position. All of its segments are vulnerable to import competition, and the problems appear so fundamental that major restructuring is required if the sector is to regain its competitiveness. Therefore, one of the most obvious conclusions of this discussion so far is that OMAs were totally inappropriate for advancing the industry's needs.

First, OMAs were not likely to limit competition. Footwear production facilities can easily be set up in developing countries, and a large number of suppliers were already exporting to the United States. As a result, it was very unlikely that singling out a few sources of "market disruption" could successfully reduce imports and have a positive impact on domestic adjustment.

Second, OMAs were not likely to inspire the confidence and investment that firms require in order to adjust. Intervention policy in the footwear industry should be designed to provide for a transition to a more competitive industrial structure. Small companies need an opportunity to modernize or to integrate with large firms; and time is important if new technologies, presently in the development stage, will be able to help the shoe industry achieve more flexibility, greater design capabilities, and a higher degree of capital intensity.[23] The Footwear Industry Team has in fact addressed itself to many of these tasks within the domestic arena. But if OMAs increase competition in the short run and force Taiwan and Korea to accelerate the upgrading of their cheap product lines into medium-priced shoes—the mainstay of American production—then most firms will lack the incentives to risk adjustment.

[23]See U.S. General Accounting Office (GAO), *The U.S. Footwear Industry—Is This the Future of U.S. Manufacturing*, p. 75.

Several questions therefore arise. Why were OMAs chosen? Were the government and the industry unaware of the problems just outlined? How could such a policy mistake be made? To answer these queries, one must examine the politics of the footwear industry. This examination will tell us why so little was done prior to 1977, and how this particular form of international policy was eventually selected.

POLITICS OF THE FOOTWEAR INDUSTRY IN THE 1970S

The government played a minor role in the footwear industry before the Carter administration's program. Industry associations, labor groups, and Congress had all argued for government intervention; but retailers, importers, and most of the government bureaucracy had resisted. The industry had at least four chances to receive protection: in 1970, footwear could have been given quantitative restrictions as part of the 1970 Trade Act; in 1971, the United States Tariff Commission found that the industry had been injured by imports; in the 1974 Trade Act, footwear problems were given extensive treatment; and in 1976, the newly named International Trade Commission again recommended some form of presidential action. Yet in each of these instances, the executive branch refused to provide substantive support to the shoe industry. Given the severe losses in domestic footwear production (much greater in relative terms than the losses in textiles or steel), why didn't the government systematically intervene to stop the decline or revitalize the industry? What changed in 1977 to reverse the previous situation? And when the time came, why were OMAs, as opposed to other forms of protection, chosen?

Most of the apparent inconsistencies in government policy can be explained politically. The lack of effective international and domestic action before 1977 was not part of a well-conceived intervention plan. The footwear industry did not receive extensive aid simply because it did not have the political clout to win such aid. Even when the industry was finally in a position to force the administration's hand, a political compromise was the best it could achieve. Thus we shall see in the next section that OMAs were not a carefully devised economic choice, but a political response to international and domestic pressures.

The Constraints

As a leader of the industrialized nations, the United States had international responsibilities and a tradition of promoting free trade that made it difficult for any administration to offer protection to the footwear industry. U.S. decision-makers have generally considered the overall gains from an open trading environment more important than the particular interests of a few groups. This was especially true in the mid-1970s during the multilateral trade negotiations. The U.S. government's organizational commitments to GATT also limited its freedom. Tariffs, tariff rate quotas, and quantitative restrictions are all regulated by this international organization. An American foreign economic policy that used any of these tools would require GATT approval, accompanied by possible compensation or retaliation.

Yet international factors suggest only in a general way why the U.S. government usually resists protection. They do not explain the details of policy, or why other industries have received government help. International conditions establish the context of governmental action: they set the stage for domestic variables to determine the specifics of government intervention.

An important domestic factor in this case was the fact that historically, the executive branch had never been predisposed to help the footwear industry. Government decision-makers saw footwear as small fish in a big economic sea; their prevalent view was that the footwear industry should have been "capable of responding to market pressures" without government interference.[24] The existence of profitable firms within the sector hurt the industry's general case. No one wanted to aid successful companies, and the very fact that some companies were doing well reinforced the government's view that the industry at large should be able to adjust. The executive branch, which has most of the authority for economic policy-making, was also the focal point of attention from importers and retailers. Without specific voting constituencies, these two highly organized groups lobbied extensively with the White House to forestall protectionist policies. In addition, they mobilized foreign governments to support their cause.[25]

The structure of the domestic industry and its labor force were probably the most critical variables behind the failure to achieve protectionist measures. Unlike the more powerful steel and textile industries, the footwear industry was never able to mobilize widespread political support. Faced by international constraints and opposed by powerful domestic groups, foreign governments, and high-level policy-makers, the footwear industry never had much chance of winning political protection. Its own ineptitude nonetheless compounded these real problems.

A major reason for the footwear industry's lack of effective organiza-

[24]Interview with Harriet Hentges, former staff member of STR and Policy Planning Division, State Department, June 22, 1979.

[25]Interview with Kay Daines, Sr. Vice-President, American Retail Association, October 9, 1979.

tion and political clout can be traced to the sector's market structure. Large, successful firms do not have the same stake in pushing for protection as the small, unprofitable companies do. The big firms are not disinterested, but their survival does not depend on getting the government to erect import barriers. Therefore, the policy of the industry's lobby—the American Footwear Industries Association (AFIA)—has tended to represent the small firms as much, if not more, than the large firms. Big companies contribute a much smaller proportion of their revenues to AFIA activities.[26] In essence, they will become "free riders" if the AFIA is politically successful.

Another problem related to the industry's organization has been its approach to politics. Footwear lobbies have followed what appeared to be their most logical strategy, given their market position and regional character: they have sought global quantitative restrictions through Congressional action. It was rational for a small, geographically based interest group to look to Congress, particularly since the legislature has always been more sympathetic than the bureaucracy to calls for protection. Also, with the industry highly concentrated in a small number of important states, footwear issues have had the support of such powerful congressmen and senators as Edward Kennedy, Howard Baker, Jacob Javits, and Tip O'Neill. Yet without the power to threaten major legislation or the support to pass new initiatives, Congress is limited in what it can do for an interest group like footwear. In most cases, Congress can act as a vehicle for special interests to obtain favors or small-scale policy changes from the executive branch and the bureaucracy. The footwear industry's goals, however, have usually been on a grander scale.

A Brief History, 1970–1976

In 1970, the shoe industry joined with the textile lobby to call for quantitative restrictions on imports as part of the 1970 Trade Act. The bill would have allowed total imports to increase by only 5 percent per year for five years, following a rollback to their 1967–1969 level. In addition, the footwear industry filed a petition with the United States Tariff Commission claiming injury due to imports. When the ITC split and the Trade Act stalled, President Nixon chose the path of least resistance: he provided adjustment assistance to eleven firms; and he simultaneously dispatched Ambassador-at-Large David Kennedy to Europe to seek a means of correcting the trade imbalance in general and the problems of the shoe industry in particular.

[26]Interview with Robert Siff, President, B-W Footwear, October 16, 1979.

Many disagree today over whether Kennedy sought a voluntary restraint arrangement on his trip to Italy.[27] Officially, the administration claimed that the ambassador discussed no more than a statistical export visa system. Indeed, after the negotiators returned to the United States with no "formal" agreement, Italy began requiring its exporters to provide information to the government about shoe production and to apply for export visas. Yet in a statement by the Italian government, the Italian Chamber of Commerce justified its action by noting explicitly that "voluntary restraints" were preferable to possible quantitative restrictions. Whatever the case, the supposed restraint system had little or no impact on Italy's exports: strikes and increased labor and leather costs hurt Italy's exports before the negotiations began. Between 1970 and 1973, the volume of Italian shoe exports to the United States remained relatively steady, and prices increased 137 percent. Clearly, the purpose of the Italian negotiations was to pacify the footwear industry and Congress. When the government sought a similar arrangement with Spain, they used no leverage or threat of unilateral action (and the Spanish government saw little to gain by implementing an OMA).[28]

The footwear industry continued to press for government intervention during the debate over the 1974 Trade Act. Supporters of the industry were able to introduce successfully an amendment that called for the establishment of an international footwear program similar to the Multifiber Agreement in Textiles; and assistance to the footwear industry was mentioned five times in the Act. But again, the industry relied too narrowly on Congress and failed to obtain a solid commitment. None of the specific legislation bound the administration. At one point, Senator McIntyre tried to introduce a more restrictive, binding commitment on the Senate floor. The amendment, however, was defeated because Senator Russell Long and Special Trade Representative William Eberle reassured the Senate that additional legislation was unnecessary.[29]

After the Trade Act came into effect, Eberle's successor as Special Trade Representative, Frederick B. Dent, met with representatives of the footwear industry. During those meetings, he urged them to file a petition with the ITC instead of seeking an international agreement. Some members of the STR office felt strongly that the footwear in-

[27]Ralph Oman, "The Clandestine Negotiations of Voluntary Restraints on Shoes from Italy: An Augury of the Future Negotiations under the Trade Reform Act of 1974," *Cornell International Law Journal* 6-7 (1974).

[28]Interview with Gloria Pratt, Director, Office of Foreign Economic Policy, Department of Labor, June 25, 1979.

[29]See the *Congressional Record*, December 13, 1974.

dustry should not be given global protection.[30] They wanted to resist any measure which they perceived as hindering or "preventing" the process of adjustment. By asking them to seek relief through the ITC, the executive would have more influence over the final form of government intervention.

In February 1976, the ITC recommended presidential action but was divided over the form it should take. This left President Ford free to decide what type of aid was appropriate.[31] In determining the proper response, the President, a free trader, was under great pressure *not* to provide import relief. In January, the ITC had recommended a quota on specialty steel; Ford responded by seeking OMAs. Internationally, this put the United States in a difficult postion. Further protectionism in footwear might have created a foreign perception of rising American protectionism. This would threaten the administration's goal of freer trade, as well as disrupt the Multilateral Trade Negotiations, and possibly lead to future retaliation against American products.

Domestically, the administration was worried about the impact of this tariff decision on an ailing economy and on inflation. With the country only slowly coming out of recession, the tariff rate quota suggested by the ITC would cost consumers at least $750 million dollars. In addition, during the decision-making process, Treasury Secretary William Simon and Secretary of State Kissinger made particularly forceful cases against import relief.[32]

When the final decision was made, Ford limited government action to additional trade adjustment assistance and a "monitoring system" for imports. Despite the large number of congressmen and senators who contacted the White House in support of import restraints, the footwear industry was unable to obtain meaningful results for the third straight time. President Ford cited increased costs to consumers, the inconsistencies of import relief with the "international economic interests of the U.S.," and the hope that assistance for small firms would be an effective "remedy."[33]

Strategically, the industry failed to mobilize the necessary support within the executive branch; and tactically, it failed by filing petitions at a time when the administration was not predisposed to provide import

[30]Interview with Harriet Hengtes, June 22, 1979.

[31]Under the 1974 Trade Act when there was a majority recommendation by the ITC (four out of six commissioners), the President would be subject to a congressional veto if Congress was dissatisfied with the presidential response. Otherwise, the President was under no legal obligation to accept the ITC recommendation.

[32]Based on three interviews: Edward Atkins, Executive Vice-President, Volume Footwear Retailers of America; Kay Daines; and a discussion with Roger Porter, former Special Assistant to Gerald Ford.

[33]STR Press release No. 222, April 16, 1976.

relief or other types of domestic assistance. Since the footwear industry did not have the power to threaten a congressional veto on other important legislation (the traditional strategy of the textile and apparel industries), executive branch interest became a critical factor in determining the government's relative inaction.

The failures of both government and industry soon became apparent. Within six months of President Ford's decision, an interagency government task force reported that domestic production continued to fall as imports gathered a larger percentage of the market. The year 1976 was a particularly bad one for the footwear industry, and the effectiveness of government action was being called into question, even from within the bureaucracy. With indications that the Senate Finance Committee was about to request a reopening of the ITC shoe case, an Executive Committee recommended that the Trade Commission reactivate the investigation. This led to an interesting and recurrent paradox in American politics: the fact that imports accounted for 49 percent of the domestic market by 1977 meant that *the industry's economic weakness was soon to become a political strength.*

The Decision-Making Process and the Carter Program

On January 6, 1977, the International Trade Commission (ITC) recommended that a tariff rate quota be imposed on nonrubber footwear to protect the industry from further damage. The major representative of the industry—the American Footwear Industries Association (AFIA)—joined by the AFL-CIO and other political interests, agreed that unless it could threaten the administration with a possible veto of the presidential order, the ITC decision would "not be enough."[34] The dominant political objective of the footwear industry was to curtail the flow of imports, and this time Congress, labor, and the industry would not be easily placated. The decline in American footwear production had become so severe that most everyone agreed that something had to be done. In addition, the AFIA had learned from its previous experiences. They hired consultants and launched a massive public relations campaign. By April, Congress was ready for a fight.

During the first month of the decision-making process, various levels of the bureaucracy debated five policy options: "voluntary" export re-

---

[34]Late in 1976, the footwear industry achieved an extremely important success in Congress. They had the law changed to state that if the ITC split by a 3-2-1 decision, as it had in 1976, a congressional override would be possible. The 1977 decision, however, was split 4-2; see USITC, February 1977, *Footwear Investigation*, No. TA-201-18. That the ITC decision might "not be enongh" was suggested in an interview with Faun Evenson, Executive Vice-President, American Footwear Industries Association, August 27, 1979.

straints, tariff rate quotas, Orderly Marketing Agreements, quantitative import restrictions, and trade adjustment assistance.[35] By the time the issue reached the President on March 25, 1977, the alternatives had narrowed to two options. Everyone favored additional trade adjustment assistance, but State, Treasury, the Council of Economic Advisers, and HUD wanted no import relief granted, whereas Labor, OMB, Commerce, and Agriculture favored the ITC recommendation for a tariff rate quota. Interestingly enough, the OMA option that was eventually chosen was not even mentioned as an alternative.

Since the administration had already decided on its domestic policy, discussion proceeded to the question of imports. The Economic Policy Group, which consisted of the Vice-President, five Cabinet secretaries, and the heads of five units within the executive branch, was moving toward a "no relief" position. At that point, Stuart Eizenstadt of Carter's staff suggested that an OMA might serve as a middle ground and avoid the otherwise inevitable conflict with Congress. The high level of import penetration (approaching 50 percent) made Congress intent upon obtaining some form of protection. The President had also made commitments to the labor movement during the election campaign, and this decision would be his first major test. On March 28, the OMA suggestion reached President Carter. He then dismissed the other options, for all practical purposes, and instructed Robert Strauss, the new Special Trade Representative, to prepare a memo on OMAs.

During the next two days a flurry of memos bombarded Carter for and against the OMA option. No one except the STR's office and the President's staff approved of the idea. The State Department suggested that voluntary export restraints were less restrictive and more acceptable for foreign policy purposes, but Labor argued that neither voluntary restraints nor OMAs would be effective. When the industry was consulted, they said that OMAs were not optimal but would be acceptable if fully implemented. The industry's consultants counseled that OMAs might be all they could achieve.[36]

The irony of the final decision in favor of OMAs is that when the President chose the domestic program, he recognized the need for re-evaluation and coherence. The April 1, 1977, press release from STR stated: "To resolve longer term problems of the shoe industry and

---

[35]This discussion is largely based on an article by David Broder that appeared in the *Washington Post,* July 23, 1977. His information came from an executive reorganization project conducted by OMB. Mac Destler, one of the consultants on this project, verified in a phone interview that Broder's information was "quite accurate." Roger Porter, who also read the report, said that a few of the dates of meetings were inaccurate, but the remainder of Broder's article was reliable.

[36]Interview with Stanley Nehmer, head of the Economic Consulting Service and commissioned Consultant by the AFIA and footwear unions, October 11, 1979.

other industries impacted by increasing imports, a new and integrated trade adjustment system will be designed and presented to Congress to revise the inadequate present trade adjustment assistance programs."[37] Yet the OMA was not considered in the same light: it was seen first and foremost as a political compromise. By not considering all the alternatives at the highest levels, it encouraged competing departments and agencies to lobby for their own bureaucratic interests.[38] The policy was chosen for its political appeal to the middle ground, not for its value in revitalizing the footwear industry.

The administration was not the only party at fault. The industry's acquiescence was a necessary condition for the adoption of the program.[39] With so many past failures, they were willing to accept any policy that was close to their goal. As one AFIA official remarked: "The industry was hungry for some kind of results. When the administration throws you a crumb to get Congress off their back, it is difficult not to accept."[40] The industry also accepted the OMA decision because of an alleged promise given by Robert Strauss that imports from non-restricted countries would be "capped." Strauss supposedly told industry representatives and several congressmen that other nations, not covered by OMAs, would receive cables telling them to hold their present import levels constant. Since the industry and its consultants were content with the OMAs and with Strauss's promise, they were not concerned about asking for this commitment in writing.[41] Strauss later told the industry that he had no authority to make such a promise, and that although he "may have made the statement," it was "unrealistic" for them to expect such a policy.[42]

The acceptance of the OMA decision and Strauss's promise reflected the political naivete and political weakness of the industry. Both the government and the industry had sufficient information available to

[37]STR Press Release No. 247, April 1, 1977. Three months later, this evolved into the Footwear Industry Revitalization Program. To elaborate on the introduction, its essential components were an "outreach program" to get firms certified; setting up diagnostic analyses for companies which were to be accompanied by technical assistance; streamlining trade adjustment assistance; promoting exports; getting retailers to voluntarily participate in the program; and creating a Footwear Center to provide education, technology transfers, and technological services for the industry as a whole. U.S. Department of Commerce, Footwear Industry *Revitalization Program; First Annual Progress Report.* (1978).

[38]This was the assessment of the Executive Reorganization Project, according to Broder.

[39]Interview with Thomas Graham, former Deputy General Counsel, STR, and Negotiator of the OMAs with Korea and Taiwan, September 4, 1979.

[40]Interview with Rita Cavenough, Senior Economist for AFIA, August 27, 1979.

[41]Interviews with Stanley Wehner; Faun Everson; Jack Lesley, Legislative Assistant to Edward Kennedy, August 29, 1979; and Anita Jenson, Legislative Assistant to Edward Muskie, August 21, 1979.

[42]Interview with Faun Evenson.

indicate that OMAs would prove inadequate. Experience with export restraints in textiles and apparel since 1957 should have foretold that an OMA might be the worst possible solution for the industry's long-term adjustment problems.

RESULTS OF OMA IMPLEMENTATION

The logic behind the OMA decision was relatively straightforward. The administration thought that limiting the imports of the two most recent entrants into the market would politically satisfy the industry and Congress. They also hoped that potential investors in the industry would be encouraged by the government's willingness to take substantive action. But as the operational deficiencies of the OMAs have become apparent, neither this psychological advantage nor the political benefits have been sustained.

The Implementation Process

When the United States government makes decisions on economic protection, the process and likely results are public. Domestic and foreign producers alike are in a position to gauge possible outcomes. When the International Trade Commission suggested a tariff rate quota, it was clear to Taiwan and Korea that regardless of the form of protection, they would be the most likely targets for a rollback in exports. Both countries had expanded production rapidly, and since 1974 had accounted for almost 100 percent of the increase in imports into the United States. Therefore, both realized the need to maximize their gains from footwear as quickly as possible in anticipation of imminent restrictions.

Before the OMA decision was announced, Taiwan and Korea began encouraging producers to increase prices and speed up exports. The Koreans went so far as to set up an "incentive system" to diversify and upgrade the existing product line. Simultaneously they established an "export check price formula" to insure a minimum price on all shoes exported to the United States.[43] The active, anticipatory role of the Taiwanese and Korean governments in their respective industries allowed them to start capturing the profits generated from rising prices in anticipation of a shortage in low-priced shoes.[44]

[43]*Korea Herald,* January 11, 1977.
[44]The very first issue at the bargaining table, and the first concession made by the United States during the negotiations, was that Korea and Taiwan would not be put at a disadvantage vis-à-vis other suppliers. This meant that the United States was guaranteeing their market shares and thus allowing their exporters to capture the scarcity gains.

After Carter decided on the OMA, bargaining within the U.S. government was necessary to establish a unified position for the forthcoming negotiations. The AFIA insisted that the United States create categories of footwear based on price, age group, sex, and material characteristics. Conflict between the government departments, however, caused a watering down of the negotiating goals. All parties did not view the use of OMAs as a well-conceived policy for revitalizing the industry and helping American consumers. In order to achieve internal agreement, a loosely devised position was all that could be obtained. Robert Strauss then informed the industry that there was "no way" their demands could be met *before* the negotiators left for the Far East.[45] At best, Strauss told them, they would receive categories of protection by materials—leather, plastic, vinyl, and others.

Another problem that arose before the negotiations highlighted one of the weaknesses of the industry's organization. "Rubber" footwear has had a history of separate organizations and special protection from the government. The American Selling Price System (ASP), a formula for higher tariffs, has allowed U.S. rubber footwear manufacturers more confidence in their market position. Particular types of rubber shoes can be registered with the Customs Bureau, to be taxed at the special rate. Therefore, the AFIA was unable to mobilize the "rubber" segment of the industry to join forces when it filed its petition with the ITC. This means that the U.S. negotiating team did not have the legal authority to include rubber footwear in the agreement.[46]

The Negotiations

American negotiators bargained intensely with the Taiwanese and Korean government representatives for almost two weeks. Each side attempted to maximize certain gains, and each was under pressure to satisfy its own domestic industries. Taiwan and Korea ultimately agreed to the OMAs in order to preserve their overall relationship with the United States.

Most of the concessions during the negotiations came from the United States. On the hardest issue, the actual export figures, the Americans rolled back the aggregate export levels of both countries by 22 percent. This was the minimum rollback consistent with Washing-

---

[45]Interview with Faun Evenson.

[46]This is a problem because "rubber" is a misnomer. The tariff classification includes as rubber various materials, including the canvas and rope-covered ladies' shoes that have recently been in vogue. In addition, to be classified as rubber, a shoe need be only 50 percent rubber by weight. Lastly, ASP does not cover all types of rubber shoes.

ton's negotiating parameters. It also appears that this was all the United States expected. Stephen Lande, the chief negotiator, reportedly leaked the government's negotiating instructions to an importing group before their trip.[47] The result was that the importers told the Koreans and Taiwanese exactly how much the United States was willing to concede. Even with this information, the United States made additional compromises to achieve the rollback. These included pipeline clauses (which allowed each country an additional 27 percent of the first year's restraint to enter the United States without being considered in violation of the quota), shorter durations for the treaties, and late starting dates for enacting the agreements. Many loopholes were also apparent, the most obvious one being the exclusion of rubber footwear. The industry, nonetheless, approved the OMA on the condition that it be "100 percent implemented."[48]

The Level of Imports

In the early stages of the quota period, vagueness and ineffective sanctions in the agreements allowed Taiwan and Korea to maintain their export levels. The pipeline clauses and flexibility built into the treaty, plus an ambiguity concerning the definition of the exporting dates, severely lessened the quota's impact. The Koreans, for example, stated in January of 1977 that their total export capacity for that year was 60 million pairs of shoes. Although the United States sought to roll back Korea's 1976 exports of 44 million pairs as much as possible, the Koreans still were able to export *58 million pairs* of shoes to the United States during 1977. Thus many of the short-run benefits of the OMAs which were supposed to accrue to domestic producers were immediately lost.

The lack of homogeneity of footwear products also quickly worked to weaken the accords. Most footwear can be made to look similar or identical by using different substances. Since rubber footwear was excluded from the OMA, the Koreans and Taiwanese found that traditionally defined nonrubber footwear could be reclassified as rubber by simply adding rubber to the sole or making other minor alterations. In addition, these "rubber" imports entered the U.S. under the normal

[47]Interview with Thomas Graham. This information about Stephen Lande was conveyed to the author by Thomas Graham, Former Deputy General Counsel, STR, and negotiator of the OMAs with Taiwan and Korea, September 4, 1979. Mr. Graham has subsequently differed with the interpretation offered here, but he did not deny the essential facts. Mr. Graham felt that the United States could have extracted additional concessions from Taiwan and Korea, and that Lande was a first-rate negotiator.

[48]Interview with Evenson.

tariff rates. The special protection of ASP did not automatically apply.[49]

Within the first year of the OMA, exports of so-called rubber footwear rose by 25 million pairs from both restrained countries. Rubber increased from 28 percent of Taiwan's overall footwear exports to almost 38 percent; and for Korean exports, the percentages went from 39 to over 50 percent. These countries' share of the U.S. rubber market rose from 45 to 63 percent in the first seven months of 1978. As American producers realized the problem, they were able to reclassify much of the imported footwear under ASP, therefore gaining additional tariff protection. However, this did not remove the incentive for circumventing the quota. During the first quarter of 1979, the Koreans were *exporting 300* percent more rubber footwear than nonrubber footwear, as compared to only one-half as much rubber versus nonrubber in the first quarter of 1977.[50]

According to the Commerce Department, the OMAs with Korea and Taiwan did provide some import relief late in the first year of the restraints. There is some question, however, as to the validity of these findings. When the monitoring system was originally constructed, it did not even consider rubber in its classification. The Commerce Department was computing the level of imports based on the standard classification of nonrubber shoes. Therefore, given the increase in rubber imports, the degree of import relief is questionable.

In the meantime, the increase in imports from unrestrained countries also made administering the domestic program more difficult. Strauss's supposed promise to cap other importers was ignored, as expected. There was a 60 percent increase—82.7 million pairs—in nonrubber imports from uncontrolled sources in 1978. Italy reversed a five-year downtrend, increasing its own imports by 58 percent over 1977. Brazil went up 55 percent, and Spain almost 20 percent.[51] In addition, when Taiwan and Korea raised their prices on low-cost shoes, there were incentives for other producers to enter the low-priced market. Hong Kong, for example, was quickly able to set up production with the help of transshipped parts from Taiwan. As a result, exports from Hong Kong jumped 225 percent in one year.[52]

[49]ASP is a rather complicated system. U.S. manufacturers must demonstrate to the Customs Bureau that an imported shoe is directly competitive with an American equivalent. Since this was the first time Korea and Taiwan exported these shoes as "rubber," manufacturers had to petition the government before a higher tariff could be levied. And this, of course, took time.

[50]Calculated from Commerce Department *Summary Tables*, and *Brimmer Reports* (1979).

[51]Calculated from *U.S. Department of Commerce News*, April 26, 1979.

[52]Data from Bulletin No. 7, February 23, 1979, Volume Footwear Retailers of America; information regarding transshipments obtained from STR Press Release No. 277, September 19, 1978.

The United States reacted to these dramatic increases by seeking and failing to negotiate an OMA with Hong Kong. They did convince the Hong Kong authorities to implement a certificate of origin in an effort to prevent transshipment, but by the time this certificate was used, production was almost fully standardized. Therefore, it was relatively easy for Hong Kong to convert to domestically produced parts and maintain their high level of exports.[53] The British Colony, however, was not alone in entering the low-priced market. The Philippines' exports of low-cost shoes also rose from less than one million pairs in 1977 to 7.7 million pairs in 1978—an increase of 800 percent.[54] There were some indications of transshipment, here, as well.

Finally, there has been a shift in the composition and value of the restrained countries' exports. Although Taiwan has not adapted as well as Korea, both have upgraded their product lines and increased the prices on their older production. For example, footwear which was valued up to $1.25 made up 40 percent of Taiwanese shipments in the first month of the OMA. In December of 1978, this price bracket represented less than 1 percent of Taiwanese exports (see Table 4). The overall unit value of Taiwanese nonrubber footwear increased almost 60 percent between 1977 and 1978; and the overall unit value of Korean nonrubber footwear went up by 43 percent in the same period.[55] Rising wage rates, raw material prices, and general inflation accounted for some of these changes; but inflation in Korea, for instance, was only 15 percent in 1978 (and the exchange rate of the Korean currency remained fixed in terms of the U.S. dollar). To maximize their trading gains within the confines of the OMA, these foreign producers had to upgrade their product lines into middle-priced footwear—the traditional mainstay of the American market. The Korean government also took an active role in pushing up the value of its exports by increasing floor prices almost every three months.[56]

Thus the Orderly Marketing Agreement operated as expected. It contributed to an increase as well as to change in the composition of foreign competition with American footwear firms. Rather than reducing market penetration, the overall result of these developments was an increase in the share of imports in the total domestic supply over the share realized before the OMAs were negotiated. In the first quarter of 1977, imported rubber and nonrubber footwear reached 52 percent of the U.S. market; in the first quarter of 1979, the level was 55 percent.

[53]Interview with Jane Hester, Office of International Commodities, Department of Labor, August 24, 1979.
[54]Calculated from *U.S. Department of Commerce News*, April 26, 1979.
[55]Calculated from *Brimmer Reports* (1979).
[56]*Footwear News*, April 8, 1979.

Table 4. Shoe imports from Taiwan, Korea, and world, by price bracket, July 1977 and December 1978 (percent)

Price brackets	Taiwan		Korea		World	
	July '77	Dec. '78	July '77	Dec. '78	July '77	Dec. '78
Up to $1.25	39.9%	0.8%	11.5%	0.05%	24.1%	9.6%
$1.26–2.50	30.9	23.2	13.1	1.06	19.2	15.7
$2.51–5.00	22.5	66.6	62.3	14.9	29.6	33.5
$5.01–8.00	6.2	8.3	9.8	59.6	13.1	21.4
Over $8.00	0.02	1.1	3.2	24.4	13.7	19.8

SOURCE: Volume Footwear Retailers of America, *Bulletin No. 7*, February 23, 1979.

As domestic production hit record lows (390 million pairs), the only real victory the Footwear Industry Team could claim for its domestic program's contribution to industrial performance was a reduction in the rate of decline.[57]

CONCLUSIONS: POLICY IMPLICATIONS

The failure of the Orderly Marketing Agreements with Korea and Taiwan to reduce import penetration has important lessons for policy-makers. The government should learn from its own history in the footwear industry, as well as from its experience in other declining sectors, that selective protection and Orderly Marketing types of arrangements are not an effective means of facilitating industry adjustment. In many ways, it is ironic that export restraints should be such a prominent way to control imports in the postwar period. The GATT, with American sponsorship, has continually reduced tariff barriers to international trade since 1945. By doing so, this international organization has made it more difficult for developed nations to use tariffs and quantitative restrictions. Tariffs, however, are the most economically efficient form of protection.[58] If import restraints are necessary for either political or economic reasons, tariffs at least maintain competition on the basis of price. The result is that the GATT has unwittingly created a more distorting form of protectionism by restricting the use of tariffs.

OMAs, unlike tariffs, are fundamentally a political tool—a method of circumventing global constraints and satisfying domestic interests. Their political value, however, is as questionable as their economic value. When initially considering export restraints, government decision-makers usually see OMAs as a temporary expedient. In theory, the

[57]*U.S. Department of Commerce News,* April 26, 1979.
[58]See any textbook on international economics.

problem should be solved within a few years, and then everyone will be happy and protection will no longer be necessary. Yet the "boomerang effect" of OMAs in labor-intensive industries means that sectoral problems may actually get worse—not better—in the long run. If the industry remains dissatisfied, then the clamor for protection will not end. The prime example is textiles, where the government has been unable to satisfy the industry for twenty years.

Therefore, the government must address two problems related to its foreign trade policy. First, OMAs are inappropriate in conception and inadequate in implementation. This demands a technical solution: OMAs must be adjusted or new policies must be devised. Second, policy choices for OMAs are a product of international and domestic constraints, and these require a political solution. If domestic footwear firms or other American industries desire protection, and these groups are capable of effectively pressuring the Congress and the executive branch, it will be difficult for the government to ignore their demands.

Under these circumstances, tariffs would be the best international policy of all the available protectionist options. A tariff would give producers an incentive to adjust by maintaining price competition; it would generate revenue for the government; and *if properly presented,* it could inspire confidence in the government's commitment to the industry. In other words, a tariff might solve the domestic political problem. The administration is understandably reluctant to employ tariffs, particularly because of the costs to consumers and the international ramifications. In the long run, however, confronting the problem directly is politically and economically preferable to the numerous hidden costs of other international options.

The central lesson of this study of the footwear industry is that *policy coherence is a necessary condition for effective trade policies.* In an age of interdependence and internationally competitive markets, the United States cannot afford the luxury of muddling through. Without well-conceived intervention policies that combine international and domestic action designed to facilitate adjustment, the continued decline of footwear and all other distressed sectors can be expected.

Improving the policy process and directing national and international policies toward the same ends should be seen as the next challenge for American leadership. President Carter's streamlined trade adjustment assistance created by the Footwear Industry Team was one step toward an integrated domestic policy; creating a foreign economic counterpart is the next task. Effective decision-making must also provide for careful consideration of the difficulties that can arise during implementation; and policy-makers should be willing to revise their positions in light of new information.[59] The failure of the present policy for the footwear industry should provoke a whole new look at the problems of trade adjustment assistance, not a simple extension of similar policies.

RECENT POLICY DEVELOPMENTS

In the first few months of the Reagan administration, the new President faced protectionist pressures very similar to those experienced by the Carter administration in its early days. In spring of 1977, the footwear, color TV, and steel industries were all demanding trade restraints; in early 1981, auto makers were insisting on restrictions and shoe manufacturers continued to push for more import barriers. The footwear industry had an affirmative ITC decision again on its side.[60] And the auto industry had strong backers in Congress threatening to legislate quotas against Japanese cars. Like Mr. Carter, Mr. Reagan professes to be a free trader. But also like Mr. Carter, Mr. Reagan did not want to jeopardize other priorities by promoting confrontation on the trade issue with Congress early in his tenure.

The Reagan answer to this dilemma was a familiar variation of an old theme: he decided to negotiate a voluntary export restraint with Japan in automobiles, then to discontinue the OMAs in footwear. The strategy, as one might expect, was to find a political compromise that would diffuse the protectionist pressure. Once Congress was satisfied with the minimum necessary restrictions in automobiles, the administration felt it could be a free trader in shoes, without major repercussions.

The Reagan political compromise, however, is simply another example of muddling through. More problems may be created by this solution than were answered. In the case of footwear, the OMAs had already done their damage. The industry remains in disarray, government policies have generally failed, and footwear's lobbying for protection will continue to be a source of difficulty for the administration. In the case of automobiles, the same logic that worked against the OMAs in shoes could work against the voluntary export restraint in cars. Since the restraint is a *selective* restriction that singled out Japan, transshipments remain a possibility; and other countries such as France and Germany could fill the void. Since it was *negotiated*, it has been filled with the inevitable loopholes that characterize these arrangements. And

[59]See Alex George, *Appendices. Commission on the Organization of the Government for the Conduct of Foreign Policy*, Vol. 2, (Washington, D.C.: Government Printing Office 1975).
[60]The ITC recommended that the OMA with Korea be abandoned and that the OMA with Taiwan be extended.

since the voluntary export restraint is a *quantitative* restriction, it seems likely that the Japanese may upgrade their products, which would present a new threat to American car manufacturers.[61]

If future government policy-makers want to get out of the vicious cycle produced by voluntary export restraints and Orderly Marketing Agreements, they must learn that the use of these arrangements to protect declining industries has one known effect: the industries keep declining.

[61]For a fuller explication of this argument, see David B. Yoffie, "Reagan's Mythical Voluntary Export Restraints," editorial, *Wall Street Journal*, May 18, 1981.

CHAPTER SEVEN

Beyond the Age of Ford:
The Strategic Basis of the
Japanese Success in Automobiles

DAVID FRIEDMAN

American automobile companies, according to the following chapter, are
fighting the wrong war with the wrong strategies. They continue to respond to
Japanese product and production strategies with ideas developed half a century
ago. Both corporate executives and government officials must change their
conceptions of the industry and of how competitive advantage is created and
maintained.

The product and production strategies of American automobile companies still
have the mass-production orientation given them by Henry Ford. Ford's success
has become part of our industrial mythology. He produced a single car in one
color in order to obtain economies of scale that reduced cost, making that one car
widely accessible. Standard parts, a single design, and an inflexible production
system were at the core of Ford's conception. General Motors used product
variety and market positioning to break Ford's domination and establish itself as
the industry leader, but the underlying conception remained the same. The idea
was still to build a limited number of basic chassis and engine packages. GM's
innovation was to vary the external finishing of the packages, creating a series
of market entries from a few designs. Differences in cars developed, but they
were more apparent than real.

This orientation shaped the response of the American industry to the market
changes brought about by the oil crisis. Both market demand and government
regulation pushed manufacturers toward smaller cars. Because the types of cars
American buyers began to seek were already being produced in Europe and
Japan, the American market was suddenly vulnerable to imports. The barriers
that separated the world auto industry into three distinct markets—Japan, the
United States, and Europe—began to erode. Since few buyers wanted the big

American road cruisers, however, the erosion of barriers between national markets released a flood of imports into the American market. As small imports began to sell well, American producers began both to design new small car lines and to downscale existing products. Their strategic conceptions, nonetheless, stayed the same. The first strategic notion was to substitute a line of smaller cars for the standard lines of road cruisers that had dominated the American market. The basic notion of a small number of auto designs varied by external features to fit into a series of market slots continued. The second notion was expressed in the "world car" strategy. If the cars demanded in several world markets were similar, then presumably even greater economies of scale could be realized. Transmissions produced in Mexico could be used for American cars, and U.S.-made parts could be used in assembly plants around the world. It is not inevitable, of course, that significant economies of scale gained from such a strategy will continue indefinitely. Indeed, after the most important scale economies are realized, one might imagine that worldwide sourcing might contain serious diseconomies and risks. Long supply lines, for example, might mean that higher levels of stocks have to be held to assure continuous production, and holding stocks costs money in finance charges. Certainly, part of the so-called world car strategy was based on the efforts of American companies to satisfy local demands that part of the cars sold in a particular country be produced locally, so that auto imports and auto exports balance. Whatever the politics, however, the world car fit the strategic conceptions of American automobile producers.

According to the analysis presented here, Japanese producers are apparently up to something altogether different. They have begun to fragment the market for standard cars into a series of distinct submarkets, producing a distinct chassis, engine, and finishing package for each submarket. In the American conception this fragmentation seems to imply higher production costs, but this does not appear to be the case. The first American reaction to this strategy was to claim that lower wages and subsidized steel give Japanese companies an advantage. More recently, however, American firms have learned that the production system behind the Japanese strategy is new. Toyota calls it the "Kanban" system and views it as a distinct step beyond the Ford-style production reasoning that still binds American companies. It amounts to a production strategy of flexibility to match a marketing strategy of real product differentiation.

Such a system implies a greater ability to deal with rapid change, whether that change comes from strategic moves by competitors or from shifting energy costs. In the analysis that follows, the central problem of the American automobile industry is identified as its emphasis on large-scale production of standardized products. This strategy is now seriously threatened by the more flexible Japanese production strategy of greater real product variety. If the analysis is correct, then the challenges for the U.S. government and U.S. companies will endure long after the introduction of the small car into the product lines of American automakers.

351

It is interesting to compare the arguments in this chapter with the arguments in the next chapter. Both chapters reflect a similar perspective on the importance of flexibility and specialization in modern industrial economies. Friedman's work reflects a viewpoint similar to that of Piore and Sabel, with whom he has been working.

THE UNPRECEDENTED crisis in the American automobile industry, dramatized by all-too-frequent announcements of plant closings, layoffs, sagging sales, and new government intervention, has reopened the question of how and what American auto manufacturers should produce. Industrialists and academic researchers, despairing of established practices, have turned to more successful producers such as the Japanese for ideas about future policy. But the lessons these people draw from cases like Japan are necessarily colored by their prior views of automobile production, so that new possibilities are overlooked. This chapter compares the Japanese and American auto industries and argues that in contrast to prevailing views, Japan's competitive edge is based not on cost advantages gleaned through greater efficiency, but on the ability to flexibly differentiate its products. Consequently, strategies for industrial rejuvenation that ignore the possibilities for future market fragmentation and instead push for greater standardization are likely to fail for the same reasons that provoked the current problems of the U.S. automobile industry in the first place.

Most studies of the contemporary auto industry have been based on the conviction that an increasing standardization of automobiles is inevitable. They have therefore concluded that the main problem facing any producer is to lower production costs through increased automation, workplace routinization, and economies of scale.[1] Voices to the contrary are few and far between.[2] In this view, differences in the national characteristics of automobiles are steadily eroding as cars be-

---

[1]See U.S. Department of Transportation, *Auto Industry 1980* (DOT Report P-10-81:02, Cambridge, Mass., March 1981); U.S. Congress, *Current Problems of U.S. Auto Industry* (Congressional Budget Office, Natural Resources Division, Washington, D.C., July 1980); statement of F.G. Seacrest before the House Committee on Ways and Means, Subcommittee on Trade, March 7, 1980; Marina V. N. Whitman, "International Trade and Imports: Two Perspectives" (Frank D. Graham Memorial Lecture, unpublished manuscript, March 5, 1981), esp. pp. 11–19; "The Auto Crisis and Public Policy: an Interview with Philip Caldwell," *Harvard Business Review*, January-February 1981, pp. 78–82; interview, Roger Smith, *Ward's Engine Update*, December 15, 1980, pp. 4–6; and for journalistic account suggestive of most media efforts, David Meheegan, "Does Detroit Have a Better Idea?" *Boston Globe Sunday Magazine*, November 22, 1981.

[2]One notable example is William Abernathy and his associates at the Harvard Business School, who have argued that continuous product innovation may well be the characteristic form of future competiton. See William Abernathy *et al.*, "The New Industrial Competition," *Harvard Business Review*, September-October 1981, pp. 68–81.

come more homogeneous in nature. Competition between firms and countries therefore centers on the need to cut costs; everyone is racing to install the newest labor-saving devices and to reach even greater scale economies. Less successful national auto industries, such as those in America, must match the products of the more successful firms—compact and subcompact cars, for instance—and at the same time meet the lowest prices on the market. Translated into a set of industrial strategies, the hope of the prevailing view is that once a short-term but massive reinvestment in new machinery is made, perhaps with temporary government financial assistance and trade protection, a new stability based on a new standardized product will obtain in the auto industry.[3]

But a strategy that seeks increased standardization of a new, smaller automobile gambles on future market stability. In the process of standardizing production, future flexibility is sacrificed because the entire industry—including the suppliers, the workforce, and the machinery—is geared to make only one type of product. We will argue here that the odds favor increased volatility in the auto market, and that consequently the standardization strategy is almost certain to produce painful consequences not unlike the current problems in the industry. Purely contingent factors such as oil price volatility, the politics of raw material supplies, pollution and safety considerations, and changing consumer tastes are enough to ensure future market shifts.

But there is an even deeper threat: the flexibility of competitors in the auto industry. We shall see that Japanese production has been organized in ways that foster the ability to change and differentiate automobiles continuously. Industrial competition with Japan, then, guarantees that any standardized product design will be under strong pressure from Japanese firms, who will try to fragment the market with new car designs. Even as American firms try desperately to impose a new standardized automobile on the market, international competition will undercut the effort and leave them in a state of chronic, perhaps fatal, readjustment.

Compounding the gravity of this view is the fact that the problems of the industry are not confined to the auto companies; they become the concern of the government as well. If U.S. auto companies fail, political demands for protection, financial assistance, and increased state in-

---

[3]The argument for temporary support, trade restrictions, and the like occurs most clearly in discussions about the Japanese trade surplus. See "Administration Splits on Auto Imports," *Fortune*, May 4, 1981, p. 162; the interview with Philip Ca   ell in *Harvard Business Review;* and of course, the statements of labor, political, and inuustrial leaders on behalf of the Chrysler bailout, U.S. Congress, House of Representatives, *Hearings on the Chrysler Loan Guarantee Board*, vols 1–2, Washington, D.C., March 1980.

volvement are practically inevitable, given the enormous importance of auto production in the economy. We shall argue that standardization creates a policy trap in America, in which the government forces painful trade-offs of an explosive and expensive nature. If U.S. firms have, a stake in sorting out the future possibilities in automobile production, the government also has an explicit responsibility to assure that all avenues are explored. Indeed we shall conclude that it is only through a complex and subtle process in which political decisions are made paramount that increased flexibility in American production, and with it relief from the dilemmas inherent in standardized production, is possible at all.

Making this argument involves several distinct steps. First, we will discuss, in the abstract, the ways in which flexible production differs from standardized production; we shall see that the flexible and the standardized auto manufacturer make very distinct uses of new product ideas, labor, and suppliers.[4] Then we will explore in detail the empirical records of the Japanese and American auto industries, and show that Japan more or less approximates the flexible model whereas the United States is much closer to the standardized form of production.[5] Finally, we draw from the past certain implications for the future of American auto production, and argue in favor of increased flexibility. We show that providing for flexibility in production requires explicit political decisions, and we assess potential policies that might bring about a change in American production given contemporary political trends.

FLEXIBLE VERSUS STANDARDIZED PRODUCTION

Any firm faces a basic choice in building a product. It can strive to build one basic unit as cheaply as possible, gaining market shares by

[4]By innovation we do not usually mean sweeping technical modifications of a product. We refer more often to a process of bringing into the market various limited innovations—such as the Wankel engine, stratified charge technology, and diesel engines—that permit a producer to make a market appeal based on a unique performance characteristic. Nor are firms that innovate in this manner technologically more sophisticated than others; indeed, many U.S. innovations found first commercial application in Japanese cars. For our purposes here, the ability to make new market appeals and to fragment a standardized market does not depend on technical virtuosity as an inventor might think of it, but rather on the more limited ability to take an existing set of technical options, modify them, and bring out a new product.

[5]Although automobile production, when compared to other industries such as ladies' fashions or software, is highly standardized in all countries, there are nonetheless significant differences in the degree that any one firm is standardized. We are arguing only that an important degree of flexibility is possible in auto production, even given the standardized nature of the industry in general.

undercutting its competitors' prices. This production strategy is one of standardization. On the other hand, the firm can try to create new market niches by continuously differentiating its products, seeking a unique market appeal by modifying the product's design. This production strategy is one of flexibility; the firm sacrifices some efficiency in scale economies for the benefits of continuous product differentiation. The choice between flexible and standardized production is not a light one, for each form of manufacture profoundly affects the firm's relations with suppliers and the division of labor in the factory.

In standardized production, the product's definition is fixed, so that manufacturing decisions center on the problem of cutting costs. Therefore, standardized firms tend to develop an arm's-length relationship with suppliers in which the primary topic of communication is the price of components; they have little use for innovative ideas offered by suppliers. Instead of initiating consultations with suppliers about design or new product ideas (which might be considered disruptive), the standardized producer seeks only to fill its component needs at the lowest cost. To do this, it will generally deal with suppliers only on a cost basis, and will vertically integrate production where possible. Thus supplier relations in standardized production tend over time to reinforce rigidity, because neither the suppliers nor the central firms have incentives for operating procedures that readily permit extensive product modifications.

The standardized firm's overriding concern with cost cutting also profoundly affects the division of labor in the factory. Standardization brings with it increasing mechanization in production, routinization of work, and hence the gradual deskilling of the workforce. High levels of skill exercised on general-purpose machines are not required by firms that want to make only one product as cheaply as possible. Instead, highly specialized machines and very limited labor tasks are established in the factory to permit economies of scale. As in the supplier case, these commitments reinforce production rigidity; a deskilled workforce and a huge investment in machinery tailored to only one product are difficult and expensive to change. A standardized market strategy thus leads to supplier and labor practices that reinforce trends toward product stability.

In flexible production, a firm's relations with suppliers are quite different. Whereas new innovations and consultations between firms are not required in standardized production, they are essential to the flexible firm. Developing new product ideas into actual market offerings lies at the heart of its competitive strategy. This produces two pressures for close contact with suppliers. First, the central firm will want to maximize the flow of new ideas, and to do this it needs to use the creative and practical talents of its suppliers. Second, constantly changing product requirements naturally promote close coordination with suppliers, because suppliers have to know what the firm's new requirements are. Over time, standardization leads to aloof, stagnant supplier contacts, whereas flexible production tends to promote close communication between the central and the supplying firms.

Similarly, the labor force in flexible firms is very different from a standardized workforce. Several factors make the deskilling required by standardized production undesirable to flexible manufacture. First, ever-changing product needs are not served by the establishment of workplace routines and the installation of highly specialized machines. Instead, skilled workers on general-purpose machinery are employed to put out rapidly changing goods. Second, any attempt to continuously modify products will inevitably lead to production snafus, but a skilled, autonomous workforce is far more capable of immediately and efficiently resolving production problems than deskilled labor. Finally, a skilled workforce is also a productive one, and a source of ideas that can help promote new designs. Thus, high skill leads both to higher productivity and to increased flexibility.[6] As in the supplier instance, then, the division of labor in a flexible firm makes possible increased future flexibility.

Thus standardized and flexible manufacture are in many ways polar opposites. Flexibility demands high skills, worker autonomy, and close supplier contacts; standardization leads to deskilling, increased hierarchy in the factory, and loose, price-oriented supplier contacts. Moreover, flexibility and standardization are often reciprocal strategies in a single industry. A firm may react to its competitor's price edge by differentiating its products, seeking a new market niche to exploit rather than engaging in pure price competition. A flexible producer might well grow out of a previously standardized industry, then, as a result of the logic of market competition. Indeed, we shall see that Japanese flexibility in auto production has in fact been enhanced by the high degree of American standardization; Japanese firms sought to fragment the market by differentiating their automobiles. Though flexibility and standardization lead to distinct patterns of production, each can grow out of the same competitive forces in an industry.

Of course, these models of flexible and standardized procedures represent abstract, ideal types. In real settings no firm is purely flexible or purely standardized; even the most flexible company has to cut costs by limiting its product range, and even highly standardized firms face at

---

[6]See the section entitled "The Division of Labor in Japan and America" for details; our argument will be that increased flexibility, worker skill, and productivity—and hence lower production costs—go hand in hand.

least minor market adjustments that compel production changes. But in any given market, there is a certain range of freedom in which a firm can decide whether to pursue a standardized or a flexible production strategy.

If we are correct in assuming that the decision to produce in a flexible or a standardized manner affects the entire character of a firm or an industry, is there any evidence that such a fundamental choice exists in the automobile industry? By looking at statistical measures and product behavior histories of Japanese and American auto firms, we can demonstrate that the Japanese change their products much more frequently and extensively than the Americans do. Indeed, so striking is the difference between Japanese and American production that the prevailing notion that products are necessarily standardized in the auto market will have to be re-examined. We will show that as a matter of scale economies, the potential for Japanese-style production flexibility is not significantly foreclosed.

Statistical Measures

One way of distinguishing American and Japanese automobile firms is to compare their product diversity over time and as a matter of production volumes. In Table 1, the diversity of engine sizes and body types as a function of volume in 1975 and 1980 is compiled for each Japanese and American manufacturer, and for each set of national producers in the aggregate.

Before we turn to the substance of Table 1, the suitability of the measures selected needs to be carefully considered. Both engine size and body data may not measure "real" diversity. Engine size data, for instance, may indicate either a new engine design or a scaled-down, rebored version of an existing design. Moreover, firms often do not manufacture important parts: both Chrysler and AMC purchase engines from suppliers. Consequently, measuring engine diversity by displacement may distort the real scope of production. These considerations are important to bear in mind when evaluating the data in Table 1, for they indicate the extent to which real diversity is being measured.

Yet there are good reasons to think that the data in Table 1 shed some useful light on the relative diversity of American and Japanese production. The decision to produce a new engine size is not a light one. Even a rebored engine requires retooling, arranging for new parts from suppliers, and rerouting the workplace to assemble the engine. Indeed, if it is thought that size diversity somehow measures only a technically trivial capacity to change engine specification by computer-aided technology, consider the billions of dollars and the difficult tran-

Table 1. Aggregate product diversity of Japanese and U.S. automobile makers, by firm, 1975 and 1980

Year and firm	Number of models	Number of bodies	Number of engines[a]	Production volume[b] (thousands)	Bodies per volume (thousands)	Engines per volume (thousands)
1975						
Daihatsu	4	19	5	92	1:4.8	1:18
Honda	3	21	4	328	1:15	1:82
Isuzu	3	13	2	64	1:5	1:37
Toyo Kogyo	6	76	6	387	1:5	1:64
Mitsubishi	5	39	8	288	1:7.3	1:36
Nissan	9	97	12	1,530	1:15	1:127
Fuji	2	23	3	108	1:4.6	1:46
Suzuki	3	18	2	50	1:2.7	1:25
Toyota	10	145	10	1,700	1:11.7	1:170
All Japanese firms	45	451	52	4,547	1:9.9	1:86
GM	27	148	10	3,700	1:25	1:370
Ford	13	62	8	1,800	1:29	1:225
Chrysler	9	79	5	902	1:11	1:18
AMC	4	11	4	323	1:29	1:180
All U.S. firms	53	300	27	6,725	1:22	1:248
1980						
Daihatsu	5	38	7	130	1:3.5	1:18
Honda	3	23	3	706	1:30	1:235
Isuzu	3	38	5	86	1:2.2	1:17
Toyo Kogyo	7	56	7	647	1:11	1:92
Mitsubishi	8	64	8	528	1:8.2	1:66
Nissan	11	219	13	1,700	1:7.7	1:13
Fuji	2	28	4	153	1:5.4	1:38
Suzuki	4	15	4	69	1:4.6	1:17
Toyota	12	234	15	2,111	1:90	1:14
All Japanese firms	55	715	66	6,130	1:8.5	1:92

GM	29	123	19	4,100	1:33	1:215
Ford	14	47	7	1,300	1:27	1:185
Chrysler	11	38	4	638	1:16	1:16
AMC	5	11	2	164	1:15	1:82
All U.S. firms	59	219	32	6,202	1:28	1:193

[a]Measured by size of displacement.
[b]1980 volume for Japan computed from 1979 figures because of unavailability of 1980 data.
SOURCES: Engine and model diversity were compiled from Automobile Club of Rome and from *World Cars 1975* and *World Cars 1980* (New York: Herald Books). Output data were taken from *Ward's Automotive Yearbook*, various issues 1975–1981, and from Japanese Automobile Manufacturers Association, *Motor Vehicle Statistics of Japan* (Tokyo, 1980).

sition U.S. firms had to make just to achieve annual increases in fuel efficiencies to meet government Corporate Average Fuel Economy (CAFE) standards.[7] Or consider the fact that about 50 percent of the staggering $60 billion that U.S. firms are to spend in retooling for small cars is dedicated to engine capacity.[8]

And even if companies do contract for engines, we are interested in how change affects the whole supplier network. If a supplier and a firm are set up to make only one engine, they are standardized. If together they aim for change, their organization would look more like that of a flexible producer. Thus the figures in Table 1, though subject to important influences, still provide at least a relative measure of diversity and change.

Similarly, the body diversity figures in Table 1 reveal important differences in Japanese and American production. In many cases, body diversity may reflect only cosmetic changes on a basic body type. General Motor's X car platform, for instance, is the basic design for several models distinguished only by very minor physical modifications.[9] However, even if many or all firms differentiate basic platforms to build "new" models, the Japanese still seem to obtain far more diversity in bodies per volume than the Americans do. Futhermore, as we shall see, the tendency to make only cosmetic changes in a standard model type is far more characteristic of American production. Small Japanese firms, in particular, build quite distinct models composed of profoundly different engines, parts, and designs.

With these caveats in mind, we can turn to the substance of Table 1. First, the aggregate country figures show that in 1980 Japanese producers on the average built one engine of the same size for every 92,000 units, whereas the U.S. firms offered one engine of the same size for every 193,000 units. In the same year, the Japanese built one distinct auto body per 8,000 units, whereas the Americans made one body serve for 28,000 units. Compared to their U.S. counterparts, Japanese auto firms made nearly three times as many bodies and engines per unit produced.

These aggregate statistics hide the real degree of U.S. standardization because they capture American firms in the midst of a transition from large to small cars. Fully 78 percent of American engine sizes in 1980 were in the obsolete range of 4,000 cc (cubic centimeters) and

---

[7]See U.S Department of Transportation (DOT), *The U.S. Automobile Industry 1980*, pp. 64–75.

[8]*Ibid.*, p. 66.

[9]See Automobile Club of Rome, *World Cars 1980*, for technical specifications of the X car, which in the trade is sometimes called "corporate car" because of its structural identity beneath cosmic diversity.

above. Japan's diversity is even more striking in the 3,000 cc and below segments, where the U.S. firms are moving to meet Japanese competition. Here, as Table 2 shows, Japan produced 715 bodies to 58 for the Americans, and 66 different engine sizes as opposed to only 7 for the Americans.[10] On a volume-adjusted basis, that translates to nearly five times the bodies and 3.5 times the engine sizes per unit produced. In the small-car segment which American firms are rapidly trying to enter, Japanese firms build a far more diverse range of products.

A closer look at the differences in Japanese and American production revealed in Tables 1 and 2 shows that, over time, U.S. producers have been much more standardized than Japanese companies. For instance, America's best-selling car in 1979 and 1980, the Chevette, has remained virtually unchanged since it was introduced in 1975. Over the five-year span, the car was produced with three basic bodies and one 1700 cc engine (although an imported Isuzu diesel engine was fitted on some units in 1981), and it has undergone no major styling changes. Its volume in 1980 was 454,000 units. The X car, which appears variously as a Chevy, a Pontiac, and an Oldsmobile, provides an even more dramatic example of standardization. All told, this auto sold over 800,000 units in 1980, but GM provided it with only two engines. In two instances of best-selling small car production, then, we see the extent to which American firms strive to achieve high sales volumes with extremely standardized designs.

Japanese firms exhibit a dramatically different pattern of production, one that is especially marked if the firms smaller than Toyota or Nissan are examined. These smaller companies are the fastest growing auto firms in Japan and have absorbed an increasing share of the Japanese auto market. Between 1975 and 1980 alone, the share of production which the small firms took rose from 29 to 39 percent.[11]

Table 1 shows that several small Japanese auto producers—including Daihatsu, Isuzu, Mitsubishi, Fuji, and Suzuki—offer from ten to twenty times the engine and body diversity of American firms on volumes of production that are a fraction of several American *models,* let alone the total output of GM or Ford. Daihatsu, on a volume of 130,000 units in

[10]Because several U.S. model sales are reported only by model type and not by engine size, some estimates of total U.S. small car sales had to be made. In instances where it was impossible to tell if a relevant model, such as Ford's Capri, had been fitted with an eight-cylinder or a four-cylinder engine, the assumption was that only 50 percent came with the smaller units. Given the panic switch in the United States to small cars in the wake of the 1979 oil embargo, this assumption would seem to understate the actual amount of small car sales, which would make the U.S. firms appear even more standardized in Table 2.

[11]Japanese Automobile Manufacturers Association, *Motor Vehicle Statistics of Japan,* 1980.

Table 2. Small car diversity, United States and Japan, 1980

Country	Number of bodies	Number of engines[a]	Production volume[b] (millions)	Bodies per volume (thousands)	Engines per volume (thousands)
United States	58	7	2.3	1:39	1:327
Japan	715	66	6.1	1:8.5	1:92

[a]Measured by displacement.
[b]1979 volume data used for Japan.
SOURCE: See sources for Table 1.

1979, made 38 body types and 7 distinct engines. Isuzu, on an 86,000 unit volume, offered 38 bodies and 5 engines. This diversity was achieved on an output only 20 to 25 percent as large as that of the Chevette alone, and it exceeded the total product diversity of the entire Chrysler Corporation.

The statistical evidence of the diversity of Japanese firms does not measure insignificant product differentiation. By and large, a different engine size or body represents a distinct market appeal. Daihatsu's products include a mini-car line, a set of station wagons, a four-wheel-drive jeep, and a standard sedan. Its mini-car comes in two-cylinder and three-cylinder engine varieties, and on different models the firm fits engines in the front and the rear of the chassis. The jeep is fitted with a diesel engine. Daihatsu's entire line of engines was redesigned in size and in some cases configuration between 1975 and 1980, as it brought the three-cylinder and diesel engines onto the market.

Mitsubishi's products include a mini-car, a jeep, and a range of six sedans with engines from 1200 to 2600 cc. It altered 75 percent of its engines between 1975 and 1980 while adding 32 body types. Another Japanese company, Suzuki, which produces only mini-cars, changed all of its engines in the 360 cc class, and added another cylinder to each version between 1975 and 1980. These new engines were then mounted in both rear and front engine placements and on a new mini-jeep.

Isuzu brought out a new diesel sedan, redesigned or altered 60 percent of its engines, and exploited a demand for recreational and business pickup trucks with new bodies between 1975 and 1980. Its diesel sedan was the smash hit of the domestic Japanese market in 1980.[12] And in yet another example of Japanese product diversity, Fuji Motors, the makers of Subaru, offered a two-cylinder mini-car, especially redesigned its four-wheel-drive sedan, and built a recreational pickup truck

[12]Kathleen K. Weinger, "Another Japanese Car Company?" *Forbes*, November 10, 1980, p. 39.

called the Brat in 1975–1980. Finally, Toyo Kogyo, with its rotary-engined sports car and a variety of four-cylinder engines, built 56 body types in 1980, which exceeded Ford's body diversity on only 50 percent of Ford's volume.

Tables 1 and 2 therefore suggest the very different approaches to product diversity that Japanese and American firms exhibit. Indeed, even where statistical measures are not so striking, Japanese firms still make product modifications that vastly exceed those of U.S. companies. Honda, despite its comparably low ratio of engine and body diversity to production volume, nonetheless undertook a massive product transformation between 1975 and 1980. It moved from economy cars into luxury sedans, modifying two-thirds of its engines in that period and completely redesigning its bodies. And Toyota and Nissan have increased body diversity by 30 percent per unit volume between 1975 and 1980, or in absolute terms by 89 and 122 types, respectively, whereas GM and Ford cut back on body diversity in the same period. Both firms are becoming more aggressive in defining new sports and recreational vehicles; Toyota's recent management shakeup was partly blamed on the conservative product-development policies of the outgoing team.[13] In different ways, then, Honda, Toyota, and Nissan offer evidence that Japanese producers change and diversify their products more rapidly than U.S. firms do.

The statistical record of American and Japanese automobile diversity also strongly indicates that Japanese companies, to a much greater extent than American firms, attempt to change products regularly and profoundly. In the aggregate, the diversity of Japanese products is three times that of American ones (per volume), and the rate and extent of product changes over time is strikingly different in each country. To further amplify these differences, the way that Japanese and American firms have responded to similar market challenges will be compared. As we shall see, analyses of historical product behavior provide convergent evidence to support the view that Japanese production is much more flexibly oriented.

Product Histories Compared

One way to suggest the differences between U.S. and Japanese auto producers is to show how each party has responded to similar challenges. Two such challenges will be explored in this section: first, the attempt to fashion a "people's car" in the United States and Japan in the late 1940s and 1950; and second, direct trade competition. In both

---

[13]"Behind the Bloodletting over Toyota's Sales," *Business Week*, June 1, 1981, p. 44.

cases, it will be argued, the Japanese exhibited the response of a flexible producer whereas the Americans acted in the manner of a standardized manufacturer.

First, take the case of the small car. In both Japan and America in the first decade after World War II, tight money and burgeoning demand for cars, along with considerable interest shown by the press and the government, generated widespread interest in a small, inexpensive "people's car." In America, producers could not find room in their standardized product lines for a new economical car. In Japan, despite a much smaller average car size to start with, a market for very small automobiles (micro-mini size) was established.

In America in the early 1960s, the auto firms did try at first to respond to the demand for a people's car by developing plans for smaller units.[14] But the big three American firms—Chrysler, Ford, and GM—were wedded to the notion that automobiles should be standardized in fact and differentiated only in price and cosmetic appointment. They conceived of their product line as a uniform set of models arrayed from least expensive to most expensive. In this view, smaller cars had to be the cheapest possible unit. But the big three could not see how a smaller, stripped-down version of their basic car could be made for an appropriately low price, and so they abandoned their plans; their ideas for radical model departures, including a four-cylinder car, were shipped to their European affiliates. Meanwhile, independent firms either failed to differentiate their own smaller cars substantially from the larger firms' standard designs, or, as in the case of the Crosley Bantam, they produced them poorly. The people's car was forgotten.

In Japan, however, similar market pressures led to a different response by the auto producers. In the early 1950s, a widely publicized report issued under MITI's auspices advocated a people's small car as part of the general Japanese postwar recovery plans.[15] Toyota, Nissan, and Prince, then the largest car makers, preferred to concentrate on larger sedans. Unlike the American independents, however, smaller Japanese producers—including Fuji, Toyo Kogyo, and Mitsubishi—saw that they could create a new demand with cars that were substantially smaller than the 2,000 cc models with two-seat capacity. These cars were so profoundly distinct from the norm that they effectively established a new market niche in Japan from which smaller firms subsequently expanded their operations. From the start of the postwar auto recovery, then, Japan's auto industry evolved from at least

---

[14]This account is taken from Lawrence White's informative study, *The Automobile Industry since 1945* (Cambridge, Mass.: Harvard University Press, 1971), pp. 178–179.

[15]This account is drawn from Miyake Sadao, "The Japanese Motor Industry," *Japan Quarterly*, January-March 1968, p. 102.

two different product poles, reflecting two different product differentiation strategies.

The different responses of Japanese and American firms to the challenge of developing a small car in the 1950s strengthen the notion that Japanese firms have been far more attuned to product differentiation and model change. In the United States, where 5,000 cc engines were the norm, no firm had both the capacity and the vision to market a distinctly smaller car. In contrast, certain Japanese firms made a successful mini-car appeal in a market where 2,000 cc units were the norm.

The second case, the responses of U.S. and Japanese firms in head-to-head competition, further confirms the extent to which Japanese flexibility has outperformed American standardization. Beginning in the mid-1950s, the Japanese and Europeans mounted an export drive with the U.S. market as its prime target. In subsequent decades, the Japanese continually attempted to gain market shares through product differentiation, while U.S. companies stuck gamely to their standardized model lines and tried to squeeze out foreign challengers by lowering their prices. The dynamics of international competition, then, show clearly American standardization and Japanese flexibility.

Foreign competition had become a crucial factor in the U.S. market by the mid-1950s, when Japan, along with European firms such as Volkswagen, began earnest export drives. By 1959, imports held 10.6 percent of the U.S. market.[16] Because, as we shall see, Japanese export strategies were largely shaped by the response of U.S. companies to this early import wave, it is convenient to begin our analysis with the way American companies treated foreign competition in the late 1950s and early 1960s.

At first, U.S. companies simply ignored foreign cars, but as imports increased they were forced to adjust. They chose not to bring out cars that would directly compete with imports on product grounds such as size, but rather offered their own six-cylinder models and stripped-down versions of large cars. The idea behind the effort was to wean U.S. consumers away from imports with dramatic price reductions, which would in turn ensure against the erosion of standardized large car tastes. The strategy seemed successful, for by 1962 imports had fallen to only 4.6 percent of the domestic U.S. market.[17] But no sooner had the imports faded than the American producers enlarged their medium-sized autos and abandoned their smaller economy cars. In the process they converted small economy cars like Ford's Falcon

[16]Automotive News, *1981 Market Data Book*, Detroit, April 29, 1981, p. 16.
[17]*Ibid.*

into a "sporty" premium-priced Mustang, which was built on the Falcon chassis.[18] In choosing to retain their product identification and in failing to exploit even a tentative move into new regions of the market, U.S. firms clearly illustrated a commitment to standardized production.

But the importers—particularly the Japanese, who suffered greatly from the defensive moves of the American firms in the 1950s—had learned a distinct lesson. If their cars had no unique product appeal, U.S. firms could beat them back with aggressive pricing. Rather than face a debilitating struggle with U.S. standardized producers centered solely on cutting production costs, many exporters opted instead for product differentiation. Following the import waves of the 1950s and 1960s, for instance, Japanese firms sought to carve out a new niche in the U.S. market. Thus Toyota suspended export operations to design a wholly new car for the American market; the Corolla, one of the world's most successful lines, resulted.[19] By the late 1960s, attempts to fragment the U.S. market had spurred a new import wave much broader than the first one. Imports claimed 11.2 percent of the U.S. market by 1969, rising to over 15 percent in 1973—even *before* the effects of OPEC could be felt on domestic tastes.[20] In the midst of U.S. standardization, Japanese firms became more flexible in order to protect themselves, and they initiated a process of market differentiation that continues to pose severe problems for U.S producers.

This second import wave in the late 1960s and early 1970s, in contrast to the first one, was fueled by aggressive market differentiation strategies pursued by the Japanese. This complicated the task of American firms, because they could not so easily use pricing tactics to drive foreign makes from the market. Their competitors were appealing to consumers on other grounds—performance, styling, technology, and economy. But the U.S. firms again tried to pursue their standardization strategy. They initiated, as one analyst at the time called it, a "comic reprise" of their response to the first import wave: they stripped their larger models and offered moderately large autos to compete with the diminutive imports on what they hoped would be price grounds alone.[21] But in the face of the foreign car makers' new model developments and new designs, the U.S. firms could not so easily duplicate their successes of the early 1960s. Indeed, imports showed grow-

[18]Louis Rukeyser, "Detroit's Reluctant Ride into Smallsville," *Fortune*, March 1969, p. 167.

[19]Shotaro Kamiya, *My Life with Toyota* (Tokyo: Toyota Motor Sales, 1976), p. 119.

[20]Automotive News, *1981 Market Data Book*.

[21]Rukeyser, "Detroit's Reluctant Ride," p. 111.

ing strength throughout the 1970s, claiming nearly 30 percent of the market by the end of the decade.[22] Partly this was due to the OPEC embargo, which accelerated the transformation of consumer tastes. But the early success of the Japanese product differentiation strategy suggests that American firms might well have been in great trouble in the 1970s even if Iran and OPEC had never existed.

American firms in international competition from 1955 to 1973, then, exhibited a commitment to standardized production strategies. This worked for them until the late 1960s, when severe U.S. price competition led foreign car makers to pursue a more flexible market strategy. The Japanese, among others, differentiated their products and helped begin a market fragmentation to which U.S. firms have yet to respond. To market uncertainty were subsequently added gasoline price shocks, environmental and safety regulations, and volatile consumer tastes. Cumulatively, these influences made standardization an increasingly risky gamble; Japanese producers, who could make more rapid shifts in design, could feed on this uncertainty and offer cars that appealed precisely to regulatory needs, such as cleanliness or economy.[23] The head-to-head competition between U.S. and Japanese producers thus clearly illustrates American standardization on one hand and the flexible mode of Japanese manufacture on the other.

Strategic Perspectives of U.S. and Japanese Producers

American automobile strategy, as we have seen above, has long reflected the ideas of standardization. Greater homogeneity of product permits increased volume, which cuts costs through scale economies. Executives of the major auto firms have approached adjustment to the present crisis in the same way. Indeed, the "world car" strategy of GM and Ford shows clearly the direction of U.S. thinking about produc-

---

[22]Automotive News, *1981 Market Data Book.*

[23]The ability of the Japanese to quickly turn regulatory initiatives into market strengths is suggested by Honda's early adoption of the stratified charge engine. This technology made it possible to satisfy both fuel-efficiency and the antipollution standards that the U.S. government had promulgated. U.S. firms, however, quickly stated that they could never meet both standards. Honda, in a well-publicized incident, shipped a stock Impala to its factory, fitted stratified technology on its V-8 engine, and then demonstrated that it would pass both economy and cleanliness tests. This idea of using technology to promote regulatory compliance and marketability was behind the advertising slogan "Do your Civic duty," which stressed the low pollution of the new car, the Civic. Sol Sanders, *Honda: The Man and His Machines* (Boston: Little, Brown, 1975), pp. 138–139.

tion: a single standardized design on a global scale is to be produced at the cheapest possible cost.[24]

Japanese car makers, though concerned with production costs, see an opportunity for product differentiation in the contemporary auto market that is in contrast to U.S. beliefs. Their notion is that by creatively changing car designs, demand can be created. As Soichiro Honda once observed of his company: "We do not make something because the demand, the market, is there. With our technology we can create the demand, we can create the market."[25] Fuji's American president, Harvey Lamm, has recently suggested that as public interest in small cars increases, firms will be able to define specialized niches to an even greater extent. Thus, Fuji's strategy would be to find "the right guy for the right car, not everybody." In Lamm's view, a flexible product strategy will be as essential in the future as it was in the past:

> Imports are here to stay because there is always going to be room for the off brand. They offer wider selection. [And as small car segments broaden in size] interest picks up. There is more interest in all small cars, not less. Our product is particular to the needs of some people. As you put more people into our segment of the market, there will be more "somes." The X cars have helped to legitimize small cars even further. They're not competition for us, but other smaller domestic cars that come along will be. . . . [But] it's like yogurt . . . the more popular it becomes, the greater the opportunity for regional producers to compete against the national brand, Dannon.[26]

That Fuji's basic strategic outlook is indicative of the general shape of Japanese thinking is revealed in Japan's response to American downsizing and "world car" development. They have increased their concern with being able to specialize and to change products rapidly. The smaller firms are seeking niches in recreational, mini, diesel, and special-technology cars; Nissan and Toyota are changing the style of their products. On size alone, the Japanese have positioned themselves both above and below the existing model of their American competition, prompting a U.S. executive to note ruefully that no matter what his design team dreams up, "They [the Japanese] have something smaller."[27] *Ward's Engine Update* lists electric cars, turbo models, computer application, diesels, recreational vehicles, and a new economy emphasis

[24]The clearest statement of the world car strategy from a G.M. president rather than an economist is found in *Ward's Engine Update*, December 15, 1980, pp. 4–6, in an interview with then President Roger Smith.
[25]Sanders, *Honda*, pp, 139–140.
[26]"Executive on the Spot," *Industry Week*, July 23, 1979, p. 71.
[27]*Wall Street Journal*, October 14, 1980, p. 1, 21.

among the production research carried out by Japanese firms.[28] Where American firms apparently seek to create a new, multipurpose standard design in their small car strategies, Japanese manufacturers are looking for added product flexibility and differentiation. Indeed, *Advertising Age* recently noted the disjuncture between American and foreign product strategies in precisely these terms: "As for market analysis, the importers have learned as much about the U.S. as the domestics have, and more about it in some areas. The imports were quick to seize on the value of market fragmentation, the splitting up of the total market into many mini-markets that provide potential for small companies with a specialized product."[29]

This brief analysis of production strategies supports the view that the Japanese seek diversification and flexible production much more actively than American firms. Both Japanese and U.S. auto firms are concerned with cost cutting and economies of scale, but the emphasis on standardization as the key to reducing production costs is much greater in the United States. And although American industrialists and analysts alike persist in arguing that homogeneity and standardization are the inevitable future of the auto industry, the contrasting patterns of Japanese and American production seem to challenge that view. In the next section, we shall show that price and production costs are in fact ambiguously related to market advantage. Furthermore, as far as economies of scale are concerned, there is no reason to suppose that market differentiation, the hallmark of flexible production, will not continue to play as important a role in the future of the auto industry as it has in its past.

Scale Economies and Production Costs Reconsidered

At the core of the notion that the world auto industry must necessarily be standardized in the American style is the belief that scale economies constrain the degree of flexibility a firm can have in production. An automobile producer, it is thought, has only two options: mass-produce one type of car cheaply, or make many distinct varieties of cars at a premium price. As one highly respected analyst has said, "You can't have great efficiency and real innovation. There's no such thing as a free lunch."[30] This view, however, exaggerates the real effects of model differentiation on price, for three reasons. First, as we shall demon-

---

[28]"Japan Adorns MPG with Talking Cars, TC and 4WD," *Ward's Engine Update*, December 15, 1980, p. 3.
[29]"When They Said It Couldn't Be Done, Foreign Carmakers Weren't Listening," *Advertising Age*, November 15, 1971.
[30]Quoted in *Business Week*, March 16, 1974, p. 80.

strate later, the greater skill of the flexible producer's workforce cuts costs by increasing productivity. Second, the available data on scale economies indicate that the negative effects of diseconomies of scale that would be felt by a flexible producer do not prohibit aggressive model differentiation. And third, production cost advantages do not translate into readily identifiable market advantages.

First, consider two of the most highly respected estimates of scale economies in automobile production, made by Lawrence White and the Charles River Associates respectively. White's study of the auto industry suggested that an optimum output would be 400,000 autos for any production unit, but at levels of 50,000 units a firm would experience only a 20 percent diseconomy.[31] In this case, a standardized firm could make 400,000 units of one car for, say, $5,000, whereas a flexible firm might make eight distinct cars at 50,000 unit volumes for $6,000. The Charles River Associates, while agreeing with White's estimate of maximum efficiency, calculated that at 150,000 units of output a firm would incur a 26 percent cost penalty.[32] On this estimate, a standardized firm could still sell one model at $5,000, whereas a flexible firm might make three models at about 150,000 unit volumes which would sell at $6,300.

If these major studies are even close to the mark, differentiation appears to be a feasible strategy. In our example, the $1,300 difference in price is not insignificant, but neither does it suggest that flexible production could have only a limited market appeal. If a fair number of consumers purchase optional features that raise the cost of a standard model by a thousand dollars or more, it is possible that they would be equally happy to pay that premium for an automobile already designed particularly for their needs—one, for example, with special snow-handling abilities. Also, as we shall see, the cost differential is further lessened by the flexible firm's increases in productivity. The available evidence, then, does not support the view that homogeneity and standardization are inevitable in auto production; on the contrary, it suggests that within broad parameters firms can still opt for greater flexibility or standardization as a matter of strategic choice rather than market logic.

These considerations help to explain another feature of the automobile market that is anomalous in the conventional picture of the industry: the fact that Japanese successes have not been due to aggressive pricing *despite* an apparent edge over U.S. firms in production costs. The relationship of production costs to price and market advant-

---

[31] White, *The Automobile Industry since 1945*, p. 39.
[32] Eric Toder, ed., *Trade Policy and the U.S. Auto Industry* (New York: Praeger, 1978), p. 137.

age, in other words, is far more ambiguous than the standardized view of the auto industry allows. For instance, the best current estimates suggest that the Japanese have a $1,000 to $2,000 edge per car produced over the Americans.[33] However, the Japanese do not seem to rely on this cost advantage exclusively, or even primarily, in competition. At least since the 1971 *yen* revaluations, Japanese cars have not been noticeably cheaper than American models. By 1981, only two of the 20 Datsun models sold in the United States were priced at or below the Chevette, America's least expensive car, and only two of the 42 Toyota models were similarly priced; and because Japanese cars sell for the full sticker price whereas U.S. cars are often significantly discounted, evidence of aggressive pricing is further diminished.[34] The Japanese must be using their cost advantage, if it exists, far more subtly than simply to underprice their competition.

Consequently, if data on scale economies suggest the continued potential for flexible production, the weak relationship of production costs to market advantage indicates that a successful automobile industry strategy can, and perhaps must, be based on something other than an overriding commitment to cut costs. In this instance, it appears that market differentiation, and the ability to act as a flexible firm in shifting product designs rapidly, is the more important factor.

We may now take a closer look at the industry, and show that both supplier relations and the way the labor force is used also differ in Japan and America. Suppliers are much more closely integrated into Japanese production than they are in America; labor is much more skilled and autonomous in Japan than it is in U.S. firms. Both of these findings are consistent with the flexible and standardized models of production developed above, and they further challenge the view that standardization is the only feasible production strategy in automobile manufacture.

Supplier Relationships Compared

This section and the next one share two objectives. The first is to amplify our analysis of the Japanese and American automobile industries from the viewpoint of flexible versus standardized production strategies. We shall see that the conventional wisdom regarding the inevitability of standardization fails to account for the deep differences between auto manufacture in Japan and in America, whereas the no-

---

[33]DOT, *The U.S. Automobile Industry 1980*, p. 40.
[34]Consumer Reports, *Annual Automobile Fact Issue*, April 1981.

tion that each country is pursuing distinct strategies does clarify our understanding. We shall try to use our analysis to identify more exactly the extent to which national differences in automobile production exist.

The second objective is more subtle: throughout the study of supplier and labor relationships in America and Japan, we will try to show how pieces of the production system in flexible and standardized industries fit together. In the previous section we painted the differences with a broad brush; now, by considering more closely how supplier firms, labor, and market strategies can become attuned to one style of production over another, we can prepare for a discussion of the prerequisites and possibilities for *shifting* from standardized to flexible strategies. When the way that prior decisions about supplier integration and labor management act to reinforce market strategies becomes clear, then the full extent of what is required to change production styles may also be evaluated.

Because central auto firms like GM, Ford, Toyota, and Toyo Kogyo meet their parts requirements through outside purchases from suppliers, the way that suppliers and central companies interact should be highly sensitive to differences in production strategy. Japanese automakers buy as much as 70 percent of their components, and U.S. companies purchase from 50 to 60 percent.[35] Applying the conventional wisdom, which holds that cost considerations are paramount in an increasingly homogeneous product market, we should expect to see that Japanese suppliers are organized precisely to cut costs, whereas U.S. firms interact with suppliers in a more inefficient manner. What we find, however, is that *both* countries have developed a system that drives costs down, and that the American system may be even more efficient on a cost basis.

Consider first the idea that by purchasing parts from others, central firms can exploit lower labor costs in smaller companies and cut total production costs. It might be thought that the greater use of outside vendors in Japan provides an advantage in price because the total production cost of an auto is reduced. But whereas wage rates in the Japanese supplier firms are 75 percent of the central firms' standard, they are even lower in the United States: American suppliers pay from 50 to 70 percent of the labor rates in central firms like GM or Ford.[36] If the key to competitive success is thought to be the development of a parts sector that takes advantage of lower wages, apparently the Americans have made as much, or more, headway than the Japanese.

The same point may be drawn with respect to the relative profits of

[35]Robert Cole, "The Japanese Lesson in Quality," *Technology Review*, July 1981, p. 32.
[36]DOT, *The U.S. Automobile Industry 1980*, p. 43; *Business Week*, September 24, 1979, p. 140.

the American and Japanese suppliers. Japanese central firms often own all or part of their parts suppliers. A former Department of Transportation analyst has shown that many Japanese parts firms have equity links to central auto firms; on the average, Japanese central auto companies had about a 30 percent stake in any given parts supplier. Some companies were owned outright, while others were completely independent.[37] Because this interlocking equity arrangement is distinct from the independent character of U.S. suppliers, it might be thought that Japanese auto firms can squeeze the profits of suppliers to cut production costs, and thus gain a price edge in global markets.

The problem is that precisely the same process takes place in America. Where central firms aim at a 7 to 8 percent return on sales, American suppliers, who face intense pressures to undercut each other for a contract, have typically had to settle for a 3 to 4 percent return on sales.[38] Thus the capacity to drive the profits of suppliers downward in order to cut production costs exists independently in both countries; it is not an exclusive result of the Japanese pattern of mutual equity holdings.

Many analysts, however, find it tempting to try to prove that there exists in Japan a coordinated, highly integrated set of firms dedicated to the production of inexpensive cars. A bank, an auto firm, and a group of suppliers, for example, could be linked in an effort to wipe out competition by achieving economies of scale among nominally independent parts firms.[39] If this were true, we would expect to find that parts suppliers sold only to a select group of central firms, and that equity, bank, and corporate holdings would determine the specific auto firms that a parts company actually supplied.

The available evidence contradicts this thesis. In a careful study of the Japanese auto industry for the DOT, Gary Saxonhouse showed that many suppliers sold parts to firms outside of their "natural" equity group, and that competing firms took equity holdings in the same suppliers. Equity ownership and the patterns of sourcing for parts appeared to be randomly associated:

> While rival automotive groups tend to use different suppliers, this is far from universally true even for significant components. Moreover, while Daihatsu and Hino are for most purposes considered to be part of the

[37]Based on figures supplied by Martin Anderson, formerly of Transportation Systems Center, U.S. Department of Transportation, Cambridge, Mass.

[38]*Business Week,* September 24, 1979, p. 141.

[39]This suggestion has cropped up in numerous informal conversations with auto analysts and industrialists alike; it also forms the basis for some widespread ideas about Japanese "cheating" in world markets through the organization of their domestic industrial base.

Toyota group, they don't necessarily use the same suppliers as Toyota. Similarly, Fuji Heaby Industries is for most purposes considered part of the Nissan group; but it does not necessarily use the same suppliers as Nissan. . . . Many major and minor assemblers are not members of the assembler's enterprise group.[40]

The fact that central firms can and do buy from various suppliers of their choice argues against the idea that the whole Japanese auto industry is divided into a few selectively managed units dedicated to reducing production costs through scale economies.

Our analysis of the way suppliers in America and Japan contribute to production costs therefore contradicts the expectations of the standardization perspective. Firms in each country show similar patterns of sourcing and cost cutting, and the interlocking equity arrangements in Japan are only ambiguously associated with cost. What, then, distinguishes Japanese suppliers from American ones? The difference seems to lie not in efficiency, but in the way suppliers are organized to serve flexibility in production.

Production Strategies and Suppliers

The major distinction between Japanese suppliers and American parts firms lies in the degree to which they have design and production access to the central firm. Japanese auto companies—which have a much more intimate relationship between the original equipment manufacturers and the suppliers—provide suppliers with a remarkable degree of technical and design assistance. This coordination, which stands in marked contrast to the near hostility that American firms show toward supplier innovations, seems to stem from the requirements of flexible production. Indeed, as we argued at the outset, the close collaboration in Japan and the aloof, cost-oriented interaction in America broadly conform to the way we would expect flexible and standardized parts suppliers to be organized.

In the United States, unchanging parts requirements—a function of standardization and the investment auto firms have made in specialized machines—make both parties unreceptive to new ideas and components. Central firms and suppliers often act independently on a strictly contractual basis, with limited communication. This degree of mutual aloofness is reflected in what one auto analyst has called the "minuscule" staff the U.S. companies devote to supplier relations, and in the

[40]Gary Saxonhouse, *Economic Statistics and Information Concerning the Japanese Auto Industry* (Department of Transportation, Cambridge, Mass., Nov. 10, 1979), p. 5-2.

propensity of central companies to threaten small parts firms through backward integration and competition.[41]

In Japan, communication is far more thorough. A flexible firm needs tight coordination with parts firms for two reasons: to ensure a steady stream of rapidly changing components, and to nurture the generation of new ideas on which auto designs can be built. Several recent studies have confirmed that close supplier coordination does follow in part from the desire to build continuously changing products through "systematic exchanges of technical, economic, and managerial information and services."[42]

Indeed, the supplier patterns in the United States and Japan reinforce market strategies. U.S. aloofness has fostered static product designs and inefficient sourcing because links between parts firms, designers, and production managers do not exist. In contrast, Japanese automakers seem to have "socialized" the costs of flexibility by jointly supporting a staggering array of highly flexible suppliers through joint equity holdings. These holdings reflect not so much cost concerns—although costs are carefully monitored—as the desire to sustain future flexibility through the existence of a host of specialized, receptive parts producers. In turn, the fact that a network of these flexible suppliers exists helps to promote future product changes; the Japanese have the links between suppliers, designers, and production managers in place. They can easily convert production to a new design. And, as an added bonus, this tight coordination also tends to cut costs somewhat by reducing inventory through a "just in time" system, whereby parts enter the factory close to the time when they will be used.[43] Whereas in America supplier relations contribute to a "vicious cycle" of stagnation, in Japan the parts industry has evolved in such a way as to promote a "virtuous cycle" of enhanced flexibility *and* efficiency. In the next section we shall see that the same pattern exists in the way Japanese and American firms make use of labor.

Differences in the Division of Labor

The management of labor in Japan has stimulated great debate in America because Japanese practices appear to offer a way out of the labor-management struggles that are so harmful to costs. In the conventional view, Japanese workers are provided with job security and a "humanized workplace"; in exchange they accept lower wages and are able to produce more goods per unit of time; and because autos are homogeneous products, the wage and productivity advantages enjoyed

[41]Robert Cole, "The Japanese Lesson in Quality," p. 32.
[42]As reproduced in *Iron Age*, January 26, 1981, p. 63.
[43]Cole, "The Japanese Lesson in Quality."

by Japanese firms give them an unbeatable market edge. As we shall see, however, wage rates are increasingly irrelevant to Japanese market advantages, and Japan's productivity cannot be explained as a result of a "happier" work environment.

The first problem is that although several studies have indicated that Japanese wages are much lower than the American norm, no one has yet conclusively determined the extent of this variance. Estimates of the differential range from 67 to 50 percent of the U.S. rate.[44] In part, this reflects the methodological problems in comparing bonuses, pensions, and the like. In one report the Department of Transportation presented a graph suggesting a 50 percent wage differential, but in a footnote it claimed that among central auto firms, rather than suppliers, the difference was in fact 67 percent.[45] Furthermore, at least half of the components in an American car are built by parts vendors in the United States; it is seldom made clear if the cost comparisons reflect the comparatively lower labor costs of producing these parts.

The problem of assessing the degree to which cheaper wages affect the cost advantage that Japanese producers seem to enjoy is important because the higher productivity of Japanese workers appears to be an even greater factor. Japanese wages have been rising at a phenomenal rate, nearly 74 percent between 1975 and 1979 alone, but productivity has been rising nearly as fast, and at double the American growth rate.[46] Average productivity gains in the U.S. auto sector were 2.75 percent in 1975–1979, whereas in Japanese auto firms they were 5.25 percent in the same period.[47] The Japanese cost advantage gained from lower wages therefore appears to be rapidly declining: even if wages were equalized between the United States and Japan, increases in productivity would assure that Japan would still produce cars at a lower cost, other things being equal. All of this suggests that low wage rates alone can provide little insight into the competitive dynamics of the auto industry, or into the comparative importance of productivity.

In the conventional view, Japanese productivity is thought to be affected by the relatively more "humane" and secure nature of Japanese manufacture. While the inherent trend toward standardization produces a similarly routinized and dull workplace in most auto firms, some companies—notably in Japan—have found a way to make work

---

[44]DOT, *The U.S. Automobile Industry 1980*, argued the point ambiguously, stating that where central firms paid about 6 percent of the American wage, suppliers in Japan drove the average wage lower (pp. 40–43). Japanese estimates generally claim a lower differential than do U.S. studies.

[45]*Ibid.*, p. 43.

[46]Mitsubishi Research Institute, *Japanese Auto Industry Employees' Wage Packages and Productivities*, September 1980, pp. 16, 55.

[47]*Ibid.*

more rewarding by rotating people around the assembly line and devolving authority. A recent *Harvard Business Review* article, for instance, commented favorably on the development of "quality of work-life" councils in GM's Tarrytown plant because they rotated people around the assembly line. This reportedly brought people to participate more and to work in a happier environment.[48] It was thought that in emulating the well-publicized quality circles in Japan, a better set of attitudes was being fostered in the workforce, and that this would improve both productivity and quality. Combined with the notion that U.S. companies have neglected capital improvements over the years in their complacency, the conventional wisdom pictures productivity as a problem of managing worker boredom amid efficient mechanization.

The problem with this view is that workplace improvement efforts seem to have had only random and limited success in the United States. Instead, it appears that what clearly affects productivity is the extent to which product change is introduced in plants. For instance, earlier attempts at "humanizing" a highly standardized workplace, as in Lordstown, had failed.[49] But at Tarrytown, where "humanization" seems to have been beneficial, the plant was in the midst of a major product change.[50] Thus it was change of the product, not merely improving worker satisfaction with a dull job, that seems to have promoted greater output and morale. This suggests that, as in the supplier case, the concern with cutting costs cannot alone explain the differences in Japanese and American labor management.

Market Strategies and the Division of Labor

Let us now examine the links between product change on the one hand and worker skill, autonomy, and productivity on the other. In our earlier discussion of standardized and flexible producers, we argued that making quick, pervasive alterations in a car produced greater skill in the workforce. Higher skill levels foster greater ease in shifting production and permit increased confidence in the capacity of the workforce to bring a new product on line smoothly. But gaining this skill and permitting product flexibility means that a worker actually has to use his training in practice. It is here that the quality circles play a key role, because they provide the employee with the ability to actually make independent decisions about production. Because in Japan the workplace is in effect changing as products change, workers can and must learn to trust their own training in building automobiles.

[48]Robert H. Guest, "Quality of Worklife," *Harvard Business Review*, July-August, 1979.
[49]Emma Rothschild, *Paradise Lost* (New York: Random House, 1973).
[50]Guest, "Quality of Worklife," p. 85.

Analysts who accept the standardized picture of the auto industry might argue that any product changes made by flexible firms in Japan are still so modest—a new transmission, engine size, or body design, for instance—that they could not possibly affect labor practices. To see why such a view understates the contribution of seemingly minor changes in production to employee confidence, skill, and hence productivity, we may consider the example of a Japanese quality council reported by Robert Cole at the Toyota Auto Body Company.[51]

In this case, the firm had designed a retractable bumper, which the workers had not produced before. Early in the production process, it became apparent that the output of the bumper was too low. This problem was traced to the length of time it took to inspect the part for defects; the key to raising output was to shorten inspection time. The workers met in a quality circle, and tore apart all the components that went into the bumper assembly. They made a catalog of the possible ways that a bumper could be put together incorrectly, of which six were identified. It was discovered that a measurement of the size of the retractor armature itself would catch all of the six errors: if the retractor was shorter than the norm, two errors would be indicated; if it was longer, the other four problems would be suggested. The circle then instituted a simple measuring operation that speeded output while retaining quality.

The skill and creativity developed in such a seemingly trivial instance severely challenges the conviction that only dramatic change can induce greater skill on the part of workers. In the process of disassembling the bumper, the workers had to learn about a new part, think about the whole assembly operation, and then devise efficient yet effective ways of inspecting the component. Multiplied across the entire factory, and among all possible work groups, this sort of experience would ensure that the level of skill and productivity of the workers would be constantly advancing as the product was modified. Thus a manufacturer seeking continuous product differentiation, as Japanese automakers do, would tend to develop a skilled, dedicated, and highly productive workforce.

Convergent evidence of the relationship between market strategy and productivity is provided by many observers of Japanese industry. Koike has shown that most Japanese firms explicitly try to develop worker skills in order to enhance flexibility and efficiency.[52] Robert Cole has further suggested that quality circles in Japanese auto firms

[51] Robert Cole, *Work Mobility and Participation* (Berkeley: University of California Press, 1979), pp. 150–155.
[52] Kazuo Koike, "Japan's Industrial Relations: Characteristics and Problems," *Japanese Economic Studies*, Fall 1978, pp. 42–90, for a full comparison with the United States.

promote ideas that benefit workers, designers, and hence the entire firm. For example, he found that Toyota's employees offer 17.8 suggestions per employee per year, of which over 90 percent are implemented, whereas GM's employees offered only .84 suggestions per worker per year, of which only 23 percent found actual use. He concluded: "The advent of quality control circles in the last decade and the rapid rise in the number of Japanese employee suggestions are closely linked with the rapid increase in Japanese auto quality and productivity."[53] These studies confirm that flexibility, productivity, and worker skill go hand and hand in Japan.

As in the supplier case, then, labor practices show how market strategies are translated into institutions that reinforce existing procedures and attitudes toward production. The deskilling of American workers and the highly routinized, mechanized character of the U.S. factory reinforce standardization by making change costly and difficult. Specialized machines have to be changed; and workers must be provided with new skills and autonomy, which they may even resent as intrusions on their workplace prerogatives. A cycle of stagnation is induced.

In Japan, worker skill and autonomy rise with product shifts, and lead to greater productivity. Efficiency *and* flexibility are simultaneously enhanced; a cycle of increasing capacity to make shifts is induced. If we add to this picture the analysis of the supplier firms, we can see how deeply market strategies and institutions tend to become attuned to a particular style of production.

This leads to an obvious question: if a firm wanted to change its strategy, what would constrain or enhance the transformation of production? Keeping the models of Japanese-style flexible production and American standardized manufacture in mind, let us now consider how U.S. automakers might avoid the difficult problems that standardization entails.

THE POLITICAL COSTS OF STANDARDIZATION

Because automobile production affects a large part of any nation's industrial base, auto industry problems necessarily become political problems as well. We will therefore round out our understanding of the Japanese and American methods of auto manufacture by considering how government is brought to interact with the industry in each country. We will suggest that if standardization is dangerous to the firms who seek it, it also poses grave problems for policy-makers. And

[53]Cole, "The Japanese Lesson in Quality." p. 38.

if America is to circumvent the negative effects of standardized production through more flexible strategies, government must play an explicit role in reshaping the auto sector.

As we suggested at the beginning, standardized production leads to the ability to make one product, and only one product, at a low cost. Firms seeking this strategy therefore gamble that the definition of their product, and also market conditions and tastes, will remain fixed over time.

In the contemporary auto industry, this seems to be a very poor bet. American firms believe that when they have adjusted tooling and worker training toward small-car manufacture, they will once again be able to standardize production. They hope that a set of basic designs like the X or J car types and a small range of engines will provide adequate market appeal for years to come. But there is a large possibility that even as U.S. firms seek to define a new small standard design, foreign car companies, including both the Japanese and certain European firms, will break up the auto market through continuous product differentiation. Furthermore, outside pressures—such as oil changes, raw material availability, and social concerns about safety or pollution— may also compel product adjustment. Market *uncertainty* seems likely to increase in the future; if this is so, flexibly organized firms will be in a much stronger market position than more standardized companies. Indeed, American companies may well create a chronic readjustment problem by trying to find a new standard product design where none can survive.

If this scenario suggests an uncertain future for U.S. firms, it also involves government in very difficult political choices. A standardized auto sector, indeed, creates a policy trap for the domestic government. Any government has a broader scope of concerns than the survival of the auto industry. It may, for instance, seek to preserve an international free trade regime, fight inflation with tight fiscal policies, or try to clean up the environment. But given the size of the auto sector, domestic and international policies inevitably affect the market for autos. Free trade can promote imports of new car designs that destabilize the standardized market; high interest rates may cut so deeply into car sales that even limited adjustment investments have to be curtailed; and social concerns may require product modifications that domestic firms cannot easily make, leading to political controversy or increased imports by producers that *can* shift designs.

These destabilizing initiatives, when supplemented by the normal competitive pressures in the auto market, put enormous pressure on a firm. In time, the rigidity of the firm inhibits its capacity to adjust its products. When failures to adjust threaten the survival of the auto sector, government will be drawn into assisting the firm in some way, as the Chrysler case and recent U.S. trade negotiations with Japan suggest. Political initiatives taken for reasons unrelated to the auto sector may compel future government intervention in the industry.

In this set of circumstances, the government risks abandoning its larger political agenda or sacrificing the health of a large chunk of the domestic economy. It can protect the firms only by abandoning long-cherished policies such as free trade, nonintervention, or inflation; it can pursue international, economic, or social concerns only at the cost of the auto firms. With one set of policies the state props up the standardized firm, and with another it brings it close to ruin.

There are grave institutional costs in this dilemma. If the government is compelled to act contrary to long-cherished notions about free trade or economic equity in order to support the auto firms, it loses prestige and legitimacy at home and abroad. If the auto firms retain their standardized character and the government fights to stabilize their markets, the probability of recurring crisis is increased. Thus the painful interventions forced on the government, often after a debilitating domestic struggle, appear to serve no end. Consequently, the government becomes perceived as an ineffective industrial force even as it is drawn to take action on behalf of its domestic firms. This weakening of the government's power to act at a time when the necessity for action is increasing means that government loses control over the sort of events it must respond to. Policy loses rational, effective design.

At the core of this trap is the fact that standardized firms cannot adjust rapidly, or at all, to market change; the government is thus forced into trying to shield them from the costs of their own rigidity. Obviously, there are great advantages to helping automakers become more flexible. It is here that we can begin to consider, briefly, how governments in Japan and America have in the past affected industrial outcomes. By seeing how prior political decisions affect industrial strategy, we can clarify what future policy might entail. It is in the politics surrounding the economic environment of automobile competition that workers, managers, designers, and suppliers can come to realize potential market possibilities.

Government and Industry in Japan and the United States

Let us consider first the American case. The U.S. government has affected the degree of standardization in the auto industry at two levels. In terms of *policy* (explicitly government decisions that affect production), the American government has either taken no action that would lead to a reappraisal of production techniques by domestic firms, or it has acted as if standardization were the only feasible strategy. In more subtle terms, in the *background politics* of labor relations, financial structure, and other rules-of-the-game decisions, American politics has further strengthened standardization trends by closing off avenues through which alternative market strategies might develop.

In the first decades of the U.S. auto industry, it was far from certain that American companies would become archetypical standardized producers. Indeed, in the 1920s, as GM challenged Ford for the market lead, American firms practiced an explicit policy of model differentiation and flexibility. To compete with Ford's standardized Model T, GM tried to build a car for every price and need.[54] So successful was the challenge that even Ford, which had championed standardization, finally had to bring out its own new model, but only after a costly factory shutdown. As GM Chairman Sloan noted of the incident, Henry Ford "had failed to master change."[55] Taking this lesson to heart, U.S. automakers introduced numerous new products, designs, and innovations.

But in the 1930s the industry experienced a set of unfortunate product designs that led it toward a fear of continued flexibility. One crucial instance was when GM had a technical failure with its experimental air-cooled engine that it called the copper-cooled engine. Sloan drew from this experience the maxim that designs should "avoid the risks of untried experiments."[56] Because GM had established itself as the industry leader by the 1930s in an increasingly oligopolistic market shared by Ford and Chrysler, its policies were rapidly adopted by its competitors. Thus, the auto industry began to take on its present standardized character. But what accounted for the industrial structure that permitted GM's recalcitrant attitude toward change to become established industrial practice? And why could standardization persevere for so long in the United States, given the omnipresent possibilities for market uncertainty?

It is here that government action, and inaction, played a key role. Throughout the prewar and postwar periods, the U.S. government maintained an essentially aloof posture toward the auto sector. Antitrust regulations, except in a few highly visible instances, were rarely enforced.[57] Later, when social concerns over safety and pollution led to increased regulation, the government's policies in fact *depended* on the continued success of the auto firms—and therefore on the success of standardization. Indeed, the specific form that the regulations took—

---

[54]William Abernathy, *The Productivity Dilemma* (Baltimore, Md.: Johns Hopkins University Press, 1978). pp. 34–35.

[55]*Ibid.*, p. 34.

[56]*Ibid.*, p. 35.

[57]See the discussion in White, *The Automobile Industry since 1945*, regarding the tentative, if often rhetorically bold, application of antitrust laws.

coercion of producers rather than consumers—could be justified only on the grounds that forcing firms to add pollution devices or to increase fuel efficiency involved only minor costs.[58] And finally, when economic and oil crises, together with changing tastes, completely undercut American auto firms in the late 1970s, government interventions such as the Chrysler bailout were undertaken in the belief that increased mechanization, UAW wage compromises, and lower costs— the hallmarks of standardized production strategies—were essential.[59] At no point, then, did *policies* reflect the possibility that standardization might not be the best market strategy; to the extent that the U.S. government considered strategy at all, it simply adopted the analyses of the domestic firms.[60]

At the same time, the background politics of the auto sector were almost completely devoid of pressures that could have led to new production strategies. Postwar American dominance in global markets, and the development of an oil industry that kept gasoline costs low, created a distinct large-car market in the United States, in which American auto firms could operate free from foreign competition. Unions were brought to accept standardization as a market objective; this could occur because they lacked a comprehensive political vision and apparently had no political vehicles, such as parties, with which to express one.[61] And finance tended to press for short-term market gains, rather

[58]There are few systematic accounts of what regulators had in mind when they designed producer-coercive laws to promote social objectives, though it does seem clear that American politics tends to apply laws that affect the least number of people in the most indirect way. Thus regulation depended on the strength of the standardized firms, so that the companies could be used in a sense as tax collectors for the cost of the environmental or safety programs, recouping in price what they had paid. But if the companies staggered, as they did, and the economy was affected as a result, regulations became a less indirect means of changing the activities of the populace and a more directly felt cost—hence the current scramble to "deregulate" the industry. For an account of the tendency in U.S. politics to adopt broad policies that affect small minorities directly, see Theodore Lowi, "American Business and Public Policy," Case Studies, *World Politics* 16 (July 1964).

[59]See the testimony and views of congressmen and industrialists in the Chrysler Loan Board Guarantee Hearings, cited in note 3 above.

[60]In fact, some congressmen did express misgivings about the Chrysler plan, but they nearly always argued from the point of view of more effective standardization; that is, they chastised the firm's management and the UAW for not proceeding with full mechanization and rationalization.

[61]This argument is necessarily speculative, and builds on the work of American political scientists regarding the nature of participation, parties, and classes in American politics since 1896. It has been convincingly argued by Burnham, for instance, that after the Republican triumph in 1896, electoral reforms so limited participatory and organizational opportunities in America that the whole underclass effectively had no voice in politics. The result has been, among workers, a very personalized view of market failure, rather than the development of a comprehensive ideology; indeed, perhaps the last real ideological challenge to the liberal, individualistic credo that has dominated American

than long-term analyses and strategies. In short, the overall effect of American international and domestic background politics was to make it possible for early standardization attempts to flourish, and to permit the standardized industry to retain its character once it was established.

A very different political process developed in Japan. In terms of *policies*, the Japanese government, working through MITI, had from the start of the postwar period expressed an explicit concern with the long-term market strategy that auto firms should follow. But this is not to say that the government knew best, or even that it promoted appropriate strategies. Indeed, in a well-documented set of instances in the 1960s, MITI continually pressed for the consolidation of domestic auto companies into two or three groups dedicated to high-volume mass production on the American model.[62] But this step toward standardized high-volume production was forestalled by pressure from recalcitrant firms, particularly smaller companies, and by the apparent success of independent firms in finding defensive financial and market positions. Moreover, profitable and growing firms such as Suzuki and Honda, which entered the auto market precisely as MITI pressed for rationalization, cut into the apparent rationale of the standardization effort. Thus, although certain firms such as Prince and Nissan did merge, and although Toyota and Nissan built cars at world-leading volumes (the Corolla and Bluebird models, respectively), the smaller companies continued to create specialized niches in the auto market.[63] The effect of policy was not to determine the industry's character. MITI did not dictate to the auto firms or define a strategy for them, but instead brought their attention to the need for a rationale behind the market strategies they followed.

These policies were supplemented by *background politics* that furthered the development of alternative market strategies, and of flexible production. First, the fact that Japanese auto producers could form close links with banks, suppliers, and politicians permitted them to resist the dominance of other companies or even government policy itself. Indeed, MITI's failure to rebuild the auto industry along standardized lines was partly a result of the internal struggles waged by

---

thought was the Populist movement in the late nineteenth century. See the following articles in *American Political Science Review* 68 (1974): W. B. Burnham, "Theory and Voting Research," pp. 1002–1023; Gerrold Rusk, "Comment: The American Electoral Universe, Speculation and Evidence," pp. 1028–1049; Phillip Converse, "Comment on Burnham's Theory and Voting Research," pp. 1024–1027; and W. D. Burnham, "Rejoinder," pp. 1050–1057.

[62]The best account of the political battles surrounding rationalization is found in William Duncan, *U.S.–Japan Automobile Diplomacy* (Cambridge, Mass.: Ballinger, 1973), pp. 83–100.

[63]*Ibid.*

banks, Liberal Democratic Party members, and firms seeking to preserve market autonomy.[64] Thus, the fact that connections between industrial actors and government provided firms with allies in industrial
disputes that were unavailable in America made new market strategies
more likely to emerge.

Second, many of the prerequisites of flexible production—notably
employee security, worker autonomy, and cooperation within and between firms—were explicitly articulated, if not sponsored, by the government. Japanese "cooperation" is not, then, an accidental development, or a function of culture, but a product of political decisions.
There was, for example, the "doubling of incomes" policy for the decade of the 1960s, which mapped out an industrial bargain between
worker and management, paving the way for flexible factory organization.[65] Another example occurred in the 1974-1975 recession, when
the government subsidized ailing auto firms so that they would not lay
off workers and hence damage the trust and investment in skill they
had developed in the workforce.[66] Whereas in America background
politics made standardization likely, in Japan they appear to have enhanced the potential for flexibility.

This very brief survey of government and industry interaction in the
United States and Japan cannot, of course, do justice to the complexity
of events in each country. But if we look broadly at politics, and hold in
mind the pictures of Japanese and U.S. production we developed
above, even a quick analysis will suggest the extent to which political
decisions intertwine with industrial strategies. The connection appears
to be quite close. If the results of standardization are severe in nations
like America, then politics is likely to be a key factor in determining
whether a new future is possible, because government decisions provide the background for and frame the consensual views in which
industrial strategies are shaped.

To see how this is so, let us reconsider American auto production in
the contemporary period. As we shall see, although industry, labor,
and government alike persist in thinking that standardization is the
only market option available, their own experiences have shown that a
profound transformation of production is feasible. Whether people are
able to interpret these experiences as pointing to the possibility of
flexible production depends on whether they have learned to see pro-

[64]Duncan, *U.S.–Japan Automobile Diplomacy.*

[65]This observation, like the earlier comments about American background politics, is
speculative, but it does seem clear that policies like the "doubling of incomes" program
launched by Kishi in 1960 contributed to the Japanese laborer's sense that industrial
strength would result in personal advantage. See Robert Cole, *Work Mobility and Participation*, final chapter.

[66]*Ibid.*, p. 262.

duction techniques in terms of choices. Political decisions, in turn, make this outcome more or less likely.

The Japanization of American Production?

The current auto crisis has forced U.S. firms to undertake a massive change from large to small cars. Although this move is conceived throughout the industry as a change from one standard design to another, it has nonetheless provoked the same kinds of supplier and labor relations that the desire for flexible products has led to in Japan. In a curious way, then, contemporary American production confirms our notion of how change affects the way manufacture is organized, and points to the potential for dramatic modifications of the U.S. automobile industry.

Consider first the supplier sector in the United States. Current trade journals have sensed that with product change there has come a revolution in the way parts firms interact with the major auto companies. Whereas for years GM, Ford, and Chrysler spurned technical contacts with suppliers, preferring to deal only on a price basis, they now seek not only cheap parts but research, development, and new ideas from their suppliers as well. Vincent Mankowsky, a vice-president of a major parts company, explained in January 1981 how product change prompted new relations between suppliers and central firms:

> Up until the last year and a half it was sometimes difficult for us to get the automobile companies to look at some new ideas. . . . But with the impact of Japanese imports we have found that people in the automotive industry have become a lot more open to our suggestions. The big change has been in the receptivity by automotive people to ideas that press manufacturers have been talking about for years. For example, we had talked to automobile representatives in the past about using large transfer presses to produce panels but were never able to develop any interest because nobody wanted to think that way. Today you can get people to listen and they are interested in what you have to say.[67]

And GM's purchasing agent noted in late 1979, "We're finding out more and more that we don't have all the ideas"—an admission, *Business Week* suggested, that would have been "anathema" but two years earlier in Detroit.[68]

The American companies' product change has also brought a new

---

[67]Mankowsky, quoted in "Detroit Turns to Suppliers for Help," *Iron Age,* January 26, 1981, p. 63.
[68]*Business Week,* September 24, 1979, p. 140.

need to coordinate and share technology with suppliers. Another parts firm manager, Owen Viergutz, has suggested that the current American product transition poses such difficult technical problems that there may be a permanent transformation of supplier and central firm interaction:

> From our experience, a lot of materials technology that is being applied to the industry is coming from outside the industry itself. A lot of basic research and some of the applied research is being done by the automobile manufacturer, but (when) it comes down to making a cross member for the k car, that tends to be done by the supplier. This work by the supplier seems to be on the increase because the automobile firms are trying to introduce technology that didn't exist or wasn't being applied five years ago. . . . We see the firms decentralizing. Companies are finding it increasingly necessary to look outside for new technology, for [except for GM] it is difficult for an automobile manufacturer to compete in all of the technology areas that are required on today's cars.[69]

This perception is echoed by a host of auto suppliers, as *Iron Age* indicated in a special article which reported that companies involved in broaching, machine tools, furnace design, and computers had each experienced unique, in-plant access to the automobile firms.[70]

In the wake of product change, the supplier relations evident in Japan are now being fostered in the United States. This suggests the connection between strategy and structure. If products are changed frequently, as in Japan, the suppliers will be brought more intimately into the production and design of automobiles.

A parallel analysis can be drawn of contemporary U.S. labor organization. As U.S. firms scale down and redesign their products, they are relying on workers to an increasing degree. As the *Wall Street Journal* observed, auto firms are "even soliciting ideas from a previously little used source: [their] own blue collar workers." GM's workers have noticed the difference; as one said, "The last time we got new equipment we didn't see it until they asked us to run it."[71] Nor are these new manager-worker liaisons merely cosmetic. In an instance akin to the Toyota Auto Body example given earlier, GM asked workers to figure out how to increase the output of brake assembly lines, and the workers found methods to build 425 units per hour where they could make but 333 before.[72]

---

[69]Viergutz, quoted in "Detroit Turns to Suppliers for Help," *Iron Age*, January 26, 1981, p. 67.
[70]*Ibid.*
[71]*Wall Street Journal*, February 3, 1981, p. 19.
[72]*Ibid.*

Again, as in the supplier case, product change has induced within the American production system some of the labor behavior we identified in Japan. Changes in products are generating unprecedented collaboration between management and labor and profound modifications of established practices. Labor techniques appropriate for standardization are giving way to those associated with flexible production. Where analysts see only the possibility for continued standardization, and the consequently debilitating labor, design, and innovation policies, American industry itself has shown that the potential for change is far greater than previously thought. American firms, then, which have been wedded to standardization for several decades, could be the source of considerable optimism regarding the future course of the industry. But will industrialists, labor leaders, or policy-makers view these developments in this light? The answer, we suggest, will depend in part on the possibility of the American government sponsoring a new debate about automobile production.

Policies for Promoting Flexibility

Politics will help determine whether recent trends toward flexible production in America will bear fruit, or lead instead to a new era of standardization, for two reasons. First, the participants in the auto industry—labor, management, financiers, suppliers, and the like—may be unable to see alternatives to the logic of standardized production, even though their own actions indicate that other production systems are possible. As we argued at the outset, and showed in the supplier and labor studies, an industry's style of production induces self-reinforcing relations between participants in the production process. Thus an industrial crisis may in fact deepen commitments to old patterns of production, because groups with a stake in the auto industry may become defensive and seek to protect the practices they know rather than face an uncertain future. Given the paucity of opportunity for alternative production experiences, and the fear of change that a crisis can induce in industrial actors, the government becomes the only force capable of encouraging a far-reaching debate on market and production alternatives.

Second, some of the circumstances that constitute a market are shaped by government; and so when standardized firms face market challenges, they seek to bring policies to bear on their dilemmas. If the government in fact restructures trade for them and bears the cost of adjustment, then firms will be encouraged to retain their standardization strategies. In that case, firms experimenting with flexible production arrangements, and workers who sense new opportunites for developing their skill, will not develop their experiences further; and the trends toward collaboration between management and the shop floor will be discounted as only transitory, affording no hope for permanent changes. Consequently, the political resources that firms can muster to protect their market strategies will affect the subsequent choices they make about manufacture and change.

The American government still possesses enormous international and domestic power. If it decided to use that power to protect the market positions of its standardized firms, it could probably succeed, though at severe political and economic cost. Indeed, as Daniel Yergin has noted, ideas about foreign "cheating" have been flourishing recently as part of an effort to provide a rationale for erecting new trade barriers against Japan.[73] Whereas a less powerful country might find standardization unfeasible on its face, then, the American government has the resources, and seems to be building the will, to restructure a host of domestic and international conditions in the direction sought by ailing standardized firms. If it does in fact implement policies of this sort, an opportunity for developing a less vulnerable industrial structure, one with more flexibility, will be lost. The consequences in the long run are incalculable, but by any estimate they would be severe, and would include trade wars, chronic unemployment, and constant but ineffective government intervention.

In the current U.S. political climate, however, a number of policies that could positively affect industrial change simply have no chance of implementation. Ironically, much of the skepticism that Americans express about the role government could take in industrial adjustment stems precisely from disappointment over past government failures at propping up standardized industries. But if the sources of government inaction are ironic, they are also real: policies such as sponsoring pilot plants on flexible lines, giving subsidies to new firms pursuing flexible strategies, and generating an explicit commitment to industrial change are officially unthinkable in contemporary America. Thus potential policies must be weighed against the likelihood of their enactment. What is possible in American politics that could help bring about a flexible auto industry?

To begin with, the government needs to escape dependence on domestic firms for its market perspectives. American policy, we have seen, has taken auto company market analyses as the last word on production possibilities, and has therefore tailored regulation, emergency subsidies, and its general attitude toward the auto sector to fit the sup-

[73]Daniel Yergin, "Sick Economy, Trade War Talk," *Boston Sunday Globe*, February 28, 1982, pp. A33–A34.

posed inevitability of standardization. Hence it has echoed the views of industrial actors that have been shaped, and perhaps fixed, by years of experience with only one form of production.

But companies are often mistaken in their assessments of the markets and production imperatives they face. If there are alternatives to standardization in the auto sector, the government needs to be able to engage the industry in a discussion about the feasibility of achieving them. This capacity is a matter of sound management and institutional preservation, if nothing else. Unless the U.S. government is prepared to pay an increasingly high economic and political price to defend its domestic auto firms' standardization strategies, it has everything to gain and nothing to lose from considering all possible ways of structuring the industry. Government ability to look critically at the market choices made by firms might also begin to stimulate labor, management, and suppliers to reassess established practices, as has been the case in Japan.

To foster a debate about potential changes in production, the government needs to be able to envision and set forth the alternatives. If a consensus emerged that sought a new kind of production process, then a host of policies might follow. These could include opening up new markets, encouraging suppliers to share technology and ideas in order to foster innovation, decentralizing production, and fostering greater labor skill, autonomy, and freedom in production. But these policies depend on the ability of the government to form an independent market vision. Without this capacity, the government can only react to the market assessments of the auto firms, and tragically try to assist adjustment with the same set of strategies that brought about the industrial crisis in the first place.

The current world auto market is extremely volatile. It is impossible to predict with confidence that American standardization will continue to decline while Japanese-style flexibility exerts an increasingly powerful influence on the auto market. But such an outcome is a real possibility. If recent trends in market fragmentation and uncertainty prevail, ensuring product flexibility is likely to become the most crucial factor in auto production, surpassing the traditional factor of cost. Accordingly, to gain a deeper understanding of the different possibilities for auto production, we need more research on the way production changes affect labor, suppliers, and company organization. Such research might make it possible to see an alternative course of action over which firms and policy-makers alike could exercise choice.

CHAPTER EIGHT

Italian Small Business Development: Lessons for U.S. Industrial Policy

MICHAEL J. PIORE AND
CHARLES F. SABEL

The previous chapter contrasted two strategies, standardization and special-ization, that are emerging in a particular industry, and suggested that special-ization is more likely to succeed in the long run. This chapter makes a similar argument with respect to the economic success of particular national economies. It examines the economic resurgence of Italy since the late 1970s and finds its source in a group of small-scale producers located in the center and northeast of the country. The authors examine the origins and successes of these small firms and connect them to problems in the organization of assembly-line work and to growth of markets for specialty products.

They argue that the tendencies which have favored Italian small-scale produc-tion in recent years reflect longer-run shifts in the market structures and under-lying technological development of advanced industrial societies. These shifts imply that among established industrial powers, the ones that will do best are those which are best able to shift production rapidly from one specialty product to another. To the extent that this is so, the authors contend, countries, such as Italy, which have long traditions of specialty production may have new competi-tive advantages.

Seen from this perspective, the authors conclude, U.S. industrial policy is courting disaster. Just as the strategy of mass production has become extremely risky, the action and inaction of the American government are encouraging industry to defend the existing model of industrial organization and to abandon those areas of the country, such as New England, whose social and industrial structure favors the emergence of flexible specialization along Italian lines.

This essay is published by arrangement with *Inc.*, Boston.

The performance of the Italian economy, like many other recent phenomena, has confounded the expectations of conventional economic analysis. Between 1979 and 1981, Italy registered a higher rate of economic growth than any of its partners in the European Common Market; it displayed the most rapid growth in overall productivity, particularly in the manufacturing sector, and its balance of payments was at least as favorable as any in the Common Market. It did this despite formidable obstacles: an inflation rate of 20 percent a year (twice as high as that of the United States, and almost three times that of Western Germany, one of its major continental competitors); a total dependence on imported oil, and a national wage structure tied to an inflation escalator in a complex way that some analysts believe actually drives up wages faster than the price inflation for which it is supposed to compensate. The wage escalator is a product of one of the strongest trade-union organizations in modern history, as are a whole series of other restrictions on managerial freedom that one might have supposed would effectively stifle national economic growth and handicap Italian manufacturers in international competition.

But ultimately, the political and economic organization of the left, the trade unions, and the Italian Communist Party (PCI), is a key to explaining the recent evolution of the Italian economy. Much of this explanation is paradoxical in the light of conventional thinking about economic development and trade-union activity, particularly in the United States. For that very reason, it contains important lessons for us: lessons for American economists, who have conspicuously failed to forecast economic events and to diagnose and prescribe for the nation's economic ills; and also lessons for American trade unions which have been steadily losing ground in those sectors of the economy over which they once had mastery, and which now find themselves on the defensive in the political realm as well.

The center of the new wave of Italian growth is a vast network of very small enterprises spread through the villages and small cities of central and Northeast Italy, in and around Bologna, Florence, Ancona, and Venice. The Italians themselves have begun to call this area the "third Italy," to distinguish it from the older industrial triangle (defined by Milan, Turin, and Genoa) and the less developed South.[1] These little shops range across the entire spectrum of the modern industrial structure, from shoes, ceramics, textiles, and garments on one side to motorcycles, agricultural equipment, automotive parts, and machine tools on the other. The firms perform an enormous variety of

[1]Arnaldo Bagnasco, *Tre Italie: La problematica territoriale dello sviluppo italiano* (Bologna: Il Mulino, 1977).

the operations associated with mass production, excluding only the kind of final assembly involved in the automobile production line. The average size of the units varies from industry to industry, but it is generally extremely small: shops of ten workers or less are not unusual.

In 1980 and 1981, we visited a number of these small shops and interviewed proprietors, workers, and trade-union officials about the history of their enterprises and their current operations. They are virtually all family firms, and many in fact employ only family members. Workers in the shops say they use artisans' methods rather than industrial techniques of production.[2] But although many of these enterprises depend in some ways on the traditional Italian family structure, and are based on traditions of small craftsmanship, their organization does not correspond to the popular image of a family of artisans at work.

Some of the small plants are simply sweatshops, where exploitation of previously unemployed or underemployed workers compensates for primitive methods of production. But there is also a significant group of firms that belong to the most sophisticated and technologically advanced sectors of the industries in which they operate. Most of the shops we visited were of this type. They work with machinery adapted to their unusual size and structure, and they yield some of the highest earnings in Italy today.

The machine-tool shops we visited near Bologna are clear examples of this second, more modern, type of firm. Here the most advanced factories have been moved out of the household into industrial parks built by the city. Some of these parks have over 300 little shops of ten to fifteen people. The equipment is modern and expensive: numerically controlled machines are increasingly common even in the smallest shops. The layout and flow of work are fully rationalized and industrial. There are also small shops in garages in residential neighborhoods; though definitely more crowded than those quartered in the industrial parks, they have modern components and plans for further modernization.

Even in a poorer and more backward area of small industry like the Adriatic province of the Marche, we saw obvious signs of technical and organizational sophistication.[3] The typical factory in the Marche pro-

[2]These and subsequent observations on Emilia-Romagna are based on plant visits in the spring of 1980 and 1981. Earlier studies of this area include Federazione Lavoratori Metalmeccanici, Sindacato Provinciale di Bologna, *Ristrutturazione e organizzazione del lavoro: Inchiesta nelle fabbriche metalmeccaniche della provincia di Bologna*, Ufficio Sindacale (Bologna, 1975); Federazione Lavoratori Metalmeccanici, Sindacato Provinciale di Bologna, *Analisi del decentramento produttivo*, Ufficio Sindacale (Bologna, 1977); and Vittorio Capecchi and Enrico Pugliese, "Due città a confronto: Bologna e Napoli," *Inchiesta* 8 (Sept.–Dec. 1978), pp. 3–54.

[3]The following is based on plant visits in February 1980. For an earlier study, see U. Ascoli and A. Trento, "Sviluppo industriale e flessibita della forza-lavoro: Il settore calzaturiero," *Inchiesta* 5 (Oct.–Dec. 1975), pp. 23–24.

duces shoes for the luxury market in Italy and abroad. It is housed in the ground floor of a building, usually constructed within the last five years. Above the factory are two or three floors of apartments for the several households of the extended family that owns the factory. The workrooms are clean and spacious. A number of hand operations are interspersed with the mechanized ones. The machinery, however, is fully modern in technology and design; sometimes it is exactly the same as that found in a modern factory, sometimes a reduced version of a larger machine. The work is laid out rationally: the workpieces flow along miniature conveyors, whose twists and turns create the impression of a factory in a doll house. Of course, not all the factories we visted in the Marche look like this. In a great many, production is still centered in the garage, and the stitching and finishing operations overflow into the dining room next door. But the tendency is toward the other form of organization. The miniature conveyors are everywhere—all factories seem to have some of the new pieces of equipment—and the announced ambition of most families is to build their own apartment-factory complex.

In all of these industries, the people work very hard. Children start to work young and are expected to work summers and after school. But the industrial sector no longer survives primarily through the exploitation of family members. The pace of work, judged by comparison with contemporary American factories producing comparable products, appears to be steady and deliberate but slow. In the shoe factories, all work stops at noon, when the workers go upstairs to their apartments for lunch. The machine-tool shops in the industrial parks often have separate lunchrooms, as well as locker rooms and washrooms. In some cases, a large industrial park is served by a collective cafeteria. People also live well: they have expensive cars—a real luxury when one simply walks downstairs to work—and sometimes seaside condominiums. They are well traveled and frequently visit the major cities of Italy, Germany, Great Britain, and France, partly for business but also for pleasure.

Two Views of Italian Decentralization

Where do these small businesses come from? How do they manage to survive?

The proximate cause of current developments was the extreme rigidity of employment and work conditions that workers had imposed on larger enterprises in the late 1960s and early 1970s. In that period, the masses of unskilled workers—drawn from firms and artisans' shops into the large Northern factories during the first economic miracle— found that a booming economy, tight labor markets, and the weakening political authority of the ruling Christian Democrats allowed them to seriously challenge, for the first time since the late 1940s, management's unilateral control over the work process. Where union organizations already existed, they were dramatically strengthened; where none existed, new ones grew up almost overnight. Generally, the new institutions grew out of and were reinforced by informal groups of workers that coalesced on the shop floor. These organizations (formal and informal but eventually backed by national legislation) made it extremely difficult to lay off or discharge workers, either for economic or for disciplinary reasons. They also exerted a degree of control over work practices and plant operations that management found (psychologically if not always technically) to be extemely restrictive. Of these restrictions, the most burdensome was felt to be the unions' capacity to limit, through plant-level bargaining, the pace of assembly-line work and the percentage of time on the job spent actually working.

At the same time, partly as a result of labor's political power but also because the Italian state found it convenient to raise revenues for many purposes through social welfare taxes, employers were forced to pay what amounts to a head tax on every employed worker: extensive social security taxes and other fringe benefits, which in Italy now amount to 49 percent of wages (compared to 26 percent in the United States and 39 percent in Germany).

The massive shift of production to small shops in the early 1970s was a response to these developments. To escape the new shop-floor restrictions, large firms began to subcontract extensively to smaller and smaller units of production. The smaller units were more economical because they escaped union organization. They were able to discharge workers when demand dropped off, and they were much freer to organize work in their own way. In addition, they escaped the union-imposed fringe benefits, and often evaded state taxes and fringe benefits as well. In the beginning, wages were also below union scale, reducing costs still further. At that time, decentralized production was less efficient in a fundamental technical sense: given comparable wages and fringe-benefits, and without the restrictions on employee discharge and work practices, the small firms would not have been able to compete. If the organized industrial sector and legislative standards could be said to define the social norm, decentralization represented a new form of exploitation.

This set of developments was the basis for the interpretation of decentralization which, with different political accents, has dominated discussions of Italian industrial structure among trade unionists and industrialists from the mid-1970s almost to the present. One presupposition of this view is that the future of manufacturing in Italy, as elsewhere in the advanced industrial countries, lies in the giant, centralized factory with its economies of scale and standard products. A second assumption is that the unions' restrictive practices in the large Northern factories (though justifiable in the trade union view as a response to management's unilateral powers) present an unnatural obstacle to efficient organization.

Decentralization, in this view, is part of management's bargaining strategy for re-establishing effective control over manufacturing plants. The threat is straightforward: unless the unions relax their grip in the main plants, they will see one phase of production after another shifted to the artisan sector—or, when economies of scale make that impossible, to subsidiaries abroad. Management and labor have not disagreed over the question of whether production ought to be eventually recentralized; both have agreed that it should be. Their dispute concerns which particular restrictions to count as inherently inefficient.

This interpretation worked best as an explanation for the spread of sweat shops and homework, the practices that most openly violated all the rules imposed on the large firms.[4] But when linked to theories of industrial dualism, it could be extended to explain at least part of the success of the more modern small firms as well.

In a world dominated, as this view supposes, by standard products sold in a mass market, it pays to invest in the highly specialized capital equipment involved in deskilled jobs and automatic (or automated) manufacturing. But in such a world, there are peaks in the demand for any one product; and because these peaks are by definition short-lived, it is senseless to make a long-term investment in highly specific equipment to satisfy them. For this demand, it is economical to use a much more flexible labor force and less specialized, more versatile tools that can be transferred to other uses when the demand for any given product drops. The production of specialty items for which demand is limited also requires a more versatile labor force, and flexible tools and

[4]Accordingly, analysis of decentralization in the earlier 1970s focused on evasion of contractual and legislative controls, the use of antiquated machinery, and more generally the retrograde character of small-scale production. See, for example, Luigi Frey, "Il lavoro a domicilio in Lombardia," in Paolo Leon and Marco Marocchi, eds., *Sviluppo economico italiano e forza-lavoro* (Venice: Marsilio, 1973), pp. 197–216; and P. David and E. Pottario, "Retroterra rurale e condizione operaia femminile: Il settore della maglieria," *Inchiesta* 5 (Oct.–Dec. 1975), pp. 9–22. For a summary of this early literature see Renata Livraghi, "Le ricerche sul decentramento producttivo," *Quaderni Rassegna Sindacale* 15 (Jan.–Apr. 1977), pp. 234–239.

equipment. In these kinds of production, the economies of scale and conglomeration are substantially smaller: in some cases, in fact, scale and conglomeration are a real handicap to firms that must continuously adapt to shifting markets and product designs. In addition, the more unstable the world economy, the more room there will be for specialty producers, since large firms will be less willing to invest in products and production facilities that might be rendered unattractive because of changes in raw materials prices, interest rates, and so on.[5] One way of understanding Italian developments since 1969, therefore, is to say that the small-scale sector in Italy has prospered by capturing, first in their own domestic market and then abroad, a growing segment of industrial demand that has been artificially enlarged by political disturbances such as the oil shocks.

There is certainly something to be said for this view. It is true that decentralization was and remains part of a larger bargaining strategy, and that the small firms have prospered as subcontractors, filling in the gaps in the production strategy of the parent firms. Nonetheless, this first interpretation slights three increasingly significant developments of the small sector, developments that can be combined with experiences in other countries to produce a wholly different understanding of the transformation of Italian industry.

The first development has to do with the organization of production. People began to develop manufacturing techniques that have made the small shops increasingly efficient. Machinery has been adapted to the small productive units. Designers have begun to specialize in solving production problems for these very small enterprises, and equipment manufacturers (themselves small operations) have begun to concentrate on providing the instruments required for small-scale production. In some cases, the placement of large machines on the factory floor is simply changed to fit the available space, or the larger equipment is miniaturized. In other cases, however, artisan-like techniques of smelting, enameling, weaving, cutting, or casting metal are designed into new machines, some of which are controlled by sophisticated microprocessors. At the same time, large enterprises have started to use sophisticated data processing techniques to reduce the cost of passing production back and forth between the mother firm and its small satellites. Together these advances have lead to a rapid increase in the productivity of the small enterprises, and have also reduced the element of exploitation—understood as conditions of employment below the

[5]Suzanne Berger and Michael J. Piore, *Dualism and Discontinuity in Industrial Societies* (New York: Cambridge University Press, 1980).

norm established by collective agreement in the large enterprises—that occurs in the competition between large and small-scale productive organization.[6]

The second development has to do with the small firms' markets and the design of their products. Initially, and despite the fact that they could bargain over prices in good times, the subcontractors were dependent on the goodwill and prosperity of the large firms. Often the large clients delivered the tools, blueprints, and starting materials necessary to make a part. And because most of a subcontractor's clients were likely to be in closely related fields, a major economic downturn tended to affect all of them at once, making it difficult for the small firm to offset the loss of some orders with an increase in others.

Partly out of fear of this dependence, partly out of the desire to expand business, and even partly out of a fascination with new technologies, many small firms have broken the hammerlock of the large clients by developing and marketing products of their own. Generally, the new product is born of the owner's expertise in the market. He realizes that some variation of a successful, mass-produced item or component part will be especially appealing to a certain group of customers, whose complaints about existing products he may have heard for years. He knows, too, that once he has begun to do business with such a group, he will gain an even more detailed knowledge of their needs, thus establishing himself as an indispensable collaborator and breaking the big firm's control over the definition of his products.[7]

Thus, in the shoe industry, the small enterprises produce for the

[6]These remarks are based on interviews with machine designers in Emilia-Romagna in the spring of 1980 and 1981. An excellent description of technological innovation in the small firms producing ceramic tiles is Margherita Russo, "La natura e le implicazioni del progresso tecnico: Una verifica empirica," *Modena*, Dec. 1980, mimeographed. Another well-documented example is the machine tool industry, which combines technological sophistication and pronounced decentralization: in 1977, 40 percent of the Italians in the industry worked in firms employing up to one hundred workers, compared to 12 percent in West Germany and 23 percent in the United States (Anna Maria Gaibisso, "Ruolo e struttura dell'industria italiana delle macchine utensili," *"Bollettino CERIS* 5 [Sept. 1980], p. 29). Italy is now the second largest producer of numerically controlled machine tools in Europe, after West Germany and well ahead of France and Great Britain. As of 1975, 20 percent of numerically controlled machines in use in Italy were located in shops employing between twenty and forty-nine workers, and their use in small firms was increasing rapidly. See Secondo Rolfo, "La diffusione del controllo numerico nella produzione italiana di macchine utensili," *Bollettino CERIS* 5 (Sept. 1980), pp. 126–129. For detailed evidence of the technological sophistication of the industry, see Roberto Taranto, Mariella Franchini, and Vittorio Maglia, *L'industria italiana della macchina utensile* (Bologna: Il Mulino, 1979), pp. 163–187.

[7]A good case study of the emergence and operation of the system of specialized, small-scale production outlined in the next paragraphs is Gianni Lorenzoni, *Una politica innovativa nelle piccole medie imprese* (Milan: Etas Libri, 1979), which is an account of the textile industry near Prato. See also Andrea Saba, *L'industria sommersa: Il nuovo modello di sviluppo* (Venice: Marsilio, 1980).

high-fashion, high-quality sector of the industry, where a premium is placed on distinctiveness and originality in design. They see themselves as mediating between the leaders of the fashion world in New York and Paris and the mass producers of cheap imitations of fashionable designs for chain stores. Local designers travel to the major fashion shows in Europe, copy the designs of the *haute couture* houses, and work from these to produce a large variety of shoe models. The models are then usually presented to high-priced specialty shops or the "quality" department stores who order particular items in small lots. The manufacturers produce almost exclusively to order; they maintain virtually no inventories. The designers are sometimes simply other small specialized firms who sell their designs to manufacturers (and often produce the patterns and cut the leather for them as well). Sometimes the manufacturers themselves design the shoe and subcontract only the pattern-making. Virtually all the manufacturers seem to travel abroad to trade shoes, partly to look at new equipment or to line up customers but also to develop an "eye" for the current fashions and to place themselves in a position to judge the designs themselves.

Similarly, the motorbike industry around Bologna produces a specialty item, a cut above the mass-market products but in no sense competitive in the professional racing market, where bikes are precision engineered and produced to order. Equipment manufacturers come a little closer to entering a customers' market, but again not a market for one-shot deals. Thus, they tend to repeat with some frequency the production of, for example, a given cigarette-packing machine; but the orders never justify the production of more than a few at one time. Single orders, which are custom designed, are adaptations of a more general model for which there is a more substantial demand. Parts production for these machines is often subcontracted to other small machine shops, which are sometimes but not always smaller than the manufacturer who sells the final equipment. And again, the machine shops are job shops, producing small lots but almost never unique pieces.

In practice, of course, designing machinery suited to small-scale production and defining new products are not isolated processes; the use of new machines stimulates the search for new products, and vice versa. One small shop we visited, which originally specialized in the production of plastic chairs, invested in a particular injection molding machine only to discover that the bottom had dropped out of the chair market. Its response was to invent a new product, a nozzle for new kinds of irrigation systems that could be produced on the same molding machines. Conversely, the design of a new product calls for modifications, sometimes substantial, of existing equipment.

This kind of cross-fertilization is carried out quite deliberately in the small consulting firms that have emerged to serve the needs of the dynamic small manufacturers: their engineers, machine designers, and draftsmen, all with extensive production experience, work alternately at increasing the efficiency of existing small-scale operations and at extending the range of those same operations, using the knowledge gained in one phase of their work to suggest solutions in the other. In one case, a particularly farsighted owner of a rapidly growing transmission firm tried to achieve this result alone; he established "industrial" and "artisan-like" production lines side-by-side, in the hope of learning more about one from the other. But most frequently, ideas are exchanged between owners, skilled workers, or consultants in different firms.

This constant innovation in products and production technologies depends on and reinforces a third development in the small sector: the emergence of forms of collaboration within and between firms which do not square well with the image of independent enterprises competing for a limited number of spaces in the market. Innovative small firms, first of all, rely on close cooperation between workers with different kinds of expertise. This reliance follows from the firm's relation to its clients. It does the small firm no good to propose a new, customized product if the new design cannot be supplied at an affordable price. Hence discussions of design must be closely linked to discussions of production; and the final blueprint, which must be available quickly, can only be drawn after consultation between technicians and production workers who trust one another's estimates and expertise.

The internal division of labor in these firms thus tends to be extremely flexible. Owners, engineers, technicians, production heads, and skilled craftsmen work in close contact with each other, and hierarchical distinctions tend to be treated as formalities. Unskilled workers, however, are often excluded from this circle, particularly in large firms.

The need to collaborate in manufacturing new products and in perfecting small-scale manufacturing technique also shapes relations *among* the dynamic small firms. Small dependent subcontractors in the same sector compete with each other, no holds barred. But the more specialized these firms become, the more likely they are to collaborate, subcontracting to each other or sharing the cost of an innovation in machine design that would be too expensive for one producer to order by himself. Often, in fact, the relations between the innovative firms resemble the collegial relation between good doctors, good lawyers, or good university teachers: each firm is jealous of its autonomy and proud of its capacities, but each is fully conscious that its success and even its survival are linked to the collective efforts of the group to which it belongs.

One source of mutual dependence between related firms, we found, is their common use of innovative strategy. At first, a subcontractor usually seeks shelter from price competition through intense specialization—by tailoring a particular part or component to special conditions. But this concentration of attention on one particular distracts attention from all the others. Therefore, the moment the firm begins to expand and move beyond its original specialty, it finds itself dependent on the help of neighbors with complementary kinds of specialties; and because the neighbors can never anticipate exactly when the positions will be reversed, the help is forthcoming.

The more the system of related, innovative small firms expands and prospers, pressing against its original limits, the more explicit the collective character of the activity becomes. The artisans realize that to expand business they must increase the sophistication and range of their products, and that the only way to do that is to increase the sophistication of their capital equipment. But investment in exotic equipment is risky. No one is likely to undertake it unless he is confident that his friends will help him use the new machine by passing along orders, even when there is no immediate profit to them from doing so. Mistrust can freeze technological progress in a whole sector, whereas trust can foster it. The same logic applies to every phase of business: where invention creates demand and invention is also collective, collaboration is a natural result.

This sense of mutual dependence is further reinforced by an appreciation of the economies of scale that can sometimes be achieved by explicit collaboration. For most aspects of production, the small firms are not at a disadvantage because of their size. They have found that economies of scale exist at the level of a very few machines: three lathes in each of three shops are at least as efficient as nine lathes under one factory roof.[8] Small firms, however, are at a disadvantage because of economies of scale in administration; they can seldom maintain white-collar staffs to handle marketing, accounting, or even technical services. To offset this disadvantage, there has been a blossoming of cooperative service organizations, associations of artisans and other small producers who pool resources. Consortiums of small employers also purchase raw materials and secure bank loans at better prices than single firms. Thus

[8]Sebastiano Brusco, "Economie di scale e livello technologico nelle piccole imprese," in Augusto Graziani, ed., *Crisi e ristrutturazione nell'economia italiana* (Turin: Einaudi, 1975), pp. 530–559.

narrow economic considerations combine with less precisely calculable ideas of collective advantage to create a sense of professional solidarity which is the backdrop and limit for competition between the firms.

To make sense of these aspects of decentralization, some observers have begun to shift perspective.[9] Instead of seeing small firms as essentially a response to disturbance in the natural operation of large-scale industry, they see their successes as a sign and result of long-term trends in the organization of factories in the most advanced industrial countries. This view, which is beginning to circulate among small industrialists and the trade unionists most closely in touch with them, rests on two related assumptions. One concerns structural impediments to the continued success of mass production in the core industrial countries; the other concerns the nature of the industrial forms that may replace it.

The first assumption is that the behavior of the labor force in the most advanced countries is in the long run an important, perhaps a decisive, obstacle to mass production there. In this view, the problems in large-scale manufacturing facilities in Northern Italy are one more example of the trends in industrial development that have led experienced industrial workers to reject the conditions of work in large, bureaucratic industrial organizations, and to seek to circumvent them through union organization and workplace restrictions. These conditions of work were accepted in the earlier postwar decades because the workforce was heavily populated by new industrial recruits drawn from rural areas or from a declining artisans sector. Many of these recruits thought of industrial work as temporary and planned to return to their rural roots; but even those who viewed their industrial commitment as permanent measured the income and the conditions against the standard of rural poverty in which they had grown up. As the realization spread in the 1960s that there was no real prospect of return, and as the industrial labor force became increasingly dominated by a second generation for whom there was no rural point of comparison, conditions in industry were increasingly seen as unacceptable and intolerable. This changing perspective, it is argued, sparked the factory riots in Northern Italy and in a number of other European countries whose industrial labor forces had previously been fed by recruits from domestic agriculture and by foreign immigrants (a

[9]See, for example, Arnaldo Bagnasco and Rossella Pini, "Sviluppo economico e trasformazioni sociopolitiche dei sistemi territoriali a economia diffusa," *Quaderni Fondazione Giangiacomo Feltrinelli,* no. 14, 1981; and Vittorio Capecchi, "Giovani, lavoro precario e organizzione del tempo," paper presented at the Convegno sul lavoro precario, organized by the CGIL, CISL, and VIL, Modena, June 1981.

large number of them Italians).[10] The "guest worker" programs that most European countries installed in the 1960s are viewed as last-ditch attempts to evade the consequences of the maturation of domestic labor forces; it is thought that they failed because the immigrant workers settled in much larger numbers than expected, and the attitudes of those settled workers changed far more rapidly than anyone had anticipated.

The upshot of this view is that labor costs in the older and more advanced industrial countries will rise relative to the costs of latecomers with labor forces new to factory work. Since standard products are generally produced with mature technologies easily installed in many parts of the developing world, this means that labor troubles in the established factories open the way for the transfer of production to developing areas.

The second assumption is that as mass production moves out of the core countries, the manufacturing industry in those countries will become increasing directed toward the kind of specialty markets now being created in Italy.[11] In part, this outcome is regarded as merely a logical result of the first assumption: as low-wage competition from developing countries grows, a reasonable response of mature industries will be to move toward producing higher value-added specialty goods suited to the particularities of local customers.

The shift to specialty production, however, is also thought to be partly the result of economic changes unconnected to the use of labor. Of these influences the most widely noted has been the rapid fluctuation in the price of raw materials, particularly oil. These fluctuations encourage experimentation in products and production processes, calling established tastes into question and clearing the way for a profusion of new designs. Increased government regulation of products and processes, which differs from country to country, works the same way. These tendencies are then seen as reinforcing the effects of labor difficulties on the large firms, setting in motion a logic of differention whereby company after company, industry after industry, each for rea-

---

[10]For the general argument, see Michael J. Piore, *Birds of Passage* (New York: Cambridge University Press, 1979). The Italian case is discussed in detail in Charles Sabel, *Work and Politics* (Cambridge: Cambridge University Press, 1982). Europeans, particularly if they are Marxist, accept the general form of the argument but put more emphasis on the rebellion of young workers (whose attitudes appear to be the product of capitalism) than on the reaction of peasant workers new to industrial work. See Benjamin Coriat, *L'atelier et le chronomètre: Essai sur le Taylorisme, le Fordisme, et la production de masse* (Paris: Christian Bourgois, 1979).

[11]Evidence for the growing importance of specialty markets in the long-term strategy of core industries in the advanced countries is presented in Sabel, *Work and Politics, pp. 194–219*.

sons of its own, has begun to specialize its production, forcing its competitors to do the same.

In this light, the success of the Italian small firms looks like a fortuitous leap forward to a new and desirable form of production. If mass markets are broken up, the capacity to make the largest number of different products at the lowest total price in the shortest total time will prove more important than the ability to turn out one standard product at the lowest possible cost. And the defining characteristics of the small Italian firm nicely meet the general specifications for such flexible production: close collaboration between manufacturer and client; close collaboration between different groups within the firm, between the firm and its neighbors; and, as a corollary to these, general-purpose machines and a broadly skilled workforce. Although there may be many institutional forms besides that of the small firm for meeting these requirements, some parts of Italy may have stumbled onto a workable solution to problems that will more and more preoccupy the major industrial countries.

In sum, then, the dynamic small-scale production in Italy apparently emerged in a three-part process. It originated in the decentralization of production from large factories in the late 1960s and early 1970s undertaken by management in an attempt to prevent rigidification of production techniques in large factories. This first phase gave rise to the first interpretation of the small firms, in which they are seen as both a club against the unions and as successful subcontractors in their own right. Two subsequent developments are conceptually distinct, though intertwined in place and time. The first was an effort by the small producers, operating at first on subcontracts from larger firms, to escape this subordination by carving out niches in the world market or by developing new, specialized products; the second was the adaptation of technology and managerial techniques, initially copied from the larger enterprises, to the peculiar needs of small-scale production. The lead in the development of new techniques came from some of the small firms themselves: having solved their own production problems, they began to specialize in developing techniques and specializing products that gave them the much sought-after independence from the demands of large-scale enterprises. This phase of adaptation and independence also saw the blossoming of new, cooperative institutions. Together these developments encouraged a second interpretation of the small firms, in which they are seen as a distinct form of production appropriate to the emergent situation of the major industrial countries.

It is hard to find conclusive proof for either of these two interpretations. Only time will tell whether the growth of the specialty firms rests on their growing share of a stable or temporarily enlarged fringe sector, or on opportunities created by the redefinition of the world market. But two strands of evidence incline us to favor the second and more radical view.

First, there is the growing significance of the modern type of small firm: the rise in wage levels, the success in international markets, and the surge in investments and technological inventiveness characteristic of some of the areas of decentralized production do not fit well with the image of the small firms as subcontractors (if not sweatshops) depending on cheap labor and old equipment. Although it is difficult to measure the relative weight of this new sector of advanced firms, some aggregate statistics will give an idea of its vitality.

From 1971 to 1973 wages in Emilia-Romagna, the center of the small metalworking firms, averaged 93 percent of the national level, whereas wages in the highly industrialized region of Piedmont were 107 percent of the national standard during the same period. Between 1975 and 1977 wages in Emilia-Romagna had risen to 99 percent of the national average for those years, while wages in Piedmont had dropped to 104 percent of the national level. Investment per employee in Emilia-Romagna was just under the average level in Piedmont between 1971 and 1973, but on the average one and a half times greater between 1975 and 1977. A further sign of prosperity was the region's tight labor markets. In 1966 the official unemployment rate was 4.0 percent for Italy as a whole, 4.3 percent in Emilia-Romagna, but just 2.5 in Piedmont. In 1976, however, both the Piedmontese and Emilian employment rates were 2.8 percent, well below the national level of 3.7 percent. A dramatic proof of the area's new riches is the ascent of Modena, regarded as the capital of the small-firm economy: ranked by per-capita income, it was the seventeenth richest province in 1970, but the second richest (after Val D'Aosta, a center of luxury tourism) in 1979.[12]

Second, there is the growing tendency among large firms in and outside Italy to move, however haltingly, in the direction of flexible production. Assembly islands and job rotation in place of rigid assembly lines, and flexible, computer programmable equipment in place of single-purpose machine-tools for example, are widely understood as a response to the growing variability and diversification of markets. The implication is that firms experimenting with these new techniques of production are trying to adapt to the same forces that are putting powerful winds in the sails of the small Italian firms.[13]

[12]Wage levels are reported in Bagansco, *Tre Italie*, p. 105; investment and value-added per employer, *ibid.*, p. 54; and unemployment rates, *ibid.*, p. 92.

[13]Frederico Butera, "La linea di montaggio: La sua logica e il suo futuro," *Politica ed economia*, Jan.–Apr. 1980, p. 43; Coriat, *L'atelier et le chronomètre*, pp. 237–261; and N.

Despite their differences, these interpretations have chastening and overlapping implications for American industrial policy. But before turning to these lessons, we must consider two background conditions of the Italian development that seem to limit or color their significance for other nations: the role of family and artisan traditions, on the one hand, and the labor movement, on the other.

The Role of Artisan and Family Traditions

Small-scale Italian industry was not, of course, originally produced only by the demand of large firms for decentralized, small subcontractors. There were certain long-established features of Italian society that facilitated the emergence of the new sector. One of these was the old artisan tradition itself, and another was the extended family that lives and works as a unit. But as we shall see shortly, the importance of both of these traditions is often overestimated: although they seem on balance to have contributed to the growth of the innovative firms in some areas, they have not been an indispensable precondition of their success.

The influence of the artisan tradition is most noticeable in areas like Emilia-Romagna, where centuries of handicraft product for international markets created a web of relations and a store of knowledge about trading practices that could be placed in the service of the new firms. In such areas many of the new entrepreneurs and skilled workers learned their trade as artisans' apprentices; and in a few instances, traditional shops gradually made the transition to modern industrial work.[14]

But the really important role of the artisan tradition seems to have been less as a reservoir of manual and commercial experience than as the mold for the legal and political vessel in which the small shops operate. The small-scale firms are included in a legal category which enables them to escape much of the tax and labor legislation that governs large enterprises. The Statuto dei Lavoratori, for example, which defines the rights of unions in the plant, does not apply to "artigiani" firms, which are defined as having fifteen or fewer employees. This obviously gives the small firms numerous opportunities for reducing the direct costs of production and increasing the flexibility of their

Altmann, P. Binkelmann, K. Düll, and H. Stück, *Grenzen neuer Arbeitsformen*, Frankfurt am Main, Campus, 1982.

[14]See, for example, the discussion of the early history of Bolognese industry in Commune di Bologna, *Macchine, scuola, industria: Da mestiere alla professionalità operaia* (Bologna: Il Mulino, 1980).

operation.[15] The crucial significance of the term "artigiani" is legal, for it confers legal privileges on small firms in the way that articles of incorporation give them to large ones.

It is, of course, difficult to assess the advantage these privileges give the small firms relative to the large ones, if only because the large ones themselves benefit from a complicated series of exemptions (including occasional forgiveness of their social security obligations), as well as from the low production costs of the small ones.[16] It is clear, however, that many small firms could not have survived in the early 1970s without some form of exemption, just as it is also clear that the most successful of the innovative small firms now pay such high wages and offer such attractive working conditions that they could survive without any special consideration. The point to be emphasized here—and we shall return to it later—is this: it was not the artisan tradition per se, but rather a set of political and legal provisions, which might have arisen in a number of different ways, that proved most helpful to the small firms.

The tradition of family enterprise—incarnated and idealized in the old artisan's workshop and the family farm, and admired from afar by landless farmhands and industrial operatives—has likewise facilitated the development of the new firms without having served as an irreplaceable foundation for them. By providing a source of labor, a source of entrepreneurship, and a source of capital, this tradition has contributed in three ways to the growth of the small sector.[17]

The tradition functions in this way almost as a matter of definition. It ensures that children will begin work in the family firm at an early age (14 or 15), and that many of them will continue to work there at wages lower than they could earn outside. In the mid- and late 1970s in Italy, it meant that some educated young people who went to school to avoid manual work, but for whom the economy could not provide white-collar jobs, would accept jobs in a family firm out of loyalty to the ideal. The same ideal has also facilitated the accumulation of capital across generations, and the pooling of resources of several different households to finance plant and equipment. Finally, generations of husbanding resources on a small plot of land, often as a sharecropper or in a small artisan's shop, served as a school for entrepreneurship, teaching people to adapt themselves quickly to the market.

[15]Berger and Piore, *Dualism and Discontinuity.*

[16]A good accounting of the legal advantages of the small firms is Marco Ricolfi, "Legislazione economica e piccole imprese," in F. Ferreo and S. Scamuzzi, eds., *L'industria in Italia: La piccola impresa* (Rome: Editori Riuniti, 1979), pp. 119–186.

[17]This interpretation is developed most clearly in Massimo Paci, "Crisi, ristrutturazione e piccola impresa," *Inchiesta* 5 (Oct.–Dec. 1975), pp. 3–8.

At the same time, however, there seem to be ways of providing small firms with entrepreneurship, capital, and labor without drawing at all on the family tradition. Some of the entrepreneurs in the metalworking sector, for example, are former skilled workers who were fired from large factories during the purges of leftists in the 1950s, They used their severance pay, skills, and connections with lower-level production managers to set up small shops, which then benefited from the wave of decentralization that broke at the end of the 1970s. In other cases, the new firms were founded more recently by younger skilled workers, with the encouragement and sometimes the financial help of their old companies; and in still others, the entrepreneurs came from white-collar families. Direct experience of entrepreneurship on the farm or in the artisan's shop does not, therefore, seem to be the only way one can acquire a taste for it.[18]

Similarly, public and semipublic institutions provide alternatives to family credit and labor. In some regions, cooperative banks have acted as a complement, and at times a substitute, for family financing. This tradition is particularly strong in the Venetian provinces, where it has been encouraged by the Church, and in Emilia-Romagna, where it has been encouraged by the leftist parties.[19] And labor reserves can be augmented in nontraditional ways—by apprenticeship programs, for example, and (where the local youth refuse unskilled employment) by the use of immigrants. Again, Emilia-Romagna makes use of both.[20]

Examples of this kind suggest that the artisan and family traditions together represent only one of several paths to the same result. In fact, it is reasonable to suspect that there were potential solutions to problems surrounding the creation of the new firms, solutions that were not tried simply because traditional mechanisms, formed under completely

[18]These remarks are based on interviews with entrepreneurs in Emilia-Romagna, the Marche, and the Venetian provinces. Bagnasco comes to similar conclusions. Using data from a survey by Demoskopea in 1974, he found that in the province of Treviso, a center of decentralized production, 14 percent of entrepreneurs in the metalworking sector were the sons of small or tenant farmers or agricultural day laborers; 16.4 percent the sons of artisans; and the rest were the offspring of workers (21.8 percent), shopkeepers (18.8 percent), white-collar workers (10.9 percent), or high managers and professionals (11.7 percent). See Bagnasco and Pini, "Sviluppo economico e trasformazioni sociopolitiche dei sistemi territoriali a economia diffusa," p. 30.

[19]On the history of the cooperative movement, see Maurizio Degl'Innocenti, "Geografia e struttura della cooperazione in Italia," in Guido Bonfante, Zeffiro Ciuffoletti, Maurizio Degl'Innocenti, and Guido Sapelli, *Il movimento cooperativo in Italia* (Turin: Einaudi, 1980), pp. 3–87.

[20]On the growing number of artisans in Emilia-Romagna (partly as a result of efforts to hire extra laborers without exceeding the official limit of fifteen full-time employees in firms qualifying for artisans' privileges), see Andrea Trevisani, "Prime note sull'artigianato metalmeccanico in Emilia-Romagna," FIM-CISL Emilia-Romagna, Bologna, June 1980, mimeographed.

different circumstances, answered the questions posed by the growth of the modern small firms almost as soon as they were asked. Conversely, as we shall see next, even institutions that appear exclusively suited to the modern, centralized factory have played a role in organizing what looks, at a distance, like a traditional form of industry.

The Union Role

Whereas the importance of the family and artisan traditions in the operation of the Italian small-firm sector is easily overestimated, the role of the trade unions is easily underestimated or distorted. That role is complex and contradictory, but it seems that on balance the trade unions have contributed to the success of the most modern small firms, above all in areas like Emilia-Romagna.

From what has been said so far, it would seem that the union contribution to the creation of the small firms was at best indirect, not to say inadvertent or unwilling. The unions endorsed and at times encouraged the rank and file pressure for shop-floor control over the organization of production in the large plants. Thus they share major responsibility for creating the organizational rigidity that led to the creation and expansion of many small firms. It is not surprising, therefore, that the unions opposed management efforts to evade the new rules through decentralization to smaller units.

But although the unions were hardly enthusiastic about these developments in the early 1970s, and are just now coming to consider in a detailed way the possible advantages of development on the Emilian model, their opposition to decentralization was and continues to be notably restrained. In some areas, in fact, the left moved from forbearance to open advocacy of modern small firms as an alternative to the sweatshops. For instance, as we saw, in Bologna and Modena many of the small machine shops are housed in industrial parks built and financed by Communist municipal governments. And these same governments use their control over zoning regulations to shut down hazardous foundries. What explains the unexpected restraint? What makes possible the still more improbable collaboration?

Ultimately, the labor movement's restraint is rooted in the deference of Communist-Socialist trade unions to the Italian Communist Party (PCI), and particularly to its interpretation of modern Italian politics. In that interpretation, Fascism succeeded in large measure because the workers were isolated from other social classes, especially the peasants and petit bourgeoisie, who were oppressed by the evolution of monopoly capitalism. The keystone of the PCI's postwar electoral strategy was thus the attempt to win over these groups, which had provided the foundations of Mussolini's political support.[21] Any effort to impose upon the small productive units, either by law or through union organization, conditions equivalent to those of the large factories would have jeopardized the future of this strategic class alliance; it would dangerously antagonize a group which, the left feels, must be neutralized if it cannot be rallied to transformative causes.

In those areas where the labor movement has begun to collaborate, however judiciously, with the small firms, it has done so partly out of strategic calculation and partly out of historical ties between the left and particular groups of entrepreneurs. Calculation, for example, encouraged the municipal governments to build industrial parks as demonstrations of their capacity to build a modern, urban environment. The labor movement's loyalty to some of the small employers in Emilia-Romagna and elsewhere grows out of an irony of history to which we referred earlier: some of the small employers began as skilled workers, part of the group that formed the core of the anti-Fascist underground during World War Two and fell victim to the purges of the organized left in the factories in the 1950s. The connection between the labor movement and the entrepreneurs, moreover, is constantly being renewed, because the tradition of union organization among skilled workers has meant that some craftsmen have moved up to start their own firms in recent years.

But by themselves, neither strategic calculations nor historical loyalties fully explain why small shopowners frequently belong to associations that bargain with the trade unions and respect many union standards, even though their workers are not always union members or have sometimes joined only at the employer's urging. In fact, on closer inspection it turns out that traditional allegiances are more the catalyst than the underlying cause of the spread of union influence to firms in which the union is not officially represented.

One way to make sense of the apparent paradox of union standards being sustained at least as much by employer pressure as by worker organization is to look at them in the light of what is known about dispersed but unionized industries in the United States—industries such as garments, trucking and construction. It seems likely that the forces at work in them have also shaped Italian developments, for two reasons.

First, in these industries a number of small firms compete with each other for small orders, and prices are constantly being changed; entry is fairly easy and the cost of labor is relatively high proportionate to

---

[21]For the PCI's alliance strategy, see Stephen Hellman, "The PCI's Alliance Strategy and the Case of the Middle Classes," in Donald L. M. Blackmer and Sidney Tarrow, eds., *Communism in Italy and France* (Princeton: Princeton University Press, 1975), pp. 373–419.

total cost. Because this situation is very unstable, there is always the potential for cut-throat competition that will lead to severe exploitation of the labor force. Hence, there is a strong incentive for employers to support any measure that stabilizes conditions in the industry and narrows the ranges of variables affecting competition. Second, however, the employers' interest in this stability is largely as a group in the long run. In the short run, any particular employer may have an individual interest in undercutting union standards, particularly if he is hard pressed to survive. And, of course, if one employer breaks ranks, all will follow suit, because even the most efficient employer cannot afford to respect union standards if his competitors are undercutting him. Thus, employers want the union, but only if it is strong enough to control the whole industry.

Given this rather delicate balance of economic interests on the employers' side, ideological and temperamental factors that contribute to the union's strength become crucially important. For example, employees who start out as craftsmen and continue to work side by side with their employers, maintaining close personal contact and a natural sympathy with them, are often reluctant to survive through labor exploitation and the violation of union rules. Shared craft experiences also help maintain the cohesion among the employers themselves. Respect for labor standards is fostered not only out of loyalty to the workforce but also out of loyalty to other members of the employer group.

Even these kinds of bonds, however, are not always enough, and unions seem to survive best in situations where there is some other factor that links workers and employers. In the New York City garment industry that bond has been common ethnicity, and one result of the United Jewish Appeal and Italian orphanage campaigns in which the union and management organizations cooperate is to cement the sentiments of unity and community within the industry, because these sentiments contribute to the industry's stability. In the factories we visited in central Italy, the common adherence of the employees and workers to the left-wing parties and ideology seems to perform a similar function. So does the complicated web of kinship that links the two groups in any small community: in Emilia-Romagna most workers seem to have an entrepreneur somewhere in the family.

Still, even in those areas where it has gone farthest toward cooperating with the small firms, the left has no coherent policy toward decentralization. The left's support and control within the small-scale industrial sector has meant that the conflict between the interests of workers in the small and the large firms, which might have been played out as a conflict between organized and unorganized workers or between the left-wing and right-wing parties, has become a conflict within the left wing itself. The rule has been that the PCI defends the artisans out of fear of offending them and in the hope of gaining from an alliance, whereas the unions try to curb the abuses in the small shops. Coordinated action between the PCI and the unions is possible only in extreme cases, such as efforts to close extremely hazardous plants. Both the unions and the party, furthermore, remain suspicious of a form of industry so apparently at odds with their vision of modern, centralized rationality. The Fiat Mirafiore works in Turin have long been their image of the factory of the future.[22] Nonetheless, the explosive growth of the small-scale sector and growing public recognition of the need to raise national productivity levels to international standards are gradually forcing the labor movement as a whole to think through the politics and economics of its de facto cooperation with the small firms; it is being slowly pushed to endorse what we have called the second interpretation of Italian developments, and to look at ways of further integrating labor and the new firms.

In the last section, we saw that Italy's family and artisan traditions were not indispensable to the creation of a sector of small-scale industry. In this one, we have seen that the unions are not necessarily inimical to it. The final two sections connect these conclusions to the two earlier interpretations of decentralization, in an effort to draw out the meaning of the Italian experience for American debates on industrial policy.

ITALIAN DECENTRALIZATION AND AMERICAN INDUSTRY

Despite their differences, the implications of *both* the interpretations of the Italian experience ought to be sobering for American policymakers. In fact, when considered in relation to what passes for industrial strategy in the United States, the difference between the two understandings of Italy is one of kind, not of degree. The first interpretation, the dualist one, suggests that American policy is needlessly wasteful; the second and more radical reading of changes in labor and product markets suggests that current American thinking on industrial structure is potentially disastrous.

In the first view, Italian developments seem broadly consistent with much current economic policy in the United States, and especially the massive relocation of industry from the North to the South. In the United States, as among many Italian industrialists, it is widely believed

[22]These remarks are based on numerous discussions with officials of the metalworkers' union in Emilia-Romagna and Turin.

that free markets are natural, self-defining entities; that managers must be given a completely free hand if they are to manage efficiently; that taxes and unions distort correct decisions; and that the future lies with the large factory. From this point of view, the major difference between Italy and the United States is simply this: where the Italians have been forced for political and geographic reasons to settle for piecemeal decentralization into a politically protected artisan sector, the Americans have been able to rebuild a major portion of their industrial base in the South, in the bargain putting extreme pressure on Northern unions to make concessions.

This fundamental agreement, however, obscures an important aspect of the dualist lesson of Italy: as the success of the new small firms shows, there is a fringe of demand that can profitably be captured by flexible specialty firms. To abandon the Northeast with its patrimony of skills, entrepreneurship, and experience in international markets could be to forfeit the possibility of competing in those markets. So even if a large part of the future does lie with the large factory, it is wasteful to reject out of hand the possibility that some of our older industrial areas may be suited to the kind of peripheral production which, on this interpretation, is making the "third Italy" rich. If the future does not lie with large firms, of course, our picture of it will look much darker.

The first implication of the radical view of Italian developments for the United States is that the U.S. policy of industrial displacement toward the South and Southwest is simply not workable in the long run. That policy *appears* workable today because it is able to draw upon a large pool of unskilled labor in those areas. American industrialists still believe that the availability of these workers creates a favorable political climate and an attractive set of attitudes toward work in general and toward unions in particular. In the Europeans' interpretation of their own experience, however, these attitudes are basically a by-product of the novelty of industrial work for a first generation of workers. In the future—which could be a good deal nearer than we suspect, considering the suddenness with which labor unrest broke out abroad—that novelty will wear off, and the newly industrialized states will impose many of the same restrictions as the old ones have. And if these restrictions are truly as crippling as industrial managers seem to believe, large-scale production will increasingly leave the United States and locate abroad, where lower labor costs and less troublesome unions can be combined with the same technology to produce the same goods at lower costs.

The second major implication of this view of Italian developments is that the current neglect of established industries in the United States

413

may prove extremely costly. In the present political climate in America, almost any proposal to aid the run-down industrial cities in the Northeast and Midwest is likely to be written off as a misguided effort to save "places, not people."[23] But in Italy, where one village specializes in ceramic tiles, the next in small tractors, and the next in numerically controlled lathes, places in fact *define* people: some kinds of business can be conducted only in certain places. And if the success of the small Italian firms is any guide to the preconditions for success in the international economy of the future, then the accumulation of skills, the knowledge of existing markets, and the habits of dealing with a mass of subcontractors and suppliers which are the patrimony of these ailing regions in the United States are also the foundations of successful competition in the specialized markets of the future. If the strategy of rejuvenated mass production fails in the South and the basis of specialized production is destroyed in the North, what industry will we have left?

Fortunately, even if this second perspective is correct, the long-run prospects for the United States are not as bleak as they might seem. For if economic policy is a good deal more important in determining outcomes than most of us seem to believe, it is also true that even the best program seldom succeeds as planned, and the most wrongheaded one is rarely as disastrous as might be expected. There is always some room for firms and individuals to play on economic currents running beneath the surface of events and thereby produce outcomes which policy, by design or by neglect, would foreclose. And thus, to the extent that some of the same forces that led to the flowering of small businesses in north-central Italy operate in the old industrial regions of our country, these regions will not necessarily atrophy, as national policy-makers have assumed they must. By a cheerless paradox, market forces may offer us some limited protection against the advocates of the market.

Industrial New England and the Middle Atlantic States have in fact begun to show an economic resilience which, though perhaps not equivalent to that of north-central Italy, is similarly surprising.[24] After several decades of decline, and a period from the late 1960s to the mid-1970s when unemployment rates were substantially higher than the national average, manufacturing employment in these regions appears to have stabilized. In several industries, such as special machines, metal fabrication, knit goods, and even textiles (in New Hampshire),

[23]See, for example, President's Commission for a National Agenda for the Eighties, *Urban America in the Eighties: Perspectives and Prospects: Report of the Panel on Policies and Prospects for Metropolitan and Nonmetropolitan America* (Washington, D.C.: U.S. Government Printing Office, 1980), esp. pp. 71–86.

[24]On the role of small business in the New England Renaissance, see Lynne E. Browne and John S. Hekman, "New England's Economy in the 1980's," *New England Economic Review*, Jan.–Feb. 1981, pp. 5–16.

employment increased sharply between 1975 and 1980. The recession of 1981 almost bypassed the area: unemployment in southern New England remained steady despite sharp increases in the national level, and in the Middle Atlantic states the increase was slight compared to what occurred in the previous two recessions that seemed to be centered there. In March 1981, unemployment in these regions was 5.8 percent, lower than that of any industrial state except Texas.[25]

This reversal of past trends is still so recent and so startling that it has yet to be carefully examined and explained, but fragmentary evidence—much of it anecdotal—suggests that it is a result of precisely those trends in international capitalistic development that underlie recent Italian developments. The 1970s did indeed see a worldwide reaction of industry to the shop-floor practices and the general social and political climate generated by an experienced, resourceful, and noncompliant industrial labor force, as well as a migration of industrial jobs to more "hospitable" regions of a country or to less developed countries abroad. But the industries that moved out were those geared to standardized industrial production, to long runs of traditional industrial products and mass consumer goods. That movement has now been completed. The industries that remain are devoted to specialty items, innovative products, high fashion goods, and perhaps the overflow of standard industrial items that will not sustain a commitment to permanent industrial facilities. In other words, these industries serve different segments of demand because of the different advantages they offer: a skilled industrial labor force working in small shops, directed by innovative entrepreneurs with a keen sense of shifting markets, located not only at the modal points of transportation and communication but also at the centers of fashion and of scientific and engineering scholarship. As in northern Italy, these characteristics confer a particular advantage.

Typical in this respect is the ladies' garment industry. Until the Second World War the industry was centered in New York City. But after the war the City steadily lost employment—to rural areas of New York State and Pennsylvania, and to the Southern states and Puerto Rico. In the 1970s there was a further transfer of employment opportunities to low-wage countries in Asia and Latin America. Most of what left the City, however, was the mass production of standardized items—blue jeans, bras, panties, and the like. For these items, it was efficient to make the garment in sections and put it together in assembly-line fashion with unskilled operators repeating the same operations again and again on special machinery adapted with jigs and fixtures to the par-

[25]For details on employment and output trends, see statistics compiled by state and industry for various years by the U.S. Department of Commerce, Bureau of Labor Statistics.

ticular production item. This movement was heightened in the late 1960s and early 1970s by a shift in fashion toward informal leisure goods and sportswear; the demand for these items was less fickle in the very short run and therefore expanded the portion of output that could be produced on assembly lines in factories somewhat distant from the fashion center. For some time, it has been taken as axiomatic that the life of the garment industry in New York is running out.

But during this same period there was a segment of the ladies' garment industry that was not moving out of the City. Part of it was composed of high-fashion items (the top of every line, the *haute couture* items sold in small numbers for the very rich who set the style for the mass industry), but part was also composed of mass-consumption items in which design and fashion are important and which, therefore, must be produced in small lots and quickly, before the fashion changes. Most dress production, for example, remained behind in the early 1970s. As one manufacturer put it, "if I tried to make it in South Carolina, before I could ship out the design and ship back the product, the style would have changed." But it is also true that given the numbers in which any given dress is produced, it does not pay to set up an assembly line, separate production of the garment into parts, specialize the equipment, and teach inexperienced operators how to do a particular stitch. Dresses are produced in small shops by operators who stitch the whole garment on general-purpose sewing machines. Moreover, what is true of the dress industry as a whole is true of a portion of every other garment segment (even blue jeans, these days) that has a high fashion component: even for standardized items, the business must be fairly close to a fashion center, and this generally implies that some part of the production process must also be located there. One executive with extensive facilities in rural Mississippi made this point as follows: "I'm not going to sit in Greenville; [New York] is where my customers are, and this is where my designers can feel the trends in air, and this is where I have got to be, and that means I've got to start the garment and work it out in some shop in Manhattan, where if the belt doesn't sit right on the coat, they can get in a cab and bring it up here in fifteen minutes. You can't have 200 women waiting at their machines while I fly down to Greenville, Mississippi, to find out we need to take another stitch in the waist."

By the late 1970s, it was this core segment of the industry that remained uniquely adapted to the urban industrial environment of New York City. Employment prospects have been strengthened by fashion shifts, which have introduced a greater element of flux and uncertainty into sportswear design, so that a portion of this production is actually moving back to the City. As risk and fashion shift with the years, garment employment in New York will no doubt continue to vary as well. But the trend has stabilized. What appeared to be a long-term decline was instead a structural adjustment that has now run its course: what remains of the industry draws on the natural strengths of the City as a commercial and industrial community.

What is true of the garment industry in New York City is probably true of a number of other industries as well, The whole string of industrial towns running up the Connecticut Valley—from Bridgeport through New Haven and Hartford, and up to Springfield and east to Worcester—houses the specialty machine shops, machinists, and machine-tool manufacturers that once composed the American machine-building industry. Long runs of standardized machine tools and equipment may no longer be profitable here, but like the machine shops in Bologna, the area has the potential for capturing specialty markets, prototype production, and innovation. The resurgence of this potential, as the geographical redistribution of mass production comes to completion, also probably explains the stabilization of employment trends in the United States. An example of a similar phenomenon is provided by high-technology firms in eastern Massachusetts, new industries with a very high rate of innovation, which produce special machine tools and place a premium on a skilled labor force, on relatively small-scale, flexible production techniques, and on entrepreneurship and an urban location (in this case, the university community around Boston). Again, this phenomenon is not new: the Boston area has been spinning off small entrepreneurial firms and spawning new technologies since the early 1950s; some of the firms, like Polaroid, are now major industrial producers. But again, it is only as the long-term locational changes in mass-production industries run their course that these developments in industries where the area retains a natural advantage have been able to dominate economic indexes and employment trends.

Though it is easy to find, in recent U.S. trends, traces of the forces that have produced the Italian model of development, one cannot *count* on these forces to prevail unassisted, let alone to reproduce the miracle of north-central Italy in New York or New England. The natural advantages of the older industrial regions in America may well sustain them against industrially underdeveloped areas such as the South and the Southwest, but it will not protect them from other equally mature urban economies. It is improbable that Atlanta or Los Angeles—let alone Greenville, Mississippi—will ever displace New York as a garment center; but Milan might well be able to do so. It is difficult to imagine Houston, Texas, capturing the markets of Bridgeport, Connecticut, or Worcester, Massachusetts; but Modena and Bologna are in very good positions to compete with those cities. They are probably less well placed to compete with Boston for the innovative high-technology markets, but there are cities in Germany, Great Britain, France, and Japan which have an academic tradition and an industrial maturity that could well mount such a competitive threat. The innovations in communications and transportation wrought by the airplane and the computer do not enable a designer sitting in New York to rearrange the belt on a dress in Greenville, Mississippi. The cognitive processes and human interactions involved in fashion, technical innovation, and precision design may be such that urban conglomerations will always have a commanding edge in these activities. But computer and air technologies do permit the very rapid communication and transportation of finished output, once production is complete. For the specialty items in which urban centers have a productive advantage, the quality of the products, measured in terms of their degree of innovation, fashion content, or efficiency in the particular specialties for which they were designed, tend to dominate cost considerations. In competition along these dimensions, it is easy to see American industry losing out to products produced abroad and shipped in. A case directly in point is the competition between New England and north-central Italy in the shoe industry.

New England was once the center of the U.S. shoe industry in very much the same sense that New York City was the garment industry center; and shoe production, like garments, has moved south in the postwar decades. But the movement in shoes went much farther than in garments, and the result is that the U.S. industry has lost the high-fashion end of the business, largely to the very small Italian firms discussed earlier. Conventional wisdom has it that the competitive advantage of these firms lies in low wages, but as we have seen, the conventional wisdom is wrong: the advantage is precisely the skill and the conglomeration that were once possessed by New England.

AMERICAN INDUSTRIAL POLICY

What does this imply for public policy? First, and most obviously, it suggests that we must reverse the current policy of abandonment in the North, and promote or enforce acceptance of public responsibilities in this region of the country. Given the strains placed upon local and state fiscal systems by the southward movement of mass production, this means providing precisely the kinds of federal aid that the Reagan administration is attempting to withdraw. Of particular concern is the deterioration of the infrastructure of roads, bridges, sewer systems, public transportation, and the like which hold urban conglomerations together and make them viable places to live and produce. The role of government is of paramount importance because the facilities are *public:* they are widely shared and no single firm or industry has the resources or incentive to provide them, if government does not. This is especially true in an area whose economy is composed of a network of small firms. Many of the mass production facilities opening in the South and Southwest are so large, compared to the communities into which they are moving, that they might provide facilities which elsewhere are publicly provided. This is clearly not the case in the North. Conceptually, one might distinguish this direct government support of business from social progams, which do not directly sustain business activity. But to the extent that local governments are forced by commanding political pressure to compensate for declining federal support in social programs with money diverted from other budgets, federal efforts to divert funds from social programs to capital outlays are likely to be self-defeating. The pressures for social programs in the older areas are, it is worth noting, a product of their own industrial maturity. The same community, religious, and family structures of the South and Southwest which generate a pliant industrial labor force also provide many of the support services that elsewhere must be provided by government.

In the end, however, the commitment of public resources may not be sufficient to sustain the small-enterprise sector of the American economy in world markets. We seem to lack intellectual categories in which to conceive of this form of business activity and to fashion policies that are likely to foster its development. These conceptual problems, moreover, reflect a structure of business institutions that makes the existence of the type of firms which seem to prosper in the "third Italy" very problematic.

In the United States, we really have two distinct, almost opposite, images of businessmen and their activities. One is the image of the independent small businessman who strikes out on his own in some kind of daring new enterprise: Schumpeter's innovating enterpreneur, Horatio Alger or Andrew Carnegie, the economic equivalent of the Lone Ranger. It is in these terms that the Western businessmen surrounding President Reagan seem to conceive of themselves. The second business image is that of the corporate executive working his way up the bureaucratic ladder in a large corporation, through cooperation and teamwork. (The cooperation, however, is supposed to stop at the organization's boundaries: a hostile, competitive external environment ensures that internal cooperation works toward efficient solutions to economic problems.) This model of internal organizational cooperation has recently been reinforced by admiring descriptions of successful Japanese firms.

The type of small business that has been so successful in Italy, however, involves a mixture of entrepreneurship and cooperation that fits neither of these models of business activity. It involves entrepreneurship in the sense that the small firms need to be continually on the lookout for new markets, jumping from one innovation to another, anticipating rapid changes in taste and style; they must be lean and versatile, always ready to drop one project and take on another. But as it developed in Italy, this type of small business involves a good deal of cooperation as well. Part of that cooperation is, in terms of American categories of thought, perfectly benign: it is expressed in cooperative associations that serve various business functions—such as purchasing raw materials, recruiting labor, and building industrial parks. Other forms of cooperation, if not actually excluded by our American models, are rendered extremely suspicious by them. Many of the small firms in Italy, for example, subcontract among one another. Some of the subcontacting firms are obviously complementary; but a number of other subcontracts have the outward trappings of sweetheart deals. Very often in the garment or shoe industry, for example, two firms will compete with each other for an order, and then the winner will turn around and subcontract to the loser. It is difficult in our terms to understand how competitors can cooperate with each other in this way; and yet it would be impossible for them to accept the risks of a high-fashion environment without the security that such fallback arrangements permit. Some of the cooperative behavior displayed by small firms in Italy would be completely foreclosed by normative models built on our two business categories. Arrangements to fix wages through top-down union organization or to fix material prices through buying cooperatives that stabilize the market for example, would be viewed as monopolistic restraints on trade, even though they might be necessary to ensure that the firms compete on the basis of product innovation and not on the basis of cost-cutting and labor exploitation.

Nonetheless, important as cooperation is among these small firms, they also require real entrepreneurship. This entrepreneurship, moreover, is continuous; it is not sufficient to invent one new product or create one successful style. These industrial sectors survive by continual radical adjustment. In the United States, we pride ourself on our business entrepreneurship, but it is not clear that it is the sort of continuous entrepreneurship required to sustain small-scale production in the long run.

The succession in small businesses from father to son is, in the United States, particularly problematic. The activities of the independent entrepreneur and of the bureaucratic corporation actually dovetail here in a manner which, from the point of view of preserving entrepreneurial tradition, is not ideal. The key institutions mediating the relationsip are the conglomerate corporation and the business school. A typical pattern is one in which the first-generation entrepreneur has relatively little formal education; often he comes from an immigrant background. The son who follows him into the business, however, goes to business school. There he develops contact and identification with other students who go directly into large corporations. The entrepreneurial son returns upon graduation to his father's business, but not with the ambition of continuing it for life. Instead, he attempts to build up the net worth of the corporation (and of the family that controls it) in the short run, and at the same time tries to develop a market position which, from the point of view of a major corporation, is strategic—a position based on a particular product innovation, or a process patent, or an especially advantageous sales location. In mid-career, this second-generation entrepreneur plans to sell out his business to a larger corporation, moving with it as an employee into the corporate hierarchy. Very often the corporation, having bought the whole of the business, closes down a number of its activities which may have been successful in the small-scale sector but which cannot in a large organization be oriented to mass markets and run in a more regimented bureaucratic fashion.

The problem, then, is really twofold: to develop a category of business that corresponds to the real requirements of small-scale production, and to find ways of populating that category on a continuing basis. The Italians, of course, did not start with a solution to this problem. They have built the solution, as we have seen, from a variety of materials: artisan and family traditions as well as the peculiar history of left-wing politics, which married entrepreneurial craftsmen with the left-wing notions of community and cooperation. Are comparable materials available in American economic history and iconography? The closest equivalent is the family farm and the network of support services built around the agricultural extension service of the federal government. These institutions have an honored, even hallowed, place in American political discourse. Less honored but probably a good deal more relevant is the network of labor and management organizations that have controlled work practices and production techniques in the garment and construction industries. We have seen that various possibilities for cooperation between labor and the advanced small firms are being explored in Italy, and have noted the parallels between the organization of industry in the American Northeast and the "third Italy." Could the labor movement become in the United States, as it has in some regions in Italy, the fulcrum for a new industrial develop: .it strategy?

CHAPTER NINE

Conclusions: What to Do Now?

LAURA TYSON AND
JOHN ZYSMAN

INTERNATIONAL trade pressures on our domestic industries will not soon be relieved, nor can the tension between a general stance in favor of free trade and a mounting number of protectionist exceptions endure. Looking to the future, it seems unlikely that the U.S. can convince its trading partners to eliminate their domestic interventions in order to create an even more perfect international market. It is more likely that the United States will be pushed into a series of sector-specific interventions, although the form of policy and its justification will undoubtedly vary with different administrations. Under these circumstances, effective policy responses must meet a double challenge. First, policy must assure that American industry does in fact adjust to international competition. The alternative is a weakened national position and pressures from higher inflation and unemployment. Second, American policy must attend to the maintenance of an open international economic regime and a workable security alliance. Protectionist policies can only undermine these dual objectives. In these concluding remarks, we wish to make some prescriptive comments about the policies we think are likely to emerge.

Industrial policies are not a substitute for proper aggregate policies, nor do they offer an easy way to avoid the pains of the industrial adjustment required if producers are to make goods that consumers and other producers wish to buy. Nor can the scope of such policies be extensive. Since, as a practical matter, a national administrative apparatus cannot grasp all the complexities of the market (nor should it want to), any industrial policy will perforce focus on broad trends or on the

422

particular difficulties of only a few industries. Moreover, the evident complexities of any single industry should restrain any extensive interventionist ambitions.

There are both economic and political circumstances, however, that make an industrial policy a useful part of the government's repertoire. There are three broad economic justifications for an active industrial and trade policy: responding to foreign industrial policies toward critical national sectors; facilitating adjustment processes for both efficiency and equity reasons; and repairing market imperfections or offsetting market features that produce specific harmful effects in specific sectors. There are two political justifications for such policies: shaping existing policies to promote competitive adjustment; and developing policies to reduce political opposition to industrial adjustment by offering alternatives to outright subsidy or protection.

There is a crucial disjuncture between the way we think about industry politically and the way we must think about it for purposes of making an industrial policy that is sensible in business terms. Trade and industry policy must reconcile these competing perspectives. Although policy will always be made for political reasons, it must be made to work in the marketplace. The question that trade and industry policy must continuously confront is this: on what terms do firms in specific business segments fight for markets, and why are some more successful than others? The capacity to answer this question analytically is essential, whatever the particular policies selected.

Without an independent ability to examine industrial dynamics, government is entirely dependent upon the views of firms and sectors that are seeking assistance. It will be forced to deal with any industrial crisis on an ad hoc basis, in a panic, without the proper resources to make informed judgments. Independent analytic capacity is needed not only to diagnose industry difficulties without bias but also to give legitimacy to policies that may be proposed.

The capacity to analyze the competitive problems of individual industries does not imply that the solutions will be sector-specific policies. Sector problems can be clues to flaws in our aggregate policies and may suggest that we might use policy to improve the functioning of our markets for capital and labor. When we confront either a sector problem or a shift in international trade that is of broad national concern, there should be a clear order for policy preferences: aggregate policies first; policies to improve the workings of markets second; and finally— and only as a last resort—industry-specific policies.

At the very least, this ordering is a practical necessity. There are thousands of different business segments, each with its own complexities. We cannot have industry policies for all of them. Consequently, every problem that can be resolved at a general level will leave us freer to apply limited resources to the problems that seem to require sector-specific solutions. There is also the real danger that sector-specific policies will highlight the problems of a few sectors to the disadvantage of many others. Thus practical necessity pushes us in the same direction as economic theory—to rely on market outcomes at a macroeconomic or sectoral level whenever possible.

The choice of any sector-specific policy depends, then, on the cost of not acting and on the feasibility of assisting firms to respond competitively. In growth-linked sectors, the choice depends in part on how broadly a particular sector affects the future of the economy as a whole. Some sectors have extensive linkages to the rest of the economy which are usually very evident. These linkages are often inputs (such as semiconductors) that one sector provides for many other industries, or transportation and communication products (such as trucks and cargo containers) that affect the size of markets. When the pace of growth in such a linked sector can affect the competitiveness or rate of productivity increase in many economic activities, a policy of market promotion may be justified. The aggregate benefits of more rapid growth may be greater than the benefits that could be captured by individual private producers. Since the terms of competition are in flux in such growing industries, policies should be aimed at lifting constraints on growth and enlarging markets. In sectors that are in transition, the problem is to assess the likelihood of maintaining national production and employment during periods of dramatic change, and to assure that these changes result in productivity increases. Here externalities—the costs of an action that are not borne directly by the actor—are often expressed politically by the resistance of workers and communities to plant closings. It is important to remember that a competitive failure can erode the infrastructure on which a national comparative advantage rests, and that a competitive victory can establish national advantage. In some industries, the costs to government of helping to re-establish a competitive position and maintaining a comparative advantage may be lower than the costs of assisting the movement of resources to new uses and supporting individuals and communities while the shift occurs. Industrial infrastructure, both physical and social, is often the base on which a competitive position is built. A collapse in a major firm may undermine its whole network of suppliers, as in Britain where the decline of the automobile assemblers has damaged the auto components industries. In these cases, the loss of potentially competitive firms may result in a change in national comparative advantage.

When government decides to respond to business demands for assistance, one objective of its policy must be to respond to political pressures for subsidy or protection with programs aimed at helping firms move into more competitive positions and then to stand strong against those who cannot. The choice, we repeat, ought not to be between a hands-off policy and protectionist intervention. Yet without a high-level bureaucratic and political commitment to international adjustment and competitiveness, government policies will be formulated by those agencies closest to industry and most receptive to special pleading. Our existing system is well designed to support the losers, and to assist with the policies that losers prefer. We must establish bulwarks against foolish anti-market policies and create the means of wresting policy definition away from losing firms in declining sectors.

If sector-specific policies are adopted in some instances—and we have argued that they should be seen as instruments of last resort—there are three basic premises that must be built into them.

1. Policies of protection should be self-liquidating. If there is any justification for protection, it is that some sudden change by international competitors has left potentially competitive U.S. firms without the time or the resources to respond. Protection, of course, reduces the incentive to adjust, but it does provide the time. Self-liquidating protection is perhaps the only means of maintaining the incentive. Adjustment or orderly exit should be the choices that firms are left with. An alternative, though a politically difficult one, would be product-specific taxes in lieu of protection. The revenues from such taxes could be distributed among U.S. producers as a tax rebate, providing them with the funds needed to adjust but not distorting their real competitive position. This would make the cost of protection clearly visible.

2. Any sector-specific programs that provide specific gains to firms in the name of facilitating adjustment should be linked to obligations to spend those funds on adjustment activities. Sector-specific policies are a statement that under present conditions markets have failed to produce socially desirable outcomes. The specific reasons for market failure must be identified, and policies must be carefully designed to accomplish very specific objectives. For example, if the externalities of research and development keep private expeditures too low, then policies designed specifically to promote research and development are needed. Simply raising company profits does not guarantee any increase in the overall level of research. Policies must be made conditional upon certain well-defined business responses, such as explicit or extraordinary tax breaks for reinvestment in research and development in a specific sector. The government need not become involved in the details of investment or research choices; it need only frame its

policy to assure that the funds are directed toward solving the supposed problem. The public policy justification of a subsidy or protection is lost if the funds are used for some other purpose.

3. Technical advisory boards or oversight boards for sector-specific policies should be drawn from a wide community. One reason for this is that cooperation between labor unions and the community will be required for successful adjustment, and these groups will need to be included at the outset. Another equally important reason is that in the case of intermediate goods such as steel or textiles, the self-interest of producers can be balanced against the expertise of users.

In conclusion, the central economic challenge of the 1980s is the stimulation of supply rather than the management of demand. At the macro level, the goal is to promote production by allocating resources to their most productive uses. At the micro level, the goal is to enhance the competitiveness of business and ensure high wages and safe jobs for labor. Liberals and neo-conservatives share these goals and even agree on some of the general policies required to achieve them. Taxes should be adjusted to encourage savings. Without sacrificing the public interest, regulation should be minimized to reduce production costs. Energy-saving production processes should be encouraged by financial incentives.

Some analysts, besides limiting their focus to the supply side of the economic equation, insist that if government were to stop tinkering with demand and regulation, the market alone would solve supply problems. They see government as the villain behind today's economic difficulties. It is true that supply problems have intensified throughout the industrialized world over the last decade. The cause, however, is not an increase in governmental villainy or stupidity, but rather genuine changes in real economic conditions, including higher energy prices and changing patterns of comparative advantage. Neo-conservatives underemphasize the significance of these real economic changes and argue that an unfettered market system can solve our economic problems. Neither economic performance in the United States prior to the New Deal nor contemporary economic performance in the most successful industrial economies, such as Japan, Sweden, or Germany, supports this view. Markets failed to guarantee growth and resource utilization during the Great Depression; and strategic government intervention and comprehensive social welfare programs, rather than free markets, have been the engines of economic success throughout the advanced industrial world.

Government can employ a variety of tools to stimulate productivity, innovation, and efficient use of resources. These tools include aggregate policies to increase savings and investment; market-promotion policies, such as sponsorship of industrial research and development and the retraining and relocation of workers in "sunset" industries; and in some cases, sector-specific policies, such as the selective use of military procurement. Such approaches can involve the financial and administrative participation of business and labor, but there is economic justification for the participation of government as well. For example, because the social gains from research and development frequently exceed the private ones, government funding is both necessary and socially desirable. Similarly, government retraining and relocation programs can facilitate the movement of workers from low-productivity to high-productivity industries, thereby limiting the structural unemployment that would normally ensue. Finally, government programs can improve our international competitiveness, which has suffered from the industrial and trade-promotion policies of foreign governments. The adverse impact of such policies on U.S. competitiveness is painfully evident in industries such as steel and consumer electronics.

Perhaps the most compelling reason for adopting supply management policies that are firmly rooted in an understanding of the dynamics of competition is this: in their absence, political coalitions will thwart the transfer of resources made necessary by changing economic conditions. Change in the distribution of resources among firms and industries will always invite political pressure. No company or industry will calmly accept its own demise as a sacrifice to be made in the national interest. When it sees itself threatened it will agitate for government programs on its own behalf, and such programs will tend to be protectionist: they will tend to retard socially desirable decline, to increase costs and prices, and to be damaging to international competitiveness.

Political coalitions to promote structural change in industry are required to avert protectionist policies and alliances. Such coalitions should guarantee collaboration between government and business and at the same time serve the interest of a population much broader than businessmen and bureaucrats. A national industrial policy can be the basis for the formation of the broad national coalition required to counter protectionism and to promote economic development.

Index

Abel, I. W., 88
Admiral Corp., 123, 137
Advertising Age, 369
AFL-CIO, 128, 286, 338
Aggregate policy, 19–21, 43–44
Agricultural Act (1956), 260
Amalgamated Clothing Workers Union, 293
American Apparel Manufacturers Association, 302
American Cotton Manufacturers Institute, 268, 270–274
American Footwear Industries Association, 335, 338, 342
American Iron and Steel Institute, 79, 87, 88, 97
American Motors Corporation, 357
American Selling Price System, 342
American Textile Manufacturers Institute, 292, 299, 302, 305
Anti-Dumping Act (1921), 81, 92
Antitrust policy, 21, 46, 51, 110, 151, 382
Arthur D. Little, Inc., 114
Asher, Norman, 155
Automobile industry: American production strategy of, 350, 364–367; and car prices, 370–371; characteristics of the labor force in, 355–356, 375–379, 385, 387–388; engine and body diversity in, 357–363; and government independence from industry, 389–390, and government policy, 40, 353–354, 380–384, 388–390; and government regulation, 49–51; 389–390; historical background of, 363–367, 382–384; Japanese, 36, 348–349, 351, 364–369, 384–385; and labor costs, 372, 375–376; re-

sponse to competition of, 365–367; and scale economies, 369–371; and small cars, 350–351, 364–366; standardization and flexibility in, 352–353, 354–357, 364–367, 369–370, 380, 388–389; and the steel industry, 86, 98; and supplier relationships, 355–356, 372–375, 386–387; technological innovation in, 355–356, 386–387
Automotive electronics, 227

Baker, Howard, 335
Baker, James A., III, 307
Ball, George, 281
Bank of Japan, 73
Barkin, Solomon, 268
Bethlehem Steel Corporation, 66–67
Blumenthal, Michael, 133
Bologna (Italy), 399, 409, 417
Branson, William, 25
Brazil, 316, 317, 324, 344
Brock, William, 306
Brookings Institution, 31
Bureau of Labor, 75
Burns Harbor plant, 66–67, 75, 99
Business Week, 386

Capital availability, 242; and growth of Japanese semiconductor industry, 195; Japanese advantages in, 197–198; planning and stability of, 196; for U.S. as compared with Japanese firms, 197
Carter, Jimmy, 132–135, 305, 314, 338–341, 342, 347; and the steel industry, 85, 89, 91, 103
Charles River Associates, 161, 370
Chase Econometrics, 196

Christian Democrats (Italy), 395
Christopher, Warren, 287
Chrysler Corporation, 37, 59, 357, 364, 381
Cole, Robert, 378–379
Comitextil, 295
Commerce Department: publications of, 331, 344
Committee to Preserve American Color Television (COMPACT), 128–130, 134, 135, 138
Community Credit Corporation, 261
Comparative advantage, 24–29, 32–34; and accumulated investment, 27–29; and adjustment costs, 26, 33; and competitive advantage, 28–29, 33; definition of, 28; and government policy, 27–32; in Heckscher-Ohlin theory, 24–26; and industrialized and developing nations, 32–34; of Japan in semiconductors, 184–187; in Ricardian theory, 25; and technological development, 27–28
Competitive advantage, 28–32; of Japanese semiconductor firms, 199
Comprehensive Program for the Steel Industry. *See* Solomon Program.
Computer technology, 207; generations of, 168; international trade in, 234–235; Japanese market for, 203, 215, 218–220; and Japanese penetration of U.S. market, 221
Consumer electronics, 213–214
Congressional Steel Caucus, 90, 91–92, 93
Corporate autonomy, 94, 133–134, 264, 276
Council of Economic Advisors, 89, 90, 92
Council on Wage and Price Stability, 81, 89, 92, 95–96
Crandall, Robert, 82

Daihatsu Motor Company, 361–362
Davignon Plan, 85–86
Debt financing: in U.S. vs. Japan, 197
Dent, Frederick B., 336
Department of Commerce, publications of, 154, 177
Department of Defense: and U.S. semiconductor industry, 150
Development Loan Fund, 261
Dillon, Douglas, 277
Dumping, 244; of steel, 79–83, 88–93, 95, 103–104; of televisions, 119, 125–126

Eberle, William, 336
Economic Policy Group, 339
Eisenhower, Dwight D., 273, 277

Eizenstadt, Stuart, 339
Electronics, 161
Electronics Industry Association, 123, 126, 131–132
Electronics Industry Committee for Fair International Trade, 125, 128
Electronics News, 131
Emilia-Romagna (Italy), 405, 408, 410, 411
European Economic Community: and renewal of the Multifiber Arrangement, 298–301, 302–304; and the steel industry, 70, 82, 84–87, 89–93; and the textile and apparel industry, 267, 295, 298–307
Export-Import Bank, 261

Federal Trade Commission: Publication of, 98
Ferry, Jacques, 92
Finan, William, 169
Flanigan, Peter, 293
Footwear industry: and the Carter program, 314–315, 338–341; characteristics of the labor force of, 324, 325–327; decline of, 323–324; design and style in, 327–328; and firm size, 328–332; and foreign policy, 316; historical background of, 335–338; import penetration of, 314–316, 324, 343–345; Italian, 316, 317, 324, 336, 344, 394, 398–399, 418; and marketing, 328–332; and Orderly Marketing Agreements, 313–316, 332–337, 339–349; 1970–1976, 333–338; political power of, 333–335, 338; and protectionism, 335–338; and Reagan policy, 348–349; regional character of, 323–324; rubber, 342, 343–344. *See also* Orderly Marketing Agreements
Footwear Industry Team, 314, 316, 332, 346, 347
Ford, Gerald, 87, 129, 130, 337–338
Ford, Henry, 350, 382
Ford Motor Company: historical background of, 350, 363, 365–366, 383
Forward integration: in the semiconductor industry, 228
Foy, Lewis, 80
France, 38, 52, 91, 250
Fuji Motors, 362–363, 364
French Planning Commission, 52

General Agreement on Tariffs and Trade (GATT): and the footwear industry, 334, 346; Kennedy Round of, 55–56, 113, 122, 125, 280, 285; and the steel

General Agreement (*cont.*)
industry, 85, 92; and the television industry, 110, 112, 113, 122, 125, 129–
132, 133; and the textile and apparel
industry, 267, 272, 277–278, 281, 299,
301, 303, 305
General Electric, 108, 113, 123, 136–137
General Motors, 350, 360, 361, 363, 364,
377, 382
Germany, 250, 295
Gesamttextil, 295
Government policy (U.S.): for adjustment,
308–309, 311–312; aggregate economic, 43–44, 200, 422–424; antitrust,
46, 51, 110; and the automobile industry, 353–354, 380–384, 388–390; and
comparative advantage, 27–32; compared to Japanese, 139; conflicting objectives of, 48–49; efficiency rationale
for, 42–43; equity rationale for, 43; and
firm-level dynamics, 41–42; in the footwear industry, 333–338, 346–349; and
free trade, 17–18, 42, 111, 262, 285,
309; for growth industries, 38–39; for
high-risk industries, 38–39, 47–48; for
high-technology industries, 44, 47; impact of, 49–51; for industries in decline, 40–41; for industries in transition, 39–40; on Japanese television imports, 122–129; legislative vs. executive,
126–127, 253, 264–265, 271, 274–275,
291–294, 305–307; macroeconomic,
19–20; and market imperfections, 46–
48; market-promotion, 35–37, 42–43,
423, 426–427; need for industry-inde-
pendent, 389–390, 423; need for coherent, 51–52, 347–348, 423–424, 427; for
the Northeast, 418–419; and Orderly
Marketing Agreements, 339–349; political pressure for, 90, 427; protectionist,
34–35, 40, 48–59; public goods rationale for, 44–45; sector-specific, 19–22,
44–46, 423–426; and the semiconductor industry, 184–191, 199, 205; short-
vs. long-term, 48–49, 52; suggested objectives for, 308–310, 311–312; supply-
side, 43–44, 426; and the support of
public services, 418–419; and the television industry, 110–111, 114–117, 129–
132, 134, 139–141; for the textile and
apparel industries, 259–262, 278–283,
296–297, 305–307. *See also* Protectionist policy

Harvard Business Review, 377
Heckster-Ohlin theory of international
trade, 24–25

Heimlich, Richard, 91
Hollings, Ernest, 306
Honda Motor Company, 363, 384
Honda, Soichiro, 368
Hong Kong: and the footwear industry,
344–345; and textiles, 265, 270, 276,
282
Hout, Tom, 37
Humphrey, Hubert, 290

Industrial policy: and business "images,"
419–421; coordination of, 21–23; definition of, 19, 21, 22; impact of, 17, 19–
20; and international trade, 24, 27–32;
political pressure for, 19–22, 51–53;
types of, 19–22
Industrial restructuring, 199
Industrial synergism, 157
Industries, trade-impacted, 15–18, 29, 33;
and adjustment costs, 26–27; government policy toward, 19–21
Integrated circuits, 206; and computer
memories, 167; consumer products
market for, 162; 166–167; decline in
price of, 157–158; development of very
large scale (VLSI), 207; development of
large scale (LSI), 153; exports of, 177;
families of, 158; first development of,
155; history of, 150–152; importance of
large scale (LSI), 161; and the Japanese
semiconductor industry, 181, 183, 189,
202, 209; learning curve in production
of, 167; and the minicomputer, 158; redundancy in design of, 235–236; trade
patterns in, 177–78; U.S.-Japanese
trade in, 192; U.S. production of, 171;
world market shares in, 231
Interagency Textile Committee, 276–277
International Cooperation Administration,
261–262
International Labor Organization, 302
International trade: and Japanese electronics, 241; and Japanese semiconductor production and consumption, 212;
and the Japanese semiconductor industry, 192–193; liberalization of, 209; and
semiconductor export opportunities,
211; structure and strategy in, 234–237
International trade, theory of: and capital
investment, 27–29; and comparative advantage, 24–28; and competitive advantage, 28–29, 30–31; and free trade,
23–26; and government policy, 24,
27–32; Heckscher-Ohlin, 24–26; Ricardian, 25; and technological development, 27–28. *See also* Comparative advantage; Industrial policy

International Trade Commission: and the footwear industry, 314, 333, 335, 336–339, 341, 342; publications of, 177; and the steel industry, 87, 93, 96; and the television industry, 129–132, 134

Iron Age, 387

Isuzu Motors, 362

Italian Communist Party (PCI), 392, 409–410, 412

Italy: economic growth of, 392; and the footwear industry, 316, 317, 324, 336, 344, 394, 398–399, 418. *See also* Small businesses, Italian

Japan: automotive industrial policy of, 36, 384–385; business strategies in, 187; consumer electronics market in, 212; domestic market structure of, 219–220; economic structure of, 60–61, 186; financing of postwar economic development in, 195; importance of government promotional policies in, 243; industrial policy of, 27–29, 32–33, 35–37, 106–108, 113, 117–120, 139, 145–147, 243; managerial skills in, 31, 37; protectionist policies of, 111–113, 175, 217; semiconductor industry in, 107–108, 176, 181–184, 188, 209; television industry in, 106–108, 112–120, 124, 127, 139; textile and apparel industries in, 252, 262, 265, 267–268, 272–274, 282, 286–288, 292–295

Javits, Jacob, 335

Johnson, Chalmers, 60

Johnson, Lyndon B., 287

Keiretsu, 193–196

Kendall, Donald, 292

Kennedy, David, 294, 335–336

Kennedy, Edward, 335

Kennedy, John F., 266, 277, 278, 279, 280–286

Kissinger, Henry, 337

Korea: and footwear agreements, 314, 315–316, 324, 325, 341, 342–345; and the television industry, 138

Korke, Kazuo, 378

Krasner, Stephen, 105

Labor: in developing economies, 33–34, 41; in the footwear industry, 324; and government policy, 21; industrialized, 394–396, 402–403, 410–411, 413, 415, and offshore productions, 58; in trade-impacted industries, 16–17, 43

Labor, steel: 72, 75, 78, 89–90; compared to Japanese, 67, 74; and protectionism, 84–85, 88, 90–93, 102–103

Labor, television: Japanese, 114, 115, 118, 119, 124; and offshore production, 106–107, 114–116, 134, 135; and protectionism, 107, 110, 122–124, 126–129

Labor, textile, 256–258, 261, 276, 312; collaboration with management of, 268, 276, 293, 297, 301–302; and protectionism, 268, 272, 286, 293

Lamm, Harvey, 368

Lande, Stephen, 343

Learning-curve economies, 31, 167

Licensing agreements, 202, 204, 223; Japanese unwillingness to enter into, 237; and problems of market growth, 224; on semiconductor technology, 176

Long, Russell, 336

Long-Term Arrangement, 281–282, 283, 286, 287–289

Long-Term Agreement in Cotton Textiles, 322

LSI. *See* Integrated circuits

Lykes Corporation, 100

McBride, Lloyd, 88

Mackintosh, Ian, 157

Magaziner, Ira, 37

Magnavox, 123, 125, 136–137

Managerial capacity, 31, 37

Mankowsky, Vincent, 386

Marche (Italy), 393–394

Market-promotion policy, 19, 21–22, 35–37, 42–43

Martin, Edwin, 286

Mass production: in the automobile industry, 352–353, 354–357, 364–367, 369–370, 380, 388–389; and labor force characteristics, 394–396, 402–403, 413, 415; and relocation to less-developed areas, 403, 413, 415–416; and specialty production, 403–405, 415–417

Mexico, 85, 114–116, 136, 137

Mick, Colin, 108

Microfabrication methods, 210

Microprocessors: development of market for, 167–168; technological advances in, 170. *See also* Integrated circuits

Mills, Wilbur, 290, 293–294

Ministry of International Trade and Industry (MITI), 145–146, 185–186, 202–207, 216, 236; and the automobile industry, 364, 384–385; and integrated circuit development, 181, 183; and the steel industry, 72, 73; and the television industry, 107–108, 118, 139

Mitsubishi Motors Corporation, 362, 364

Modena (Italy), 405, 409, 417

Morse, True D., 273

Motorola Inc., 117, 123
Multifiber Arrangement, 252, 265–266, 267, 279, 294–296, 306–307; and the European Economic Community, 298–310, 302–304
Multilateral Trade Negotiations, 85, 88–89, 91, 92, 337
Murchison, Claudia, 272
Murphy, Peter, 307
Murray, Albert, 155
Mutual Security Act, 261

National Aeronautics and Space Administration (NASA): and U.S. semiconductor industry, 150
National Association of Blouse Manufacturers, 272
National Retail Merchants Association, 129
National security, 41, 45, 88, 283
Nevin, John, 136
New York Times, 133, 136
Nippon Telephone and Telegraph (NTT) 181–182, 215, 216; and integrated circuit development, 181
Nissan Motor Company, 363, 364, 368, 384
Nixon, Richard, 290, 291, 293–294, 298, 335

Office of Technology Assessment, 45, 48, 68
Offshore production: in the semiconductor industry, 173, 177; of televisions, 109, 112, 114–117, 120–122, 125–126, 134, 136–137
O'Neill, Thomas P. (Tip), 355
Orderly Marketing Agreements, 17, 37, 53–54; characteristics and purpose of, 317, 321; failure of, 314–316, 332; in the footwear industry, 313–316, 319–320, 332, 337, 339–349; foreign adjustment to, 320–322, 341, 343–344; problems of, 317–327, 332, 340; and the relocation of production, 317–318; and scarcity gains, 318–319, 341; in the steel industry, 87, 91; in the television industry, 106, 109, 121–122, 134–138
Organization for Economic Cooperation and Development, 85

Pastore, John, 275
Pastore hearings, 268, 270, 275–276, 285
Phillips, Lawrence, 285–286
Policy: aggregate, 19–21, 43–44, 422–424; antitrust, 21, 46, 51, 110; market-promotion, 19, 21–22, 35–37, 42–43, 423, 426–427; sector-specific, 19–22, 44–46; 423–426; trade, 19. *See also* Government policy; Industrial policy; Protectionist policy
Predatory pricing, 244
Protectionism, steel: alternative strategies to, 101–103; and competitiveness, 96–100, 101, 104–105; cost to consumers of, 98, 104, 105; and dumping, 79–83, 88–93, 95, 103–104; and foreign industry, 104–105; industry argument for, 79–81; and the Solomon Program, 93–100; and trigger-pricing, 93, 94–95, 96, 103–104; and unfair trading practices, 79–81. *See also* Solomon Program
Protectionist policy, 48–59; alternatives to, 252; conditional, 425–426; European, 111–113; foreign adjustment to, 84, 106–107, 253–254, 265, 279, 280, 289–290, 320–322, 341, 343–344; and government policy, 17–18, 34–35, 40, 48–59; history of, 55–56; and industry adjustment, 17, 18, 40, 54, 56–58; Japanese, 111–113, 175, 217; legislative vs. executive, 253, 264–265, 271, 274–275; and Orderly Marketing Agreements, 53–54; oversight of, 426; political pressure for, 18–19, 51–53, 90, 309; self-liquidating, 425; and the semiconductor industry, 174–175, 199, 217; snowball effect of, 259–261, 264, 265–266, 279, 297, 308; suggestions for, 425–426; and the textile and apparel industry, 253–254, 265–266, 268–280, 289–290, 308; and the theory of international trade, 23–27; and U.S. commitment to free trade, 331–334, 337, 348. *See also* Industrial policy; Orderly Marketing Agreements

Rayburn, Sam, 272
RCA Corporation, 107, 108, 113, 117, 118, 123, 131, 136–137
Reagan, Ronald, 306, 347, 418–419
Reciprocal Trade Agreement Act, 272
Reconstruction Finance Corporation, 47

Saccio, Leonard, 262
Sadlowski, Ed, 88
Sato, Eisaku, 287, 292
Saxonhouse, Gary, 373–374
Schultze, Charles, 89
Sector-specific policy, 19–22, 44–46. *See also* Protectionist policy
Semiconductor industry: acquisitions in, 225; and antitrust legislation, 46; capital

Semiconductor industry (*cont.*)
  availability for, 47–48, 144, 174, 198–
  199; capital equipment for, 210; changing technology in, 144, 148, 154, 159–
  160, 169, 179; comparative advantage
  in, 36–37, 54–55, 144–146, 147–148;
  competition in, 152, 163; and computers, 156–157; development of, 150–
  153; and the economics of large scale
  integration, 161, 163–165; effects of
  company integration in, 186, 227, 228,
  231; and government policy, 39, 45,
  47–48, 54–55, 145; international structure of, 173, 178, 201, 217–221; and
  Japan, 145–147, 153–154, 176, 182,
  196; and long-term corporate planning,
  240; market segmentation in 232–233;
  and military procurement, 149, 154–
  155; and national security, 45; and offshore operations, 173; performance of,
  143–144; research and development
  in, 179; restructuring of, 232; role of
  ATT and IBM in, 144–145
Semiconductor Industry Association, 222
Senate Committee on the Judiciary:
  "Merger Movement in the Textile Industry," 258
Short-Term Arrangement, 266, 278, 279–
  281
Simon, William, 130, 337
Simonet Plan, 85
Sloan, Alfred, 382
Small businesses, Italian: and the artisan
  tradition, 406–407; near Bologna, 393,
  399; cooperation between, 400–402,
  404, 420; and economies of scale, 396–
  397, 401–402; in Emilia-Romagna, 405,
  408; and the family tradition, 407–408;
  flexibility of, 396–397; historical background of, 394–395, 406–412; and the
  industrial labor force, 394–396, 402–
  403, 410–411; and interpretations of
  decentralization, 395–397, 402, 404,
  412–414; and the Italian Communist
  Party, 409–412; labor force characteristics of, 393–394, 400; and labor unions,
  394–396, 402, 409–412; legal advantages of, 395–396, 406–407; in the
  Marche, 393–394; machine-tool, 393;
  organization of production of, 397–
  398; product and technology innovation
  in, 398–400, 404; prosperity of, 405;
  shoe, 394, 398–399, 418; and specialty
  markets, 396–397, 398, 404; structure
  of, 393–394; and U.S. factory relocation, 412–414; and U.S. specialty markets, 415–418

Software: and distributed processing, 230;
  types of, 169–170
Solomon, Anthony, 91
Solomon Program, 93–100; and steel
  competitiveness, 96–100; and trigger-
  pricing, 93, 94–95, 96
Spain, 85, 86, 317, 324, 336, 344
Special Trade Representative, 87, 88–89,
  134, 136, 339–340; and the steel industry,
  87, 88, 89, 92. *See also* Strauss, Robert
Speer, Edgar, 88–89, 91, 99
Stans, Maurice, 291–292
Steel Communities Coalition, 90
Steel industry: anti-dumping suits by, 88–
  93, 95, 103–104; financing of, 75–76;
  growth of, 68–69; historical background
  of, 68–78, 84–93; and import penetration, 69, 77; and inflation, 89, 94; Japanese, 28, 29, 35–36, 60–61, 66–70, 72–
  74, 84, 87–93, 96; modernization of, 71,
  97–100, 104; non-steel investments of,
  97–100, 104; oligopolistic structure of,
  71, 72, 75–76, 77–79; political power of,
  62–63, 102–103; pricing practices of, 71,
  72, 75–76, 77–79, 96; profitability of, 75–
  76, 78–79, 96, 103–105; and protectionism, 84–86, 87–93, 97, 103–104; segments of, 65–68, 101–102; and the Solomon Program, 91–100; and steel export,
  68, 69–70, 77–78; structure of, 64–65;
  technology of, 63, 66–68, 71, 74–75, 76;
  and trigger pricing, 93, 94–95, 96; and
  Voluntary Restraint Agreements, 84. *See
  also* Labor, steel; Protectionism, steel
Steel Tripartite Advisory Committee: *Report to the President on the United States
  Steel Industry*, 103–104
Stobaugh, Robert, 120
Strauss, Robert, 88–89, 90, 92, 135, 339–
  340
Strom, Leland, 155
Suzuki Motor Company, 362, 384
Sylvania Corporation, 123, 125, 128, 129–
  132

Taiwan: and footwear agreements, 314,
  315–316, 324, 325, 341, 342–345; and
  the television industry, 114–116, 136,
  137, 138
Tariff Commission: publications of, 123–
  125
Tariff Schedules of the United States,
  173–174
Technology transfer: in the semiconductor industry, 176, 183, 203, 223; in the
  television industry, 112, 117, 121, 124
Technology-Development Contracts, 226

Telecommunications, 230

Television Digest, 136, 137

Television industry: color, 117–120; decline of, 116–117, 120–121, 127–128; domestic vs. multinational, 109, 122, 125–126, 128–129; export market of, 110, 112, 116, 119; and fair trade laws, 122, 125–126; and foreign components, 109, 116, 121, 124; and government policy, 110–111; historical background of, 110–121; and import relief, 122–124, 128, 129–132, 134, 137; and imports, 114–116, 117, 124–126, 127–128, 132–133; Japanese, 106–108, 112–120, 124, 127, 139; and labor, 107, 110, 114–116, 120–121, 124, 128–129; marketing and production strategies of, 106, 119–120; monochrome, 112–117, 119; and offshore production, 112, 114–117, 120–121, 134, 136–137; Orderly Market Agreements in, 106, 109, 121–122, 134–138; and related markets, 108–110; and the Sylvania fair trade suit, 129–132; and tariffs, 112, 114–116, 131; technology of, 106, 107, 117–118; and technology transfer to the Japanese, 112, 117, 121, 124. *See also* Labor, television

Textile and apparel industry: apparel segment of, 269–270, 285–286, 310–311; and bilateral agreements, 265, 266–267, 282, 289, 292–294, 299; cotton segment of, 268–269, 279–280; domestic problems of, 268, 275, 279–280, 297, 299, 301, 311–312; and the European market, 277–278, 285, 291, 294–295, 298–301; export market of, 250–252, 310; and fiber substitution, 255–256, 265, 279, 289–290; and firm size, 255, 258–259, 263, 311; and government policy, 253, 264–265, 271, 274–275, 291–294, 305–307; and the Kennedy plan, 278–279, 280–283, 296–297; and labor, 261, 286, 293; and labor adjustment, 276, 297, 312; ladies garment segment of, 415–417; man-made fiber segment of, 269, 283–285, 289–290; in the mid-1950s, 255–259; and the Mills trade bill, 293–294; and the Multifiber Arrangement, 294–296, 298–307; and multilateral agreements, 277–279, 294–295; 1955–1961, 266, 267–279; 1974–1980, 267, 298–304; 1961–1973, 266, 279–298; and outward processing, 301–302; and plant relocation, 256–258, 415–417; protectionist coalition in, 253, 264–265, 268–270, 272, 276–277, 293, 297, 308; protectionist strategies of, 252–253, 268, 270–279, 290–294, 309; and quotas, 273–274, 275–277, 285, 293; and restrictions of Japanese imports, 252, 265, 267–268, 272–274, 282, 292–294; segments of, 263, 264, 268–270, 277, 283–285, 310; and the Short and Long Term Arrangements, 278–282, 288–289; and the snowball effect of protection, 259–261, 264, 265–266, 279, 308; and U.S. cotton policy, 259–261, 282–283; and U.S. foreign policy, 261–262, 271, 272, 277, 279–280, 288, 297–298, 311; wool segment of, 283–285, 286–288, 289

Textile Surveillance Body, 296

Textile Workers Union of America, 276, 286

Thurmond, Strom, 306

Tilton, 203

Toyo Kogyo Company, 363, 364, 372

Toyota Motor Company, 351, 363, 364, 366

Trade Act (1962), 279, 297

Trade Act (1974), 43, 58; and steel, 82, 85, 87

Trade Agreements Extension Act, 273, 283

Trade Expansion Act (1962), 122–124

Trade Reform Act (1974), 126–127, 128, 130, 132

Tran van Thinh, 303

Truman, Harry S, 72

United States Steel Company, 68, 71, 88, 98–99, 103–104; and protectionist policy, 87, 89, 91

United Steelworkers of America, 69, 84, 85, 88

Ushiba, Nobukhio, 293

Utterback, James, 155

Vanik, Charles, 90, 92–93

Viergutz, Owen, 387

Vinson, Fred, 283

Vision of MITI Policies in the 1980s, 145

Voluntary Restraint Agreements, 84

Wallace, George, 290

Wall Street Journal, 387

Ward's Engine Update, 368–369

Washington Post, 93

Weidenbaum, Murray, 306

White, Lawrence, 370

White House Conference on Steel, 91–92

Zenith Radio Corporation, 107, 118, 123, 125, 128, 133, 136–137

Zysman, John, 72

Library of Congress Cataloging in Publication Data

Main entry under title:
American industry in international competition.

   (Cornell studies in political economy)
   Includes index.
   Contents: American industry in international competition / Laura Tyson and John
Zysman—Slow growth and competitive erosion in the U.S. steel industry / Michael
Borrus—Decline in an expanding industry : Japanese competition in color television /
James E. Millstein—[etc.]
      1. United States—Industries—Case studies. 2. United States—Commerce—Case
studies. 3. Industrial promotion—United States—Case studies. 4. Competition—Case
studies. I. Zysman, John. II. Tyson, Laura D'Andrea, 1947-   . III. Series.
HC106.8.A45   1983   382'.3'0973   82-22044
ISBN 0-8014-1577-2